Post-Imperial Democracies

Ideology and Party Formation in Third Republic France, Weimar Germany, and Post-Soviet Russia

STEPHEN E. HANSON
University of Washington, Seattle

CAMBRIDGE
UNIVERSITY PRESS

CAMBRIDGE UNIVERSITY PRESS
Cambridge, New York, Melbourne, Madrid, Cape Town, Singapore,
São Paulo, Delhi, Dubai, Tokyo, Mexico City

Cambridge University Press
32 Avenue of the Americas, New York, NY 10013-2473, USA

www.cambridge.org
Information on this title: www.cambridge.org/9780521709859

First published 2010

Printed in the United States of America

A catalog record for this publication is available from the British Library.

Library of Congress Cataloging in Publication data

Hanson, Stephen E., 1963–
Post-imperial democracies : ideology and party formation in Third Republic France, Weimar
Germany, and post-Soviet Russia / Stephen E. Hanson.
    p.   cm. – (Cambridge studies in comparative politics)
Includes bibliographical references and index.
ISBN 978-0-521-88351-1 (hardback)
1. Ideology – Political aspects – Europe – Case studies.   2. France – Politics and government –
1870–1940.   3. Germany – Politics and government – 1918–1933.   4. Russia (Federation) –
Politics and government – 1991–.   5. Comparative government.   I. Title.   II. Series.
D397.H32   2010
320.5–dc22   2010015178

ISBN 978-0-521-88351-1 Hardback
ISBN 978-0-521-70985-9 Paperback

Post-Imperial Democracies

Ideology and Party Formation in Third Republic France, Weimar Germany, and Post-Soviet Russia

This book examines the causal impact of ideology through a comparative-historical analysis of three cases of "post-imperial democracy": the early Third Republic in France (1870–1886), the Weimar Republic in Germany (1918–1934), and post-Soviet Russia (1992–2008). Stephen E. Hanson argues that political ideologies are typically necessary for the mobilization of enduring, independent national party organizations in uncertain democracies. Clear and consistent ideologies can artificially elongate the temporal horizons of their adherents. By presenting an explicit and desirable picture of the political future, successful ideologues induce individuals to embrace a long-run strategy of cooperation with other converts. When enough new converts cooperate in this way, it enables sustained collective action to defend and extend party power. Successful party ideologies thus have the character of self-fulfilling prophecies: by portraying the future polity as one organized to serve the interests of those loyal to specific ideological principles, they help to bring political organizations centered on these principles into being.

Stephen E. Hanson is the Vice Provost for Global Affairs and the Herbert J. Ellison Professor in the Department of Political Science at the University of Washington. Hanson is the author of *Time and Revolution: Marxism and the Design of Soviet Institutions* (1997), which received the 1998 Wayne S. Vucinich book award from the American Association for the Advancement of Slavic Studies. His more recent publications include *Postcommunism and the Theory of Democracy* (2001, with Richard Anderson Jr., M. Steven Fish, and Philip Roeder) and articles in journals including *Comparative Political Studies*, *Comparative Politics*, *Communist and Post-Communist Studies*, and *East European Politics and Societies*. He also served as Assistant General Editor of the Cambridge Studies in Comparative Politics series until 2008.

Cambridge Studies in Comparative Politics

General Editor
Margaret Levi *University of Washington, Seattle*

Assistant General Editors
Kathleen Thelen *Massachusetts Institute of Technology*
Erik Wibbels *Duke University*

Associate Editors
Robert H. Bates *Harvard University*
Stephen E. Hanson *University of Washington, Seattle*
Torben Iversen *Harvard University*
Stathis Kalyvas *Yale University*
Peter Lange *Duke University*
Helen Milner *Princeton University*
Frances Rosenbluth *Yale University*
Susan Stokes *Yale University*

Other Books in the Series

Continued after the Index

Contents

Acknowledgments

This book has been in gestation for a very long time, and to list all the people I should thank for their intellectual and personal contributions to the project might by now require a short monograph of its own. If I have failed to acknowledge anyone in particular who helped me at some stage of the research or writing of this book, I apologize in advance. Naturally, too, those who are mentioned here bear no responsibility for any of the book's remaining shortcomings.

The initial argument about ideology and party formation that ultimately inspired this book was developed while I was a Research Scholar at the Kennan Institute for Advanced Russian Studies in Washington, D.C. The Kennan Institute's director, Blair Ruble, has been a continuing source of professional and personal inspiration to me. Further work on the comparison of post-imperial democracies was carried out at the Minda de Gunzburg Center for European Studies at Harvard University. I would like to thank in particular Grzegorz Ekiert, who helped to make my sabbatical at Harvard so productive – and who soon became a coauthor and close friend as well. I would also like to thank Timothy Colton, Peter Hall, Charles Maier, and Daniel Ziblatt for their support and insightful feedback. I was able to complete the writing of the theoretical portion of the manuscript while working as a Visiting Scholar in the Department of Politics and International Relations at Corpus Christi College, Oxford University, and I am deeply grateful to Giovanni Capoccia, who invited me to Oxford and agreed to read my early draft chapters, for his incisive commentary and his warm friendship. I also received useful comments at Oxford from Paul Chaisty, Stephen Whitefield, and David Priestland.

I have been truly blessed in my career to be integrated into a network of scholars of postcommunist societies that is populated by brilliant, principled, and wonderfully supportive colleagues. Many of the key ideas for this work were first developed as short essays for the Program on New Approaches to Russian Security (PONARS), a group of leading Russian, Ukrainian, and American analysts of post-Soviet affairs. I am deeply and abidingly indebted to my friends in PONARS, and most of all to PONARS's founder and long-time executive director, Celeste Wallander, whose intellectual leadership and unfailing loyalty have played an incalculably positive role in my life and career.

I would also like to thank Jeffrey Kopstein of the University of Toronto, whose suggestion that we coauthor an article on "The Weimar/Russia Comparison" in *Post-Soviet Affairs* in 1997 set me on the course that eventually resulted in this book. Jeff's steadfast friendship, sage counsel, and occasional commiseration over the past twenty years have been among the most reliable joys of my professional and personal life. The same can be said about my friend and University of Washington colleague Steve Pfaff, whose generosity in reading nearly all of my work, helping me frame my ideas, and supporting my overall vision means more to me than he probably realizes.

Yoshiko Herrera read an early draft of the manuscript in its entirety and provided me with amazingly detailed and precise commentary. John Gerring also took a close look at the theoretical chapters, and I have returned to reexamine his criticisms more than once. Laura Belin graciously offered to let me use her large collection of post-Soviet Russian party programs and other campaign materials. Henry Hale read through the penultimate draft of the book manuscript, and his suggestions have helped me immensely. In our continuing debates over the years, Steve Fish has pushed me to consider alternative explanations for outcomes in postcommunist politics, for which I am deeply grateful. Other colleagues who kindly took time out of their busy schedules to provide comments on portions of this book include Michael Bernhard, Venelin Ganev, Andrew Gould, Ken Jowitt, Marc Howard, Marcus Kreuzer, Jan Kubik, Rudy Sil, and Lucan Way. I also received copious very useful suggestions from the anonymous referees chosen to review my book for Cambridge University Press.

The University of Washington has been my academic home for the entirety of my career, and I owe much of my intellectual development to my friends and colleagues there. First and foremost among them, I would like to thank Margaret Levi, who has been a mentor and supporter since I first came to Seattle in 1990 – even when I was pursuing theoretical paths that she no doubt saw as blind alleys. Working under her leadership as assistant general editor of the Studies in Comparative Politics series of Cambridge University Press for much of the past decade has been an honor and a privilege. Without Margaret, the UW Political Science Department would have been a far less stimulating place to make a career. Other past and present UW colleagues who read parts of the manuscript or participated in discussions of this project are Jim Caporaso, Daniel Chirot, Michael Hechter, Bob Huber, Raymond Jonas, Bryan Jones, Edgar Kiser, Jamie Mayerfeld, Scott Radnitz, Michael Taylor, Susan Whiting, Erik Wibbels, and John Wilkerson. Michael Biggins, the UW's stellar head Slavic librarian, went out of his way to collect campaign ephemera for me during his various trips to Russia. Christian Boulanger and Kristin Bakke also provided outstanding research assistance during their stay in the UW political science department. I am grateful to them, and to everyone at UW, for their continuing support.

Drafts of various chapters of this book have been presented at numerous institutions of higher learning and academic conferences over the past several years. I have benefited greatly from the commentary I received at Yale University's seminar on comparative politics, the University of Chicago's comparative politics lecture series, the Davis Center for Russian and Eurasian Studies at Harvard University, the University of Michigan's Department of Political Science, Indiana University's Department of Political Science, the University of Illinois's Center for Russian, East European and Eurasian Studies, the University of Notre Dame's Kroc Center for International Studies, Seoul National University, the University of Strathclyde, the University of Miami's campus in Luxembourg, the Conference of European Studies, the American Association for the Advancement of Slavic Studies, and the American Political Science Association. I also presented a nearly complete draft of the book to a workshop organized by Margaret Levi at the University of Washington, where I received excellent feedback from Jason Wittenberg and Steve Pfaff, UW graduate students Will Murg and Audrey Sacks, and a variety of other faculty and graduate student colleagues.

It has been my profound good fortune to be able to work with the best political science editor in the business, Lew Bateman, both at the University of North Carolina Press, where he published my first book, and now at Cambridge University Press. Lew's incredibly sound intellectual judgment – and equally incredible work ethic – have played a key role in shaping the political science discipline. To have had the opportunity to work closely with Lew, both on my own projects and in the preparation of so many other books in the field, has been one of the highlights of my career as a political scientist.

Some passages in this book have appeared in print previously in various articles and chapters written over the past decade. I would like to thank the editors of the *Journal of Communist Studies and Transition Politics, East European Politics and Societies*, and Cambridge University Press for permission to republish short sections of these works.

Finally, there is one person to whom I would like to express something much more than mere gratitude – for her good humor in difficult times, her indefatigable spirit of adventure, her willingness to put up with my authorial mood swings and my far-too-frequent travel, and, most of all, for her unwavering faith in me. My wife, Jennifer Stevenson, is the real reason this book has actually made it into print. I therefore dedicate it to her as an expression of my undying love.

Preface

As the first decade of the twenty-first century came to a close, Russia's political party system was in a parlous state. Despite repeated proclamations by top Russian leaders that building strong parties was crucial for the stability of the state and the future of Russian democracy, party organizations no longer played any independent role in Russian political decision making by the end of Putin's second term as president. The one political party with a mass membership, United Russia, clearly owed its power to the direct financial and institutional backing of the Kremlin and used its overwhelming dominance of both the central and most regional legislatures to slavishly support any and all Kremlin initiatives. Russia's erstwhile liberal parties, Yabloko and the Union of Rightist Forces, had dwindled into splinter groups of no significance. The Communist Party of the Russian Federation led by Gennadii Ziuganov, which had come close to seizing power in the turbulent 1990s, continued to voice opposition to the Putin-Medvedev regime and to sponsor occasional protests but, with public support in the low teens and only 57 seats in the 450-seat State Duma, was essentially impotent. The Liberal Democratic Party of Russia, led by theatrical nationalist Vladimir Zhirinovskii, continued to combine radical rhetoric with faithful support of the Kremlin in all key parliamentary votes. And the rest of the Russian party system was made up of various "parties of power" designed to serve the temporary interests of one or another faction within Russia's ruling circles.

Few, if any, Western theorists of democratic transition and consolidation expected this outcome nearly two decades after the collapse of the USSR. Indeed, a review of the initial predictions of political scientists specializing in postcommunist democratization shows that most were quite optimistic about the future of Russian party organizations, arguing that the adoption of a new democratic constitution in 1993 and the experience of several reasonably free and fair elections were gradually solidifying the emerging links between social groups in Russia and the new parties working to mobilize them, as well as providing increasingly effective coordination of partisan factions within the legislature.[1] Even Putin's initial consolidation of state power was seen by some analysts as potentially strengthening the party system by providing clearer institutional rules governing party activities; indeed, Putin himself said as much in arguing for the adoption of such rules during his first term in office.[2] More pessimistic analysts of post-Soviet Russia, meanwhile, tended to predict a return to an explicitly anti-Western form of dictatorship, of either the communist or nationalist variety.[3] The emergence of an explicitly anti-ideological authoritarianism in Russia in the second decade after communism's collapse in Eurasia is thus a puzzle worthy of sustained theoretical investigation.

The central thesis of this book is that these two phenomena – the decline of Russian political parties and the absence of coherent Russian ideologies – are in fact logically connected. Put simply, I argue that political ideologies, defined as clear and consistent definitions of the principles of membership in a desired political order, are typically necessary (although not sufficient) for the mobilization of enduring, independent national party organizations in uncertain democracies. In highly turbulent social environments of the sort generated by the collapse of the Soviet Union, the formation of large-scale parties requires the solution of a massive collective action problem: while everyone who belongs to or is represented by a political party might benefit from its existence, no single individual will ordinarily find it rational to contribute to the initial formation of such a party on her own. For this reason, new parties in uncertain democracies cannot emerge simply because of opportunities provided by formal political institutions or demands from particular social groups. There must also be some individualized incentives to motivate initial party builders to join in sustained, collective sacrifice for common party goals. Yet, in the absence of stable state institutions, the organization of "selective incentives" to promote such behavior seems itself individually irrational.

Clear and consistent ideologies, I argue, can have the effect of artificially elongating the time horizons of those who embrace them. By presenting an explicit and desirable picture of the political future, successful ideologues can induce at least some instrumentally rational individuals to embrace a long-run strategy of cooperation with other converts. When enough new converts cooperate in this way, sustained collective action to defend and extend party power becomes possible. Successful party ideologies thus have the character of self-fulfilling prophecies: by portraying the future polity as one organized to serve the interests of those loyal to specific ideological principles, they help

---

[1] M. Steven Fish, "The Advent of Multipartism in Russia, 1993–95," *Post-Soviet Affairs* 11(4, 1995): 340–383; Moshe Haspel, Thomas F. Remington, and Steven S. Smith, "Electoral Institutions and Party Cohesion in the Russian Duma," *Journal of Politics* 60(2, May 1998): 417–439.

[2] See, for example, Peter Lavelle, "The Poor Political Lexicon of Russia's Liberals," RIA-Novosti, September 26, 2005, http://en.rian.ru/analysis/20050926/41512468.html, accessed on January 15, 2006.

[3] Jerry F. Hough and Susan Goodrich Lehmann, *The 1996 Russian Presidential Election* (Washington, DC: Brookings Institution Press, 1996); Stephen Shenfield, *Russian Fascism: Traditions, Tendencies, Movements* (Armonk, NY: M. E. Sharpe, 2001).

to bring political organizations centered on these principles into being. If this reasoning is correct, the failure of Russia's postcommunist political parties can be traced to the absence of successful party ideologies in the wake of the discrediting of Marxism-Leninism. In short: no ideologies, no parties.

This central argument is reasonably simple. To sustain it, however, requires an extended and complex exposition, because the claim that ideology can be seen as a crucial "independent variable" for explaining institutional outcomes directly contradicts much of mainstream social science thinking about the role of ideas in history. Despite their myriad differences, the three social science paradigms that have dominated the political science discipline over the past century – modernization, Marxism, and rational choice theory – are generally unified in their assumption that political ideologies should be understood not as causes of social outcomes but as reflections of more fundamental social forces (be these cultural, class based, or strategic). The ironic result, as Kathryn Sikkink has pointed out, is that scholars who spend their entire lives developing, disseminating, and defending their own ideas nevertheless vehemently insist that ideas have no systematic social impact.[4]

Indeed, there is a kind of methodological catch-22 facing social scientists who wish to argue for the theoretical importance of ideologies as explanatory variables in particular empirical contexts. We might term it the "suicide test." To wit: mainstream social scientists, attuned to discovering the hidden strategic or material interests lurking behind every profession of political principle, quickly conclude that ideology is irrelevant the moment they discover that so-called ideologues have acted in a self-interested manner.[5] Apparently, only those politicians who march like lemmings to their own political or personal destruction can truly be considered "true believers." Ideologues who do commit political or personal suicide, however, no longer play any role in real-world politics – and therefore they can be safely ignored. In short, the only "proof" of ideology's independent effect currently accepted by the social science mainstream automatically also proves that ideology is irrelevant.

On top of this catch-22, there is an element of intellectual "path dependence" at work in the continuing marginalization of research into political ideology. Because the dominant social science paradigms downplay the causal significance of ideas, few political scientists bother to spend much time learning the specific nuances of ideological discourses. For this reason, even leading scholars frequently possess stereotyped, inaccurate conceptions of major ideological

---

[4] Kathryn Sikkink, *Ideas and Institutions: Developmentalism in Brazil and Argentina* (Ithaca, NY: Cornell University Press, 1991).

[5] For example, note the way in which the alternative explanations based on "ideology" are quickly dismissed in Stathis Kalyvas's very fine book about the origins of Christian Democratic parties in Western Europe. Because the Catholic Church officially opposed the creation of such parties, Kalyvas assumes that ideological beliefs played no role in their formation, which must instead be explained by strategic factors. Left out of account in this analysis is any effort to ascertain the political beliefs of the actual founders of new Christian Democratic parties themselves. Kalyvas, *The Rise of Christian Democracy in Europe* (Ithaca, NY: Cornell University Press, 1996).

traditions, such as Marxism-Leninism, Nazism, liberalism, and social democracy. These incorrect folk understandings of major ideologies are then compared to the political strategies pursued by their adherents to gain political power, economic resources, and international influence – with the result that the irrelevance of "ideological beliefs" for explaining political behavior *appears* obvious. This naturally reinforces the standard initial assumption that ideology is not worth sustained analytic attention – and the cycle continues.[6]

To counter both the suicide test and the resulting general inattention to ideological specifics in contemporary social science research, two analytically distinct steps are necessary. First, it must be shown theoretically that ideologically principled actors, genuinely committed to their belief systems, can under certain conditions be "selected for" in social and political competition, defeating their more pragmatic competitors – in other words, that lemming-like ideological consistency can lead actors to the pinnacle of power and not only to the bottom of the cliff. Second, it must be demonstrated that the substantive content of the ideological principles upheld by victorious ideologues can have a demonstrable empirical effect on the kinds of policies they adopt after taking power – that is, that principled ideologues do not immediately turn into stereotypical Machiavellians the moment they gain control of the state.[7]

In my first monograph, *Time and Revolution: Marxism and the Design of Soviet Institutions*, I attempted to respond to the second of these two imperatives by demonstrating the empirical importance of Marxist theoretical principles in accounting for many otherwise puzzling features of Soviet political and economic institutions from the founding of the Soviet state in 1917 through its collapse in 1991.[8] In particular, I traced the impact of Hegel's and Marx's philosophical understandings of time on the later institutional development of Leninism and Stalinism, arguing, in short, that the incentive structures of both Lenin's Bolshevik Party and Stalin's planned economy were explicitly designed to realize Marx's vision of communist society by synthesizing the "rational" time discipline of Western capitalism with incentives for "revolutionary" time transcendence by party members, managers, and workers. From this perspective, I demonstrated, political debates among Marxist theorists of the Second International after the deaths of Marx and Engels, among Bolshevik Party leaders

---

[6] Of course, this depiction of mainstream political science should not be taken to imply that there are no good contemporary studies of political ideology whatsoever. The works of Peter Hall and his collaborators, for example, remain seminal; see especially Peter A. Hall, ed., *The Political Power of Economic Ideals: Keynesianism across Nations* (Princeton, NJ: Princeton University Press, 1989). As discussed in Chapter 2, in the past decade or so pioneering scholarship on the role of ideas and ideologies has begun to emerge in all major subfields of political science. Still, the situation facing advocates of idea-based explanations in most leading U.S. political science departments remains largely as I have described.

[7] A similar point has been made by Mark Blyth, "Any More Bright Ideas? The Ideational Turn of Comparative Political Economy," *Comparative Politics* 29(2, January 1997): 229–250.

[8] Stephen E. Hanson, *Time and Revolution: Marxism and the Design of Soviet Institutions* (Chapel Hill: University of North Carolina Press, 1997).

after Lenin's death, and among Soviet leaders after Stalin's death showed a strikingly consistent pattern of division into three competing tendencies: a "left" faction promoting an immediate revolutionary leap to communism; a "right" faction arguing for an evolutionary socialism consistent with modern, rational notions of time; and an "orthodox center" faction arguing for simple fidelity to the foundational principles of Marxist and Leninist theory. I concluded by showing how Gorbachev's perestroika reforms, which ultimately destroyed the Soviet Union, were in fact designed as a last-ditch attempt to resurrect the synthesis of revolutionary and rational time use in the Soviet economy through the encouragement of "socialist enthusiasm" from below.

The arguments advanced in *Time and Revolution*, which were first developed in my doctoral dissertation in the late 1980s before the breakdown of the USSR, have stood the test of time reasonably well.[9] The evidence of previously secret Soviet archives and of countless memoirs by Soviet leaders after the collapse of communism suggests that ideology did play a far greater role in Soviet politics and society, even toward the end of the Soviet period, than had been previously acknowledged by most Western analysts.[10] Indeed, the contemporary historiography of the Soviet period has increasingly focused squarely on the question of ideological discourse, revealing the remarkable degree to which it penetrated every facet of life in the Soviet Union.[11] Stalin himself, we now know, was busy making notations in the margins of Karl Marx's works even at the end of his life, when nobody was in any position to monitor or sanction his behavior.[12] And Gorbachev tells us in his memoirs, written four years after the Soviet Union's collapse, that "the most cherished of all his awards" – more important to him, apparently, than the Nobel Peace Prize he received in 1990 – was the Order of the Red Banner of Labor he received for his heroic work as a combine operator on the collective farm at the age of seventeen![13] For scholars who expected that the collapse of the USSR

---

[9] In an essay written in 1990 based on my dissertation research, for example, I accurately predicted that if Gorbachev continued to pursue a strategy of "disciplined dismantling" of Leninist institutions, the Soviet system would soon cease to exist. See Stephen E. Hanson, "Gorbachev: The Last True Leninist Believer?" in Daniel Chirot, ed., *The Crisis of Leninism and the Decline of the Left: The Revolutions of 1989* (Seattle: University of Washington Press, 1991), p. 54.

[10] See, for example, Stephen Kotkin, *Magnetic Mountain: Stalinism as a Civilization* (Berkeley: University of California Press, 1995); Alexei Yurchak, *Everything Was Forever, Until It Was No More: The Last Soviet Generation* (Princeton, NJ: Princeton University Press, 2006).

[11] In addition to the works cited, see Igal Halfin, *From Darkness to Light: Class, Consciousness and Salvation in Revolutionary Russia* (Pittsburgh: University of Pittsburgh Press, 2000); Halfin, *Communist Autobiographies on Trial* (Cambridge, MA: Harvard University Press, 2003); and Jochen Hellbeck, "Working, Struggling, Becoming: Stalin-Era Autobiographical Texts," in Igal Halfin, ed., *Language and Revolution: The Making of Modern Political Identities* (London: Frank Cass, 2002), pp. 135–159.

[12] Nigel Gould-Davies, "Rethinking the Role of Ideology in International Politics during the Cold War," *Journal of Cold War Studies* 1(1, Winter 1999): 92–93.

[13] Mikhail Gorbachev, *Memoirs* (New York: Doubleday, 1996), p. 49.

would reveal its leadership to be utterly uninterested in theory or principle, such revelations have contributed to a serious rethinking of their fundamental assumptions about politics.[14] For the small number of us who predicted such findings in advance, it is hard to avoid the conclusion that our initial theoretical assumptions have been essentially validated.

Yet, as I acknowledged in *Time and Revolution*, the study of the Soviet Union, however suggestive for the comparative study of ideology's influence elsewhere, in the end represents only a single case. With the end of the Cold War, the political science mainstream has tended to focus on topics where ideology's putative role initially seems far less clear. Indeed, even within the post-Soviet milieu, the near absence of any coherent ideological basis for politics after communism's collapse – as I argue later in this book – has been one of the most striking features of political life. Even for those who now acknowledge the importance of Marxist-Leninist ideology (and its disintegration) for explaining Soviet political behavior, the need to devote sustained attention to the analysis of ideology in comparative politics more generally is still far from clear.

Moreover, *Time and Revolution* did not address in any depth the first of my two analytical imperatives. That is, I did not endeavor to demonstrate in detail that Lenin's ideological commitment to Marxist conceptions of time was causally linked to his successful revolutionary takeover of power in 1917, explaining that a full account of the dynamics of the Russian Revolution itself would be beyond the scope of my case study. This lacuna in the argument could perhaps bolster the conclusion that, even if Lenin and his successors were genuinely committed ideologues, their victory after the fall of tsarism was an idiosyncratic event unlikely to be repeated in other social and historical contexts – and, therefore, that the rise and fall of the Soviet system contain few lessons for comparativists.

This book focuses squarely on explaining why ideologically committed elites come to power not only in very atypical situations but also quite frequently, and for predictable theoretical reasons. In doing so, I introduce a new, more precise definition of ideology. As Berman has emphasized, the social science literature on the role of "ideas" has long suffered from a conceptual fuzziness that has made empirical testing of causal claims very difficult – and the concept of ideology in particular is certainly no exception in this respect.[15] Far too frequently, scholars of ideology have seen their subject matter as an intrinsic and all-pervasive aspect of social life, insisting that practically every social phe-nomenon is "ideological" at some level. Meanwhile, the materialist mainstream insists that *nothing* is really ideological at its core, because ideologies are mere reflections of underlying interests. What is needed for testable causal analysis, however, is a definition of ideology that allows social scientists to distinguish

---

[14] See, for example, John Lewis Gaddis, *We Now Know: Rethinking Cold War History* (Oxford: Clarendon; New York: Oxford University Press, 1997).

[15] Sheri Berman, *The Social Democratic Moment: Ideas and Politics in the Making of Interwar Europe* (Cambridge, MA: Harvard University Press, 1998).

empirically between ideological and nonideological politics – in other words, one that allows for variation on the independent variable.

Ideologies can best be understood as proposals made by individuals to define clear and consistent criteria for membership in a proposed polity.[16] Because most people tend to understand their political affiliations in informal, fuzzy, and inconsistent ways, such proposals very rarely succeed. Indeed, genuine ideologues will often strike ordinary people as obnoxious and repugnant, precisely because demands for political consistency are usually unwelcome in everyday social interaction. Adopting a clear and consistent definition of one's own political identity can also foreclose future political options that might prove personally advantageous. From this perspective, it becomes clear that establishing a coherent new ideology is itself a collective action problem: those individuals who share a clear and consistent definition of political membership will find it easier to mobilize collectively than individuals with no ideology, but no single individual typically has an interest in sacrificing her own political flexibility for the collective success of an ideological movement.

Would-be founders of new ideologies, I argue, are typically able to overcome this collective action problem only when social uncertainty is so high and pervasive that ordinary instrumentally rational actors are unable to stick to any consistent political strategy for long. In such environments of social chaos, the clear and consistent visions of the political future set out by ideologues can artificially elongate the time horizons of those who join their cause, making it rational for them to forgo their short-term individual interests in favor of pursuing the potential long-term benefits available to early converts in the event of an ideological movement's ultimate victory. Thus, in chaotic social conditions, ideologues will usually be the only political entrepreneurs capable of mobilizing large-scale networks of committed activists, giving them a key strategic advantage over their nonideological competitors. The victory and subsequent political hegemony of ideological movements in times of social chaos is thus not anomalous but a typical outcome of social change in uncertain environments. If so, the study of ideology must be placed at the very center of political science inquiry.

To test such an argument empirically, I analyze the problem of political party formation in new, uncertain democracies. Political scientists have long understood that the creation of a viable, well-institutionalized system of competitive political parties is vital to successful democratic consolidation. Well-organized parties have also been crucial to the establishment of many of the most powerful modern dictatorships. Recently, scholars have focused on the formidable

[16] The range of possibilities for defining such criteria is, of course, vast: ideological Leninists demand a polity based on the proletariat and led by Marxist revolutionary professionals; Nazis fight for the political supremacy of racially pure "Aryans"; and ideological liberals set out a vision of politics built around rational individual citizens and property owners. All three ideologies, however, can be usefully understood as proposing clear and consistent principles of political membership.

collective action problems that would-be party builders confront in the task of building national party organizations.[17] It is fair to say, however, that the mystery of where successful, enduring parties come from is still far from resolved in the literature. The role of ideology in this puzzle has been explored to some extent: we know, for example, that most European political parties have had relatively consistent ideological platforms for most of their history; we know that ideologically "left" parties in Western Europe differ systematically from "right" parties in terms of their social welfare and taxation policies; and we have a sense that theoretically, ideologies must play a key role as "information shortcuts," allowing voters to choose rationally among the parties competing in democratic elections.[18] However, the argument that ideology can be a central independent variable causing party formation in the first place is, to my knowledge, new.

Thus, the primary dependent variable in this study is the formation or nonformation of successful national networks of party activists in times of extremely high social uncertainty. To be clear at the outset, I have no wish to argue that ideology alone can explain the type of regime, democratic or undemocratic, that emerges in any given chaotic environment. To insist on such a monocausal explanation of democracy and authoritarianism would vastly understate the complexity of political and social change. Nevertheless, focusing on ideology as an independent variable leading to party formation in uncertain democracies can still shed important new light on the crucial problem of explaining patterns of democratic consolidation and democratic breakdown.[19]

Specifically, if I am right that clear and consistent definitions of membership in the polity are necessary to mobilize committed party activists for sustained collective action in periods of great social turbulence, it follows that new democracies born in such circumstances will frequently confront at some stage a zero-sum struggle between irreconcilable ideological organizations for control over the key institutions of the polity.[20] I argue that the outcome of such struggles depends ultimately on decisions by the military, powerful state officials, and

[17] John H. Aldrich, *Why Parties? The Origin and Transformation of Political Parties in America* (Chicago: University of Chicago Press, 1995); Herbert Kitschelt et al., *Post-Communist Party Systems: Competition, Representation, and Inter-Party Cooperation* (Cambridge: Cambridge University Press, 1999).

[18] See, among many other works on these topics, Ian Budge, David Robertson, and Derek Hearl, eds., *Ideology, Strategy, and Party Change: Spatial Analyses of Post-War Election Programmes in 19 Democracies* (Cambridge: Cambridge University Press, 1987); Harold Wilensky, *The Welfare State and Equality: Structural and Ideological Roots of Public Expenditures* (Berkeley: University of California Press, 1975); Anthony Downs, *An Economic Theory of Democracy* (New York: Harper, 1957); Melvin J. Hinich and Michael C. Munger, *Ideology and the Theory of Political Choice* (Ann Arbor: University of Michigan Press, 1994).

[19] The argument here is thus consistent with that of Dankwart Rustow, who emphasized the importance of consensual definitions of the boundaries of the state for democratic consolidation. See Rustow, "Transitions to Democracy: Toward a Dynamic Model," *Comparative Politics* 2(3, April 1970): 337–364.

[20] A related argument has been made in Giovanni Capoccia, *Defending Democracy: Reactions to Extremism in Interwar Europe* (Baltimore: Johns Hopkins University Press, 2005).

economic elites to back one or another opposed ideological party – or, instead, to support the executive branch against all forms of partisan opposition. Once we move from explaining the formation of national party networks to examining regime outcomes, then social "structure" comes inexorably back into the analysis. However, political and economic elites obviously cannot fight for the victory of a party that is no longer on the playing field. Indeed, the success of ideologues in mobilizing effective party organizations in the initially chaotic environments created by the collapse of old regimes, and the concomitant failure of more "pragmatic" party builders, can later present bureaucrats, officers, and capitalists with very uncomfortable political choices, none of which may reflect their initial preferences. Whether economic elites support democrats or authoritarians during crucial periods of political polarization and crisis can be deeply influenced by how such elites evaluate their interests under the potential future ideological hegemony of the parties that are still available to choose among at that point.

Given the admittedly ambitious scope of my argument, this book necessarily covers a rather broad theoretical and empirical territory. Part I is devoted to a detailed examination of central conceptual and theoretical issues that are fundamental to the claims I am advancing. Fair warning: the novelty of many of these claims forces me to take the reader through a fairly extensive tour of social science theory over the past century or so. Because the major paradigms that have historically dominated the social sciences have tended to downplay the importance of ideology, I must first explain how the rather paradoxical scholarly consensus on the ineffectuality of "ideas" in politics first arose. In Chapter 1, I begin with an account of the century-long marginalization of the one great social theorist who most clearly put ideas at the center of social scientific explanation, Max Weber. I outline the key features of the Weberian theoretical approach, showing how Weber's unique combination of methodological individualism and attention to nonstrategic types of human social action sets his theory apart from Marxism, modernization theory, and rational choice theory alike.

Building on this foundation, in Chapter 2 I turn to an examination of the political science literature on ideology, showing how Marxist, modernization, and rational choice approaches have all ended up "explaining" ideology in unacceptably functionalist terms. Building in part on more recent works on the role of ideas in comparative politics, I set out and justify my new definition of ideology as *any clear and consistent definition of the criteria for membership in a desired political order*. I argue that the formation of new ideologies in this sense constitutes a previously unrecognized collective action problem whose solution requires "principled" (or, in Weberian terms, "value-rational") conduct on the part of an ideology's initial advocates.

In Chapter 3, I review current theories of political party formation, showing how my analysis of ideology and collective action contributes to, and improves upon, recent literature that focuses on the supply of – and not only the demand for – new party organizations. Again, I show how previously dominant approaches to the study of comparative political parties tend to ignore or downplay the initial problem of party formation in environments of institutional uncertainty. Building on recent works by Aldrich and Kitschelt, I show how party ideology can play a crucial causal role in allowing partisans to sustain collective action in the initial phases of party building. I conclude Part I with a discussion of some of the methodological issues involved in testing my hypothesized relationship between ideology and party formation and justify my use of a comparative historical approach to the subject matter.

In Part II, I examine the causal impact of ideology through a comparative-historical analysis of three theoretically chosen empirical cases. Specifically, I argue that post-Soviet Russia can be analyzed as an example of a more general phenomenon I term "post-imperial democracy" – that is, a situation in which a new democratic regime is born within the core nation of a formally imperial polity immediately after its disintegration, and where reasonably fair and open democratic elections are held for at least a decade after imperial collapse. In particular, I engage in a comparative historical analysis of the first sixteen years of the Third Republic in France (1870–1886), the Weimar Republic in Germany (1918–1934), and post-Soviet Russia (1992–2008).[21] In all three of these cases, the continuation of formal democracy well after the initial period of social chaos generated by imperial defeat or collapse led to a distinct environment of prolonged uncertainty governing key institutional features of the new regime – including constitutions, electoral rules, national symbols, and even national borders – that gave rise first to political stalemate between competing parties and then to a decisive crisis, before the eventual consolidation of a new regime type. The three cases share other features that make them particularly fruitful for comparative analysis: each had experienced some degree of parliamentary liberalization in the final years of imperial rule; each saw a prolonged competition between the executive and legislative branches of government for institutional supremacy in the period after imperial collapse; each adopted a constitution that was widely seen as lacking initial legitimacy; each struggled with both institutional and cultural legacies of empire that interfered with democratic politics; and each suffered through major economic crises that had the potential to undermine the constitutional order. However, the outcomes of party formation in these three cases – the emergence of a dominant republican party in France, the establishment of Nazi dictatorship in Germany, and the systematic failure of all independent political parties in Russia – were dramatically different.[22]

---

[21] Mark J. Gasiorowski and Timothy J. Power have found that the rate of democratic failure drops off significantly once a new democracy has endured at least twelve years. In this respect, then, the time period examined here in each case includes the years that are most crucial for democratic consolidation. See Gasiorowski and Power, "The Structural Determinants of Democratic Consolidation," *Comparative Political Studies* 31(6, December 1998): 740–771.

[22] Other cases that could be added to the list of post-imperial democracies by my definition would be Austria and Hungary after World War I – because both were "cores" of the Austro-Hungarian Empire – and Portugal in 1974. Cases where national sovereignty was gained through the defeat and collapse of foreign empires, such as interwar Poland or the post-Soviet

If I am right that ideology is a necessary condition for political party formation in situations of intense social uncertainty, then we should expect to find
in cases such as those examined here that ideologues with clear and consistent
definitions of criteria for membership in the future polity are initially more
successful than nonideological "pragmatists" in mobilizing activists for collective action to build national party networks – even where such pragmatists
begin the process of party building with seemingly superior material and organizational resources. We should also expect that conflicts among competing
ideological parties will be extremely difficult to resolve, given that each such
party advocates a different, incommensurable definition of the polity itself. In
the end, too, we can expect that the victory of any given ideological party – or,
conversely, the failure of any ideological party to establish political hegemony –
will have a profound effect on the institutions that are built and policies that
are adopted after regime consolidation.

The empirical chapters present findings that are largely consistent with these
theoretical predictions.[23] In Chapter 4, I analyze the early Third Republic in
France, a case that has been unjustifiably neglected in most studies of comparative democratization. I show that ideological consistency allowed French
republicans and legitimists to outflank the more "pragmatic" Orléanists and
Bonapartists, despite the latter two parties' initial resource and personnel
advantages. The emergence of the legitimist-republican partisan cleavage generated a deep political struggle between supporters of divine-right monarchy and
Catholic hegemony and advocates of a secular state and radical social inclusion.
Given the unpalatable choice of backing French president Patrice MacMahon,
who appeared to sympathize with the ideological agenda of the legitimists, or
the radical republicans led by Léon Gambetta, most of the French bourgeoisie
reluctantly sided with the latter. The eventual victory of the republican party
generated a consolidated democratic polity that, remarkably, endured for seven
decades. Indeed, republicanism remains the ideological foundation of French
democracy through the present day.

In Chapter 5, I review the better-known case of democratic breakdown in
the Weimar Republic. Again, I show that parties with no clear and consistent
definition of the polity – in particular, the two German liberal parties of this
period – failed to overcome the collective action problems of party organization,
splintering into fragments by the mid-1920s. By contrast, the most successful

---

Baltic states, or where empire collapsed only gradually, as in twentieth-century Britain, pose
different theoretical issues, because they are not necessarily marked by systematic institutional
and social uncertainty.

[23] I should note that, while the initial hypothesis of this study was developed from a comparison
of the Weimar and post-Soviet Russian cases, coauthored with Jeffrey Kopstein, the case of
the French Third Republic was chosen for purely theoretical reasons, with no prior knowledge
of its dynamics on the part of the author. Thus, the finding that here, too, ideological parties
defeated pragmatic ones is a striking confirmation of the initial hypothesis. See Stephen E.
Hanson and Jeffery S. Kopstein, "The Weimar/Russia Comparison," *Post-Soviet Affairs* 13(3,
July–September 1997): 252–283.

parties of Weimar – the Social Democrats, the German National People's Party, the Communists, and ultimately the Nazis – were all quite ideologically consistent, generating the political stalemate Sartori famously analyzed as "polarized pluralism."[24] In the end, this stalemate was broken by the ideologically committed activists of the Nazi Party, strongly supported by President Paul von Hindenburg and the German aristocracy – with devastating consequences for humanity.

In Chapter 6, I return to the case of post-Soviet Russia, utilizing the comparative theoretical perspective developed throughout the book. Once again, I argue, the only parties to endure in the same form over the first fifteen years after the collapse of the USSR were those that were founded with distinctive official ideologies: the Communist Party of the Russian Federation and the Liberal Democratic Party of Russia. Once again, efforts to form independent democratic parties on the basis of political "centrism" and "pragmatism" systematically failed. In comparison with the ideological elites of the nineteenth and early twentieth centuries, however, even the most successful post-Soviet party leaders of the 1990s did not remain clear and consistent about their ideological commitments for long; instead, they made highly public political compromises with the state that undermined the initial principled commitment of their party activists. The ultimate failure of efforts to articulate a new Russian political ideology – whether democratic or antidemocratic – thus generated a situation in which all political parties were too weak to challenge even a very weak state. Whereas in both France and Germany initially weak presidents were forced to rely on the mobilized activist networks of one or another powerful ideological party in an attempt to defend their political position, thereby marginalizing the role of the presidency itself, in Russia the absence of consistent ideological parties with effective national support allowed President Vladimir Putin to establish an independent hegemony. Powerful business elites who had previously hoped to influence Russian politics by backing one or another political party learned – particularly after the arrest and imprisonment of billionaire Mikhail Khodorkovskii in 2003 – that support for the president was the only instrumentally rational political option. Thus, Russia developed neither a consolidated democracy nor a consolidated fascism, but rather a "pragmatic" presidential authoritarianism in which the state-sponsored "party of power" simply carried out the directives of the executive branch.

Chapter 7 concludes the book with a recapitulation of the main findings of the study and an exploration of their consequences for our understandings of democratic – and autocratic – consolidation. The primary hypothesis that

---

[24] Giovanni Sartori, *Parties and Party Systems: A Framework for Analysis* (Cambridge: Cambridge University Press, 1976). The Catholic Center Party provides the single disconfirming case for my hypothesis: although the party leadership never managed to decide on a clear and consistent conception of how membership in the German polity should be defined, it did hold together organizationally until Hitler's takeover of power in 1933. I discuss the implications of this observation for my argument in the Conclusion.

ideology promotes collective action by artificially elongating the time horizons of converts holds up even when subjected to some rather rigorous empirical tests. Indeed, the comparative-historical method adopted here controls for several of the most important alternative explanations for the fate of party systems in the cases examined. Neither the formal institutions of presidential-parliamentary rule, nor antidemocratic legacies of empire, nor even levels of cultural support for authoritarianism differed substantially at the outset of the Third Republic, Weimar Germany, or post-Soviet Russia, yet the outcomes of party formation and consolidation were decisively different.[25] What does seem to explain the success or failure of major political parties in these three cases – as can be demonstrated through careful process tracing – is the extent to which their founding elites were clear and consistent about their definitions of membership in their proposed versions of the political order. In conditions of high social and institutional certainty, then, ideological party builders generally win, and "pragmatists" generally lose. Moreover, ideologues do not drop their ideological commitments the moment they gain power: for good or ill, they tend to implement the most significant elements of their initial political visions.[26]

Russia is the exception that proves the rule. Although the most ideologically consistent Russian party builders were still more successful than their pragmatic competitors in forging national networks of party activists, in the end they all made obvious short-term tactical compromises that blatantly contradicted their professed principles. In part, this outcome reflects the cumulative cultural disgust with "ideology" in general in Russia, in a country where Marxism-Leninism has become farcical, fascism is associated with the horrors of the Second World War, and liberalism is seen by many as a plot hatched in the West to destroy the country. The failure of all post-Soviet ideology, as predicted by the theory advanced here, has ultimately led to the failure of the entire political party system, rendering the parliament politically powerless. Yet Putin, lacking any ideology of his own, could not find a way to forge national networks of committed activists that might ensure the consolidation of his authoritarian regime and was forced instead to rely on the personal loyalty of a small circle of longtime friends and associates. The result is the establishment of a novel form of "weak state authoritarianism" – with unpredictable consequences for the future political stability of Eurasia.

If I am right that ideological clarity and consistency are necessary but not sufficient conditions for party formation in uncertain democracies, certain

---

[25] Other major factors mentioned in the literature on party formation and democratic consolidation do vary among the three cases but not in ways that fit existing theoretical predictions of party or democratic success; thus, France was comparatively more agricultural in 1870 than Germany in 1918 or Russia in 1990, but no one argues that high levels of agricultural production are good for democratic party building. Electoral systems also differed widely in the three cases but also do not seem to explain persuasively differences in party formation among them. See Chapter 7 for further details.

[26] Daniel Chirot, *Modern Tyrants: The Power and Prevalence of Evil in Our Age* (New York: Free Press, 1994).

long-standing explanations in comparative politics for the empirical distribution of democracies and dictatorships must be rethought. The argument sheds new light, for example, on important political phenomena such as the initial establishment of the Taliban regime in war-torn Afghanistan, the revolutionary success of ideologues such as Khomeini in Iran and Pol Pot in Cambodia, and even the historical emergence of liberal capitalism itself. Moreover, the relationship between ideology and collective action has important implications for politics in more stable institutional and social contexts. For at least some marginalized individuals in every society, uncertainty about the future is high enough that ideological conversion may be instrumentally rational; this helps to account for the continuing influence of radical ideological parties and social movements even in the most successful, established democracies.

Finally, the argument here may potentially reshape our understanding of the relationship between "structure" and "agency" in social life. It is true that ambitious politicians eventually require the backing of moneyed interests and of military or police forces in order to rule the state; these structural factors inevitably limit political choices to a greater or lesser extent in all societies. We must reject any "great-man theory of history" that fails to reckon with these limits. Yet the argument defended here shows that in uncertain periods, when collective action problems undermine the strategic coherence and consistency of economic and coercive elites alike, principled agents with long-term visions of the political future can play a decisive historical role. Perhaps, then, if this book is convincing, social scientists may begin to take into account the potential political and social importance of ideas – including their own.

Post-Imperial Democracies

Ideology and Party Formation in Third Republic France, Weimar Germany, and Post-Soviet Russia

PART ONE

CONCEPTUAL AND THEORETICAL ISSUES

I

Weberian Methodological Individualism

It might seem odd to devote an entire chapter of a book on the origin and causal impact of ideologies to an analysis of Max Weber's political sociology. After all, Weber is one of the acknowledged giants of classic social theory whose work has been ritualistically cited by social scientists for more than a century. One might assume that, by now, Weber's key concepts and definitions would be so widely understood as to render a detailed account of them superfluous. Remarkably, however, this is far from being the case. Indeed, as this chapter helps to demonstrate, Weber is almost certainly the most commonly misinterpreted theorist in the history of social science.

To correct such misinterpretations is a lonely task. Despite near-universal acknowledgment of Weber's intellectual genius, self-described Weberians form a distinct minority of contemporary Western social scientists.[1] Among political scientists, in particular, only a tiny handful of scholars embraces a self-consciously Weberian paradigmatic approach.[2] Nor is this result due simply

---

[1] An outstanding exception here is Stephen Kalberg. See especially Kalberg, *Max Weber's Comparative Historical Sociology* (Chicago: University of Chicago Press, 1994). Other contemporary sociologists who make explicit use of Weberian theory include Alan Sica, *Weber, Irrationality and Social Order* (Berkeley: University of California Press, 1988); Julia Adams, *The Familial State: Ruling Families and Merchant Capitalism in Early Modern Europe* (Ithaca, NY: Cornell University Press, 2005); and Philip S. Gorski, *The Disciplinary State: Calvinism and the Rise of the State in Early Modern Europe* (Chicago: University of Chicago Press, 2003).

[2] Weber's influence has been perhaps stronger among political theorists than among the other subfields of political science. See in particular the excellent recent book by Sung Ho Kim, *Max Weber's Politics of Civil Society* (Cambridge: Cambridge University Press, 2004). Within comparative politics, Reinhard Bendix stands out for his explicit Weberianism. Weberian theory was later applied to the study of comparative communism by Ken Jowitt and his school. See especially Reinhard Bendix, *Max Weber: An Intellectual Portrait* (Berkeley: University of California Press, 1977); Bendix, *Kings or People: Power and the Mandate to Rule* (Berkeley: University of California Press, 1978); Ken Jowitt, *New World Disorder: The Leninist Extinction* (Berkeley: University of California Press, 1993); and Vladimir Tismaneanu, Rudra Sil, and Marc Howard, eds., *A World without Leninism* (Seattle: University of Washington Press, 2006). The

to the length of time elapsed since Weber's day. In fact, most social scientists continue to profess allegiance to competing social science paradigms also developed in the nineteenth century: Marxism, Parsonian modernization theory (rooted in the works of Emile Durkheim), and the neoclassical economic approach to social scientific analysis (initially derived from Adam Smith) that is now called rational choice theory. The academic marginalization of Weberian analysis is thus a striking intellectual puzzle. The paucity of Weberians within the political science discipline is perhaps particularly surprising, because of all the classical social theorists Weber would seem to have been the one most directly concerned with politics as an independent social force.

The task of this chapter, therefore, is to reclaim original Weberianism as a worthwhile starting point for contemporary comparative political analysis. To do so, I first show how the theoretical foundations of Weber's social theory differ from those of its three main paradigmatic competitors: Marxism, modernization theory, and rational choice. Specifically, I argue, Weber's theory uniquely combines a thoroughgoing methodological individualism with an emphasis on the nonstrategic, irreducibly cultural sources of individual motivation – a theoretical combination that for some reason has been almost entirely unexplored in social theory of the past century, and which is therefore ignored in influential presentations of the history of the discipline. Second, I show how Weber's theoretical analysis of the four main types of social action – instrumental rationality, value rationality, affect, and habit – builds explicitly on rational choice theory, which confines its attention solely to the first of these types. Finally, I attempt to improve upon Weber's own admittedly confusing account of the connection between the four types of individual social action and his three types of "legitimate domination" – traditional, rational-legal, and charismatic – by explicating the deductive logic that links Weber's "microfoundations" and his macropolitical analysis. I conclude with some observations about how supporters of the Weberian approach might reply to criticisms from adherents of the other three social science paradigms.

The Four Major Social Scientific Paradigms

Any effort to categorize the intellectual history of social science in a few pages is bound to be controversial. Depending on which schools of thought and which theoretical controversies one wishes to emphasize, the past century and a half of social scientific inquiry can be characterized in potentially infinite

use of key Weberian concepts in comparative politics has also been promoted by Juan Linz and those influenced by him. See especially H. E. Chehabi and Juan Linz, eds., *Sultanistic Regimes* (Baltimore: Johns Hopkins University Press, 1998); Robert M. Fishman, "On Being a Weberian (after Spain's 11–14 March): Notes on the Continuing Relevance of the Methodological Perspective Proposed by Weber," in Laurence McFalls, ed., *Max Weber's "Objectivity" Reconsidered* (Toronto: University of Toronto Press, 2007), pp. 261–289.

ways.[3] The utility of any particular subdivision of the literature, then, depends upon its ability to shed light on the implicit conceptual and methodological principles uniting diverse authors into coherent scientific communities – what Thomas Kuhn famously called "paradigms" – so as to give the reader a sense of her own position within and among them.[4] A successful categorization of competing paradigms should act as a sort of map to guide further intellectual exploration rather than imposing rigid barriers that only perpetuate the division of the world of scholarship into warring camps.[5]

Of course, even the very idea that social science is "mature" enough to have developed successful paradigms in Kuhn's sense is controversial. Kuhn himself famously considered social science to be preparadigmatic – that is, lacking any consensus whatsoever about how to define conceptually and measure empirically the field's main objects of study, and therefore doomed to endless and unproductive debates about abstract theoretical and methodological principles.[6] Clearly, the history of social science does demonstrate a tendency toward ongoing conflict among several competing paradigms rather than the sort of universal scholarly acceptance of a single paradigm that Kuhn saw as necessary for the pursuit of the "normal science" of cumulative, empirical puzzle solving.

Yet, upon closer examination, Kuhn's quick dismissal of social science as preparadigmatic fails to take account of several remarkably enduring theoretical traditions that have guided social science research in identifiable and consistent ways. In particular, four great social theorists – Adam Smith, Karl Marx, Emile Durkheim, and Max Weber – arguably identified the main contours of the great paradigms that have competed for intellectual supremacy since the late nineteenth century: rational choice theory, Marxism, modernization theory, and the Weberian approach. Of course, these four theorists did not anticipate every new theoretical innovation in later social science. Advocates of such approaches as psychoanalytic theory, postmodernism, pragmatism, and pluralism might wish to add to the list of "great theorists" presented here. Yet it is remarkable how much of contemporary mainstream social science inquiry

---

[3] See, for example, the disparate accounts of paradigmatic boundaries given by Andrew C. Janos, *Politics and Paradigms: Changing Theories of Change in Social Science* (Stanford, CA: Stanford University Press, 1986), and Mark Irving Lichbach and Alan S. Zuckerman, *Comparative Politics: Rationality, Culture, and Structure*, 2nd ed. (Cambridge: Cambridge University Press, 2009).

[4] Thomas Kuhn, *The Structure of Scientific Revolutions* (Chicago: University of Chicago Press, 1962).

[5] In this way, the effort to delineate major scholarly paradigms in social science may be seen not as hindering but as promoting research into more tractable empirical issues, thus answering the objections of Barbara Geddes, who argues that social science progresses more through a focus on tractable empirical puzzles than through debates about grand theoretical concepts. See Geddes, *Paradigms and Sand Castles: Theory Building and Research Design in Comparative Politics* (Ann Arbor: University of Michigan Press, 2003).

[6] Kuhn, *Structure of Scientific Revolutions*, pp. 164–165.

TABLE 1.1. *The Four Social Science Paradigms*

	Strategic Motivation	Expressive Motivation
Structuralism	Marxism	Durkheimian/Parsonian theory
Methodological individualism	Rational choice theory	Weberianism

still fits quite comfortably within the theoretical rubrics set out in detail by these four authors more than a century ago.

The longevity of the rational choice, Marxist, modernization, and Weberian paradigms is due to the fact that together they represent the four logically possible responses to two central and unavoidable questions facing all social scientists: the unit-of-analysis problem, and the problem of understanding human motivation. On the first dimension, every analyst must decide either to accept individual action as a methodological starting point or to examine social groups as actors in and of themselves – that is, to adopt a "structuralist" perspective on social action. On the second dimension, analysts must decide whether actors should be seen as essentially strategic – that is, oriented toward achieving identifiable ends with available physical and social means – or as essentially expressive, frequently behaving in ways that lack any strategic element whatsoever in order to convey their subjective sense of identity to others. These two theoretical choices cannot be determined simply by examination of empirical social situations. Good social science is equally possible from a methodologically individualist or a structuralist perspective, and one can plausibly interpret the same observed social behavior as primarily strategic or expressive, depending on one's conceptual starting point. Placing these two dimensions on a two-by-two matrix (Table 1.1), we see how the four major social scientific paradigms occupy unique and competing cells.

To be sure, such a categorization cannot do full justice to the myriad theoretical debates within each of these four traditions. It is true that there are some Marxist cultural theorists who see expressive motivations as significant in their own right, and other Marxists who embrace methodological individualism; there are rational choice theorists who take collectivities such as states or classes as actors and who accept some types of nonstrategic motivation as consequential; and so on. However, even in such cases of paradigmatic cross-fertilization, the classification in Table 1.1 helps to illustrate precisely where the boundaries of each school of thought lie.

It should be noted at the outset that this two-by-two matrix has much in common with those recently presented by Alexander Wendt and by Rudra Sil.[7] However, while these authors agree that one of the key paradigmatic divides in

---

[7] Alexander Wendt, *Social Theory of International Politics* (Cambridge: Cambridge University Press, 1999); Rudra Sil, "The Foundations of Eclecticism: The Epistemological Status of Agency, Culture, and Structure in Social Theory," *Journal of Theoretical Politics* 12 (July 2000): 353–387. A rather different sort of categorization of social scientific theories is presented in Craig Parsons, *How to Map Arguments in Political Science* (Oxford: Oxford University Press, 2007).

social science is the unit-of-analysis problem, both Wendt and Sil take as their second dimension a supposed division between "materialist" and "idealist" social science approaches. This, I believe, is a mistaken characterization of the main debates about the nature of human motivation among social scientists. In particular, rational choice theorists are by no means necessarily materialists. They generally postulate only that actors maximize "utility"; this may frequently take the form of wealth maximization, of course, but rational actors can also maximize status, personal security, their chances for salvation, or myriad other things.[8] It is true, however, that social scientists are generally divided between those who see actors (individual or collective) as essentially strategic – instrumentally calculating the best means to attain their goals while taking into account as much as possible the likely actions of others – and those who see actors as primarily oriented toward conduct that is expressive of their personal or shared subjective beliefs, often only secondarily considering such behavior's strategic consequences.

Thus, rational choice theory embraces both methodological individualism and a view of individual social behavior as, at the core, strategic in nature. The main goal of social analysis, from this paradigmatic perspective, is to understand how collective outcomes – whether socially optimal or suboptimal – reflect the strategic choices of reasoning individuals who, whatever their cultural or social environment, are savvy enough to pursue their self-interest in a reasonably consistent manner. Such a characterization of the foundations of rational choice theory, I think, will not be controversial.[9] Note that the characterization of individual action as generally "strategic" applies even to the growing number of rational choice analysts who see cultural norms or identities as important. Indeed, the primary goal of most rational choice analysis of culture is to show that seemingly "irrational" cultural behavior actually makes good strategic sense for the individuals who engage in it.[10]

---

[8] Margaret Levi, "Reconsiderations of Rational Choice in Comparative and Historical Analysis," in Lichbach and Zuckerman, *Comparative Politics*, 2nd ed., pp. 127–128.

[9] One sees precisely these two theoretical elements set out explicitly as foundational for rational choice theory by such well-known practitioners of this approach as Michael Hechter, Jeffrey Frieden, and Barbara Geddes, for example. See Hechter, *Principles of Group Solidarity* (Berkeley: University of California Press, 1987); Frieden, *Debt, Development, and Democracy: Modern Political Economy and Latin America, 1965–1985* (Princeton, NJ: Princeton University Press, 1991); and Geddes, *Paradigms and Sand Castles*. Geddes, it should be noted, objects that rational choice theory should be seen not as a paradigm but rather as an "approach," because "it includes uncountable numbers of hypotheses and theories, many of which are inconsistent with each other"; ibid., p. 22. In fact, such a situation is typical of all scientific paradigms, according to Kuhn. It is certainly also true of the Marxist, modernization, and Weberian paradigms as well.

[10] David M. Kreps, "Corporate Culture and Economic Theory," in James E. Alt and Kenneth A. Shepsle, eds., *Perspectives on Positive Political Economy* (Cambridge: Cambridge University Press, 1990), pp. 90–132; Avner Greif, *Institutions and the Path to the Modern Economy: Lessons from Medieval Trade* (Cambridge: Cambridge University Press, 2006); and David Laitin, *Identity in Formation: The Russian-Speaking Populations in the Near Abroad* (Ithaca, NY: Cornell University Press, 1998).

Karl Marx and most subsequent theorists in the Marxian tradition essentially embrace the rational choice view of social action as strategic but insist that the main actors in social history are collectives: social classes rather than individuals. Indeed, Marx analyzes the dynamics of class conflict precisely in order to uncover previously hidden mechanisms of collective exploitation that are obfuscated by conventional individualist political economy. As in the case of rational choice theory, too, Marxism frequently places an important emphasis on the role of "ideological" or "cultural" factors in human history – but, in the end, such forces are always analyzed as having a strategic function in upholding a given mode of production. The very notion of the isolated individual as a rational actor – for Marx himself and for cultural Marxists in the Gramscian tradition – reflects the dominance of bourgeois ideology that works to camouflage the systematic nature of capitalist domination by portraying it as the product of free individual choices.[11] Similarly, from this paradigmatic perspective, the eventual revolution of the working class against the capitalist system will occur not because of any "moral beliefs" or "principles" motivating particular groups of workers but rather because revolution is in the collective strategic interest of the proletariat.[12]

The common orientation of Marxism and rational choice theory toward a view of class motivation as primarily strategic rather than expressive accounts for the strong affinity between these two scholarly traditions. Indeed, practitioners of "analytical Marxism" hold that Marx's theory is fully compatible with methodological individualism; some interpreters insist that Marx himself was a methodological individualist.[13] In my view, a careful reading of Marx's own writings makes it clear that he really did see classes, rather than individual members of classes, as the key actors of history. For the purposes of an overarching analysis of social science paradigms, however, the resolution of this debate is not crucial. We can simply say that to the extent that analytical

---

[11] Karl Marx and Friedrich Engels, "The German Ideology," in Robert C. Tucker, ed., *The Marx-Engels Reader* (New York: Norton, 1978), pp. 176–193; Antonio Gramsci, *Prison Notebooks* (New York: Columbia University Press, 1992).

[12] Note that this summary of Marx's views refers only to his analysis of class-based society – that is, of human history from the earliest empires through the end of capitalism. With the final victory of the proletariat and the resulting end of class struggle under communism, Marx thinks, humanity will finally be free to act in fully self-expressive ways, which will be in some sense a return to our true "species-being." Moreover, seeds of free self-expression exist even within class-based society, to the extent that ascendant revolutionary classes are able to break the chains of the past through collective action against the ruling class. However, the preceding categorization of Marx's theory as postulating strategic behavior by collective actors is generally adequate for describing his analysis of precommunist history, and this is Marx's main legacy in contemporary social science. See Marx, "Economic and Philosophic Manuscripts of 1844," in Tucker, *The Marx-Engels Reader*, pp. 67–125; Stephen E. Hanson, *Time and Revolution: Marxism and the Design of Soviet Institutions* (Chapel Hill: University of North Carolina Press, 1997).

[13] See, for example, John Roemer, ed., *Analytical Marxism* (Cambridge: Cambridge University Press; Paris: Edition de la Maison des Sciences de l'Homme, 1986).

Marxism replaces structural units of analysis with individuals, it moves from the top left to the bottom left cell in Table 1.1 and should be seen as a variant of rational choice theory – as, in fact, most analytical Marxists themselves tend to claim.

Moving to the top right-hand cell in Table 1.1, we arrive at the paradigmatic viewpoint that dominated Western social science for most of the postwar period: modernization theory. This paradigm, like Marxism, accepts that social structures should be seen as the primary units of social analysis but rejects the notion that human action is best understood as strategic in nature, insisting that expressive behavior based on diverse human cultural norms has an autonomous influence in social life. The roots of this approach can be traced back to the initial formation of sociology in France by such figures as August Comte and Herbert Saint-Simon, but the best and most comprehensive explication of what is now known as the modernization paradigm was presented in the works of Emile Durkheim. Like Marx, Durkheim argued that "individualism" itself is a product of historical changes in social organization; thus it is a mistake to see the individual actor as somehow ontologically or methodologically prior to social structures. Unlike Marx, however, Durkheim insisted that the essential ties binding human beings together in communities of solidarity are expressive, not strategic; indeed, strategic actors bereft of any "higher" form of social solidarity would find themselves in a state of anomie – isolated, adrift, and prone to various forms of mental illness and social pathology.[14] The chief task of sociology, Durkheim insisted, is to chart new, "organic" forms of cultural solidarity adequate to the individualism, impersonalism, and interdependence of the modern age, to replace the "mechanical" forms of cultural solidarity that dominated earlier stages of human history; in this respect, he sees the goal of social science as analogous to that of medicine in its diagnosis of "diseased" social forms resulting from "disequilibrium" within society as a whole.[15]

Talcott Parsons's effort to systematize European social theory in the postwar period, which exercised an unparalleled influence on the later development of global social science, also fits squarely within the "expressive-structuralist" cell of Table 1.1. Although Parsons saw himself as synthesizing the main contributions of Durkheim, Weber, and Freud into a single overarching theory of the "social system," almost all of his central claims were contained within, and anticipated by, Durkheimian theory. Like Durkheim, Parsons sees the key divide of human history as lying between "traditional" forms of social organization based upon ascription at birth to cultural roles prescribed by particular communities and "modern" forms of social organization based upon achievement orientations and legal universalism.[16] Like Durkheim, Parsons explicitly upholds a Spencerian interpretation of "social evolution" as involving progress

[14] Emile Durkheim, *Suicide: A Study in Sociology* (New York: Free Press, 1966).
[15] Emile Durkheim, The *Division of Labor in Society* (New York: Free Press of Glencoe, 1964); Durkheim, *The Rules of Sociological Method* (New York: Free Press of Glencoe, 1962).
[16] Talcott Parsons, *The Social System* (London: Routledge and Kegan Paul, 1951), pp. 182–191.

from "lower" to "more complex" forms of organization, culminating in liberal capitalist democracy.[17] And while Parsons formally insisted on the importance of avoiding "value judgments" in science, like Durkheim, he still saw the role of social science as contributing in an essential way to the maintenance of system stability and integration.[18]

That Parsons nevertheless claimed to be a Weberian – indeed, becoming the first translator of many of Weber's major works into English – was of inestimable significance for the future course of social scientific intellectual history. Generations of Western social scientists who were trained within the Parsonian tradition naturally tended to accept Parsons's characterization of Weberian sociology as in essence paralleling the Durkheimian and Spencerian views of modernization. Certainly, several key themes in Weber's work, such as the emphasis placed on "the rise of the West" for understanding global social change and on the progressive "rationalization" of modern capitalist societies, appeared to fit neatly within the structural-functionalist view of modernization theory. Even in Germany, where Weber's own sociology had been tarnished by its perceived association with the failures of Weimar democracy, leading scholars such as Wolfgang Schluchter and Jürgen Habermas tended to build on Parsons's reinterpretation of Weber's work, emphasizing the linear process of rationalization in modern society and deemphasizing Weber's concurrent insistence on the unpredictable political and social effects of new belief systems articulated by charismatic individuals.[19] The result is that most social scientists tend to equate Weberianism with modernization theory – greatly complicating the task of resurrecting Weber's distinctive theoretical approach for contemporary audiences.[20]

[17] Parsons, "Evolutionary Universals in Society," *American Journal of Sociology* 29(3, June 1964): 339–357.

[18] Parsons, *The Social System*, pp. 348–359.

[19] See Wolfgang Schluchter, *The Rise of Western Rationalism: Max Weber's Developmental History* (Berkeley: University of California Press, 1981); Jürgen Habermas, *The Theory of Communicative Action* (Boston: Beacon Press, 1984–1987). The broad and enduring influence of Wolfgang Mommsen's scurrilous and highly misleading critique of Weber's supposed great-power statism, originally published in the 1950s, was particularly damaging. It is surely one of the great ironies of intellectual history that Weber – a committed liberal democrat who died more than a decade before Hitler's rise to power – is now more frequently associated with the failure of Weimar democracy than the committed Nazi theorists Karl Schmitt and Martin Heidegger, whose works are approvingly cited by contemporary left-wing academics. See Wolfgang Mommsen, *Max Weber and German Politics, 1890–1920* (Chicago: University of Chicago Press, 1984); for a thoughtful recent critique of Mommsen's views, see Sung Ho Kim, *Max Weber's Politics of Civil Society*.

[20] Another influential conflation of Weberianism and modernization theory was offered by Edward Said, who argued that Weber's reliance on nineteenth-century scholarship about the non-Western world led him "perhaps unwittingly" to replicate Orientalist categories of analysis. Edward Said, *Orientalism* (New York: Pantheon, 1978), p. 259. For an insightful refutation of Said's interpretation of Weber's work, see Mohammad Nafissi, "Reframing Orientalism: Weber and Islam," in Ralph Schroeder, ed., *Max Weber, Democracy, and Modernization* (Basingstoke: Macmillan; New York: St. Martin's, 1998), pp. 182–201.

As the matrix in Table 1.1 demonstrates, however, the distinction between Weber's approach and that of Durkheim and Parsons is simple and fundamental: both paradigms see expressive motivations for human social action as primary and strategic motivations as secondary, but Weber – like rational choice theorists and unlike modernization theorists – is a staunch methodological individualist. As he puts it succinctly, "For sociological purposes there is no such thing as collective personality which 'acts.' When reference is made in a sociological context to a state, a nation, a corporation, a family, or an army corps, or to similar collectivities, what is meant is, on the contrary, *only* a certain kind of development of actual or possible social actions of individual persons."[21] In a nutshell, Weber sees collective social outcomes as generated by the actions of individuals who are motivated by their diverse subjective interpretations of their positions in the social world. Because of the conflation of Weberianism and Parsonian modernization theory, this theoretical viewpoint has been remarkably unexplored in the history of social science. "Culturalists" are almost invariably assumed – usually correctly – to be methodological structuralists, and methodological individualists are almost always assumed to accept a primarily strategic view of human motivation.[22] The new wave of "constructivism" in international relations and, increasingly, within the comparative politics subfield of political science has unfortunately only further reinforced this divide.[23] Only a few scholars have been willing to embrace methodological individualism while accepting that people are essentially interpretive and expressive beings.[24]

[21] Max Weber, *Economy and Society*, trans. Guenther Roth and Claus Wittich, 2 vols. (Berkeley: University of California Press, 1968), p. 14 (emphasis in original).

[22] The affinity between culturalism and structuralism has endured across multiple changes of intellectual fashion among interpretivists. Whatever their other theoretical differences, an essentially collectivist approach to the units-of-analysis problem unites cultural approaches ranging from Parsonian structural-functionalism, to Geertzian and Huntingtonian primordialism, to Gramscian cultural theories of "hegemony," to Foucauldian studies of "discourse," to Bourdieuian studies of "habitus." Scholars in all of these camps tend to reject "methodological individualism" as a simple synonym for rational choice theory.

[23] For representative works, see Wendt, *Social Theory of International Politics*; Ted Hopf, *Social Construction of International Politics: Identities and Foreign Policies, Moscow, 1955 and 1999* (Ithaca, NY: Cornell University Press, 2002); Mark Blyth, *Great Transformations: Economic Ideas and Institutional Change in the Twentieth Century* (Cambridge: Cambridge University Press, 2002). An important work that examines the microfoundations of emerging belief systems in rather more detail is Yoshiko Herrera, *Imagined Economies: The Sources of Russian Regionalism* (Cambridge: Cambridge University Press, 2005).

[24] Note, for example, that both Wendt and Sil in their works cited previously reject the "individualist/idealist" cell of their own two-by-two matrices. Wendt associates this cell with the liberal school in international relations theory – which he then compellingly demonstrates is actually rooted in an essentially rationalist ontology, thus leaving the methodologically individualist/expressive cell in effect empty. Sil, meanwhile, describes individualistic idealism as the terrain of social psychologists but does not cite any scholars working in this tradition by name; he sees Weber, like Giddens and Bourdieu, as adopting a pragmatic "middle ground" among all four competing approaches. See Wendt, *Social Theory*, and Sil, "The Foundations of Eclecticism."

As a result, the most influential efforts to synthesize and summarize competing paradigms in political science tend to ignore or misunderstand the distinctive Weberian approach. Andrew Janos's generally insightful account of the development of Western political science, for example, follows Parsonian convention in treating Weber as one of the founders, along with Durkheim, of main stream modernization theory.[25] So do Anthony Giddens's and Jeffrey Alexander's frequently cited surveys of the classic works of sociological theory.[26] Lichbach and Zuckerman's influential volume quite succinctly and powerfully explores the divisions among rational choice theorists, Marxist and post-Marxist structuralists, and culturalists who embrace a collectivist approach – that is, three of the four cells in Table 1.1 – but does not explore the possibility of a methodologically individualist culturalism.[27] Hall and Taylor's influential article on the three kinds of "new institutionalism" distinguishes among a neo-institutionalism that focuses on individual rationality under institutional constraints, a historical institutionalism that emphasizes the legacies of past institutional structures for contemporary state-society relations, and a sociological institutionalism that emphasizes the power of informal cultural norms and the diffusion of collective cultural practices; again, the possibility of a theoretically distinct "Weberian new institutionalism" is unrecognized.[28] In perhaps the most egregious misrepresentation of Weber's theory, James Coleman's magnum opus, *The Foundations of Social Theory*, opens with a criticism of *The Protestant Ethic and the Spirit of Capitalism* as lacking clear theoretical "microfoundations" to link Calvinism to the ultimate macrosociological outcome of modern capitalism, thus showing the imprecision of cultural theory as compared to rational choice theory – this despite the fact that the entire thrust of Weber's book is precisely to explain why *individual* Calvinists might find it rational to work in a methodical and disciplined way given their theological beliefs, and why the organization of capitalist enterprise by such individuals must necessarily produce incentives for ordinary workers to "punch the clock" in a disciplined manner themselves.[29]

---

[25] Janos, *Politics and Paradigms*.

[26] Anthony Giddens, *Capitalism and Modern Social Theory: An Analysis of the Writings of Marx, Durkheim, and Max Weber* (Cambridge: Cambridge University Press, 1971); Jeffrey C. Alexander, *Structure and Meaning: Rethinking Classical Sociology* (New York: Columbia University Press, 1989).

[27] This remains true in the recently issued second edition of their volume of essays, notwithstanding the editors' frequent invocation of Weber in their introductory chapter. See Lichbach and Zuckerman, *Comparative Politics*.

[28] Peter A. Hall and Rosemary C. R. Taylor, "Political Science and the Three New Institutionalisms," *Political Studies* 44(5, December 1996): 936–957.

[29] James Coleman, *The Foundations of Social Theory* (Cambridge, MA: Harvard University Press, 1990), pp. 7–9. It is true that Weber provides less empirical evidence to illustrate the link between Calvinist entrepreneurship and broader incentives for time discipline in capitalist societies than he does concerning the theological content of Calvinist belief systems, but there is no ambiguity about the nature of the causal mechanism linking micromotives to macrosociological outcomes in Weber's argument: once some capitalist enterprises were organized in

To explain the entrenched resistance on all sides to acknowledging – let alone embracing – Weber's logically consistent combination of theoretical axioms would perhaps require a separate treatise in the sociology of knowledge.[30] Suffice it to say that reclaiming this paradigmatic ground for contemporary Weberianism necessarily opens up a battle that must be fought simultaneously on many intellectual fronts. Parsonian (and Habermasian) scholars will insist on the superiority of their own collectivist interpretations and operational-izations of Weber's conceptions of "rationalization" and "culture." Rational choice theorists may find common ground with Weber on the issue of method-ological individualism but will tend to resist the idea that strategic rationality is only one of several possible types of social action that must all be examined within specific cultural contexts.[31] Marxists and neo-Marxists must logically reject Weberianism in toto, objecting both to its methodological individualism and to its willingness to see ideology, religion, philosophy, and other forms of cultural self-expression as autonomous causal factors rather than as reflec-tions of class interests. Indeed, even some contemporary scholars who consider themselves Weberians will no doubt object to my account of Weber's legacy here. It must therefore be demonstrated both that such a characterization of the Weberian paradigm is an accurate reflection of Weber's own theoretical intent and that it can serve as the basis for a productive alternative approach to empirical social scientific research.

Weber's Four Types of Social Action

That Weber was a committed methodological individualist should be clear enough from his explicit statements to this effect cited earlier. However, his simultaneous embrace of the importance of nonstrategic forms of motivation shapes his theoretical version of methodological individualism in several dis-tinct ways that must be clarified at the outset for contemporary readers. In particular, Weber's methodology must be distinguished from his ontology; Weber's distinctive definition of individual "social action" must be parsed; and Weber's understanding of "instrumental rationality" must be differentiated from that adopted in rational choice theory.

---

terms of rational discipline, others were forced to do the same or go out of business. See Max Weber, *Protestant Ethic and the Spirit of Capitalism*, trans. Stephen Kalberg (Chicago: Fitzroy Dearborn, 2001), p. 68.

[30] For some speculations on the reasons for the continuing marginality of Weberianism in polit-ical science, see Stephen E. Hanson, "Weber, Prediction, and Social Science Methodology," in Laurence McFalls, ed., *Max Weber's "Objectivity" Reconsidered* (Toronto: University of Toronto Press, 2007), pp. 290–308.

[31] Some rational choice theorists now argue for an "analytic Weberianism" emphasizing strategic rationality in human behavior. See Edgar Kiser and Justin Baer, "The Bureaucratization of States: Toward an Analytical Weberianism," in Julia Adams, Elisabeth Stephanie Clemens, and Ann Shola Orloff, eds., *Remaking Modernity: Politics, History and Sociology* (Durham, NC: Duke University Press, 2005), pp. 225–245.

First, Weber's methodological individualism is genuinely *methodological* in intent. He is by no means an *ontological* individualist – that is, he does not insist, à la Margaret Thatcher, that "society does not exist" and only individuals are real. On the contrary, Weber clearly accepts the need to analyze social collectivities as such. However, he argues that, when doing so, one must always bear in mind the ultimate dependence of such collectivities on individual action:

> For . . . cognitive purposes – for instance, juristic ones – or for practical ends, it may . . . be convenient or even indispensable to treat social collectivities, such as states, associations, business corporations, foundations, as if they were individual persons. Thus they may be treated as the subjects of rights and duties or as the performers of legally significant actions. But for the subjective interpretation of action in sociological work these collectivities must be treated solely as the resultants and modes of organization of the particular acts of particular persons, since these alone can be treated as agents in a course of subjectively understandable action.[32]

Sociological depictions of collective social entities thus necessarily take the form of "ideal types" – that is, abstract, simplified models based on one's interpretation of the underlying types of individual social action that probabilistically combine to generate and reproduce such collectivities. Any depiction of social collectives as "actors" in and of themselves, in Weber's view, necessarily results in misleading reification. In this sense, Weber's methodological individualism is of a more thoroughgoing variety than that adopted in rational choice theory, whose practitioners frequently take collective social units such as states, classes, or even societies as their "individual" strategic units, methodologically sidestepping the collective action problems involved in maintaining and reproducing such units over time.[33]

Second, strictly speaking, it is not the individual per se who serves as Weber's central methodological building block but rather individual *social action*. "Action is 'social,'" Weber states, "insofar as its subjective meaning takes account of the behavior of others and is thereby oriented in its course."[34] To the extent that individuals act in ways that involve no conscious effort to influence other people's behavior – for example, because of biologically conditioned reflexes – sociological analysis is unnecessary and out of place. A simple cough is not social action, for example, unless the individual cougher is attempting consciously to influence her audience – perhaps signaling that she wishes to interrupt a speaker who has worn out his welcome, feigning illness so as to avoid work, or demonstrating various techniques for most effectively clearing one's throat.[35]

---

[32] Weber, *Economy and Society*, p. 13.
[33] Fritz Scharpf, "Games Real Actors Could Play: The Challenge of Complexity," *Journal of Theoretical Politics* 3(3, July 1991): 277–304.
[34] Weber, *Economy and Society*, p. 4.
[35] This point, of course, recalls Clifford Geertz's gloss on Ryle's discussion of the various meanings of winking in Geertz's famous essay "Thick Description." However, Geertz, unlike Weber,

Third, as this latter point implies, Weber's methodological individualism is irreducibly interpretive in character. The "same" social action can mean very different things in different cultural contexts, and understanding the individual motivation for a given action is thus an essential component of explaining it. Note that this methodological insistence on *Verstehen*, or understanding, need not preclude the possibility – central to rational choice theory – that much of human social action is instrumentally rational in nature. Indeed, interpretive sociological analysis of actors' subjective motivations will generally demonstrate that the desire simply to advance one's material or ideal interests is one of the most common forms of social action in almost every cultural setting. Weber acknowledges that the interactions of people who strive to maximize their money, power, status, or chances for salvation may be usefully analyzed through models that assume universal instrumental rationality, as in neoclassical economics; he even encourages the use of models based on rationality as the best starting point for most macrosociological analysis. For Weber, however, instrumental rationality itself must ultimately be understood as a form of expressive, subjectively meaningful behavior. Thus, rational choice models are themselves "ideal types" whose applicability will be limited to the extent that individuals in a given social setting act according to nonstrategic, rather than instrumental, motivations: "For purposes of a typological scientific analysis it is convenient to treat all irrational, affectually determined elements of behavior as factors of deviation from a conceptually pure type of rational action."[36]

With these preliminary clarifications out of the way, we may now turn our attention directly to Weber's theory of social action, which outlined four basic types: instrumental rationality, value rationality, affect, and habit.[37] Instrumentally rational action involves the calculation of the most effective or efficient means to obtain certain ends. Value-rational action involves engaging in behavior that is seen as an end in itself, regardless of payoffs. Affectual action is behavior motivated out of a sense of emotional loyalty or antipathy to others. Finally, habitual social action involves engaging in established ways of interacting with others that have become ingrained or unquestioned.

Although Weber sets out these four types of social action fairly clearly, it must be admitted that his theory of how these interpretive microfoundations relate systematically to the macrosociological analysis carried out in the rest of his work remains rather fuzzy. Weber seems to have arrived at his list of types of action in an essentially inductive way, wishing to remain open-minded about the possibility that additional types might prove to be sociologically important.

makes no attempt to introduce theoretical limits on the range of possible interpretations of social meaning through utilizing ideal types of collective action. See Clifford Geertz, "Thick Description: Toward an Interpretive Theory of Culture," in *Interpretation of Cultures: Selected Essays* (New York: Basic Books, 1973), pp. 3–30.

36 Weber, *Economy and Society*, p. 6.
37 Ibid., pp. 24–25.

TABLE 1.2. *Weberian Types of Social Action*

	Degree of Deliberation	
	Low (Emotional)	High (Rational)
Degree of time salience		
Low (sacred)	Affect	Value rationality
High (profane)	Habit	Instrumental rationality

He does consistently refer back to all four types in his analyses of his ideal-typical models of the types of legitimate domination, and these in turn serve as the theoretical starting point for his well-known analyses of bureaucracy, the state, the city, religion, and so on. But the absence of any precise theoretical account in Weber's work of how instrumental rationality, value rationality, affect, and habit at the individual level systematically relate to the emergence of traditional, rational-legal, charismatic, and nonlegitimate forms of domination is clearly a major lacuna in his sociological theory, which may account in large part for the later misunderstandings of his work by modernization theorists, Marxists, and rational choice theorists alike.

The four-cell matrix in Table 1.2 clarifies how one can present Weber's four types of domination as built quite explicitly on the four types of social action.[38] In doing so, I have expanded somewhat upon Weber's own theoretical presentation; however, I think I have remained essentially faithful to the original tenets of Weber's sociological method.

Here Weber's four types of social action are seen as derived from the possible combinations of two variables: whether the *degree of time salience* for the action is high or low, and whether the *degree of deliberation* associated with the action is high or low. High time salience means that the motivation of action is perceived as firmly embedded in the context of concrete events connecting past, present, and future. Low time salience means that the action is perceived as being governed by, or oriented toward, timeless principles or loyalties. Following the work of Mircea Eliade, I term action motivated by time-bound concerns as "profane" and actions where time is seemingly unimportant as "sacred."[39] A high degree of deliberation means that the principles of an action are evaluated, pondered, and processed at length; at some point, highly deliberate action becomes simply thinking. A low degree of deliberation, by contrast, means that the motivation for action is more directly connected to impulses or instincts. At the risk of oversimplification, one can understand

[38] I would like to thank Arista Cirtautas for the initial inspiration to think about Weber's four types of social action as representing deductive combinations of more fundamental dimensions of individual social motivation, presentable on a two-by-two matrix of the sort described here.

[39] Mircea Eliade, *The Sacred and the Profane: The Nature of Religion* (New York: Harper and Row, 1961).

highly deliberate action as "rational" and action that is less highly deliberate as "emotional."[40]

Weber's four types of social action can then be derived deductively from the axes depicted in Table 1.2. Highly deliberate, highly time-salient social action is what Weber – along with most contemporary social scientists – terms "instrumental rationality." In other words, instrumentally rational action involves a careful evaluation of how to pursue one's interests in a given time period. This is the classic form of means-ends rationality on which modern economic theory and rational choice models of social organization focus. Instead of seeing instrumental rationality as universal or taking it as axiomatic, however, Weberian theory insists that this type of human social action exists empirically only where actors subjectively process information in a deliberate and goal-oriented manner in deciding to act.

Highly time-bound social action that does not involve much deliberation is what Weber terms "traditional" action. To avoid confusion with Weber's ideal type of traditional legitimate domination, I term this form of social action "habit." Habit is action that is motivated very much by day-to-day concerns, but without the actor being clearly aware of the principle according to which she is acting or the precise costs and benefits that are involved. The decision to do what one has typically done in the past does not require much deliberation; nor is it likely to be associated with explicit religious or philosophical principle. Explorations of "bounded rationality" in economics and political science have shown that decision making based upon "rules of thumb" or "standard operating procedures" are empirically more common than fully rational utility-maximization.[41]

Highly deliberate social action that does not take temporal context into account is what Weber terms "value rationality." Value-rational action thus involves conduct based on a well-thought-out decision to uphold ethical ideals or philosophic maxims that are perceived to be timelessly binding, without regard to the potential future payoffs or costs posed by the concrete social situation. This is perhaps the rarest form of individual action, but despite its

---

[40] How far this two-by-two chart corresponds to new findings in neuroscience concerning human brain functioning is a fascinating topic that deserves additional research. My preliminary effort to survey this literature suggests that Weber's categorization of types of social action as I have synthesized it here connects rather well to neurobiological findings about human cognition. Of course, as neuroscience develops, we may find good reasons to modify or complicate Weber's original scheme of types of social action to include other, previously unrecognized dimensions of cognition that turn out to be salient for social science. In any case, Weber's four types of social action certainly connect more successfully to contemporary scientific accounts of individual brain function than standard rational choice theory, with its wholly unrealistic assumptions about individual information processing. See, for example, the findings reported in Joseph Henrich et al., eds., *Foundations of Human Sociality: Economic Experiments and Ethnographic Evidence from Fifteen Small-Scale Societies* (Oxford: Oxford University Press, 2004).

[41] Herbert A. Simon, *Models of Bounded Rationality* (Cambridge, MA: MIT Press, 1982).

infrequency, it may exert a disproportionate influence on social outcomes – as the subsequent analysis of ideology in this study will show.

Finally, social action that does not involve much deliberation but which is experienced as being out of the ordinary flow of events in time is what Weber terms "affect." The classic example of affectual action is the behavior of people who are newly in love. While new lovers may, of course, scheme instrumentally to spend more time together, they subjectively experience their moments of blissful union as utterly outside of ordinary temporality – as the frequent deployment of such phrases as "I feel as if I've always known you" or "we will love each other for all eternity" suggests. Of course, affectual action can also take forms we would generally judge as negative, as in the case of action motivated by a "timeless" desire for revenge or by addictions to mind-altering substances.

In short, then, Weber's four types of social action can be thought of as synonymous with profane rationality (instrumental rationality), profane emotion (habit), sacred rationality (value rationality), and sacred emotion (affect). It remains to show how this deductive scheme for interpreting social action can clarify Weber's "microfoundations" of legitimate and illegitimate domination. In the next section, I demonstrate that Weber's famous division of traditional, rational-legal, and charismatic types of legitimacy can be understood as involving the successful institutionalization of different combinations of individual instrumental rationality, value rationality, habit, and affect in the pursuit of political ends. Note that this procedure is precisely analogous to the search for microfoundations of macropolitical phenomena within rational choice theory; the range of possible types of individual action that are seen as significant for explaining collective outcomes is simply expanded to include motivation that is neither time salient nor deliberative.

Weber argues that the proper starting point for comparative political analysis is an understanding of the nature of domination, which he defines simply as "the probability that certain specific commands (or all commands) will be obeyed by a given group of persons."[42] From this point of view, if subordinates are 100 percent likely to obey the commands of a superior, then domination is total; if the likelihood of obedience drops below a certain point, domination ceases to exist. In politics, "legitimate domination" refers to the subjective belief by the "staff" of the state or ruling group that those who give orders have a "right" to do so; Weber argues that subjective belief in the legitimacy of commands tends to increase the probability they will be carried out.[43] Note that this way of looking at domination focuses analytic attention on individuals within elite-staff relationships rather than on the state-society relationships often studied by scholars interested in problems of legitimation.[44] Thus, from a Weberian

---

[42] Weber, *Economy and Society*, p. 212.
[43] Ibid., p. 213.
[44] Stephen E. Hanson, "Defining Democratic Consolidation," in Richard Anderson Jr., M. Steven Fish, Stephen E. Hanson, and Philip Roeder, *Postcommunism and the Theory of Democracy* (Princeton, NJ: Princeton University Press, 2001), pp. 126–151.

point of view, a state can be highly legitimate among its staff while being simultaneously hated by much of its subject population.

For Weber, there are three main types of "legitimate domination."[45] Pure charismatic authority rests upon the acceptance by followers of a leader's claim to possess miraculous, superhuman, and extraordinary powers; charisma thus stands opposed to all "routine" bureaucratic or communal ways of life. Traditional authority rests upon the legitimacy of historical customs, familial bonds, and accepted practices. Rational-legal authority rests upon the legitimacy of impersonal rules and procedures governing individual behavior. Finally, there is the nonlegitimate type of instrumental domination, in which elites sustain themselves in power through sheer coercion or material payoffs.[46] Like charismatic authority, however, instrumental domination is comparatively fragile, because it inspires no loyalty among those who act as its agents of enforcement and who are therefore likely to defect the moment immediate payoffs or penalties are withdrawn.

Weber did not intend for these four ideal types to be utilized in reified, static terms, as complete and accurate descriptions of actual political regimes. In fact, according to Weber, no pure charismatic, rational-legal, traditional, or even instrumental form of domination can ever exist. Instead, Weber sees his ideal types of collective order as built out of the aggregated social action of individuals. When the actions of many individuals are patterned along standardized lines over time and space, we can say that an organization exists. When such standardized patterns of behavior are seen as authoritative, we can say that the organizational order has become legitimate. But all of these designations are subject to change as the bases of individual action toward others in society themselves change. To say that an organization exists, in this sense, is in effect to assert that there is a high probability that individuals within a given social location will act toward others in accordance with a particular set of formal and informal rules or norms. If the probability of action conforming to such rules or norms decreases below a certain point, the organization collapses.

Charismatic domination is based on the combination of value rationality and affect, the two forms of "sacred" or timeless social action.[47] When a charismatic movement is established, those involved in it feel that an affectual bond between members of the group is wholly consistent with self-conscious and explicit principles of justice, morality, or religion. At the same time, such movements must oppose both instrumental rationality, which is seen as introducing egoistic calculation capable of poisoning the purity of the group's affectual bond, and habit, which is seen as eroding the clarity of deliberation necessary to grasp

---

[45] Weber, *Economy and Society*, p. 215.

[46] Although Weber does not develop the concept of instrumental domination at length, it does appear in his work when describing, for example, the emergence of authority in the medieval European city as an "usurpation" of the traditional authority of feudal elites. See Weber, "The City (Non-Legitimate Domination)," in *Economy and Society*, pp. 1212–1372.

[47] See also Hanson, *Time and Revolution*.

the group's sacred principles. As a result of pure charisma's basis in forms of social action for which temporal outcomes have very low salience, charismatic movements tend to be highly unstable.

Sometimes, however, charismatic forms of domination undergo the process Weber termed "routinization."[48] From the perspective adopted here, routinization can be understood as the gradual replacement of whichever sacred category is less important in the original formation of a charismatic movement with the profane form of action diagonally opposed to it in Table 1.2. If value rationality is less important than affect, as in the case of a charismatic leader who finds a followership primarily because of the influence of his powerful personality, followers may over time begin to obey that leader (or his successors) primarily out of habit, though still preserving the affectual core of the charismatic bond.[49] In this case, charisma has been routinized in a traditional direction. If affect is less important than value rationality, as in the case of a religious or ideological sect in which the charismatic leader's authority is seen primarily as derived from his doctrine, followers may over time begin to pursue mundane interests instrumentally, though still within the ethical framework mandated by that doctrine. In this case, charisma has been routinized in a rational-legal direction.

The two stable forms of legitimate authority – the rational-legal and traditional types – thus tend to emerge initially out of charismatic movements. *Traditional domination*, based on the combination of affect and habit, tends to repress or institutionally limit all highly deliberate forms of social action, whether value rational or instrumentally rational. *Rational-legal domination*, based on the combination of value rationality and instrumental rationality, tends to repress or institutionally limit all emotional forms of social action, whether affectual or habitual. Because both of these forms of domination weld together a "sacred" principle and a "profane" principle, they are capable of providing an unchanging focus of identity and a mechanism for channeling the time-bound interests of those who find that focus of identity legitimate. Rational-legal and traditional authority are thus relatively stable compared to the charismatic and instrumental types of domination. However, it is important to emphasize that even these more stable types of legitimate domination endure only contingently, because human beings in all societies act on diverse motivations and tend to resist strict institutional control.[50]

---

[48] Weber, *Economy and Society*, p. 246.

[49] This is consistent with the theoretical and empirical analysis of Douglas Madsen and Peter G. Snow, *The Charismatic Bond: Political Behavior in Time of Crisis* (Cambridge, MA: Harvard University Press, 1991).

[50] By no means should Weber's ideal types of rational-legal and traditional domination be confused with Parsons's analysis of traditional and modern social "systems," which wrongly assumes that the legitimating principles governing elite-staff relationships must somehow functionally fit with underlying cultural values common to entire societies. See Parsons, *The Social System*.

Moreover, the dynamic that produces the routinization of charisma does not end with the creation of rational-legal or traditional domination. Instead, the gradual erosion of the sacred bases of social action within any routinized context continues after stable institutions are established. Thus, the process of routinization is followed by a process of corruption, characterized by the decay of the dominant principle of legitimation – affect or value rationality – within a routinized social order.[51] Under traditional authority, this means the decay of the affectual bond between the staff and the leader. Under rational-legal authority, corruption involves the decay of the value-rational principle of legitimacy that generates the rules for order following in a given bureaucratic organization. Thus, different forms of individual behavior are considered corrupt in different political settings. Using one's office to benefit family members, for example, is corrupt from the point of view of rational-legal norms of bureaucratic rectitude, but it may be perfectly legitimate within the context of traditional authority based on communal affective ties. Indeed, the upholding of legal procedures at the expense of personal loyalties itself can be considered "corrupt" by those enmeshed in traditional norms of legitimation.

Nevertheless, corruption within both traditional and rational-legal organizations ultimately leads to the same end result: domination becomes illegitimate, generating *instrumental domination*. This form of domination combines habitual and instrumentally rational bases of social action. In other words, instrumental domination occurs when an elite continues to pursue its worldly interests within roles to which it has become habituated. Such an elite cannot possibly inspire any "timeless" loyalty; therefore, instrumental domination lasts only as long as those who might oppose it are coerced into obedience or bought off. The corruption of a routinized legitimate form of domination into purely instrumental domination thus leads ultimately to the final breakdown of organizational order. It is in environments of breakdown that new charismatic movements, which appear to reinfuse social life with sacred meaning, can have both cultural power and material success. The cycle of charisma, routinization, and corruption thus continues indefinitely, or at least as long as human social action is governed by deliberation and time perception.

Although admittedly the preceding summary of the microfoundations of Weber's types of legitimate domination never appears in precisely this form in Weber's own writings, the major dynamics it describes are nevertheless consistently present in various ways in his ideal-typical accounts of major social institutions. In particular, as many commentators have noted, Weber's sociology

---

[51] Weber, it is true, did not discuss the concept of corruption in great detail. However, the dynamics of decaying legitimacy that I summarize in this section are implicit in his treatments of how "the pursuit of wealth, stripped of its religious and ethical meaning, tends to become associated with purely mundane passions," and of the ways in which traditional forms of legitimacy allow "a wide scope for actual arbitrariness and the expression of purely personal whims on the part of the ruler and members of his administrative staff." See Weber, *The Protestant Ethic and the Spirit of Capitalism*, p. 182; Weber, *Economy and Society*, p. 239.

tends to emphasize the "conflicting imperatives" underlying all forms of social organization.[52] From the perspective outlined here, we can understand these conflicts as rooted in contradictions between the primary types of social action combined in various macrosociological structures. Thus, enforcers of charismatic domination are inevitably faced with divisions between followers who emphasize the purity of doctrine (value rationality) and those who venerate the personage of the charismatic leader (affect) – in other words, between those who interpret charisma as built on powerful deliberation about timeless insights and those who interpret it as built around an emotional bond with a time-transcendent personality. Efforts to reinforce rational-legal domination are torn between the imperatives of "formal" and "substantive" rationality – that is, between the need to ensure, through the enforcement of appropriate rewards and punishments, that bureaucrats individually follow the formal rules on a day-to-day basis (instrumental rationality) and the need continually to reorient bureaucratic activity toward the underlying, defining "purpose" of the bureaucracy itself (value rationality). Traditional domination is forced to confront the conflicting imperatives of preserving and protecting ordinary people's time-honored customs (habit) while ensuring an extraordinary, not merely habitual, veneration of the traditional leadership (affect). Failure to cope with one or another side of these conflicting imperatives generates internal organizational divisions that can ultimately lead to a rupture of the legitimate order itself.

Weberian Theory and Competing Paradigms

Obviously, it is impossible to summarize all of Weber's diverse theoretical and empirical contributions in a single chapter, and the model of Weberian microfoundations of the ideal types of domination sketched in the preceding section is by no means intended to stand in as a substitute for a careful reading of Weber's own work. However, because Weber himself places the problem of political order giving and order following at the center of his own comparative sociology, this somewhat streamlined account of Weber's version of methodological individualism may help to clarify precisely how the Weberian paradigm differs from, and in some ways intersects with, existing mainstream approaches in social science.

Indeed, on the basis of the discussion of two dimensions of paradigmatic controversy in social science with which this chapter began, the main objections to Weber's theoretical approach from all three major competing paradigms can be anticipated. Rational choice theorists, to begin with, will object that the expansion of types of individual social action beyond the time-bound,

---

[52] Bendix, *Max Weber: An Intellectual Portrait*, p. 438; Kenneth Jowitt, *The Leninist Response to National Dependency* (Berkeley: Institute of International Studies, University of California, 1978); Andrew Gould, "Conflicting Imperatives and Concept Formation," *Review of Politics* 61(3, Summer 1999): 439–463.

deliberative realm of instrumental rationality is likely to make Weberian theory less parsimonious and potentially unfalsifiable. Specifically, Weberian analysts may be tempted to invoke the categories of "value rationality" and "affect" to explain every initially puzzling form of social behavior, before first seeing whether a simple instrumentalist explanation might suffice. Particularly given the subjective element of Weberian methodology introduced by the reliance on interpretive understanding of individual motivation, such an approach could end up producing simple tautologies, in which seemingly noninstrumental individual behavior is "explained" by ascribing it to unobservable, nonrational types of motivation. Some rational choice theorists may even doubt the ontological possibility of individual action that is truly lacking any concern with temporal outcomes whatsoever, insisting that underlying every profession of "value-rational" principle and "timeless" devotion lurks a self-interested desire to influence one's audience for personal gain.

These objections can be answered successfully, I think, by emphasizing the ways in which Weberian theory is consistent with much of existing rational choice theory. Indeed, cutting-edge approaches to rational choice already explore interactions among actors with different time horizons (i.e., "discount rates"), even if the rational choice paradigm at present lacks a theory of where these time orientations come from. To arrive at the Weberian concept of "value rationality," we need only accept that some rational actors elongate their time horizons past the time scale of their own life-spans – a postulate that would appear to be hard to deny in an era of endemic suicide bombings.[53] Similarly, that actors empirically vary in the degree to which they consciously deliberate

---

[53] At least some headway in assessing the ontological possibility of value-rational action can be made, I think, simply through introspection. I, for example, have been a vegetarian since 1988, with only a couple of misguided episodes of seafood consumption after that date. I subjectively believe that I have adopted this lifestyle for "ethical" reasons: after long debates in my mid-twenties with two respected friends, I came to the conclusion it is always wrong to kill animals when one does not have to. I once had an argument about this account of my motivation with an academic colleague who was committed to rational choice theory. My colleague insisted that my vegetarianism must actually be motivated by my desire to live a longer life, because it simply could not be motivated by ethical reasoning in the form I described to him! Of course, a more sophisticated rational choice interpretation of my conduct might involve an effort to show that I gain positive utility from trying to impress others with my relatively consistent purity on this issue, or perhaps that my vegetarianism provides me with a trustworthy community of other like-minded individuals who can help me find good restaurants in foreign cities. But I was quite unaware of these latter effects of my decision to give up meat eating at the time I made it. Subjectively, the decision has seemed a very costly one that has forced me to abjure many of my once-favorite dishes, to inconvenience my family and friends, and to separate myself from many of the central rituals of ordinary society. Indeed, not only do I now dread rather than welcome my inevitably awkward conversations about the ethics of vegetarianism, but I also have only a small handful of vegetarian friends and family members. All things considered, an explanation of my lifestyle choice in terms of my subjective sense of duty to defend "sacred principles" seems more parsimonious and persuasive to me than any instrumentalist explanation. Obviously, readers will have to judge for themselves the extent to which their own behavior is best characterized as consistently instrumental.

about the relationships between means and ends is already the focus of important work on the role of "bounded rationality" in explaining political and social outcomes.[54] The role of affect, finally, has been experimentally demonstrated to have systematic effects on the behavior of subjects in a wide variety of game theoretic situations.[55] Weberian theory thus merely endogenizes these three types of motivation that are treated as exogenous in standard rational choice theory – and it does so parsimoniously, simply by allowing individual time orientations and degrees of deliberation to vary past the axiomatic limits prescribed in conventional neoclassical economics. As for the problem of falsifiability, there is actually little to distinguish Weberianism and rational choice theory here at the abstract, paradigmatic level. The assumption of individual strategic rationality is no more and no less falsifiable, in and of itself, than the assumption that individual social action can be usefully characterized in terms of Weber's four types. If anything, experimental research on cognitive psychology seems to indicate the superior empirical accuracy of Weber's view.[56] Ultimately, however, the primary test of a theoretical paradigm's utility is whether it can generate hypotheses that do a better job of explaining outstanding empirical puzzles than its competitors – as I hope this book will demonstrate is true of the Weberian approach.

A second set of objections to the Weberian paradigm will arise from advocates of Parsonian modernization theory, as well as from other culturalists who reject methodological individualism. Surely, such scholars will insist, individuals do not autonomously "choose" the values, emotions, and habits that shape

---

[54] Bryan D. Jones, *Politics and the Architecture of Choice: Bounded Rationality and Governance* (Chicago: University of Chicago Press, 2001).

[55] A particularly interesting example is presented in Iris Bohnet and Bruno S. Frey, "Social Distance and Other-Regarding Behavior in Dictator Games: Comment," *American Economic Review* 89(1, March 1999): 335–339. In the dictator game, subjects are asked simply to divide a set sum of money between themselves and a recipient; rationally, dictators should offer the recipient nothing. Bohnet and Frey found that 25 percent of their subjects offered an equal division when both partners were anonymous; 39 percent did so when they could identify the other party in the division (but not vice versa); but fully 71 percent offered an equal division when participants were asked to look at each other silently for a few seconds prior to the experiment *before* the roles of "dictator" and "recipient" were assigned, even though there was no way for recipients later to discover who had played the role of dictator.

[56] Daniel Kahneman, Paul Slovic, and Amos Tversky, eds., *Judgment under Uncertainty: Heuristics and Biases* (Cambridge: Cambridge University Press, 1982); Robert P. Abelson, "The Secret Existence of Expressive Behavior," in Jeffrey Friedman, ed., *The Rational Choice Controversy: Economic Models of Politics Reconsidered* (New Haven: Yale University Press, 1996), pp. 25–36. A particularly interesting refutation of the rationality assumption, based on the real-life behavior of contestants in a game show with high potential payoffs in which there are determinate predictions from expected utility theory, is Thierry Post et al., "Deal or No Deal? Decision Making under Risk in a Large-Payoff Game Show," Paper presented at the annual meeting of the European Finance Association, April 2006. Post et al. found that contestants who had turned down large cash offers at the beginning of their game but later suffered a streak of bad luck were likely irrationally to reject comparatively good offers – presumably because these objectively good offers were now framed as losses as compared to the earlier higher ones.

their daily social lives. Given that the very notion of "individualism" is a product of modern history, particularly in Western Europe and North America, it seems a mistake to utilize it – even "methodologically" – to analyze social life in diverse global cultural contexts. Empirical research in the Parsonian tradition has demonstrated, after all, that social values tend to go together in coherent cultural packages that correlate strongly to levels of socioeconomic development.[57] How can such findings be explained from a theoretical perspective that denies the independent causal role of collective social units of analysis?

The objection that it is impossible to understand collective identities from a methodologically individualist perspective, I think, is based on a misunderstanding of precisely what that perspective does and does not imply about human identity. Again, methodological individualism for Weber is not ontological individualism. It is an analytical technique for breaking social collectives into the more basic units of social action that make them up. Thus, it is quite possible that a group of individuals, each of whom sees the other as connected in an eternal affective bond, and none of whom deliberates very much about this emotional connection, will interpret their collectivity as representing a "higher community" that possesses a collective identity and a capacity for autonomous action. To say this, and even to acknowledge the emotional and social power that is generated by such an interpretive framework, does not require the social scientist herself to share in this interpretation of the origins and inner dynamics of the group.[58] In fact, it is unlikely that anyone who does see her community in these terms will possess the necessary detachment to analyze it scientifically. A steadfast commitment to methodological individualism can thus act as an important corrective against bias generated by powerful commitments to particular communitarian social doctrines. Moreover, Weberian analysis also allows for analysis of social situations where individuals' motivations are not shared so symmetrically – for example, where most members of a group see their bond in affectual terms, but a few treat their fellows in an instrumentally rational manner, pretending to be loyal to the community only to exploit it more effectively. Modernization theory is forced to treat such a mixed situation as one of "disequilibrium" or "anomie"; Weberian theory expects such environments to be the norm in social life. As for the empirical findings of modernization theory about the correlations between levels of development and collective value systems, most can also be accounted for fairly easily in Weberian terms. Thus, for example, the fact that people who have grown up under the powerful political and socioeconomic institutions of rational-legal

---

[57] Ronald Inglehart, *Modernization and Post-Modernization: Cultural, Economic, and Political Change in 43 Societies* (Princeton, NJ: Princeton University Press, 1997).

[58] Contrast this approach to that of John Searle, who makes an unjustified logical leap from the observation that individuals can choose to see each other as part of a larger "we" to the assumption that collective actors themselves can be said to have "intentionality." See Searle, *The Construction of Social Reality* (New York: Free Press, 1995), p. 24.

liberal capitalism tend to see themselves as "rational individuals" who reject "tradition" and "superstition" and embrace individual "liberty" is hardly surprising, given that the expression of such beliefs is generally consistent with prevailing value-rational principles, frequently helps to further one's individual interests, is easy to repeat habitually after years of exposure, and may even make one feel good emotionally. Weberian analysis improves upon modernization theory, however, by also allowing for interpretive understanding of otherwise seemingly anomalous cultural combinations, such as the "revolutionary" modernization program of Soviet Marxism-Leninism, which required individuals to profess a simultaneous belief in rational planning and miraculous overproduction, or "traditional" capitalism governed by personal loyalties among key business families rather than rational-legal impersonalism in the enforcement of property rights.[59]

In some ways, Marxist and structuralist critiques of Weberian theory are the most difficult to respond to, given the completely different starting point of such theories in collective strategic behavior rather than individual subjectivity. Marxists and structuralists will thus object that the brute facts of the global distribution of resources, the geographic concentration of major trade networks and sources of capital in the developed West, and the dominant modes of labor exploitation do much more to explain the trajectory of contemporary history than do the subjective imaginings of "expressive" individuals.[60] The danger, then, is that Weberian methodological individualism may devolve into a kind of German idealist "science of spirit" (Geisteswissenschaft) with no grounding in analysis of what is actually possible in a given physical and socioeconomic environment. Worse yet, to focus on individual subjectivity rather than objective constraints may have the effect of obscuring these brute structural facts for scholars and ordinary people alike, contributing to the perpetuation of currently hegemonic forms of domination.

Weber himself was actually quite sensitive to this kind of criticism of his work, and there is much evidence to show that he accepted the need to incorporate a certain degree of "structuralism" within interpretive sociology. Thus, he insists that individuals are initially drawn to adopt specific belief systems because of an "elective affinity" between such beliefs and their existing ways of life.[61] Calvinism, for example, flourished in European cities where a certain degree of economic rationalism had already been attained by burghers

59 Hanson, Time and Revolution; Gary Hamilton and Nicole Woolsey Biggart, "Market, Culture, and Authority: A Comparative Analysis of Management and Organization in the Far East," American Journal of Sociology 94 (supp., July 1988): S52–94.

60 Immanuel Wallerstein, Geopolitics and Geoculture: Essays on the Changing World System (Cambridge: Cambridge University Press; Paris: Editions de la Maison des Sciences de l'Homme, 1991); Wallerstein, "The Rise and Future Demise of the World Capitalist System?" Comparative Studies in Society and History 16(4, September 1974): 387–415; Charles Tilly, Coercion, Capital, and European States, AD 990–1990 (Cambridge, MA: Basil Blackwell, 1990).

61 Weber, The Protestant Ethic and the Spirit of Capitalism.

during the Middle Ages. He concludes the *Protestant Ethic* by reminding the reader that by no means is it his intention to substitute for a "one-sided materialistic an equally one-sided spiritualistic causal interpretation of culture and history."[62] Similarly, Weber's analysis of the three types of legitimate domination is accompanied by a lengthy analysis of associational interactions based on economic rationality that shape the environmental conditions within which relations of political domination are initially formed. And Weber's *General Economic History*, compiled from lecture notes to his students, emphasizes "material" factors at least as much as religious and cultural identities.[63]

What differentiates Weber's approach to "material" factors in social change from that of Marxists and other structuralists, however, is that Weber never loses sight of the ultimate dependence of all collective social outcomes on the patterns of individual social action that generate them. A "class," for Weber, is not a collective unit with its own autonomous ability to act but rather a set of individuals who subjectively feel that their position in the economic system of a given society binds them together in a common identity.[64] A "state," he argues, is constituted in the final analysis by specific interactions of political leaders and their "staffs" that reproduce institutions that can monopolize the means of legitimate coercion in a given territory.[65] If individual workers in sufficient numbers no longer see themselves as being part of the "working class," then "class" ceases to be a useful sociological category for analyzing their behavior. If enough individual agents who wield coercion on behalf of a state no longer believe subjectively that the "state" they serve has any legitimate claim on their loyalty, then the state disappears. Thus, for Weberian theory there can be no "problem of false consciousness" in which individuals fail to recognize their "true" structural position. Nor are there any indispensable "structural units" in the global system, immune to eventual collapse as a result of defections by the individuals who defend them. Indeed, Weber's key point is that all macrostructures, no matter how powerful or enduring, are themselves originally the products of previous successful coordination of individual interpretive actors.

Weber's consistent awareness of the essential contingency of all macrostructures in social life also explains his refusal to subordinate the task of scientific analysis to the cause of human liberation (or any other nonscientific value). In doing so, social scientists wittingly or unwittingly present themselves as charismatic leaders who assert their own "timeless" political principles as the only path forward for humanity. Even if they succeed in gaining a following,

---

[62] Ibid., p. 183.

[63] Max Weber, *General Economic History* (New York: Greenberg, 1927); Randall Collins, *Weberian Sociological Theory* (Cambridge: Cambridge University Press, 1986), pp. 19–44.

[64] Max Weber, "Class, Status, Party," in H. H. Gerth and C. Wright Mills, *From Max Weber: Essays in Sociology* (New York: Oxford University Press, 1953), pp. 180–195.

[65] Weber, "Politics as a Vocation," in ibid., pp. 77–128.

such academic "prophets" thereby simply become part of the empirical subject matter of comparative sociology. Thus, the spirit of Weber's interpretive
historical sociology can be captured by reversing Marx's famous aphorism:
the social scientists have, in various ways, attempted to change the world; the
point, however, is to understand it.[66]

[66] Karl Marx, "Theses on Feuerbach," in Tucker, *The Marx-Engels Reader*, p. 145.

2

A Weberian Theory of Ideology

Many of the central theoretical themes in Weber's work as analyzed in the previous chapter are succinctly conveyed in one of Weber's most widely cited passages, in ways not always evident from a merely cursory reading: "Not ideas, but material and ideal interests, directly govern men's conduct. Yet very frequently the 'world images' that have been created by ideas have, like switch-men, determined the tracks along which action has been pushed by the dynamic of interest."[1] To begin with, as Weber makes clear here, his sociology is by no means an "idealist" one: he does not see "ideas" as somehow possessing causal force in the absence of any connection to everyday individual interests. In terms of Weber's four types of social action, then, habit and instrumental rationality – that is, time-bound forms of human conduct – are most relevant for explaining the ordinary patterns of daily social life. Of the two "time-transcendent" types of social action, moreover, nondeliberative affect – that is, motivation from heightened emotional states – is probably more common among ordinary social actors than the value-rational defense of cherished ideals.

Nevertheless, as Weber's metaphor implies, at critical historical turning points, value-rational commitments to political ideals may play a decisive role in channeling individual behavior motivated by instrumental interests of various types (whether these interests be "material" or "ideal"). Although action based on fidelity to "timeless" rational values is sociologically rare, under conditions of institutional, economic, and cultural uncertainty such conduct may exert a powerful impact on the behavior of those who encounter it. This seems clearest in the case of the great world religions, which are not coincidentally the subject of the essay by Weber from which his famous quotation is taken. Religious elites typically take paradigmatic cases of value-rational conduct – Jesus's acceptance of his crucifixion, Buddha's rejection of his comfortable life

---

[1] Max Weber, "The Social Psychology of the World Religions," in Hans Gerth and C. Wright Mills, eds., *From Max Weber: Essays in Sociology* (New York: Oxford University Press, 1958), p. 280.

to struggle for enlightenment, or Mohammed's conscious submission to the will of Allah – as models for general emulation, with long-term consequences for how individuals perceive and pursue their instrumental interests. Precisely because such "pure" models of human fidelity to time-transcendent values are so rare, they can persuasively be interpreted as reflections of divine or eternal forces ordinarily inaccessible to human beings, generating theologies with powerful impacts on diverse societies. It is certainly plausible, from a social scientific point of view, that a counterfactual history – one in which Jesus, Buddha, and Mohammed had never individually committed themselves to what they saw as timelessly valid principles but had instead pursued their short-term instrumental interests – would have turned out very differently from how history did in fact unfold.

Nevertheless, Weber's enticing metaphor of "ideas as switchmen" cannot substitute for a fully developed, testable theory of just how ideas matter. Because Weber's own best-known work focused on world religions, the relevance of his sociological framework for the analysis of modern political ideologies is not immediately obvious. Indeed, Weber himself never devoted systematic attention to the term "ideology" itself. Of course, this is in part due to the fact that he died in 1920, before the full impact of modern ideologies such as Marxism-Leninism and Nazism was felt on a global scale. Still, the absence of a fully developed Weberian theory of ideology, combined with Weber's tendency to indulge in rather broad speculation about the long-term social impact of religious belief systems, may have contributed to later confusions about his theory and methodology, making it seem as if Weberians must attribute every aspect of modern politics and society to Calvinism – and, conversely, to blame all failures of modernization outside the West on the influence of "traditional religious cultures."[2]

This is unfortunate, because the Weberian theoretical framework lends itself very well to the task of constructing a clear, generalizable theory of ideology and its effects on social action. It is the task of this chapter, therefore, to develop such a theory in detail. In the first section, I review the main approaches to the subject of ideology developed within the three competing grand social scientific paradigms: Marxism, modernization theory, and rational choice theory. I demonstrate that all three approaches to the topic have to date ended up advocating indefensibly functionalist explanations for the phenomenon. I then turn to the problem of defining the term ideology itself, arguing that our failure to do so clearly has been responsible for much of the weakness of the comparative politics literature on the impact of "ideas"; I argue for a new ideal-typical definition of ideology as "any clear and consistent definition of the criteria for membership in a desired political order." Finally, I explicate the central thesis of this book: that ideology exerts its causal effects by

[2] Mohammad Nafissi, "Reframing Orientalism: Weber and Islam," in Ralph Schroeder, ed., *Max Weber, Democracy, and Modernization* (Basingstoke: Macmillan; New York: St. Martin's, 1998), pp. 182–201.

artificially elongating the time horizons of new converts who had previously seen the social future as highly uncertain, facilitating collective action among them. Thus, ideological groups that originally mobilize around value-rational fidelity to political principles are gradually able to cohere for instrumentally rational reasons as well.

Ideology and Social Theory

The term "ideology" entered the social science lexicon, ironically, with a certain amount of ideological baggage. The original *ideologues* were French intellectuals of the revolutionary era who, inspired by the potential application of Enlightenment ideas to human affairs, endeavored to discover what they assumed were the universal scientific laws governing human social beliefs, in order then to reorder society in a more rational way and thus to secure perpetual social happiness. This project struck the ascendant Napoleon Bonaparte as a ridiculous academic exercise – at least in part because the ideologues publicly opposed his plans for dictatorship – and he disparaged them as mere intellectuals with no true understanding of political reality. The association of "ideology" with an unrealistic, academic point of view stuck, exerting its influence on interpretations of the concept up through the present day.[3]

The notion that ideology represents a distortion of underlying reality was powerfully reinforced by Marx and Engels, whose theoretical approach has exerted perhaps the greatest single influence over subsequent inquiry on the topic.[4] As noted in Chapter 1, Marxism is built around the combination of a structural perspective on the units-of-analysis problem and a strategic, rather than expressive, view of human motivation. Classes, the key actors in Marx's theory of history, perpetually struggle over the distribution of the "surplus value" generated by a given mode of production, with the property-owning class systematically exploiting the propertyless. According to Marx's "materialist conception of history," mere "ideas" cannot exert any independent causal influence over this economic reality; in fact, "the ruling ideas of each age have ever been the ideas of its ruling class."[5] The goal of a systematic radical analysis of ideology, then, is always to show its function in maintaining the position of the dominant class. It should not surprise us to find, for example, that

[3] This story has been recounted many times by scholars of ideology. See, for example, Karl Mannheim, *Ideology and Utopia: An Introduction to the Sociology of Knowledge* (San Diego: Harcourt, Brace Jovanovich, 1936).

[4] Thus, Marx and Engels wrote that "the phantoms born in the human brain are also, necessarily, sublimates of their material life process, which is empirically verifiable and bound to material premises. Morality, religion, metaphysics, all the rest of ideology and their corresponding forms of consciousness, thus no longer retain the semblance of independence." Karl Marx and Friedrich Engels, "The German Ideology," in Robert C. Tucker, ed., *The Marx-Engels Reader* (New York: Norton, 1978), pp. 154–155.

[5] Karl Marx and Friedrich Engels, *The Manifesto of the Communist Party*, in Tucker, *The Marx-Engels Reader*, p. 489.

slave owners promote theories defending slavery as "natural"; that aristocrats embrace myths of "noble bloodlines" differentiating them from commoners; and that capitalists promote laissez faire economics and philosophical individualism. In Gramsci's influential reformulation of this approach, ideologies are comprehensive social worldviews that exert intellectual "hegemony" over the thinking even of subaltern classes, such that challenging class domination appears conceptually impossible.[6]

Over the past half century, an instinct to "unmask" the hidden class interest behind each and every expression of political, religious, or economic ideology has become the implicit starting point for most social scientific discussions of the topic.[7] Logically, however, the Marxist approach to analyzing ideology suffers from the functionalist fallacy – that is, it "explains" the existence of ideology according to its social function, without also demonstrating the precise causal mechanisms through which adoption of an ideology in the first place generates feedback effects that encourage sustained ideological commitment in a given society.[8] Indeed, there is little analysis in the Marxist literature concerning just how new ideologies are originally generated and reproduced within particular social groups; generally – in line with the structuralist approach to the units-of-analysis problem – ideologies are seen as mere "reflections" of class domination that somehow emerge automatically along with the class whose interests they represent. This sort of argument thus becomes a simple tautology: ideology is "explained" in terms of its function of class domination over the sphere of ideas, but ideology is defined in the first place as "ideas that function to preserve the rule of the dominant class." It is hard to see how such a hypothesis could ever be falsified.

To the extent one does allow for the possibility that ideologies may first emerge for reasons other than their role in preserving class hegemony, it seems far from clear that the link between ideology and class interest is either automatic or even causally primary. Nazism, for example, may initially have been welcomed by some German agricultural, business, and military elites as a bulwark against communism, but in the end Hitler destroyed the entire German economy in pursuit of his ideological vision. In the case of Marxism-Leninism, the problem is equally acute: far from representing the "class interest" of the proletariat, as Lenin and later Soviet leaders claimed, Marxist-Leninist ideology promoted the rise of a party of "revolutionary" bureaucrats and managers whose control over ordinary workers was even more absolute than that of the tsarist bourgeoisie they replaced. Efforts to resolve this problem by inserting

[6] Antonio Gramsci, *Prison Notebooks* (New York: Columbia University Press, 1992).

[7] This is noted in Michael Freeden, *Ideology and Political Theory: A Conceptual Approach* (Oxford: Clarendon, 1996).

[8] For extended criticisms of functionalist logic, see David Hackett Fischer, *Historians' Fallacies: Toward a Logic of Historical Thought* (London: Routledge and Kegan Paul, 1971), and Jon Elster, *Explaining Technical Change: A Case Study in the Philosophy of Science* (Cambridge: Cambridge University Press; Oslo: Universitetsforlaget, 1983).

ad hoc adjustments to Marxist theory – by claiming either that the Leninist intelligentsia itself represented a "new class" or that the Stalinist elite somehow "betrayed" a genuine proletarian revolution that would eventually return to its rightful historical path – are clearly unsatisfying.[9]

The empirical evidence seems to suggest, in fact, that what people believe about the political world has often only a tenuous connection to what might seem to be the "brute facts" of material reality. Indeed, the vast majority of people are almost entirely ignorant about global politics – including, unfortunately, many political elites. In a world of inadequate information and typically high uncertainty, individuals' often idiosyncratic interpretations of the nature of social and political change play an inescapably important role in their decision making. To believe that some hidden force nevertheless compels every class, or even its leading representatives, to uphold consistently the "dominant ideology" that preserves class rule requires a remarkable leap of faith in the power of economic structures to shape individual cognition. In fact, not even Marx and Engels were able to deny the independent role of individual theorizing entirely, arguing that certain representatives of the ruling class could free themselves from the grip of the dominant ideology by theoretically embracing the interests of the oppressed:

[I]n times when the class struggle nears the decisive hour . . . a small section of the ruling class cuts itself adrift, and joins the revolutionary class, the class that holds the future in its hands. Just as, therefore, at an earlier period, a section of the nobility went over to the bourgeoisie; so now a portion of the bourgeoisie goes over to the proletariat, and in particular, a portion of the bourgeois ideologists, who have raised themselves to the level of comprehending theoretically the historical movement as a whole.[10]

Such reasoning may convince steadfast devotees of a particular conception of historical destiny; from a scientific point of view, however, Marx and Engels fail to provide even a cursory description of the causal mechanism through which advanced "theoretical" abilities might allow actors suddenly to switch sides in the class struggle. A more straightforward interpretation of Marx's and Engels's rejection of their own bourgeois backgrounds seems much more plausible: namely, that they, like many other people, developed their theoretical viewpoints for intellectual and psychological reasons having little or nothing to do with their initial class interest.

Despite its logical problems, Marxist analysis has continued to shape interpretations of ideology in more recent, influential works of comparative politics.

---

[9] Leon Trotsky, *The Revolution Betrayed: What Is the Soviet Union and Where Is It Going?* (London: New Park, 1967), and Milovan Djilas, *The New Class: An Analysis of the Communist System* (New York: Holt, Reinhart and Winston, 1957). See also George Konrad and Ivan Szelenyi, *The Intellectuals on the Road to Class Power* (Brighton: Harvester, 1979), which ultimately departs from Marxism in order to make a persuasive argument about the corporate rule of revolutionary intellectuals under Leninist regimes.

[10] Marx and Engels, *Manifesto of the Communist Party*, in Tucker, *The Marx-Engels Reader*, p. 481.

Thus, Theda Skocpol in her magisterial *States and Social Revolutions* insists that "it cannot be argued that the cognitive content of ideologies in any sense provides a predictive key to the outcomes of the Revolutions."[11] To be sure, Skocpol admits, as did Marx, that a common belief in revolutionary ideas can serve to coordinate collective action among revolutionaries. In the end, however, she argues that the institutional outcomes of revolutions are determined by "structural" forces – in particular, the geopolitical imperative of modern state building – that make the specific intellectual content of ideologies causally irrelevant. Again, Skocpol never analyzes where new revolutionary ideologies come from in the first place; thus, there is no causal mechanism provided to show how exactly ideologies might cement the cohesion of revolutionary vanguards. Given Skocpol's theoretical assumptions, she sees no need to examine at length the specific content of revolutionary ideologies as they have been articulated prior to revolutionary victory.

Yet detailed examination of the intellectual substance of ideologies would seem to be logically necessary in order to assess whether ideological beliefs are consistent with the institutions imposed by new revolutionary elites. In fact, from a scientific point of view, to test the impact of ideologies in revolutionary situations, one should ideally sample a wide range of revolutionary ideologies developed before instances of state breakdown – in other words, one should sample on the independent variable.[12] Doing so, however, would generate a sample of beliefs including not only Jacobinism, Bolshevism, and Maoism, but also the worldviews of the eighteenth-century Polish parliamentary nobility, the Khmer Rouge in Cambodia in the 1970s, or supporters of radical market reforms in postcommunist Europe – all of which, in various ways, worked to undermine central state power rather than to reinforce it. Even a cursory glance at this somewhat wider sample of revolutionary ideologies would seem to provide prima facie evidence that the content of belief systems does have a consistent relationship to the kind of state building that emerges after revolutionary victory.[13]

A second essentially structuralist approach to ideology, that of modernization theory, has exerted nearly as much influence on social science as the Marxist approach. Given the emphasis of modernization theory on expressive, and not only strategic, forms of human motivation, one might expect this paradigm to be well equipped to address the causal factors leading to the

---

[11] Theda Skocpol, *States and Social Revolutions* (Cambridge, MA: Harvard University Press, 1979), p. 170. See also William H. Sewell Jr., "Ideologies and Social Revolutions: Reflections on the French Case," and Theda Skocpol, "Cultural Idioms and Political Ideologies in the Revolutionary Reconstruction of State Power: A Rejoinder to Sewell," *Journal of Modern History* 57(1, March 1985): 57–85, 86–96.

[12] Gary King, Robert Keohane, and Sidney Verba, *Designing Social Inquiry: Qualitative Inference in Qualitative Research* (Princeton, NJ: Princeton University Press, 1994).

[13] In later works, Skocpol began to admit the need to take the substantive content of ideology more seriously as a possible causal variable. See, for example, her essay "Rentier State and Shi'a Islam in the Iranian Revolution," *Theory and Society* 11(3, May 1982): 265–283.

formation and reproduction of diverse political belief systems. Unfortunately, as with Marxism, its collectivist approach to the units-of-analysis problem works against any sustained effort to trace contemporary ideologies back to their initial origins. Building on Durkheimian sociology, modernization theory has tended instead to portray the emergence of ideology as a collective sign of social "disequilibrium." In this literature, ideology is portrayed as a false, dogmatic style of thought that provides psychological comfort to societies disrupted by the breakdown of tradition and, at the same time, promotes the political power of antiliberal revolutionary vanguards who capitalize on social anomie.[14] The style of explanation here remains functionalist – except that whereas Marxism explains ideology in terms of its function in preserving class domination, modernization theory focuses on its function in preserving the rule of revolutionary dictatorships in the context of early modernization.

The link between ideology and dictatorship in most of modernization theory obviously owes much to the historical context of the Cold War, during which the Parsonian paradigm rose to intellectual prominence in the West.[15] Hannah Arendt's early influential efforts to analyze the origins of Soviet "totalitarianism" argued forcefully – again, building on Durkheim – that both Nazism and Marxism-Leninism were reflections of the anomie permeating the "mass society" generated by incomplete modernization in both the German and Russian contexts.[16] Deprived of the moral values inculcated in traditional peasant communities, yet not fully integrated into a new modern social system built around individual liberty and tolerance, confused German and Soviet citizens found comfort in an ersatz morality generated by emotional identification with a "great leader." From this it was but a short step to argue that Nazism and Marxism-Leninism – and by implication, ideology in general – had no causally significant substantive content but instead should be understood as merely reflecting underlying cultural dislocations. In the influential work of Friedrich and Brzezinski, for example, ideology is presented as a mere instrument of totalitarian rule; Nazism and Marxism-Leninism, notwithstanding their obvious theoretical differences, are seen as functionally equivalent.[17]

The logical implication of this approach was that ideology should disappear entirely once social modernization is complete on a global scale.[18] Studies of development in the "Third World" seemed to suggest that as previously parochial populations were educated, integrated into new urban centers, and exposed to new forms of mass communications, their levels of political

---

[14] See, for example, Chalmers Johnson, *Revolutionary Change* (Boston: Little, Brown, 1962).

[15] This point is emphasized in Michael Freeden, *Ideology: A Very Short Introduction* (Oxford: Oxford University Press, 2003).

[16] Hannah Arendt, *The Origins of Totalitarianism* (New York: Harcourt, Brace, 1951); see also William Kornhauser, *The Politics of Mass Society* (Glencoe: Free Press, 1959).

[17] Carl J. Friedrich and Zbigniew K. Brzezinski, *Totalitarian Dictatorship and Autocracy* (Cambridge, MA: Harvard University Press, 1965).

[18] Daniel Bell, *The End of Ideology: On the Exhaustion of Political Ideas in the Fifties* (Glencoe: Free Press, 1960).

tolerance and flexibility would increase, making them decreasingly suscepti-
ble to the appeals of ideological radicalism.[19] Even in the formally Marxist-
Leninist Soviet Union, modernization theorists argued, ideology was quickly
eroding, being replaced by "development" as a policy priority.[20] With the collapse of the USSR under Gorbachev, avowed modernization theorist Frances
Fukuyama could even argue that ideological "history" itself had come to a
close.[21]

That the end of ideology is still, apparently, nowhere in sight, more than half
a century after the first confident predictions of the structural-functionalists,
is obviously a serious problem for the modernization approach. As explored
in detail in the next chapter, most political parties today continue to advocate
clear, diverging political ideologies that do have measurable impacts on their
policy choices. Even in the most prosperous state in the world, the United States,
a marked resurgence of ideological polarization appears to have emerged in
the early twenty-first century. Meanwhile, the emergence of new revolutionary
ideologies such as the Islamic radicalism of Al-Qaeda has had an undeniable
impact on politics in both the developing and the developed world.

Moreover, as in the case of Marxist versions of structuralism, the absence
in modernization theory of any clear causal mechanism to explain precisely
how ideologies are initially promulgated and reproduced sharply limits the
theory's explanatory power. Again, the functionalist fallacy plagues much of
this literature: the emergence of ideologies such as fascism and communism is
explained as functional for the consolidation of totalitarian regimes, but there
is generally little effort to demonstrate precise feedback loops that promote the
reproduction and reinforcement of ideology within such regimes after its initial
articulation by revolutionary leaders. As in the case of Marxism, too, analysis of
ideology in the Parsonian paradigm usually selects on the dependent variable:
only the belief systems of successful revolutionary movements are analyzed.
A more scientifically persuasive approach would be to begin by examining as
wide as possible a sample of ideologies, in order to assess the likelihood that
adopting an ideological worldview promotes the political success of aspiring
totalitarian rulers. Such an exercise would quickly demonstrate that the initial
promoters of new ideologies are in fact much more likely to end up dead, in
prison, or teaching for little pay at state universities than they are to rule over
powerful regimes.

The criticism that both Marxism and modernization theory lack clear causal
mechanisms to explain the proposed link between social conflicts and ideological success is not new. In fact, a critique similar to the one advanced here was
already proposed by Clifford Geertz in a justly famous essay from the early

---

[19] Alex Inkeles and David H. Smith, *Becoming Modern: Individual Change in Six Developing Countries* (Cambridge, MA: Harvard University Press, 1974).

[20] Richard Lowenthal, "Development vs. Utopia in Communist Policy," in Chalmers Johnson, ed., *Change in Communist Systems* (Stanford, CA: Stanford University Press, 1970), pp. 33–117.

[21] Frances Fukuyama, "The End of History?" *National Interest*, no. 16 (Summer 1989): 13–16.

1960s.[22] Analysis of ideology, he argued, tended to rely on either "interest theory" or "social strain theory," without taking the time to look directly at how ideology might shape people's cognitive viewpoints in a way that might either serve group interests or address social strain effectively. In short, Geertz's essay was a passionate plea to take the substantive content of ideologies seriously as a guide to understanding their political impact. Yet Geertz, too, still taking social collectivities as the primary unit of social analysis, refused in the end to discard the functionalist approach to ideology. In fact, he explicitly argued that once the cultural significance of ideological worldviews was taken into account, the "function" of ideology in promoting political integration in the developing world would become more readily apparent.

Despite the relative loss of influence of both orthodox Marxism and Parsonian modernization theory, the majority of self-described "culturalists" in contemporary social science remain wedded to a structuralism – and, hence, also to a functionalism – of either the Marxist or Durkheimian sort. One school of thought continues to examine the ways in which political myths, values, and symbols express deeper principles of social integration that work to legitimate various political systems.[23] A competing viewpoint, building primarily on Gramsci, argues that political discourse should instead be seen as "constructed" by elites and enforced through the visible or invisible exercise of power, but it continues to insist that once constructed, political ideologies inevitably function to reinforce hierarchical rule.[24] The main subject of theoretical debate, in short, remains the degree to which human collective behavior should be understood as primarily expressive or primarily strategic. Few culturalists ever consider seriously the possibility of a methodologically individualist approach that might remedy the functionalist fallacies encountered so frequently in this literature.

Rational Choice Approaches to Ideology

In this light, the recent explosion of interest in ideology, culture, and identity by rational choice theorists would seem to be a welcome development. After

[22] Clifford Geertz, "Ideology as a Cultural System," in David Apter, ed., *Ideology and Discontent* (London: Free Press of Glencoe, 1964), pp. 47–76. The essay was also later reprinted in Clifford Geertz, *Interpretation of Cultures: Selected Essays* (New York: Basic Books, 1973), pp. 193–233.

[23] The most prominent representative of this approach within the discipline of political science remains Ronald Inglehart. See Inglehart, *Modernization and Postmodernization: Cultural, Economic and Political Change in 43 Societies* (Princeton, NJ: Princeton University Press, 1997).

[24] James C. Scott, *Seeing Like a State: How Certain Schemes to Improve the Human Condition Have Failed* (New Haven: Yale University Press, 1998); Lisa Wedeen, *Ambiguities of Domination: Politics, Rhetoric, and Symbols in Contemporary Syria* (Chicago: University of Chicago Press). For a useful contrast between Geertzian and Gramscian approaches to the study of political culture, see also Wedeen, "Conceptualizing Culture: Possibilities for Political Science," *American Political Science Review* 96(4, 2002): 713–728.

all, advocates of rational choice theory have long argued for the superiority of their paradigm in part because of its ability to remedy the functionalism of earlier, modernization theoretic scholarship. The seminal work of Mancur Olson, in particular, demonstrated logically that groups do not spontaneously cooperate in defense of their collective interests. Rather, rational individual actors will always have an incentive to defect from proposals for cooperation to obtain pure public goods, because the effect of any one individual's decision to participate in such collective action on the success or failure of the effort is negligible, and all members of a successfully organized group will benefit whether or not they individually participated. The only way to overcome such "free riding" behavior, Olson argued, is to impose "selective incentives" that make participation in the collective cause individually rational, by monitoring individual behavior carefully and either punishing those who do not contribute or providing additional rewards to those who do.[25]

Seen in light of Olson's well-known theory, the creation of new ideologies, too, would appear to involve serious problems of collective action. If successful ideologies do indeed perform the important functions they are assigned in both Marxism and modernization theory, they can be understood as "public goods" in Olson's sense. If so, however, the logic of free riding surely applies here as well. No single individual can meaningfully affect the probability that a new ideology takes hold over a society; at the same time, if a new ideology that works to integrate and legitimate some social group does emerge, all members of that group will benefit regardless of whether they participated in the ideology's initial articulation and reproduction. Thus, we should predict that in the absence of selective incentives to ensure individual ideological conformity, no new ideologies should ever emerge. The task for research, then, is to identify and isolate the ways in which this seemingly insuperable problem of collective action is overcome in practice in various social and political contexts.

Unfortunately, this promising line of argument has been entirely absent in the rational choice literature on the impact of ideas and ideologies to date. Instead, the concept of ideology proposed in this literature has generally been every bit as functionalist as that of previous authors. Ideology or "ideas" are frequently defined as forces that somehow help individual rational actors overcome various problems of collective action – making the argument that ideologies promote successful collective action a circular one. No author has yet examined the problem of how rational actors might generate the collective good of ideology in the first place.

Thus, Douglass North, whose learned and insightful works have played a crucial role in reintroducing the concept of ideology into the rational choice literature, argues that ideology plays a key causal role in the formation of new institutions, which then in turn determine the diverging paths of development experienced by different societies in history. However, the causal mechanisms

---

[25] Mancur Olson, *The Logic of Collective Action: Public Goods and the Theory of Groups* (Cambridge, MA: Harvard University Press, 1965).

that lead from ideology to institution building are never clearly specified. In *Structure and Change in Economic History*, North argues that ideology helps rational actors overcome collective action problems by somehow overriding the instrumental rationality of the social groups who adopt it: "Ideology's fundamental aim is to energize groups to behave contrary to a simple, hedonistic calculus of costs and benefits. This is the central thrust of major ideologies, since neither maintenance of the existing order nor its overthrow is possible without such behavior."[26] But how this process takes place in practice is left entirely vague. Even very energetic rational actors will still face the same logic of free riding; wanting a public good even more intensely does not constitute a rational reason for sacrificing one's short-run interests in order to achieve it.

Realizing the inadequacy of this argument, North, along with his collaborator Denzau, has more recently turned to an analysis of ideology not as a force that directly generates group mobilization but as a "shared mental model" that lowers information costs among believers.[27] The causal mechanism here is better defined: if multiple rational actors share a picture of the world that is clear and consistent enough to obviate the need for lengthy information gathering before joint action, then such "ideological" groups will indeed have an advantage over nonideological collectivities that cannot coordinate so effectively in situations of strong uncertainty. Again, however, from the rational choice point of view, shared mental models of this sort also represent collective goods that are subject to the free-rider problem. In practice, any cognitive model of the social world privileges some actors over others. A belief that the industrial working class will liberate humanity has certain negative implications for members of the petty bourgeoisie; a contrary belief that the wealth of nations is generated by the freedom of rational individuals to pursue their self-interest under market conditions will tend to generate spirited opposition from the leaders of craft guilds. Even within smaller social groups that might appear to be advantaged in similar ways by a particular shared mental model, divergences of opinion on ideological specifics with direct implications for political and economic payoffs will inevitably emerge. Thus, Marxists may all share a model of the world in which class struggle is the motor of history, but – as the history of Marxism amply demonstrates – this by itself does not prevent bitter disputes about the role of intellectuals in this process, the proper attitude toward the bourgeois state, the degree to which revolutionary action requires leadership from a party elite, and so on. Each of these questions has direct implications for who will gain and lose political power within the Marxist movement.

Adopting a new cognitive picture of the world – unlike, say, driving on the left-hand side of the road rather than the right – is a potentially costly individual

---

[26] Douglass C. North, *Structure and Change in Economic History* (New York: Norton, 1981), p. 53.

[27] Arthur T. Denzau and Douglass C. North, "Shared Mental Models: Ideologies and Institutions," *Kyklos* 47(1, January 1994): 3–31.

decision that forecloses many future options for strategic behavior. And those who initially choose to convert to a new ideology that does not succeed may well end up as "suckers."[28] In other words, the situation of individuals who all wish to establish a "shared mental model" is best modeled as an n-person prisoner's dilemma, not a game of pure coordination.[29] The best outcome for the collective in this game, as Denzau and North suggest, is for everyone to choose to "convert" to a new ideology, so as to reduce information costs and thus promote mutually beneficial forms of collective action. For any single individual, however, an even better outcome would be for everyone else to convert to the new ideology, except herself. Such an individual will still gain the collective, nonexcludable benefits of the enhanced collection action of other members of her group, while maintaining the ability to exploit the group for personal gain whenever possible. Indeed, for such an individual, exploitation of the group should theoretically become much easier as a result of the new predictability of its members' interpretations of the world.

For purposes of illustration, imagine a situation in which all workers in a given industry are faced with a choice of adopting a Marxist mental model of history. Full conversion to Marxism by the entire group will lower transaction costs among them, allowing for more successful collective action vis-à-vis the factory bosses. If a single individual chooses not to convert to Marxism while everyone else does, however, that person will enjoy the increased benefits from her colleagues' better coordination and solidarity – but will also be able to maintain the flexibility to pursue fundamentally self-interested plans. By the same logic, the worst possible outcome for an individual facing such an ideological prisoner's dilemma is to be the only loyal convert to Marxism when everyone else rejects it. In such a case, one will lose the cognitive flexibility of a nonconvert, while gaining no advantage from any new shared mental model among one's group. Rational actors in this situation, then, should always choose to defect from proposals to enforce a shared mental model, and new ideologies should never emerge in the absence of other selective incentives that induce this result – even though this leaves them all worse off than if everyone had converted.

[28] In this respect, the situation facing would-be builders of a new ideology is different from that encountered by individuals deciding whether to uphold the rules of their local ethnic culture. Russell Hardin has argued that the latter sort of decision can be understood as a problem of pure coordination, because, once local cultural norms arise, there is typically no individual advantage in unilaterally flouting them. The relative consistency and formality of ideologies, by contrast, requires converts to pay the start-up costs of learning and adapting to new modes of political identification. Once a new ideology has been established, then, a single individual who "sells out" his more ideologically consistent colleagues can receive a large short-run payoff, whereas those who still pay the costs of maintaining an ideology after others have abandoned it have, in effect, been played for "suckers." See Russell Hardin, *One for All: The Logic of Group Conflict* (Princeton, NJ: Princeton University Press, 1995).

[29] That Olson's problem of collective action is mathematically equivalent to an n-person prisoner's dilemma game has been shown by Michael Taylor, *The Possibility of Cooperation* (Cambridge: Cambridge University Press, 1987).

Similar problems beset other attempts to reintegrate ideology into the rational choice paradigm. Garrett and Weingast, for example, have argued that "ideas" should be understood in rational choice terms as playing the role of "focal points" that can help to solve problems of pure coordination.[30] Prominent ideas in cultural discourse may act to coordinate otherwise indeterminate political expectations in situations of social uncertainty – just as in Schelling's famous example, where two people who must meet in New York City, but with no other information about where or when, each decide to go to Grand Central Station at exactly noon.[31] This admittedly creative hypothesis, however, fails to explain why ideological debates in politics are generally so bitter and prolonged. Far from serving as neutral, consensual guideposts for otherwise uncoordinated strategic action, ideologies instead generally introduce deep new divisions that can make cooperation with nonconverts even more difficult than before. Certainly the empirical examples cited by Garrett and Weingast – the idea of the European common market after World War II and the emergence of the norm of state "sovereignty" in the Westphalian period – became relatively consensual coordinating devices only after decades of bloody ideological war, waged by committed elites who wished to prevent the emergence of institutions based on these very ideas. Given the poor empirical prospects and often disastrous personal consequences of most ideological proposals for political coordination, surely instrumentally rational actors should generally avoid ideological commitments rather than quickly coordinating around them.[32]

In sum, the notion that ideology somehow solves rational actors' collective action problems, whether through energizing individuals or through lowering their information costs, only reintroduces the collective action problem at the level of ideology itself. Yet the question of how rationally strategic actors might somehow combine to generate new ideologies in the first place has received little

---

[30] Geoffrey Garrett and Barry Weingast, "Ideas, Interests, and Institutions: Constructing the European Community's Internal Market," in Judith Goldstein and Robert O. Keohane, eds., *Ideas and Foreign Policy: Beliefs, Institutions, and Political Change* (Ithaca, NY: Cornell University Press, 1993); Barry R. Weingast, "A Rational Choice Perspective on the Role of Ideas: Shared Belief Systems and State Sovereignty in International Cooperation," *Politics and Society* 23(4, December 1995): 449–464.

[31] Thomas C. Schelling, *Micromotives and Macrobehavior* (New York: Norton, 1978).

[32] This is also the problem for Kathleen Bawn's effort to account for the role of ideology in strategic interaction by emphasizing the importance of forming and maintaining political coalitions over the long run. While I agree that ideologies attain their causal influence in large part through their effect on defining sustainable political communities, Bawn simply makes commitments to specific long-term coalitions part of the initial strategies of "ideological" actors – thus rendering the argument for ideology's influence over coalition formation tautological. It is certainly true that rational actors who know precisely with whom they should combine to pursue common interests will conduct themselves differently from those who maintain coalitional neutrality. But the problem is to explain why any rational actor under strategic uncertainty would ever commit herself in advance to long-run cooperation with a particular set of coalition partners, rather than free-riding on the coalitional commitments of others. See Bawn, "Constructing 'Us': Ideology, Coalition Politics, and False Consciousness," *American Journal of Political Science* 43(2, April 1999): 303–334.

to no attention in this literature. Indeed, a remarkable number of leading rational choice analysts have recently introduced conceptions of ideology, ideas,
norms, and culture that closely resemble the functionalist arguments of Parsonian modernization theory. For Jon Elster, social norms act as the "cement of
society," because without them the Hobbesian problem of social order cannot
be overcome.[33] According to North's latest work, "a common cultural her-
itage ... provides a means of reducing the divergent mental models that people
in a society possess and constitutes the means for the intergenerational transfer of unifying perceptions."[34] For Avner Greif, "cultural beliefs" should be
understood as "the shared ideas and thoughts that govern interactions among
individuals and between them, their gods, and other groups," which generate uniform strategic orientations that largely determine a society's subsequent
institutional developmental trajectory.[35]

In all these works, ideology, ideas, norms, "common knowledge," or culture
are seen as somehow exogenously operating outside the universe of instrumental rationality, emerging when needed to account for nonstrategic forms of
human cooperation and solidarity. Because these rational choice approaches
to the role of ideas provide no rational choice microfoundations to explain
their emergence and social power, they subtly depart from methodological
individualism to introduce structural units of analysis for examining cognitive
frameworks. But rational choice theory is not a bus from which one can dis-
embark temporarily in order to address the problem of collective cognition.
If nonstrategic forms of individual behavior matter in explaining the emergence of ideology in times of uncertainty, crisis, or institutional origin, then
surely they must also exist in ordinary, stable, well-institutionalized environments as well. If so, we need a theory that tells us the precise conditions under
which noninstrumental behavior tends to trump strategic rationality.[36] This is

---

[33] Jon Elster, *The Cement of Society: Study of Social Order* (Cambridge: Cambridge University
Press, 1989). Ironically, this latter argument is essentially identical to that made by Talcott
Parsons decades earlier: "Analysis of ... the Hobbesian problem of order shows conclusively
that competitive allocation cannot operate without institutionalization of a set of norms defining
the limits of legitimate action"; Parsons, *The Social System* (London: Routledge and Kegan Paul,
1951), p. 188. Thus, rational choice theory, confronted with the need to explain how strategic
actors ever coalesce initially around shared cognitive frameworks that make coordination and
cooperation possible, has unwittingly arrived back at the starting point of postwar structural-
functionalism.

[34] Douglass North, *Understanding the Process of Economic Change* (Princeton, NJ: Princeton
University Press, 2005), p. 27.

[35] Avner Greif, *Institutions and the Path to the Modern Economy: Lessons from Medieval
Trade* (Cambridge: Cambridge University Press, 2006), pp. 269–270. See also Michael Suk-
Young Chwe, *Rational Ritual: Culture, Coordination, and Common Knowledge* (Princeton,
NJ: Princeton University Press, 2001).

[36] This point has also been made by Michael Taylor: "We should not assume that cooperative
(and other) behavior must rest on rational choice. We should instead at least consider the
possibility that though we sometimes act in an instrumentally rational fashion, we are also
capable of acting from normative, expressive, and intrinsic motivations." See Taylor, "When
Rationality Fails," in Friedman, *The Rational Choice Controversy: Economic Models of Politics
Reconsidered* (New Haven: Yale University Press, 1996), p. 233.

precisely the advantage of the Weberian paradigm, which endogenizes noninstrumental forms of social action and thus uniquely provides microfoundations for a general theory of how new ideologies initially emerge.

The Problem of Definition

As is apparent from the preceding review of the literature, functionalism is very frequently built into the definition of the concept itself.[37] Scholars have defined ideology as a kind of thinking that is inherently functional for the ruling class, for totalitarian regimes, or for solving problems of collective action – but this inevitably leads to circular reasoning in any causal account of ideology's hypothesized political effects. To use the concept of ideology fruitfully in comparative research, we must first define it in a way that does not depend upon observing its later role within established political systems. In addition, such a definition must allow us to distinguish clearly between ideological and nonideological kinds of political orientation, in order to allow for systematic testing of ideology's hypothesized causal effects. If every form of politics is defined as in some sense ideological, then by definition we can have no causal theory of the effects of ideology's presence or absence.[38]

Providing a definition of ideology that meets these scientific criteria, however necessary, is bound to generate controversy, as the terminological confusion within this branch of political science is particularly severe. At present, such terms as "ideology," "culture," "ideas," "worldview," "norm," "identity," and "schema" are used more or less interchangeably in the comparative politics literature, even though scholars using these terms may intuitively wish to highlight quite different empirical phenomena and processes.[39] Moreover, in reading the literature that focuses on any of these terms, one is struck by the multiplicity of competing definitions they are given – a situation obviously hindering social science cumulation and reinforcing scholarly suspicion of "ideational" approaches.[40] Efforts to resolve definitional controversies by trying to isolate a common conceptual core to all existing usages, however

---

[37] This has been pointed out in John Gerring, "Ideology: A Definitional Analysis," *Political Research Quarterly* 50(4, December 1997): 957–994.

[38] Michael Freeden is perhaps the most prominent advocate of the opposite view, that we should interpret all politics as in some basic sense "ideological" – but he is also skeptical about the possibility of a causal theory of ideology. See Freeden, *Ideology and Political Theory: A Conceptual Approach* (Oxford: Clarendon Press; New York: Oxford University Press, 1996); *Ideology: A Very Short Introduction* (Oxford: Oxford University Press, 2003).

[39] The confusion of contemporary terminology in ideational scholarship has been noted by Mark Blyth, "'Any More Bright Ideas?': The Ideational Turn of Comparative Political Economy," *Comparative Politics* 29(2, January 1997): 229–250; Sheri Berman, *The Social Democratic Moment: Ideas and Politics in the Making of Interwar Europe* (Cambridge, MA: Harvard University Press, 1998); and Stephen E. Hanson, "From Culture to Ideology in Comparative Politics: A Review Essay," *Comparative Politics* 35 (3, April 2003): 355–386.

[40] A welcome recent effort by several leading scholars to define the term "identity" more precisely for social science research is Rawi Abdelal et al., *Measuring Identity: A Guide for Social Scientists* (Cambridge: Cambridge University Press, 2009).

helpful in mapping this contested terrain, generally end up generating lengthy, catchall definitions of ideational variables that are still too vague to be useful in comparative research.[41]

An additional problem in crafting a scientifically useful definition of ideology is what Russell Faeges has called the dilemma of "classificatory perversity."[42] Faeges notes that because social science terminology is laden with words used in ordinary language – unlike, say, physics, which has developed a whole scientific lexicon in which the mathematical precision of concepts allows scholars to use nonsense words such as "quark" with no loss of understanding – any effort to provide theoretical clarity to the definition of social science concepts is bound to run afoul of at least some everyday linguistic usages. Thus, no contemporary chemist would argue against the definition of "water" as H_2O by retorting that the "water" we use in our bathtubs each morning actually contains copper, fluoride, and iron, too; such a complaint would be seen, rightly, as irrelevant to the modern scientific understanding of water. Social scientists, on the other hand, quite frequently reject conceptual definitions on the grounds that they do not fit some of the empirical features associated with words in that definition as they are utilized by ordinary English speakers. Thus, would-be crafters of more precise social science definitions are inevitably confronted with a difficult dilemma. Should they choose to invent neologisms to label their carefully defined concepts or to avoid confusion with ordinary language understandings, they are likely to be seen as obtuse or bizarre. Should they continue the common practice of utilizing ordinary language terminology in their social science definitions, however, they run the risk of misunderstandings based on the charge of "classificatory perversity" outlined previously.

I have chosen in this book not to invent any neologisms but rather to do my best to give the ordinary language word "ideology" a specific theoretical definition. It is therefore important to distinguish my use of this term from earlier definitions in the scholarly literature – all of which have had an impact on the common understanding of ideology now present in everyday English language. In particular, I wish to differentiate my use of the term ideology from earlier works defining "ideology" as "world view," as "flawed thinking," or as "position on a left-right scale."

The first of these definitions – of ideology as a "world view" or "belief system" – is by far the most widespread.[43] Indeed, the notion of an ideology as a "world view" is ubiquitous to the point of becoming a part of ordinary

[41] See, for example, the synthetic definition given in Malcolm B. Hamilton, "The Elements of the Concept of Ideology," *Political Studies* 35(1, March 1987): 18–38.

[42] Russell Faeges, "Theory-Driven Concept Definition: The Challenge of Perverse Cases," paper presented at the annual meeting of the American Political Science Association, Atlanta, September 2–5, 1999.

[43] Leon Baradat, *Political Ideologies: Their Origins and Impact* (Englewood Cliffs, NJ: Prentice Hall, 1991); Arthur T. Denzau and Douglass C. North, "Shared Mental Models: Ideologies and Institutions," *Kyklos* 47 (1, Spring 1994): 3–31.

language. But such a fuzzy definition is unlikely to help us very much in exploring the empirical impact of specific political ideologies in concrete historical situations. For one thing, it is difficult to imagine any political elites who have no "world view" or "shared mental model" whatsoever. "Nonideological" politicians, by this definition, would literally have to approach their professions with no preconceptions at all, changing their orientations toward their local and global environments constantly in response to changing circumstances. For another, even apolitical people have basic understandings about the world around them to help negotiate their lives; the notion of ideology as "world view" thus requires us to assume that every social actor has an "ideology" – and there are therefore, potentially, billions of different ideologies at any point in time.

Thus, most analysts in this tradition refine their definition of ideology to emphasize the relative consistency and formality of "ideological" as opposed to other kinds of "world views."[44] This is a step forward but still leaves many methodological problems unresolved. Theologies, scientific paradigms, and certain kinds of paranoid delusions can be quite internally consistent too, but it is not clear that there is much theoretical utility in grouping together as political "ideologies" phenomena such as Sufism, quantum mechanics, or the "world view" of mass murderer Gary Ridgway. In addition, such a definition of ideology demands that the analyst develop clear conceptual criteria for distinguishing degrees of "consistency" in political *Weltanschauungen* – something rarely attempted in comparative analyses of this sort.

The second most common definition of ideology applies the term to "flawed" or "rigid" forms of thought. This definition of ideology shows up in studies of the ways in which ideological "blinders" can inhibit perception of "reality" among "closed-minded" individuals.[45] It also permeates the literature on comparative foreign policy, in which the political philosophies of anti-Western leaderships are frequently described as "ideological" in order to distinguish them from the presumably "pragmatic" views of actual or potential Western allies.[46] Such an approach, unlike the definition of ideology as a "world view," does have the virtue of allowing analysts in principle to distinguish empirically between ideological and nonideological actors. Unfortunately, this definition of ideology also gets us into sticky methodological difficulties. Fundamentally, in order to assess reliably which beliefs of political actors are "ideological" and which are "realistic," the analyst herself must presume

---

[44] Philip Converse, "The Nature of Belief Systems in Mass Publics," in David E. Apter, ed., *Ideology and Discontent* (New York: Free Press, 1964), pp. 206–261; Clifford Geertz, "Ideology as a Cultural System," in *The Interpretation of Cultures* (New York: Basic Books, 1973); Gerring, "Ideology: A Definitional Analysis"; Franz Schurmann, *Ideology and Organization in Communist China* (Berkeley: University of California Press, 1966).

[45] Milton Rokeach, *The Open and Closed Mind: Investigations Into the Nature of Belief Systems and Personality Systems* (New York: Basic Books, 1970).

[46] See, for example, R. K. Ramazani, "Ideology and Pragmatism in Iran's Foreign Policy," *Middle East Journal* 58(4, Autumn 2004): 549–559.

to know just what reality *is*, in all times and places. Otherwise, one person's "ideology" will be another person's "foresighted strategy" – and vice versa.

The third common definition of ideology is taken primarily from studies of American and West European electoral politics, and this is to equate political ideology with self-placement on a "left-right" numerical scale. In the delimited context of consolidated Western electoral democracies, studies based on this operational definition can, of course, be extremely useful. On a broader comparative level, however, such a definition begs the question of just why "left" and "right" are given their particular political connotations in different social environments. At best, the left-right scale can measure ideological positions in Western European and North American polities since the French Revolution, when the original National Assembly happened to place the Jacobins at the extreme left of the hall, and the Legitimists at the extreme right, generating the core associations of "left" with radicalism and "right" with conservatism. Even after 1789, however, the precise political content of "left" and "right" has demonstrably changed over time and varied from place to place – despite heroic attempts to find some consistent and stable meaning to these terms.[47] In postcommunist Russia, to take an illustrative case, Boris Yeltsin's self-identified "left" defeated the pro-Gorbachev forces, whom it labeled part of the "right" (over Gorbachev's strenuous objections).[48] A few years later, supporters of Yeltsin's Westernization policies, acknowledging the influence of Margaret Thatcher, called themselves the "right," while Ziuganov's pro-imperial communist party appropriated the term "left" (more precisely, according to Ziuganov, the "patriotic left"). Public opinion polls taken at the time, not surprisingly, also demonstrate a remarkably wide range of public understandings of the meanings of "left" and "right" – at least, until the success of the Communist Party of the Russian Federation (CPRF) in claiming the term "left" for itself brought some clarity to the entire Russian political spectrum.[49] In this case, we see political ideology generating institutionalized definitions of left and right, rather than conceptions of left and right somehow generating coherent ideological positions.

All of these considerations lead me to propose a new definition of "ideology" that improves upon these common approaches. Specifically, I define ideology as "any clear and consistent definition of the criteria for membership in a desired

---

[47] See, for example, Noberto Bobbio, *Left and Right: The Significance of a Political Distinction*, trans. by Allan Cameron (Chicago: University of Chicago Press, 1996). Kenneth Benoit and Michael Laver have also recently broken with the idea that there is any way to develop a single, meaningful left-right scale for transnational comparative research and instead choose to rely on country experts to classify the specific dimensions of partisan competition in each democracy. Benoit and Laver, *Party Policy in Modern Democracies: Expert Survey Results from 47 Countries, 2003–2004* (London: Routledge, 2006).

[48] Mikhail Gorbachev, *Memoirs* (New York: Doubleday, 1996).

[49] Timothy Colton, *Transitional Citizens: Voters and What Influences Them in the New Russia* (Cambridge, MA: Harvard University Press, 2000).

political order."[50] This definition takes its cue from the literature on "formal and consistent" worldviews in the first school of thought examined here and excludes from the concept the fuzzy, inconsistent, and informal norms and practices typical of most ordinary social actors (political and apolitical alike).[51] I go a step further, however, in focusing attention here on how certain formal, consistent political viewpoints also set out clear rules for defining just who is a "member" of one's political "community" and who is "alien." From this perspective, ideologues are people who explicitly choose to politicize their identities by designing recognizable and enforceable group boundaries that can be "policed."[52] It is not surprising, then, that ideologues are frequently interested in claiming control over a "state" – that is, the monopoly of the legitimate means of coercion within a given territory – in order to institutionalize such identity boundaries.[53]

Formal and consistent religious worldviews that focus on a world beyond this one, therefore, are not "ideologies" by this definition; neither are scientific paradigms or personal philosophies or delusions that do not claim to articulate criteria for political membership. Nor, despite their desire for state representation of a chosen "people," are all nationalists necessarily ideological in my sense; on the contrary, most nationalisms are remarkably fuzzy concerning the philosophical criteria that determine who does, and does not, belong to the "nation." Ideologues, by this definition, are actually quite rare: few social actors in any given social context are able to set out clear and consistent definitions for membership in the political community they favor. By this definition, moreover, ideologies are neither "incorrect" nor "correct"; one's approbation or condemnation of a given ideology will instead depend upon one's particular values. Finally, the term "ideology" as defined here is meant to be employed as a Weberian "ideal type"; no political actor or set of actors is ever absolutely clear and absolutely consistent about criteria for defining political membership,

[50] I have developed this definition in several essays: Stephen E. Hanson, "Ideology, Uncertainty, and the Rise of Anti-System Parties in Post-Communist Russia," *Journal of Communist Studies and Transition Politics* 14(1–2, March–June 1998): 98–127; Hanson, "Defining Democratic Consolidation," in Richard Anderson Jr., M. Steven Fish, Stephen E. Hanson, and Philip Roeder, *Postcommunism and the Theory of Democracy* (Princeton, NJ: Princeton University Press, 2001), pp. 126–151; and Hanson, "Instrumental Democracy: The End of Ideology and the Decline of Russian Political Parties," in Vicki Hesli and William Reisinger, eds., *The Elections of 1999–2000 in Russia: Their Impact and Legacy* (Cambridge: Cambridge University Press, 2003), pp. 163–185.

[51] My definition of ideology fits what Goertz calls the "necessary and sufficient conditions" approach to concept formation, rather than the Wittgensteinian "family resemblances" approach. See Gary Goertz, *Social Science Concepts: A User's Guide* (Princeton, NJ: Princeton University Press, 2006).

[52] Thus, ideologues make the criteria for boundary formation explicit, whereas ethnic groups have boundaries that are generally left implicit. See Frederick Barth, ed., *Ethnic Groups and Boundaries: The Social Organization of Culture Difference* (Boston: Little, Brown, 1967).

[53] Max Weber, "Politics as a Vocation," in Gerth and Mills, *From Max Weber: Essays in Sociology*, p. 78.

but nonetheless certain political actors orient their behavior toward each other in ways that more or less closely approximate this ideal-typical definition.

No doubt some scholars will object that this definition of ideology classifies some belief systems or worldviews in ways that do not fit their intuitions. However, as explained previously, clashes with existing usage are the inevitable fate of all carefully articulated definitions of social science concepts, because no definition can encompass all the multiple and conflicting meanings carried by words in both scholarly and ordinary communication.[54] That said, the definition of ideology as any formal, consistent definition of the criteria for membership in a desired polity does happen to encompass a very large number of the key individuals, and movements, generally associated with this term. Revolutionary leaders such as Cromwell, Robespierre, Lenin, Hitler, Pol Pot, and Khomeini clearly count as ideologues in this sense; so, too, would "extremist" politicians in mainstream democracies such as Le Pen, Haider, and David Duke. At the same time, more positive figures from the liberal perspective, such as Locke, Montesquieu, or Madison, can be understood as ideological innovators by this definition as well.

Ideology and Collective Action

It remains to show how this new definition of ideology, combined with the Weberian theory of social action presented in the previous chapter, can provide microfoundations for a theory of how ideologies first emerge and then subsequently affect political outcomes. Three points will be emphasized: first, ideology as conceptualized here is initially a product of individual, not collective, social action; second, ideology is in essence a form of value rationality; and, third, the ultimate success of an ideology depends on its intersection with both affectual and instrumentally rational motivations for conversion and adherence.

The fact that the definition of ideology as "any clear, consistent definition of the criteria for membership in a desired political order" is fully compatible with a thoroughgoing methodological individualism is perhaps its greatest single advantage over competing conceptions. Anyone, after all, can propose a new political order – and people do so all the time. That such proposals are usually fated to disappear once those who utter them leave the dinner table, café, or seminar room should not obscure the fact that successful ideologies also have their origins in individual action. Indeed, one of the greatest obstacles to a truly causal theory of ideology in the social sciences has been the overwhelming tendency of scholars to insist on the "inherently collective" nature of ideology – in effect forcing scholars to "select on the dependent variable" by definitional fiat.[55] True, the cultural and linguistic materials used by individuals

---

[54] Faeges, "Theory-Driven Concept Definition."
[55] For examples, see Freeden, *Ideology: A Very Short Introduction*; Mark Blyth, *Great Transformations: Economic Ideas and Institutional Change in the Twentieth Century* (Cambridge: Cambridge University Press, 2002).

who propose new ideologies are inherently collective products, and existing cultural modes of expression do place certain constraints on what kinds of political orders can be articulated in any given social context.[56] Nevertheless, the range of individual creativity displayed by ideologues in reordering ordinary language and culture – as we will see in the empirical section of this study – is much greater than typically recognized.

If our definition forced us to see every individual as an ideologue, though, it would have the same methodological problems as the "world view" approach discussed in the preceding section. This is where the elements of clarity and consistency become definitionally important. Most people, after proposing a viewpoint on membership in a preferred polity – perhaps one where "foreigners don't take our jobs" or where "the bureaucrats get off our backs" – make no effort to formalize its various elements, nor do they take care to remain consistent with it in each and every subsequent political conversation. On the contrary, most people in any society possess only fuzzy, inconsistent notions of politics – what we may define as "cultural" as opposed to "ideological" views.[57] Against this background, the few individuals who manage consistently and precisely to articulate who belongs in their desired political order, in various social settings at different points in their lives, become empirically relatively easily to identify.

As this account implies, individual articulation of an ideology is an analytically value-rational form of social action in Weberian terms. The formality and consistency involved in articulating ideologies requires a high degree of deliberation; heightened emotional states or habitual stereotypes alone do not suffice to produce standardized definitions of the political order. In addition, the articulation of a formal and consistent definition of the polity inevitably involves disengagement with contingent temporal factors in order to connect to values seen as "timeless" on some level. After all, in the flux of everyday life, no stable or consistent way of defining membership in any political order can endure for long: as patterns of demography, migration, and economic development change, so too will individual interests connected with policies toward citizenship and exclusion. Ideologues, by contrast, see their desired political orders as existing in some sense outside of such ordinary temporal considerations. Indeed, empirically one often finds that ideologues describe the "timelessness" of their political proposals in explicit terms, claiming that the establishment of their favored conceptions of political membership will cause previous human history to end and time itself to begin again.[58]

---

[56] Hannah Fenichel Pitkin, *Wittgenstein and Justice: On the Significance of Ludwig Wittgenstein for Social and Political Thought* (Berkeley: University of California Press, 1972).

[57] Converse, "The Nature of Belief Systems"; Ann Swidler, "Culture in Action: Symbols and Strategies," *American Sociological Review* 51(2, April 1986): 273–286; Hanson, "From Culture to Ideology."

[58] Stephen E. Hanson, *Time and Revolution: Marxism and the Design of Soviet Institutions* (Chapel Hill: University of North Carolina Press, 1997).

If the promotion of a new ideology is a subtype of value-rational action, nevertheless ideologies do not succeed or fail solely on the basis of their philosophical or religious appeal in the abstract. Simply repeating a clear and consistent definition of one's favored polity, obviously, does not automatically lead to one's attainment of an important leadership role in real politics. Instead, as would be expected in Weberian theory, other types of social action intersect with the value-rational core of ideologies to account for their acceptance or rejection by others in the social environment. Thus, to the extent that formal, consistent definitions of the criteria for political membership resonate with deeply felt symbols and loyalties in a surrounding culture, some individuals may "convert" to a new ideology for predominantly affectual reasons. Cultural racists who have not deliberated much about the rationality of their views, for example, may find themselves strangely thrilled to hear a systematic, consistent presentation of history by a fascist ideologue. In a parallel manner – although with diametrically different political implications – undergraduates in Western universities who were raised with vaguely liberal sympathies may decide to "convert" to Rawlsian or Habermasian definitions of membership in the political order without fully grasping their philosophical underpinnings. In any case, an ideologue who does not succeed at all in connecting to local actors' emotions seems highly unlikely to gain many converts, regardless of her degree of philosophical consistency.

Still, even ideologues who manage to gain converts on the basis of affectual appeals must find some way to satisfy the short-term instrumental interests of converts in order to sustain their movements. Ideological sects built on value rationality and affect constitute a subtype of charismatic domination, relying solely on "timeless" social orientations, and thus are vulnerable to sudden collapse in the face of adverse economic and social circumstances. In cases such as the Jonestown massacre, ideological leaderships may even choose mass suicide rather than compromising the purity of value-rational principles of membership in the organization – quickly eliminating their future political impact. We must explain, then, how initially value-rational commitments to particular formal definitions of political membership can also change the instrumental calculations of rational actors who encounter them in ways that reinforce, rather than undermine, organizational power.

The key to this mechanism is how ideological commitments affect the time horizons of rational actors under conditions of high uncertainty. Typically, one would expect that instrumentally rational actors subjected to situations where the future is not only highly uncertain but where even ordinary risk assessments are made impossible by changing institutional and social circumstances will discount the benefits of future cooperation very highly.[59] Given generally high discount rates of this sort, we would expect instrumental actors to "defect" from cooperation to produce collective goods, in the absence of other selective

---

[59] Frank H. Knight, *Risk, Uncertainty, and Profit* (Boston: Houghton Mifflin, 1921).

incentives that make such cooperation individually rational. Yet, where social uncertainty is pervasive enough, systems of selective incentives of the necessary sort can also be analyzed as public goods: such selective incentives would indeed benefit the entire group, but no single individual has any rational incentive to sacrifice to produce them.[60] In short, given high enough uncertainty, social life truly does begin to resemble the Hobbesian world. Yet, as rational choice theory demonstrates, Hobbes's own "solution" to this dilemma – the introduction of Leviathan – involves collective action dilemmas that rational actors alone can never solve.[61]

The various solutions to this problem that have been introduced over the past several decades are legion, and there is insufficient space here to address all of them in detail.[62] Some of them are tautological, relying on ad hoc assumptions about unusual actors who participate in collective action to gain "expressive benefits" or who act as "heroic" enforcers of norms others do not consistently follow.[63] Those solutions to the Hobbesian dilemma that are not tautological, in one way or another, all involve efforts to show how certain actors begin to cooperate for long-term benefits rather than pursue short-run payoffs as a result of the lengthening of their time horizons. Michael Taylor, for example, has demonstrated in a rigorous formal model that cooperation under anarchy is possible for "conditional cooperators" whose discount rates are sufficiently low.[64] Robert Axelrod has shown that a strategy of "tit for tat," rather than simple defection, will win out over time in iterated prisoner's dilemma simulations.[65] Building on this result, computer simulations based on agent-based modeling have illustrated how small groups of "cooperators" can eventually "colonize" regions of society where individual strategies of defection previously dominated.[66] Finally, various authors have explored the ways

---

[60] This point is emphasized in Michael Taylor, *The Possibility of Cooperation* (Cambridge: Cambridge University Press, 1987).

[61] Thomas Hobbes, *Leviathan*, ed. Richard Tuck (Cambridge: Cambridge University Press, 1996); Russell Hardin, *Indeterminacy and Society* (Princeton, NJ: Princeton University Press, 2003).

[62] Particularly useful treatments include Russell Hardin, *Collective Action* (Baltimore: Johns Hopkins University Press, 1982); Michael Hechter, *Principles of Group Solidarity* (Berkeley: University of California Press, 1987); Elinor Ostrom, *Governing the Commons: The Evolution of Institutions for Collective Action* (Cambridge: Cambridge University Press, 1990).

[63] Dennis Chong, *Collective Action and the Civil Rights Movement* (Chicago: University of Chicago Press, 1991); James Coleman, *Foundations of Social Theory* (Cambridge, MA: Harvard University Press, 1990).

[64] Taylor, *The Possibility of Cooperation.*

[65] Robert Axelrod, *The Evolution of Cooperation* (New York: Basic Books, 1984).

[66] See, for example, Robert Axelrod and Scott D. Bennett, "A Landscape Theory of Aggregation," *British Journal of Political Science* 23(2, April 1993): 211–33. For recent efforts to show how agent-based modeling intersects with central concerns in macrosociological theory, see Ian S. Lustick and Dan Miodownik, "The Institutionalization of Identity: Micro Adaptation, Macro Effects, and Collective Consequences," *Studies in Comparative International Development* 37(2, Summer 2002): 22–51; and Lars-Erik Cederman, "Computational Models of Social Forms: Advancing Generative Process Theory," *American Journal of Sociology* 110(4, January 2005): 864–893.

in which "trust" and "social capital" may allow instrumentally rational actors to pursue long-term benefits from cooperation rather than short-term benefits from defection.[67]

The problem for all of these arguments is that the elongation of time horizons involved in each case happens fundamentally for reasons exogenous to the theory. The first person, after all, to adopt a low discount rate and "trust" others to cooperate in an environment where others are operating on short-run instrumental rationality, or to employ a tit-for-tat strategy when typical interactions with others are a one-shot affair rather than an iterated game, will surely end up as a sucker. In a world where every rational actor immediately defects from any proposed system of long-term social cooperation in order to pursue short-run payoffs, such a "trusting" actor is in the position of the single person who waits at a red light at an intersection in Naples at rush hour – gaining neither the benefits of long-term cooperation to enforce social order in traffic regulation nor the short-term benefit of inching ahead of competing drivers.[68] When not only traffic laws but all institutional rules are being systematically violated, such naive behavior can have personally tragic results.

In short, to solve the initial Hobbesian dilemma, we need a theory of where low discount rates in environments of social uncertainty come from in the first place. Here, I argue, is where ideologies – defined in the terms already set out – play their crucial causal role. Ideologues, by providing clear and consistent definitions of who belongs to the future political order they propose, in effect offer instrumentally rational actors the chance to "gamble" on the truth of their ideological prophecies. In a social world characterized by pervasive distrust and clear evidence that most of one's fellows are thinking in terms of only short-term interests, the clarity and consistency of small groups of committed ideologues who have joined for value-rational or affectual reasons can provide prima facie evidence that "conversion" to the ideology may be worthwhile. The fact that such groups already can be seen empirically to cooperate in advancing their ideological beliefs – despite rapidly changing social conditions – makes

---

[67] The most famous of these authors is Robert Putnam. See in particular Putnam with Robert Leonardi and Raffaella Y. Nanetti, *Making Democracy Work: Civic Traditions in Modern Italy* (Princeton, NJ: Princeton University Press, 1993). See also the discussion in Russell Hardin, *Trust and Trustworthiness* (New York: Russell Sage Foundation, 2002), and Karen S. Cook, Russell Hardin, and Margaret Levi, eds., *Cooperation without Trust?* (New York: Russell Sage Foundation, 2005).

[68] As one eyewitness describes the situation: "Driving in Napoli can make any perfectly normal and happy person go mad and insane! Neapolitans have no respect for traffic laws, in fact they have made up their own. Such as: 1. Ignore the traffic lights, unless police is present. 2. Honk your horn as often as you can, just for fun. 3. If you see a person trying to cross the street, make sure NOT to stop. 4. Always drive where the Taxi and Buses are supposed to drive and make even more traffic chaos. 5. Make sure to park in a way that always makes it impossible for the other 10 cars to get out! But to the Neapolitans' defence, even though they are very arrogant drivers, they are good at it! I say, if you can drive in Napoli – you can drive anywhere, seriously!" Posted by Calista, http://www.virtualtourist.com/travel/Europe/Italy/Campania/Naples-147332/ Transportation-Naples-BR-1.html, accessed on June 23, 2006.

their commitment to advance the interests of new converts potentially credible. There is, of course, still a chance that joining a group that professes to have clear and consistent political principles may lead to one's exploitation and abandonment by that group. But given the high personal costs of remaining within a fundamentally Hobbesian environment with no reliable networks of support, the gamble of ideological conversion may nevertheless seem to be a risk worth taking.

Once an instrumentally rational individual decides to adopt the formal, consistent definition of membership in the future polity articulated by a new ideological elite, the effect is artificially to lower her discount rate in evaluating the future benefits from cooperation with her fellow converts. Secure in the "knowledge" of long-term political success, such an individual can now rationally forgo the benefits of short-term egoistic behavior in order to advance the cause of the ideological collective. "Selling out" one's comrades might generate a short-term "sucker's payoff," but the ease with which such a defector can be identified among a group of clear and consistent ideologues makes it likely that she will thereafter be excluded from all networks of cooperation established among ideological believers. In a sufficiently uncertain environment, maintaining one's bond with an ideological movement in order to reap the smaller, but longer-term, rewards of cooperation may be in fact the instrumentally rational choice.[69]

Of course, in order to convert to a new ideology, one must see oneself as possessing social characteristics that are reasonably consistent with the formal criteria of political membership proffered by the ideological elite. Feudal nobles, for example, will typically find it difficult to convert to orthodox Marxism; members of traditional guilds are unlikely to join liberal movements for free trade. Naturally, therefore, we would expect the majority of initial ideological converts to belong to social groups explicitly identified by the ideology in question as crucial to the establishment of the desired future polity. The fuzziness and plasticity of most individuals' informal cultural identities, however, can sometimes allow for ideological conversion even among members of seemingly unlikely social groups – as in the case of marginalized intellectuals in preindustrial societies in the developing world identifying with Marx's call for a future "proletarian dictatorship" emerging out of advanced capitalism. While most clear and consistent definitions of desired political orders have direct implications for who is likely to be accepted as "members" of such orders, those ideologies which are relatively specific about their criteria for membership in the future polity – and which therefore define more precisely just who does and does not belong to the "trustworthy" group of future cooperators in

---

[69] Another way of putting this point is that once the number of believers in a new ideology passes a certain critical threshold, the benefits available to adherents of that ideology change from nonexcludable pure public goods to excludable "club goods" – making collective action among believers considerably easier to enforce. I thank Henry Hale for bringing this point to my attention.

the new order – may paradoxically inspire more powerful forms of conversion than ideologies that describe the preferred future political order in relatively inclusive terms.

Where sufficient numbers of people do join ideological groups for instrumentally rational reasons, the effect is to make initial ideological prophecies about the future definition of the polity appear to be correct – inspiring others to convert in turn, for both affectual and instrumental reasons. Indeed, once an ideological movement acquires sufficient momentum, even relatively secure social actors with stable material and personal resources may find it in their interest to join as well. Over the course of time, highly marginal politicians with tiny followings can, in this way, be hailed by vast numbers of people as uniquely perspicacious leaders who have somehow grasped the true "destiny" of the nation. Of course, scientifically, such retrospective interpretations are always incorrect, because for every ideologue who succeeds in generating a new core group of cooperators and then attracting large numbers of instrumentally rational converts, many other would-be ideological leaders have failed altogether. Put differently: providing a clear and consistent definition of the future polity is a necessary but not a sufficient condition for success in mobilizing collective action under Hobbesian conditions.

Another important implication of this line of argument is that ideologies can never be created by purely strategic actors who do not actually believe in the principles of political membership they formally espouse. Under conditions of high social uncertainty, instrumentally rational actors who are concerned with attaining payoffs within some definite interval of time will be unable to sustain the consistency necessary to make their ideological commitments credible. Given rapidly changing social circumstances, strategic politicians will inevitably be forced repeatedly to repudiate ideological "principles" they have earlier embraced, for fear of ending up in a marginalized political position. Because adoption of a new ideology is *not* a sufficient condition for mobilizing a political movement under Hobbesian conditions, it is foolish to try to adopt and publicize a formal, consistent view of the future polity in advance, on the off chance that one will be the fortunate ideologue whose message is actually successful. For every ideologue who emerges as a "charismatic leader," hundreds of other ideologues may end up on the streets, in prison, or dead; an instrumentally rational politician should never take such a bad bet.[70] If so,

---

[70] The only way to avoid this conclusion and defend a strict rational choice account given this problem, I think, is to argue that there are a few very unusual actors who have preference schedules that assign an overwhelmingly high utility to becoming a charismatic leader with a mass following and to evaluate any other personal outcome as nearly worthless. For such actors, it may be instrumentally rational to adopt an ideology and stick with it no matter what, in order to maximize their chances of attaining their only desired result. I have no logical objection to such a line of reasoning but would argue that the historical role of actors who behave as if they did possess such "preference schedules" is much better understood in Weberian terms. For a similar argument against describing the behavior of revolutionary ideologues in rational choice terms, see Barbara Geddes, *Paradigms and Sand Castles: Theory Building and Research Design in Comparative Politics* (Ann Arbor: University of Michigan Press, 2003), pp. 181–182.

only ideologues with genuinely value-rational orientations toward their conceptions of political membership can succeed in catalyzing the dynamic of collective action described here.

If this theory of ideology and collective action is correct, it may help to explain why ideologies seem to most observers to be "collective products" rather than the results of individual action. Once significant numbers of social actors have converted to an ideology, its origins in the academic scribblings or café conversations of marginal intellectuals will likely be forgotten, replaced with a myth that the ideology has emerged directly from the "will of the people" itself. Neither ideological elites nor followers will generally possess the necessary analytic distance to describe the process of conversion in more neutral social scientific terms. In the end, even dispassionate scholars will likely encounter a documentary record heavily biased in favor of the view that particular ideologies naturally "represent" their favored social constituencies. The lack of serious research into failed ideologies has thus created a severe problem of selection bias that has obscured the causal mechanisms that can lead – in a small number of cases – from ideological consistency to widespread collective action.[71]

A final advantage of defining ideology as any formal, consistent definition of the criteria for membership in a desired polity is that such an approach allows us to analyze not only the rise of new belief systems in politics but also reasons for their eventual decline and fall. If the initial articulation of a new ideology and conversion of a small group of converts can be understood in Weberian terms as a subtype of charismatic domination, then its dynamics of routinization and corruption can be analyzed in a similar way. Specifically, one would expect that over time, the early perception that ideological principles are "timelessly valid" will tend to erode, replaced by ritualistic obeisance to ideological norms combined with conformity for instrumentally rational and habitual reasons. The formality and consistency of ideology will tend, gradually, to decrease; ordinary people living within polities initially founded on ideological principles will increasingly hold fuzzy, informal understandings of just what those principles are. In this way, even successful ideologies tend to lose their "ideological" quality over time, becoming part of a society's political culture. However, if this process continues for too long, enforcers of ideological definitions of political membership may themselves begin to abandon their earlier clarity and consistency, upholding their professed ideology only on a case-by-case basis. Where no new converts to formal ideological principles can be found to keep such dynamics of political "corruption" in check, a formal ideology may disappear entirely.

In sum, the Weberian definition and analysis of ideology offered in this chapter can potentially shed new light on a wide variety of political phenomena that have been neglected or misunderstood by competing social science paradigms.

[71] See Stephen E. Hanson and Jeffrey S. Kopstein, "Regime Type and Diffusion in Comparative Politics Methodology," *Canadian Journal of Political Science* 38(1, March 2005): 69–99.

It remains to be shown, however, that the Weberian theory of ideology and collective action set out here can be deployed successfully in empirical social science research according to accepted methodological standards. In the following chapter, I turn to an examination of the literature on political party formation, in order to demonstrate that the hypothesis that ideology artificially elongates the time horizons of rational actors in uncertain environments can advance our present understanding of a long-standing, unresolved problem for students of comparative party systems: namely, explaining just where new political parties come from in the first place.

3

Ideology and Party Formation

The link between political parties and ideology is well established, in both social science theory and empirical research. Indeed, if representative democracy without a system of well-organized political parties is "unthinkable," as Schattschneider famously argued, genuine electoral competition without competing ideologies seems equally hard to imagine.[1] If parties have no stable ideological positions whatsoever, then party labels cannot convey any meaningful information to party activists and voters about the kinds of policies particular party elites are likely to pursue in office. Electoral campaigns in such a situation become a charade, with politicians merely pretending to stake out positions they had no intention of defending once in power – with the result that voters must quickly learn that their participation in the entire game of electoral politics is irrational. Thus, in any stable democracy there will always be some limits in practice on just how much freedom party elites have in "choosing" positions on the ideological spectrum.[2]

Despite this logic, it is fair to say that the primary focus of most of the literature on comparative political parties has been to emphasize not the ideological limits that the need for credibility places upon party behavior but the tendency of partisan "entrepreneurs" to abandon quickly their professed principles for reasons of electoral and political expediency. Thus, the first serious social scientific analyses of comparative party politics at the turn of the twentieth century focused on the rise of unprincipled mass party "machines" in the United States and Western Europe. Ostrogorski bemoaned the power of the British Conservative Party caucus to "whip" independent MPs to conform to the party line, hindering their ability to represent the views of local constituencies in parliament.[3] Michels saw the gradual abandonment of socialist

[1] E. E. Schattschneider, *Party Government* (New York: Holt, Reinhart and Winston, 1942).
[2] David Robertson, *A Theory of Party Competition* (London: J. Wiley, 1976).
[3] Moisei Ostrogorski, *Democracy and the Organization of Political Parties* (London: Macmillan, 1902).

principles by the German Social Democratic Party in favor of bureaucratic centralization as evidence of an "iron law of oligarchy" operating in all modern party organizations.[4] Weber himself, in a period of disillusionment with German party elites in the immediate wake of defeat in World War I – and heavily influenced by Ostrogorski's and Michels's earlier analyses – argued that the dominance of unprincipled party machines typical of the United States was becoming the norm in German parliamentary politics as well, with potentially fatal consequences for the newly established Weimar Republic.[5]

As might be expected, later theorists in the rational choice tradition have generally been in full agreement with these early cynical assessments of the motivations of party politicians – except that whereas Ostrogorski, Michels, and Weber saw the unprincipled conduct of party machines as in some basic sense a departure from democratic ideals, most rational choice accounts denied that "principled" behavior by career-oriented politicians should be expected in any case. The electoral "market," Schumpeter insisted, should be seen as closely analogous to the capitalist market; parties were like firms trying to "sell" their "products" to voters, with all the same kinds of marketing tricks.[6] Maurice Duverger's magisterial comparative overview of party politics, which shaped the research agenda of countless later scholars, focused its analytic attention on the incentive systems for party formation within different electoral systems rather than on the ideological belief systems of party builders.[7] This general line of reasoning was systematized in Anthony Downs's seminal work on party competition, which used the economic theories of Hotelling and Smithies to argue that in a two-party electoral systems with a single dimension of policy competition and a single-peaked distribution of voter preferences, rational party elites should gravitate toward the very center of the political spectrum – essentially eliminating any initial ideological differences between them.[8] Despite the plethora of proposed modifications to Downs's simple model in the half century since its publication, the tendency within rational choice accounts of party competition to discount the independent causal effects of partisan ideological commitment remains very pronounced.

Thus, most political scientists now work with a basic image of party politicians as driven by career ambitions that inevitably override the demands of the principles they supposedly embrace.[9] Of course, there can be no denying the important empirical insights that have been gained by adopting this image,

4 Robert Michels, *Political Parties: A Sociological Study of the Oligarchical Tendencies of Modern Democracy* (New York: Free Press, 1966 [1915]).
5 Weber, "Politics as a Vocation," in Hans Gerth and C. Wright Mills, eds., *From Max Weber: Essays in Sociology* (London: Routledge and Kegan Paul, 1970), pp. 77–128.
6 Joseph A. Schumpeter, *Capitalism, Socialism, and Democracy* (London: Allen and Unwin, 1947).
7 Maurice Duverger, *Political Parties: Their Organization and Activity in the Modern State* (London: Methuen; New York: Wiley, 1954).
8 Anthony Downs, *An Economic Theory of Democracy* (New York: Harper and Row, 1957).
9 Joseph A. Schlesinger, *Ambition and Politics: Political Careers in the United States* (Chicago: Rand McNally, 1966).

which surely does capture the realities of modern democratic politics to some extent. Yet no general theory of party competition has managed to discard entirely the assumption of at least some degree of ideological "sincerity" on the part of party elites. Indeed, for the early theorists of party organization, tendencies toward machine politics and oligarchy were striking precisely because they so clearly contradicted the strongly antibureaucratic principles professed by the ideologues who built the first mass parties. Ostrogorski, Michels, and Weber, despite their despair about the instrumentalism of modern democracy, all nevertheless concluded their analyses by calling for a return to "principled" politics that might reinfuse representative institutions with political meaning. And although this is rarely noted today, even Duverger was careful to insist that, in accounting for party formation, "ballot procedure has no driving power. The most decisive influences . . . are aspects of the life of the nation such as ideologies and particularly socio-economic structure."[10] Thus, Duverger argued that the fundamentally antidemocratic ideology of the French and Italian communist parties remained a serious threat to representative institutions in these countries that would not necessarily be attenuated simply through repeated elections.[11]

For Downs, too, some degree of ideological consistency was a necessary assumption in order to justify the idea that ideology might serve as an "informational shortcut" for rationally ignorant voters. Thus, Downs stipulated that, at a minimum, parties could not "leap" over their competitor's ideological positions on the left-right scale – that is, socialist parties should not be able to adopt more radical promarket positions than their liberal opponents, nor should parties ideologically committed to laissez faire economics suddenly argue for nationalization of industry.[12] Why such leapfrogging should be prohibited for purely instrumentally rational politicians, however, is never really made clear in Downs's work.

Some prominent later scholars, recognizing the conceptual problems involved in excluding ideology altogether from analysis of party competition, have therefore endeavored to reincorporate political value commitments into their theories. Within the tradition of comparative historical analysis, the most important contribution along these lines was Giovanni Sartori's *Parties and Party Systems*, which argued that assessing the range and intensity of partisan ideological commitments was fundamental to any empirically plausible classification of types of party system.[13] In particular, Sartori demonstrated, the combination of a strong degree of ideological polarization combined with the centrifugal effects of a five-party system played a crucial causal role in generating the dangerous dynamics of "polarized pluralism" in cases such as

---

[10] Duverger, *Political Parties*, p. 205.
[11] Ibid.
[12] Downs, *Economic Theory of Democracy*, pp. 122–123.
[13] Giovanni Sartori, *Parties and Party Systems: A Framework for Analysis* (Cambridge: Cambridge University Press, 1976).

the Weimar Republic.[14] More recent studies within the comparative-historical tradition include Panebianco's theory of party organization, which argues that the initial "collective incentives" provided by ideologies during the "genesis" period of new party organizations tend to generate long-term constraints on the degree to which later party elites can depart from their parties' professed ideological positions.[15] Shefter, building on an insight from Duverger, has hypothesized that "external" parties – that is, parties built from outside the existing state structure – must depend on ideological appeals in order to sustain activists' commitment despite the inability of party elites initially to tap state resources for patronage purposes.[16] None of these important works, however, devotes sustained attention to the problem of explaining precisely where new party ideologies come from in the first place.

Efforts to reincorporate the ideological factor have also emerged within the Downsian tradition. A seminal contribution in this respect was made by David Robertson, who argued that in place of a view of party politicians as either wholly principled or utterly cynical, parties should be understood as oriented toward "problem solving." In his model, different parties propose policy prescriptions for key social problems that, if electorally and institutionally successful, provide parties with long-term reputations for competence in these policy arenas. For such a model to fit democratic reality, there must be some empirical evidence that initial party programs really do anticipate the policies adopted by party elites in power. Robertson's initial test of this hypothesis, utilizing content analysis of Labour and Conservative party manifestos in British postwar politics, demonstrated a remarkably high correlation between parties' stated electoral positions and their actual policy stances in power.[17] Building on Robertson's insights, Budge, Crewe, and Farlie called for a new comparative approach to party identities that might reveal the key policy dimensions underlying European electoral competition.[18] Since then, work by these and other scholars in the comparative party manifestos research project has provided ample evidence of the importance of party ideologies for later party behavior. In a wide range of policy arenas in both domestic and foreign policy, party politicians really do "mean what they say" in electoral campaigns.[19] However, this literature focuses almost exclusively on highly developed party systems in

---

[14] Ibid., pp. 131–145.
[15] Angelo Panebianco, *Political Parties: Organization and Power* (Cambridge: Cambridge University Press, 1988).
[16] Martin Shefter, *Political Parties and the State: The American Historical Experience* (Princeton, NJ: Princeton University Press, 1994).
[17] David Robertson, *A Theory of Party Competition* (London: J. Wiley, 1976).
[18] Ian Budge, Ivor Crewe, and Dennis Farlie, *Party Identification and Beyond: Representations of Voting and Party Competition* (London: Wiley, 1976).
[19] The vast literature spawned by work within this project – first known as the Manifesto Research Group (MRG) and later renamed the Comparative Manifestos Project (CMP) – is impossible to cite in a single footnote. For representative works, see Ian Budge, David Robertson, and Derek Hearl, eds., *Ideology, Strategy, and Party Change: Spatial Analyses of Post-War Election Programmes in 19 Democracies* (Cambridge: Cambridge University Press, 1987), and Hans-Dieter Klingemann et al., *Parties, Policies, and Democracy* (Boulder, CO: Westview Press, 1994).

North America and Western Europe; its relevance for understanding the role of ideology in the initial stages of party formation is thus limited.

Another important effort to restore ideology to a prominent position in the analysis of party competition can be found in Hinich and Munger's *Ideology and the Theory of Political Choice*.[20] Taking seriously Sartori's critique of the Downsian model as lacking a convincing account of how party ideologies become credible to voters, but endeavoring to retain the rigor of spatial theories of voter choice, Hinich and Munger argue that the influence of consistent, comprehensive ideological worldviews should henceforth be placed at the very center of our understanding of democratic politics. Building on the work of Douglass North, they argue that both the credibility of candidates' campaign promises and the willingness of voters to offer support to their favored political parties can be understood only if we assume that both politicians and voters possess quite consistent, comprehensive ideologies that constrain their choices to a remarkably high degree: "Ideological success demands two types of consistency. First, the same ideology must justify the same action, and vice versa, in all similar situations. Second, as the ideology evolves over time and becomes more sophisticated, it must avoid contradictions."[21] Moreover, the central dimensions of party competition should be analyzed not as reflecting a postulated universal "left-right" spectrum but as emerging empirically from the salient lines of ideological opposition within given societies.[22] Hinich and Munger's innovative analysis does not, however, explain either how new ideologies are created by rational actors or how powerful ideologies sometimes lose their grip on the political and social actors who once embraced them. Ironically, then, this rational choice argument brings us back full circle to the initial concern of Ostrogorski, Michels, and Weber – namely, to explain how ideological visions are compromised and corrupted in the course of building up successful party organizations.

Taken as a whole, then, the vast literature on the role of ideology in party politics leaves us in something of a quandary. It is clear both theoretically and empirically that party ideologies do exert an independent role on party behavior in modern democracies, as the seminal works cited here have demonstrated. It is equally clear that politicians do sometimes abandon their professed ideological principles in order to pursue their short-term instrumental ambitions. As of yet, however, we possess no integrated theory specifying precisely how ideological and instrumental motivations interact within party organizations in order to produce these diverging empirical results.

To develop such an integrated theory for application to all party systems would take us far beyond the confines of the present work. Instead, my goal here

---

[20] Melvin J. Hinich and Michael C. Munger, *Ideology and the Theory of Political Choice* (Ann Arbor: University of Michigan Press, 1994).

[21] Ibid., p. 15.

[22] Fortunately for parsimonious analysis, Hinich and Munger contend, the number of such dimensions in most stable democratic polities is empirically generally limited to one or two. Ibid., p. 144.

is more modest: to illustrate how the Weberian theory of ideology sketched out in the previous chapter can shed light on the specific role of ideology in catalyzing party formation in conditions of high institutional uncertainty. I examine existing approaches to the problem of party formation "from scratch" on the basis of Marxism, modernization theory, and rational choice theory and show that, in all three cases, party formation (like the formation of ideologies examined in the previous chapter) is ultimately explained in functionalist rather than adequately causal terms. Building on the recent works of Aldrich and Kitschelt, I argue that we must focus our attention on the initial problems of collective action that would-be party builders must solve in order to mobilize diverse ambitious politicians around a single, enduring party label. I then set out the working hypothesis of my empirical case studies: that ideology is a necessary condition for building national party organizations in highly uncertain social environments. In such cases, I argue, party ideology cannot be a reflection of underlying class or social cleavages, or merely a tool chosen strategically by instrumental and ambitious politicians; it must reflect the genuinely value-rational commitments of initial party builders. Where such commitments exist, ideological parties in turbulent new democracies tend to emerge as the winners in a process of "social selection" that eliminates their nonideological competitors, which are relatively more vulnerable to the free-rider problem. If this argument is correct, it may help to explain why successful political parties even in more established democracies also tend to have relatively stable ideologies; because the costs of developing and enforcing new ideological frameworks are high, it is generally easier to "piggyback" on those developed in earlier, less stable times. I conclude the chapter with a methodological discussion of the principles of case selection and comparison that I use to test this theoretical hypothesis empirically in Part II of this book.

Where Do New Parties Come From?

For the century or so that Western social science was dominated by structuralist approaches to the units-of-analysis problem, the issue of how party organizations were developed and maintained could be answered in a rather direct way, simply by pointing to the collective actors that presumably generated them. The assumption that parties in some sense did reflect the interests of powerful social groups – whether by representing these groups in a democratic manner or by enforcing their political hegemony through more nefarious means – was seen as unproblematic in most of the classic literature.

The direct relationship between political parties and group interests is especially clear in the Marxist tradition. For Marx himself, "bourgeois" parliamentarianism was little more than a facade behind which different parties merely represented different factions of the bourgeoisie.[23] Of course, such an analysis

---

[23] See, for example, Karl Marx, *The Eighteenth Brumaire of Louis Bonaparte* (New York: International Publishers, 1963).

was quite defensible in the mid-nineteenth century, when no European country had extended the suffrage in a meaningful way beyond the property-owning elite. Even after witnessing the first signs of working-class inclusion in Western Europe during the later stages of his life, however, Marx remained convinced that parties and parliaments served only as instruments of the broader class struggle – even if the proletariat might now more effectively organize its own revolutionary communist parties using legal democratic methods.[24] Indeed, the possibility that party elites could somehow develop and pursue organizational interests separate from, and even potentially opposed to, class interests was, for Marx, theoretically excluded a priori. While revolutionary intellectuals would naturally tend to take the lead within newly formed working-class parties, Marx and Engels argued that communists could "have no interests separate and apart from those of the proletariat as a whole," even if they did "have over the great mass of the proletariat the advantage of clearly understanding the line of march, the conditions, and the ultimate general results of the proletarian movement."[25] In this respect, Vladimir Lenin's depiction of communist party organization in *What Is to Be Done?* – seen by many commentators as a direct departure from Marxism for its emphasis on the role of intellectual leadership in guiding ordinary workers – is quite consistent with Marx's own comments on the issue.[26]

Few if any scholars today would accept Marx's and Lenin's simple equation of party interest with class interest. The key problem for this position was analyzed by Michels and Weber nearly a century ago: once communist intellectuals or leading workers became party bureaucrats, their interests as elites within the party organization would inevitably tend to trump the collective goals of the proletariat as a whole. Indeed, paradoxically, the more successful Social Democrats were in mobilizing electorates and attaining political representation within "bourgeois" parliaments, the more powerful were the organizational incentives to abjure "revolutionary" goals in favor of the status quo. Moreover, if this logic operated within the competitive electoral context, it was incomparably more powerful within Leninist single-party regimes, where not even the threat of electoral defeat could check the "iron law of oligarchy." And if the problem of organizational bureaucratization bedeviled left parties, it surely was equally an issue for parties of the right, whose leaders would also be forced to contradict the desires of some of their more vocal capitalist backers in order to maintain their political and electoral viability.[27]

---

[24] Marx, "The Possibility of Non-Violent Revolution," in Robert C. Tucker, ed., *The Marx-Engels Reader* (New York: Norton, 1978), pp. 522–524.

[25] Karl Marx and Friedrich Engels, *Manifesto of the Communist Party*, in ibid., pp. 483–484.

[26] Vladimir I. Lenin, *What Is to Be Done? Burning Questions of Our Movement* (New York: International Publishers, 1969).

[27] Within the Marxist tradition, however, this latter point was usually made about the capitalist state, not about the leaders of capitalist parties per se. See, for example, Fred Block, *Revising State Theory: Essays in Politics and Postindustrialism* (Philadelphia: Temple University Press, 1987).

These theoretical shortcomings of Marx's and Lenin's efforts to analyze parties as simple instruments of class interest have tended to limit the influence of the Marxist paradigm in the analysis of comparative party politics. Far more important for contemporary scholarship is the modernization approach to understanding party systems developed originally by Seymour Martin Lipset and Stein Rokkan.[28] In line with Parsons's emphasis on the cultural, and not only the material, dimensions of social modernization, Lipset and Rokkan saw Western party systems as reflecting the collective identities of major social groups that were mobilized at critical junctures in the modernization process. The class cleavage between labor and capital, to be sure, did play a key role in shaping the dimensions of party competition in most of Europe, but Lipset and Rokkan argued that three other social cleavages – between modernizing national core regions and ethnic or linguistic peripheries, between the church and the state, and between industrial and agricultural sectors of the economy – were initially more important. Different patterns of early modernization in Western democracies thus generated distinct dimensions of electoral competition, which in time generated strong and enduring forms of party identification that continue to exert an influence over contemporary democratic politics. Indeed, Lipset and Rokkan famously argued that the initial shape of party systems formed during the early process of modernization tended to become "frozen" – at least until even higher stages of modernization generated new social cleavages, expressed in the formation of new social movements and parties such as the West German Greens.[29]

Lipset and Rokkan's analysis of the social cleavages underlying the dimensions of party competition, with its ability to account for the diversity of party systems in Western democracies and its emphasis on the importance of subjective party identification as well as objective interest representation, surely marks a major theoretical advance in the field. Nevertheless, Lipset and Rokkan, following Parsons, still take social groups as their primary units of analysis; thus, they do not devote sustained attention to explaining precisely how social cleavages originally become "represented" within specific party organizations. Instead, they assume that where there is a social demand for parties, supply will follow automatically. Thus, Lipset and Rokkan miss the alternative hypothesis that the key dimensions of competition within developed party systems are not simply a reflection of the nature of social cleavages within democratizing societies but may also result from the conscious efforts of political entrepreneurs to define and mobilize precisely these cleavages and not others. A focus on the specific dynamics of initial party formation appears especially crucial for analysis

---

[28] Seymour Martin Lipset and Stein Rokkan, "Cleavage Structures, Party Systems, and Voter Alignments," in Lipset and Rokkan, eds., *Party Systems and Voter Alignments: Cross-National Perspectives* (New York: Free Press, 1967), pp. 1–64; Stein Rokkan, *Citizens, Elections, Parties* (New York: McKay, 1970).

[29] Ronald Inglehart, *The Silent Revolution: Changing Values and Political Styles among Western Publics* (Princeton, NJ: Princeton University Press, 1977).

of non-Western democracies, where the well-defined and enduring social cleavages characteristic of modern Europe and North America are often absent.

A similar kind of functionalism weakens Inglehart's hypothesis about the importance of "new social movements" such as environmentalism in generating new parties such as the Greens. As Simon Hug has demonstrated, for example, sociological conditions and public opinion in the Netherlands appeared every bit as supportive of environmentalism in the 1970s as within West Germany, yet no electoral Green party emerged in the former case until 1986.[30] A full account of party formation thus apparently requires a theory of how parties are "supplied" by political entrepreneurs and not only a theory of the social demand for them.

A focus on party supply as well as demand forces us to move from the structuralist level of analysis typical of Marxism and modernization theory to a methodologically individualist perspective on the formation of party organizations. To be sure, the classic works on party organizations have always recognized the need to account for the decisions of self-interested individuals who choose to undertake the project of political party building on behalf of some broader group. The fact that party leadership might lead to individual, and not merely collective, advantages in power, status, and material resources is crucial to Michel's argument about the "iron law of oligarchy" within party organizations. The rational self-interest of parliamentary politicians in organizing electoral campaigns is also the key causal variable in Duverger's account of how mass parties emerge historically out of parliamentary clubs or groupings.

Mancur Olson's argument about the logic of collective action, however, renders these classic accounts of party formation problematic. Party organizations, to the extent they are successful, constitute collective goods for those they represent. Because all members and social constituents of a party necessarily benefit from its success whether or not they have contributed to it individually, rational politicians and citizens should "free ride" on the efforts of others to build and maintain political parties. If so, it is not clear why any individual, instrumentally rational parliamentarian should ever initiate the process of national party formation in the manner described by Duverger. Nor is it clear why rational political entrepreneurs should initially try to build "external" parties outside the state structure. Only where specific systems of selective incentives already exist to promote party formation should politicians undertake the party-building process; the mere existence of collective benefits to be gained after successful party formation cannot explain why individuals unite within distinct party organizations in the first place.

Much of the rational choice literature on party politics assumes away this problem by simply treating parties as unified rational actors. Such an assumption may, of course, be justified for research on stable democratic regimes, where strongly institutionalized selective incentives already exist to discipline

---

[30] Simon Hug, *Altering Political Parties: Strategic Behavior and the Emergence of New Political Parties in Western Democracies* (Ann Arbor: University of Michigan Press, 2001), p. 16.

the behavior of party members. For an analysis of party building in less stable environments, however – both in the initial period of democratization in the West and within most of the developing world – the assumption of party unity does not get us very far. Indeed, a comparative analysis of new democracies shows that successful party formation is by no means a sure thing. Even after repeated free elections, parties do not always "close the electoral market"; instead, "party substitutes" ranging from local electoral machines to slates sponsored by powerful businesses can interfere with the process of institution-alizing representative national party systems.[31] To explain why national party formation is nevertheless successful in some uncertain new democracies, then, we need an account of the microfoundations that underlie successful solutions to the daunting collective action problems involved in initial party building.

The Microfoundations of Party Organization: Aldrich and Kitschelt

Two scholars, working within different social science paradigms, have recently tackled the problem of explaining the initial process of party formation head on. John Aldrich, working within the rational choice tradition, has contributed a pathbreaking historical analysis of the formation of national political parties in the world's first mass democracy, the United States.[32] Herbert Kitschelt, working within a modified version of modernization theory that incorporates key Weberian concepts, has along with his coauthors undertaken a massive comparative study of the determinants of party formation in a wide variety of democracies.[33] Both make crucial contributions to our understanding of the process by which party entrepreneurs overcome Olsonian collective action problems in party building. Neither, however, devotes much attention to the possible role of ideology in this process – a factor that, I will attempt to show, helps to address certain remaining theoretical questions arising from their thought-provoking works.

Aldrich's *Why Parties?* has become something of an instant classic in the field, and deservedly so. Aldrich begins by carefully outlining the various ways in which political parties solve collective action problems that might other-wise make representative democracy unworkable. Building on V. O. Key's famous tripartite distinction among the role of parties in parliament, par-ties as organizations, and parties in the electorate, Aldrich notes that each of these roles involves the solution to distinct collective action problems.[34] Within

[31] Henry Hale, *Why Not Parties in Russia? Democracy, Federalism, and the State* (Cambridge: Cambridge University Press, 2006). I present a more detailed discussion of the literature on postcommunist party building in Russia in Chapter 6.

[32] John Aldrich, *Why Parties? The Origin and Transformation of Political Parties in America* (Chicago: University of Chicago Press, 1995).

[33] Herbert Kitschelt, *The Transformation of European Social Democracy* (Cambridge: Cambridge University Press, 1994); Kitschelt et al., *Post-Communist Party Systems: Competition, Repre-sentation, and Inter-Party Cooperation* (Cambridge: Cambridge University Press, 1999).

[34] V. O. Key, *Politics, Parties, and Pressure Groups* (New York: Crowell, 1964).

parliaments, strong partisanship solves problems of social choice – in particular, the problem of "cycling" discovered by Kenneth Arrow – by coordinating parliamentary votes around preformed partisan agendas.[35] Strong partisan loyalties within party organizations also solve problems of coordination among ambitious politicians, allowing for central strategic direction by party leaders of the diverse local electoral campaigns of a large representative democracy. Finally, well-established parties also potentially help to solve problems of free riding among voters, because party affiliation provides an "initial reputation" that helps voters reduce the information costs involved in making decisions at the ballot box.[36]

Because parties solve all three of these problems of collective action at once, strong party organizations are crucial for the successful functioning of modern electoral democracy. However, unlike earlier authors in the modernization and Marxist paradigms, Aldrich recognizes that the functional importance of party systems cannot by itself constitute an explanation for their emergence. The "demand" for new party organizations in mass democracies is clear, but the problem of party "supply" must be analyzed independently. Hence, Aldrich undertakes an original study of the formation of the very first national system of mass parties, namely, that of the United States. Aldrich finds that party organizations – as would be expected, given the various problems of collective action involved in forming new parties cited previously – remained either weak or nonexistent through the first few decades of United States history. The early partisan divide between the Hamiltonian Federalists and Jeffersonian Anti-Federalists had dissolved by the early nineteenth century into a de facto one-party system, in which the "Virginia squirearchy" and its supporters dominated both the presidency and the Congress with little effective opposition. During this so-called "Era of Good Feelings," local electoral "machines" were built on the basis of personalistic networks within local and state electoral districts, but no overall coordination of these separate power structures into overarching national party organizations was established.

The situation changed, Aldrich argues, only when a remarkable political entrepreneur, Martin Van Buren, hit upon a successful strategy for overcoming all three collective action problems involved in party building in order to found the Democratic Party. To overcome indifference at the level of the electorate, Van Buren backed the presidential candidacy of a popular war hero, Andrew Jackson, in the 1828 electoral campaign. Jackson's mass popularity – combined with the vagueness of his policy positions – then provided a focal point for coordination of ambitious politicians throughout the country, who could be convinced to come out in support of the Democrats in order to further

---

[35] Kenneth Joseph Arrow, *Social Choice and Individual Values* (New York: Wiley; London: Chapman and Hall, 1951); Richard McKelvey, "Intransitivity in Multidimensional Voting Models and Some Implications for Agenda Control," *Journal of Economic Theory* 12 (June 1976): 472–482.

[36] Aldrich, *Why Parties?*, p. 50.

their own electoral chances. The great electoral success of this strategy in 1828 also provided a foundation for partisan loyalty within Congress among elected Democratic legislators, who now saw their future political prospects as tied to their affiliation with the triumphant Democratic Party. This initial coordination, however, might have quickly dissolved because of opportunism and free riding among party members after attaining office. To stave off this possibility, Van Buren promoted the idea of the "party principle": individual Democrats must equate the collective interests of the party with their own, thus binding themselves to long-term coalitions with other Democratic partisans. Once established, Aldrich argues, such a principle quickly became self-enforcing, as politicians who adhered to it were also more likely to attain office, pass legislation, and gain the party's backing in future electoral campaigns than those who defected.

The success of Van Buren's strategy naturally attracted imitators. The Whig Party, Aldrich claims, was constructed in a similar way, through coordination of local opposition politicians around the presidential candidacies of war heroes William Henry Harrison in 1840 and Zachary Taylor in 1848.[37] When the Whig Party fell apart after the death of party leader Henry Clay, the resulting vacuum was soon filled by the Republican Party, which successfully coordinated ambitious northern politicians around a platform of opposition to the extension of slavery to the new Western territories. From that point onward, the basic bipartisan structure of American democracy, with the Republican and Democratic parties effectively monopolizing access to political office, was set.

Aldrich's powerful argument, as can be seen from this brief review, tends to downplay the independent effect of political beliefs on the formation of the United States party system. Indeed, the key to Van Buren's success, Aldrich argues, was the choice of a politically inexperienced war hero with no clear platform, Andrew Jackson, as the Democratic Party's first presidential candidate. Moreover, the "party principle" Van Buren promoted, according to Aldrich, had no substantive content other than simple fidelity to Democratic Party coalition building itself.[38] The Whig Party was, if anything, even more careful to avoid announcing a substantive program during their successful popular campaign to elect Harrison in 1840. And Lincoln's Republican Party, according to Aldrich, was more pragmatic in articulating its stance on slavery than other movements associated with abolitionism, avoiding any distinct ideological commitments.[39] If this account is right, then ideological vagueness, not value-rational commitment, is the key to party building.

However, closer examination reveals lacunae in Aldrich's theoretical and empirical arguments that appear to highlight the role of ideology after all. To begin with, it must be noted that despite the rather unsettled shape of the

---

[37] Ibid., pp. 123–135.
[38] Ibid., p. 108.
[39] Aldrich writes that the Republican Party was "focused in appeal, but it was not an ideological party. That is, it was not solely antislavery or extremist." Ibid., p. 156.

American party system in the early nineteenth century, the country's other core political and economic institutions in general were by that stage reasonably well established – in large part because of the general ideological consensus of leading American politicians around the basic principles of Lockean liberal republicanism articulated in the United States Constitution.[40] Still, Aldrich is surely right to emphasize the formidable collective action problems facing would-be organizers of disciplined national parties in this period. Indeed, given the seriousness of these problems, Aldrich's account never entirely clarifies the logic that led ambitious politicians in different regions of the country initially to agree to coordinate their behavior with Van Buren's Democratic Party leadership – even at some potential cost to their own local political prospects. After all, Jackson had also run for the presidency in 1824, losing to John Quincy Adams when no candidate won a majority of the popular vote and the election was thrown into the House of Representatives. Yet Van Buren's early success as an organization builder was achieved during the middle years of the Adams administration, well before anyone could have been entirely confident about Jackson's ultimate political fate.[41] Thus, rather than Jackson's election in 1828 being the "sure thing" that provided an incentive for ambitious politicians to bandwagon with the Democratic Party, the successful prior organization of the Democratic Party served to ensure Jackson's success in his second presidential campaign. If so, we still need to explain just how Van Buren's initial organizational success was first achieved, despite the continuing uncertainty about the party's future electoral chances.

Even if we accept Aldrich's account of the galvanizing effect of Jackson's presidential election in 1828, however, his argument about the importance of Van Buren's "party principle" for the Democratic Party's ability to overcome free-rider problems after this date seems problematic from a strict rational choice perspective. After all, for an ambitious politician, the voluntary decision to subordinate oneself to a party organization for the long term would appear to be irrational, even in the wake of a great electoral victory. Changed future circumstances, after all, might devalue any currently popular partisan affiliation. There is no doubt that parties as a whole would benefit collectively from the general acceptance of such a norm – but for any given individual, surely it would be preferable to let others make binding partisan commitments while reserving the right to form extrapartisan coalitions oneself. To say, in effect, that the collective action problems in party building among rational politicians can be overcome through general acceptance of a norm not to defect from one's party colleagues is only to restate the problem at the level of the norm

---

[40] Louis Hartz, *The Liberal Tradition in America: An Interpretation of American Political Thought since the Revolution* (New York: Harcourt, Brace, 1955).

[41] As Remini notes, during 1826–1827 "a cleavage among Republicans did emerge, but few contemporaries regarded it as irreconcilable.... All opponents of Adams did not rush into the Jackson camp." Robert Vincent Remini, *Martin Van Buren and the Making of the Democratic Party* (New York: Columbia University Press, 1959), p. 124.

itself. Otherwise, "norm emergence" can be invoked as a catchall explanation whenever rational choice theory fails.

In this respect, Aldrich's entire argument can be reinterpreted in light of the Weberian theory of ideology presented in this book, with no loss of explanatory power or elegance, with one key revision: Martin Van Buren's subjective political beliefs must be taken more seriously. Aldrich's account of events tends to present Van Buren as primarily a self-interested politician.[42] Many historians, however, see Van Buren's goals in mobilizing the Democratic Party as far more explicitly ideological in nature, in the sense put forward in this book: Van Buren, throughout his life, was a committed Jeffersonian republican who knew precisely what criteria defined a true member of the sort of polity he wished to defend.[43] Van Buren's personal experience growing up in a poor, Dutch-speaking region of New York deeply impressed upon him the need to attack new forms of elite privilege in the American Republic; thus, he saw the gradual reemergence of Federalist forms of centralism in the "Era of Good Feelings" not merely as an obstacle to his individual political ambition but also as a disgraceful departure from original Jeffersonian ideals. The Democratic "party principle" he advocated did not simply involve a pledge to support future Democratic partisan coalitions; rather, joining Van Buren's Democratic Party required a willingness to declare oneself publicly as a sworn enemy of schemes to expand the power of the federal government in order to facilitate democratic participation by ordinary male, property-owning citizens. Andrew Jackson himself, of course, had also openly declared himself in favor of this quite consistent Jeffersonian definition of the criteria for membership in the American polity, well before 1828. Jackson's vagueness on other policy issues before his election may well have been a tactical advantage for early Democratic party activists – but only in the context of Van Buren's clarity about the sort of political coalition of "planters of the South and plain republicans of the North" for which the party ultimately stood.[44]

Once such an ideological commitment on the part of Van Buren, Jackson, and other key party leaders to this new vision of American democracy had

---

[42] To be sure, Aldrich acknowledges that "these rational political actors were self-interested in the narrow sense, but not merely that. They were also actors with broader and richer goals, and their actions could be understood only by the interplay of these two sorts of motivations." Aldrich, *Why Parties?*, p. 67. Still, the thrust of Aldrich's argument is focused almost entirely on the self-interested side of political action rather than on substantive political goals.

[43] Even Remini, whose account forms the basis for much of Aldrich's analysis, emphasizes that Van Buren "had been arguing principles long before he became a Jacksonian; and they were the same principles after he became a Jacksonian. With him, the principles and the party came first; after that he found his candidate." Remini, *Martin Van Buren*, p. 125. Such an interpretation is developed in more detail by Jerome Mushkat and Joseph G. Rayback, *Martin Van Buren: Law, Politics, and the Shaping of Republican Ideology* (DeKalb: Northern Illinois University Press, 1997). Mushkat and Rayback note that even in his teenage years, for example, Van Buren turned down a prestigious legal internship rather than work for a local attorney with Tory and Federalist affiliations; at great personal cost, he sought out more reliably republican mentorship.

[44] Mushkat and Rayback, *Martin Van Buren*, p. 131.

emerged, both affectual and instrumental motivations for partisan allegiance could function in the ways described by Aldrich. On the emotional level, many ordinary American voters found attacks on the Washington "elite" resonant with their own less fully deliberated political beliefs; this, combined with Jackson's image as the Hero of New Orleans in the War of 1812, certainly did contribute to the momentum of his presidential campaigns in 1828 and 1832. As the support for Jacksonian Democracy swelled, instrumentally rational politicians also began to declare themselves for the Democrats. The end result was the creation of a mass party that did solve collective action problems among voters, politicians, and legislators alike, enduring through the present day. But this happened only because Van Buren had committed himself in advance to beliefs that were, at the outset, politically risky and consequential, thus making his long-term political vision credible to Democratic Party activists.[45]

This alternative explanation for the emergence of the Democratic Party also helps to explain the comparative organizational failure of the Whig Party, whose 1840 campaign against the incumbent Van Buren to elect "Tippecanoe and Tyler too" was notable for its utter lack of ideological content.[46] Clay's emulation of the earlier Van Buren strategy of running a popular war hero against the new "Democratic Party elite" – however absurd it might have seemed, given Van Buren's own humble origins and Harrison's background of wealth and privilege – did produce short-term success through the effective manipulation of voters' emotions. But the unprincipled nature of the campaign generated no comparable process of sincere partisan identification among Whig activists. Indeed, party loyalty within the Whig leadership seems to have been enforced primarily through personal ties to Clay himself – in Weberian terms, creating an organization built around affectual bonds to the leader rather than ideological value rationality. Once Clay himself passed from the scene, the Whig Party predictably disintegrated.

Only with the emergence a new core of activists who were truly committed to a clear and consistent vision of the criteria for membership in the American republic – in particular, to a vision of that republic that absolutely excluded any further extension of slavery to the Western territories – could a

---

[45] Mushkat and Rayback point out that during Van Buren's early legal career, his "crusade against the prevailing landlord system in the Upper Hudson Valley . . . posed considerable risk to a budding politician." Ibid., p. 182. Van Buren's unwillingness to depart from strict, Anti-Federalist republicanism has also been seen as a key reason for his political failure in responding to the economic crisis during his term as president; during his unsuccessful reelection campaign, too, he insisted that the Democratic Party campaign "not on the attractiveness of either candidate, but on their claim of the superiority – and rightness – of their ideas." Joel H. Silbey, *Martin Van Buren and the Emergence of American Popular Politics* (Lanham, MD: Rowman and Littlefield, 2002), p. 150.

[46] Aldrich himself notes that the ideological gyrations of the Whig Party made it "appear to lack conviction," thus contributing to its eventual disintegration. Aldrich, *Why Parties?*, p. 141. Holt argues that the Whigs were united by principled opposition to Jacksonian Democrats – but this does not constitute an "ideology" in terms of the definition I have set forth. See Michael F. Holt, *The Rise and Fall of the American Whig Party: Jacksonian Politics and the Onset of the Civil War* (New York: Oxford University Press, 1999).

second, enduring mass party organization be built. With the founding of Abraham Lincoln's Republican Party, party competition in the United States now revolved around not only competing political ambitions but also competing visions of the polity: one appealing to a Jeffersonian conception of state's rights and the "traditional liberties" of white men, and the other to a very different conception of political liberalism advocating a strong central government that might improve the nation's industry and curtail the power of the "slave system." Diverging "party principles" might well have been resolved through carefully crafted compromises; diverging visions of the nation itself ultimately could not be.[47]

Aldrich's analysis thus explains a great deal about the microfoundations of national political parties, but it falls short in accounting for their diverging political programs. Here the contributions of Herbert Kitschelt and his collaborators have greatly advanced our understanding of the party-building process. Kitschelt's theoretical point of departure is the nuanced modernization theory of party cleavages developed by Lipset and Rokkan; at the same time, however, Kitschelt directly incorporates elements of both rational choice and Weberian theory in order to study the microfoundations of party formation. Unlike most analysts, too, from his earliest work on the formation of ecological parties in Western Europe Kitschelt has emphasized the importance of the ideological motivations of party activists in helping to determine the ultimate political stances taken by party leaderships.[48] In the years since, Kitschelt has developed a distinctive, comprehensive approach to the study of comparative party systems, in both stable and emerging democratic contexts, in which partisan programmatic commitments play a central role.[49]

---

[47] It would take us too far beyond the focus of the current study to discuss the mechanisms of partisan dealignment and realignment in mature party systems. Naturally, the specific ideological content of bipartisan party competition between the Republican and Democratic parties has changed over the past 150 years. Indeed, today's Republican Party embraces "states' rights," while the Democratic Party now stands for a stronger federal government. The problem of maintaining a credible ideological stance once a stable party systems already exists is analytically different from the problem of creating such organizations in the first place. Even so, a certain degree of ideological consistency may still be necessary to preserve party organizational unity through periods of crisis. John Gerring has argued, for example, that underlying each subsequent ideological redefinition of the Democratic and Republican parties since the Civil War has been a fundamentally consistent divide between Democratic Party advocacy of "equality" and Republican Party advocacy of "prosperity." See Gerring, *Party Ideologies in America, 1828–1996* (Cambridge: Cambridge University Press, 1998). I return to this issue in the Conclusion.

[48] Herbert Kitschelt, *The Logics of Party Formation: Ecological Politics in Belgium and East Germany* (Ithaca, NY: Cornell University Press, 1989); Kitschelt and Staf Hellemans, *Beyond the European Left: Ideology and Political Action in the Belgian Ecology Parties* (Durham, NC: Duke University Press, 1990).

[49] Kitschelt, *The Transformation of European Social Democracy*; Kitschelt, *Party Systems in East-Central Europe: Consolidation or Fluidity?* Studies in Public Policy No. 241 (Glasgow: Centre for the Study of Public Policy, University of Strathclyde, 1995); Kitschelt et al., *Post-Communist Party Systems*.

Following Weber, Kitschelt sees the problem of explaining order following among the "staff" that enforces the rules of an organization as the starting point for developing useful analytic typologies for comparative analysis. Thus, Kitschelt postulates three basic types of party organization built around Weber's three types of legitimate domination: programmatic, clientelistic, and charismatic.[50] Programmatic parties of the type generally found in developed Western democracies are rational-legal in nature: such parties are oriented toward substantive goals that are clearly defined in value-rational terms and governed by formal, procedural rules that clearly delimit each member's personal authority. Clientelistic parties, by contrast, are analytically traditional; they are built around personalistic ties to the party leadership and maintained through particularistic payoffs to loyal subordinates. Finally, in line with the mainstream Parsonian interpretation of Weber's concept of charisma, Kitschelt sees charismatic parties as mobilized simply around affect toward a single leader and therefore as ephemeral.

Utilizing this overarching typology, Kitschelt and his collaborators have undertaken a global survey of empirical patterns of party building, focusing in particular on the degree to which party officials in various democracies can be said to understand and orient their conduct toward clear programs. Kitschelt et al. examine this issue through surveys of party members, in order to ascertain the extent to which their assessments of their party's official policy positions are generally consistent or inconsistent; they then compare these results with surveys of the wider electorate to ascertain the degree to which party programs are conveyed to voters.[51] The authors plausibly argue that where ordinary party members cannot agree on what their party's programmatic positions actually are, the mechanism binding the party organization together over time must be clientelistic or charismatic rather than rational-legal in nature, hindering the development of programmatic linkages with the electorate. As might be anticipated from modernization theory, strong programmatic parties are rarely found in new non-Western democracies; fundamentally personalistic forms of authority, instead, underlie the clientelistic parties of postcommunist Eurasia.[52]

Nevertheless, programmatic parties obviously do sometimes emerge in newly established electoral contexts. Recognizing, as Aldrich does, the immense collective action problems confronting party organizers in unstable democratic societies, Kitschelt and his collaborators argue that programmatic parties can still emerge in such contexts where previous regimes have already developed and sustained elements of rational-legal bureaucratic order that can be

---

[50] Kitschelt et al. also mention a fourth possible type, the protoparty built out of parliamentary factions with no mass organization, but do not devote a great deal of attention to it in their empirical analysis. Kitschelt et al., *Post-Communist Party Systems*, pp. 47–48.

[51] Ibid., pp. 133–154; Herbert Kitschelt and Regina Smyth, "Programmatic Party Cohesion in Emerging Postcommunist Democracies: Russia in Comparative Context," *Comparative Political Studies* 35(10, 2002): 1228–1256.

[52] Kitschelt et al., *Post-Communist Party Systems*, p. 401; Kitschelt and Smyth, "Programmatic Party Cohesion in Emerging Post-Communist Democracies."

remobilized by ambitious politicians for party-building purposes. Within post-communist Europe, variation in party building thus reflects differences among the legacies of the various types of communism experienced in these countries. In "bureaucratic authoritarian" Leninist regimes, such as Czechoslovakia, high levels of state coercion were used to control societies with substantial democratic experience. In "national accommodative" Leninist regimes, such as Hungary and Poland, a more inclusive relationship between party and populace was established within a comparatively procedural framework. Finally, the "patrimonial communism" found in most of the former Soviet Union was characterized by high levels of both state coercion and personal corruption. These legacies, Kitschelt et al. argue, help to explain the empirical finding that programmatic parties developed most rapidly in the Czech Republic, where the old communist regime imploded and procedurally oriented civil servants rapidly took over the state. Party building also proceeded relatively quickly in Hungary and Poland, with their relatively liberalized forms of communism. However, party building in Bulgaria, with its previous domination by patrimonial communism, showed relatively lower degrees of programmatic structuration.[53]

Kitschelt et al. argue that these historical legacies should be understood not as reflections of deep "political cultures" affecting contemporary politics in these nations but rather as empirical patterns of elite-staff interaction that have been transmitted over time through the preservation of rational-legal and clientelistic organizational practices from the imperial past, throughout the Leninist period, and into the postcommunist era.[54] Where such legacies of organizational proceduralism are absent, they conclude, only institutional openness along with continuing social modernization might over time allow for the creation of a sociological basis for modern programmatic party building. The near-term prospects for programmatic party competition in much of the former Soviet Union – and, thus, for democratic consolidation – are in this respect rather bleak.[55]

As in the case of Aldrich's important book, any criticism of Kitschelt's massive research project expressed here must be taken in the context of deep admiration and indebtedness to the line of argument and research developed therein. Nevertheless, Kitschelt's work again raises certain theoretical and empirical questions that a focus on the causal role of ideology can help to address. To begin with, Kitschelt and his coauthors' postulated causal link between the presence of inherited rational-legal organizational legacies and subsequent programmatic party building is not entirely persuasive. The coding of previous regime types in the postcommunist world is one potential concern. Kitschelt et al.'s categorizations of Czechoslovak and Hungarian Leninism as more

---

53 Kitschelt et al., *Post-Communist Party Systems*, pp. 69–92.
54 Kitschelt, "What Counts as a Good Cause?" in Grzegorz Ekiert and Stephen E. Hanson, eds., *Capitalism and Democracy in Eastern and Central Europe* (Cambridge: Cambridge University Press, 2003).
55 Kitschelt and Smyth, "Programmatic Party Cohesion in Emerging Post-Communist Democracies."

consistently rational-legal than, for example, Titoism in Yugoslavia or even the planned economy of the USSR seem sensible in retrospect, perhaps, but few scholars of comparative communism before 1989 would have agreed with this classification scheme. Indeed, the scholarly consensus during the 1970s, for example, was that Tito's version of Leninism was more "modern" than that found in the rest of East Europe, while Czechoslovakia was seen simply as a bastion of orthodox Stalinism.[56]

Even if one accepts Kitschelt et al.'s coding of the organizational legacies of past regimes, the precise microfoundations of their argument about the mobilization of these legacies for contemporary party building are never made entirely clear. After all, not every regime legacy survives forever; sometimes, spiraling individual defections from former organizational orders can lead to their complete and irreversible disintegration. Taking the problem of collective action seriously requires us to explain how individuals within the formally defunct organizational networks of collapsed Leninist regimes sometimes managed to maintain their procedural orientations, even in environments of massive social uncertainty, until they could once again commit themselves to nascent party organizations with fundamentally new political programs. Granted that past personal experience working in rational-legal bureaucratic contexts may well produce skills that are crucial for successful party building in new democracies, why should any individual former bureaucrat make the risky decision to commit herself initially to serve a new party organization with no guarantee of future success?

Like Aldrich, Kitschelt never takes seriously the possibility that the content of political programs themselves might play an independent role in the mobilization of organizational staffs within new programmatic parties. Yet in the case of the new democracies of East-Central Europe, the ideological power of the vision of the "return to Europe" as the goal of anticommunist revolutions provided a crucial element of confidence about the future that elongated the time horizons of programmatic party builders in the region.[57] European Union officials buttressed this ideological vision by initiating membership talks with most East-Central European postcommunist democracies, while insisting that the enforcement of rational-legal proceduralism in many key policy arenas was the key to eventual admission.[58] Given the high degree of elite consensus about

[56] Anna Grzymala-Busse has persuasively demonstrated how the legacy of orthodox Stalinism hampered efforts to reform the Czech Communist Party after the breakup of Czechoslovakia. See Grzyamala-Busse, *Redeeming the Communist Past: The Regeneration of Communist Successor Parties in East-Central Europe after 1989* (Cambridge: Cambridge University Press, 2002).

[57] Stephen E. Hanson, "Defining Democratic Consolidation," in Richard Anderson et al., eds., *Postcommunism and the Theory of Democracy* (Princeton, NJ: Princeton University Press, 2001).

[58] Grzegorz Ekiert and Stephen E. Hanson, "Time, Space, and Institutional Change in Eastern and Central Europe," in Ekiert and Hanson, *Capitalism and Democracy in Eastern and Central Europe* (Cambridge: Cambridge University Press, 2003); Milada Vachudova, *Europe Undivided: Democracy, Leverage, and Integration after Communism* (Oxford: Oxford University Press, 2005).

the desirability of this goal, both former communist parties and liberal parties in the region began to recruit members and entice voters by arguing that they, rather than their competitors, would be more successful in bringing a "return to Europe" to fruition.

If this argument is correct, the creation of programmatic parties in much of East-Central Europe reflects not only domestic sociological factors but also internationally appealing ideological visions. Here Kitschelt neglects to consider the possibility that ideological party programs themselves may contain charismatic as well as rational-legal elements. Kitschelt's interpretation of Weber's three types of legitimate domination is essentially a Parsonian one; thus, he sees charisma as entirely based on affect for an individual leader rather than potentially including value-rational elements as well. In light of the argument presented in previous chapters of this book, we can slightly reformulate Kitschelt's Weberian classification of party types to take into account the independent role of political ideology. All new parties, from this point of view, are ideal-typically charismatic: a novel effort to redefine partisan identities must always involve an appeal to extraordinary, timeless values or emotions that are held to require a reorientation of existing political affiliations. However, would-be party builders differ in the degree to which they articulate such claims on the basis of the "miraculous" abilities of the party leadership (affect) or, instead, on the basis of appeals to defend "eternal" political principles (value rationality). The former type of charismatic party either can disintegrate quickly as popular affect for the leader dissipates – as in the case of the Tyminski party in postcommunist Poland, or the Reform Party led by H. Ross Perot in the United States – or can routinize into a clientelistic organization that is maintained through the reinforcement of habitual, informal class, ethnic, and/or regional loyalties.[59] The latter type of charismatic party – that is, a party whose leadership articulates a clear and consistent new ideology – can potentially routinize in a rational-legal direction, welding value rationality to ordinary instrumental rationality in a stable procedural organization.

To be sure, as Kitschelt's research persuasively demonstrates, the existence of significant social groups already trained in norms of bureaucratic proceduralism and impersonal law may greatly facilitate programmatic party formation. Yet even where regime legacies appear conducive to such a process, ideologues who articulate clear and consistent visions of the criteria for membership in the polity also play an important causal role. Moreover, if this argument is correct, new programmatic parties may sometimes emerge even in environments where high institutional and social uncertainty might otherwise appear to block all prospects for national party organization. The ultimate political consequences of programmatic party formation, finally, may sometimes be

---

[59] Steven Levitsky argues that this is what explains both the staying power and the remarkable programmatic flexibility of the Peronist Party in Argentina. See Levitsky, *Transforming Labor-Based Parties in Latin America: Argentine Peronism in Comparative Perspective* (Cambridge: Cambridge University Press, 2003).

dangerous for, rather than conducive to, democratic consolidation – depending upon the specific substance of the ideological principles advanced by successful party builders. Indeed, the universalistic ideology of Marxism-Leninism itself generated quite powerful, programmatically antiliberal party organizations in practically every European country – a factor oddly missing from Kitschelt's historical account of the legacies of communism.

Testing the Hypothesis: Methodological Reflections

The remainder of this book endeavors to demonstrate how the Weberian theory of ideology advanced in Chapter 2 complements the analyses of Aldrich and Kitschelt to provide a more comprehensive explanation for initial party formation in environments of uncertainty. To restate the main thesis of this book: ideologies, I have argued, are best understood as clear, consistent definitions of the criteria for membership in a desired polity that are articulated by individuals. The motivation for articulating and defending a new ideology is value rational in essence; ideologues thus argue for the timeless truth of their carefully deliberated principles for defining political membership. However, successful ideologies can also trigger affectual motivations for conversion, to the extent that they resonate with the strongly held prejudices and/or psychological predispositions of particular subcultures. Eventually, even instrumentally rational actors may then choose to affiliate with ideological definitions of their identity, if they perceive the chances for the eventual success of a new ideology to be reasonably good.

The problem of party formation in uncertain democracies should theoretically be an ideal one for observing this process empirically. As the preceding discussion has demonstrated, the strong relationship of party competition and ideology is a consistent theme in the literature, but the reasons for this connection have not been fully explained. Given the various collective action problems involved in welding together national parties, the reasons for the initial decisions of ambitious politicians to affiliate with new party organizations remain analytically unclear. The hypothesis that ideology can act as an independent variable in accounting for the success or failure of political parties might resolve both of these theoretical issues, and thus seems well worth investigating.

The problem, however, is to test this hypothesis in a way that might convince the skeptical social scientific mainstream. As Berman and Blyth have recently emphasized, ideational arguments have in the past too frequently discarded the baby of methodological rigor along with the bathwater of outmoded materialism.[60] Fortunately, recent advances in the field of qualitative methods, which have begun to attract the attention of a growing number of political

---

[60] Sheri Berman, *The Social Democratic Moment: Ideas and Politics in the Making of Interwar Europe* (Cambridge, MA: Harvard University Press, 1998); Mark Blyth, *Great Transformations: Economic Ideas and Institutional Change in the Twentieth Century* (Cambridge: Cambridge University Press, 2002).

scientists, are well suited to the sort of empirical problems I am examining here. In particular, I investigate the relationship between my independent variable, the presence or absence of political ideology, and my dependent variable, the formation or nonformation of national party organizations with strong activist networks, by using the comparative-historical method.[61] Such an approach has several advantages, given my subject matter. First, the "large *n*" statistical samples most often used in the study of comparative democratization consist mainly of states after 1945; among postwar democracies, high degrees of institutional certainty tend to limit the observable role of ideology in party politics.[62] Second, the comparative historical approach is particularly appropriate for the study of necessary causal conditions, as opposed to linear correlations between variables.[63] The deterministic hypothesis "no ideology, no parties" – understood as an ideal-typical statement that can nevertheless be used fruitfully to analyze the dynamics of empirical cases of democracy that approach a situation of "pure" social and institutional uncertainty – can in principle be falsified if the independent variable is absent in a single instance of successful party building under such conditions. Thus, as an initial test of the hypothesis's plausibility, a "medium *n*" study – based on observations of sixteen political parties in three historical cases – seems appropriate.[64] Third, historical case studies are ideal for undertaking careful "process tracing" of a proposed causal mechanism – such as the artificial extension of individual time horizons among converts to a new party ideology.[65] Finally, whereas single-case studies can be criticized for their potentially idiosyncratic nature and lack of generalizability, "structured, focused comparisons" of the sort advanced here allow us to "hold constant"

---

[61] James Mahoney and Dietrich Rueschemeyer, eds., *Comparative Historical Analysis in the Social Sciences* (Cambridge: Cambridge University Press, 2003).

[62] See, for example, Adam Przeworski et al., *Democracy and Development: Political Institutions and Well-Being in the World, 1950–1990* (Cambridge: Cambridge University Press, 2000). For a study utilizing data that extend back further into the nineteenth century, which generate quite different theoretical implications, see Carles Boix and Susan C. Stokes, "Endogenous Democratization," *World Politics* 55(4, July 2003): 517–549. See also Daniel Ziblatt, "How Did Europe Democratize?" *World Politics* 58 (January 2006): 311–338.

[63] This point is emphasized in Charles Ragin, *The Comparative Method: Moving Beyond Qualitative and Quantitative Strategies* (Berkeley: University of California Press, 1987). In my own view, deterministic causation in comparative historical research of the sort characterized by hypotheses about "necessary" and "sufficient" conditions in social life should always be understood as having heuristic value only at the level of ideal types of collective order constructed through simplifying assumptions about individual motivations.

[64] The utility of single-case studies for testing deterministic causation was first emphasized by Harry Eckstein, "Case Studies and Theory in Political Science," in Fred Greenstein and Nelson Polsby, eds., *Handbook of Political Science* (Reading, MA: Addison-Wesley, 1975), 17: 79–123. See also John Gerring, *Case Study Research: Principles and Practices* (Cambridge: Cambridge University Press, 2006).

[65] Alexander L. George and Andrew Bennett, *Case Studies and Theory Development in the Social Sciences* (Cambridge, MA: MIT Press, 2005); Jon Elster, *Nuts and Bolts for the Social Sciences* (Cambridge: Cambridge University Press, 1989); Robert Bates et al., *Analytic Narratives* (Princeton, NJ: Princeton University Press, 1998).

many of the institutional and structural factors that might otherwise muddy the analysis.[66]

Specifically, in order to examine the hypothesized relationship between ideological conviction and low individual rates of time discounting among activists within ideological parties, we need to find cases that combine extremely high levels of social uncertainty and an extended period of relatively free and fair elections within which parties might potentially form. This combination is empirically rare, because most highly unstable polities formed in the wake of autocratic collapse quickly disintegrate or generate new forms of authoritarianism, making it harder to demonstrate the possible independent role of ideological beliefs in the process of party formation.

The three cases chosen for analysis in Part II of this book – Third Republic France, Weimar Germany, and post-Soviet Russia – are thus methodologically ideal for a number of reasons. First, the three cases are similar in theoretically relevant ways, involving the sudden and unexpected collapse of a previously powerful empire in war and/or revolution, which generated empirically observable, extremely high levels of political, economic, and cultural uncertainty. All three countries found themselves confronted with deep political and social divides about the future orientation of the post-imperial regime, territorial uncertainty including the possible secession and/or annexation of important regions considered symbolically important to national identity, the need to make massive debt payments to former enemies, and revolutionary threats from extremists on both the left and the right. At the same time, Third Republic France, Weimar Germany, and post-Soviet Russia also managed to maintain relatively competitive, inclusive democratic elections (albeit, in the French case, ones that excluded women) for at least the first decade of the post-imperial period. Politicians in all three countries were also able to build to some extent on previous party organizations developed during periods of relative liberalization during the late imperial period. Finally, the post-imperial polity in all three cases was initially formally governed by a presidential-parliamentary system in which the relative power of the executive and legislative branches of government was hotly contested.

The high uncertainty and relative political openness of these polities should, in principle, make it possible to distinguish empirically between committed ideologues, who alone will be able to maintain consistency with their professed principles, and "pragmatists" whose political positions will shift quickly along with the rapidly changing political circumstances. Thus, within each country, among that group of parties generally recognized by contemporaries as having some prospect of joining the ruling government coalition or of blackmailing it through threats of revolution, it is possible to distinguish between parties that entered the post-imperial period with relatively clear and consistent

---

[66] Alexander George, "On the Method of Structured, Focused Comparisons," in Paul Gordon Lauren, ed., *Diplomacy: New Approaches in History, Theory, and Policy* (New York: Free Press, 1979); George and Bennett, *Case Studies and Theory Development*.

definitions of the criteria for membership in the future polity and parties with only vague, inconsistent positions on the nature of the political order.[67] If we were to discover within any of these cases that stable networks of national party activists emerged within independent electoral parties that articulated no clear and consistent ideology, the central hypothesis of this book would be called into question.[68] Conversely, while the success of the more consistently ideological parties in each case cannot "prove" the theory advanced here – for this, analysis of a far greater number of appropriate cases as well as logically related auxiliary hypotheses would be necessary – direct empirical evidence of the proposed process by which ideology generates partisan loyalty in these diverse historical contexts would seem to provide prima facie evidence of its validity.

Finally, while the three cases are similar in their degrees of institutional and social uncertainty, facilitating the comparison of ideological and pragmatic parties within each case, they also obviously vary in terms of ultimate regime outcomes: France by the mid-1880s had become a consolidated democracy; Germany by 1934 was under consolidated Nazi rule; and Russia by 2008 had become a personalistic autocracy with no independent political role for party organizations. To be clear, the proposed causal link between ideology and party formation advanced in this book is not meant as a monocausal explanation for the overall success or failure of democratic transition in these countries. Ideology may be a necessary condition for party formation in uncertain democracies, but articulating an ideology is not a sufficient condition for party success – much less for the creation of a new political order. As the case studies amply demonstrate, many other causal factors influenced the ultimate victory of the French Republicans, the German National Socialists, and the Putin presidential administration over their political rivals.

However, the role of ideology in generating national party organizations in the French Third Republic and Weimar Germany, along with the absence of successful ideologies and of strong parties in post-Soviet Russia, does help to explain the shape of the political "playing field" across in the three cases. The Republican victory in France and the Nazi victory in Germany were, I

---

[67] Following Sartori, I confine my analysis to the four to six parties in each case generally considered, both by contemporaries and by later historians, to be politically relevant – that is, potentially able either to serve as part of a ruling governmental coalition or, for opposition parties, to "blackmail" the regime by virtue of their strong electoral support. Theoretically, it would be ideal to examine a broader sample of the parties operating in the post-imperial period, but in each case this would require historical examination of dozens of additional groupings, most of which had no discernible long-term political influence. Sartori, *Parties and Party Systems*, pp. 121–123.

[68] As will be seen in the case studies, the working hypothesis that ideology is a necessary condition for national party building in times of high social and institutional uncertainty holds for fifteen of the sixteen party organizations I examine; the lone exception is the Center Party in Weimar Germany, which survived from 1918 to 1933 without any clear and consistent definition of the criteria for membership in a future German polity. The implications of these findings for the generalizability of my argument are discussed in the Conclusion.

argue, due in large part to the fact that powerful elites perceived competing ideological organizations as even more threatening. The presence of strong ideological parties in these two cases also prevented the president from exerting independent dominance over all political opposition. By contrast, the weakness of post-Soviet Russian ideologies generated a weak party system that was no match for an executive branch determined to rebuild its own political hegemony over the state. Thus, the initial organizational advantages of ideologues in the chaotic period after imperial collapse had important implications for the ultimate trajectory of regime change across these three cases.

No doubt there will still be some powerful objections to the methodology and principles of case selection used in this study. Some critics will point out that despite the explicit theoretical reasons for selecting these three post-imperial, uncertain democracies for analysis, not every potentially relevant variable is thereby held constant. In particular, changes in the degree of global economic interdependence and the technologies of mass communication over the past 150 years have had dramatic effects on modern democratic parties. Surely twenty-first-century Russia, in these respects, cannot be meaningfully compared to nineteenth-century France or early twentieth-century Germany.

Here I can only note that such problems of comparability and inadequate controls affect all social science research, with the partial exception of laboratory experiments in social psychology; no two historical situations are ever fully alike. The key question is whether the alternative variables that are inevitably left uncontrolled in a given comparative-historical analysis might plausibly affect outcomes on the dependent variable in a way that undercuts one's favored hypothesis. As is discussed at length in the Conclusion, this does not appear to be the case for the three countries examined in Part II.

Others may be skeptical of qualitative process tracing on the grounds that interpretation of the historical record is inherently subjective. Human beings are inclined to see patterns, after all, even in empirically random data. There is no reliable way to "get inside people's heads" to discern the precise psychological state of political actors in three different countries over the course of two centuries. It is entirely possible, then, that a single author with a strong incentive to find evidence supporting his theory will magically discover "ideological consistency" and "pragmatic inconsistency" wherever they happen to fit his argument. This danger is particularly serious given the fact that politicians in all countries at all times have tended to accuse their opponents of ideological incoherence, whether or not this charge is true; thus, it will always be possible to quote some contemporary observer who declares that a presumed "ideologue" was actually a self-serving opportunist.

Comparative historical analysis should, I think, take concerns such as these very seriously. Indeed, I am acutely aware of the limitations of my evidentiary base, particularly concerning the motivations of early party activists in each case, which are not always preserved in the historical record. One method for limiting this problem is to read as wide a range of historical scholarship on one's topic as possible – particularly when one's argument rests to a great extent on secondary sources, as is the case in this study – so as to avoid the form of selection bias in which one cites only those historians whose interpretations of the evidence fit one's preconceptions.[69] Definitional clarity is also very important; as argued in Chapter 2, vagueness in defining key variables such as "ideology" and "culture" has been a consistent methodological problem for the comparative politics literature on the role of ideas. If my study shows that political parties led by people with relatively clear and consistent definitions of political membership systematically outcompete more "pragmatic" parties in uncertain post-imperial democracies, this should provide at least prima facie evidence that my proposed causal mechanism – the elongation of time horizons among ideological party activists – is also a plausible one. Ultimately, of course, readers will be free to judge for themselves where I have adequately demonstrated the clarity and consistency – or lack thereof – of various party ideologies in the cases under examination.[70] I will permit myself to note, however, one additional reason for confidence about the argument advanced here, notwithstanding its qualitative methodology: it has already generated several accurate, falsifiable predictions in advance about future trends in contemporary Russian politics.[71]

Finally, some analysts will object that like all comparative-historical research, my study cannot fully take into account the problem of "world time" – that is, the possible causal influence of earlier cases on the outcomes of later ones.[72] Thus, the fact that Third Republic France defeated and occupied

---

[69] Ian Lustick, "History, Historiography, and Political Science: Multiple Historical Records and the Problem of Selection Bias," *American Political Science Review* 90(3, 1996): 605–613.

[70] Ultimately, it might be possible to develop tools for judging ideological consistency that would attain high degrees of intercoder reliability, limiting the influence of the subjective bias of any single researcher. It seems sensible, however, first to make a plausible initial case for more elaborate future research along these lines, before engaging in the sort of costly, extensive training of graduate students in the Weberian theory of ideology such a project would require.

[71] In an essay written in 1997, for example, I predicted that both the Our Home Is Russia party of Viktor Chernomyrdin and the fledgling Truth and Order party of Aleksandr Lebed would disintegrate because of their lack of ideological clarity and consistency, while the relatively ideologically consistent Liberal Democratic Party of Russia led by Vladimir Zhirinovskii and Communist Party of the Russian Federation led by Gennadii Ziuganov would endure for a longer period. In an essay written in 2001 and published in 2003, I argued that, by the beginning of Putin's first presidential term, all party ideologies had failed; I therefore predicted the final demise of Russia's independent party system. Neither of these accurate predictions was in line with mainstream analysis among Russia specialists at the time. See Stephen E. Hanson, *Ideology, Uncertainty, and the Rise of Anti-System Parties in Post-Communist Russia*, Studies in Public Policy No. 289 (Glasgow: Centre for the Study of Public Policy, University of Strathclyde, 1997), and Stephen E. Hanson, "The End of Ideology and the Decline of Russian Political Parties," in Vicki Hesli and William Reisinger, eds., *The Elections of 1999–2000 in Russia: Their Impact and Legacy* (Cambridge: Cambridge University Press, 2003), pp. 163–185. For more on the importance of prediction in social science methodology, see Stephen E. Hanson, "Weber and the Problem of Social Science Prediction," in Laurence McFalls, ed., *Max Weber's "Objectivity" Reconsidered* (Toronto: University of Toronto Press, 2007), pp. 290–308.

[72] Theda Skocpol, *States and Social Revolutions* (Cambridge, MA: Harvard University Press, 1979), p. 288.

Germany had clear implications for the ideological viability of post-imperial republicanism in the latter country; similarly, widespread knowledge of, and debates about, the basic dynamics of Weimar's collapse arguably affected the outcome of political transition in post-Soviet Russia. Problems of institutional diffusion that limit the independence of cases – also known as Galton's problem – surely undercut the power of comparative historical analysis of regimes from very different time periods.[73]

However, my decision to focus on cases in moments of extreme institutional and international uncertainty tends to limit the problem of diffusion for explaining the divergent outcomes of post-imperial democracies in Third Republic France, Weimar Germany, and post-Soviet Russia. Because all of these countries were relatively isolated internationally, with few obvious allies to emulate and no guarantee of foreign support for any particular long-term strategy of party building, the effects of institutional diffusion on their emerging party systems were less powerful in comparison to many other transitional democracies.[74] As for the problem of elite learning from the past, because historical lessons matter only to the extent that political actors subjectively perceive them to be important, this is a less serious objection to my argument. Indeed, I show that, in all three cases under examination, ideological party leaders developed quite clear and consistent interpretations of the historical record, while nonideological party leaders were unable to do so. In this respect, as I argue in the Conclusion, "world time" is actually endogenous to my theory: it exerts its influence primarily through the ideologies that shape broader social interpretations of the past. Indeed, the overall trajectory of the ideological debates analyzed here – revolving around struggles between monarchists and republicans in France, then centering on a choice among social democrats, communists, nationalists, and fascists in Germany, and finally involving a post-ideological milieu in Russia in which no ideology at all seems credible – tells us something important about the fate of ideology in the modern world. If the fate of postcommunist Russia is any indication, a genuine "end of ideology" on a global scale would undermine democratic consolidation just as much as it inhibits totalitarian rule. If so, the disintegration of independent political parties and general public cynicism under Putin may provide some indication of disturbing trends for democracy in general in the twenty-first century.

In chapters that follow, the analysis will proceed in four stages. First, after a brief discussion of the treatment of each case in the general literature on

---

[73] Stephen E. Hanson and Jeffrey S. Kopstein, "Regime Type and Diffusion in Comparative Politics Methodology," *Canadian Journal of Political Science* 38(1, March 2005): 69–99.

[74] This is not to say that international diffusion effects were entirely absent, of course. In the French case, for example, Bismarck's decision tacitly to support the republicans under Gambetta in the latter part of the 1870s played an important role in the final defeat of MacMahon; however, by no means did imperial Germany build the French republican party in the first place. In the Weimar and post-Soviet Russian cases, Western efforts to support prodemocratic parties and politicians against their antiliberal competitors certainly existed but were given relatively meager resources and had no ultimate success.

TABLE 3.1. *Stages of Development in Uncertain Democracies*

	Chaos	Stalemate	Crisis/Resolution
Third Republic	1870–1873	1874–1876	1877–1886
Weimar Germany	1918–1923	1924–1928	1929–1934
Post-Soviet Russia	1992–1993	1994–1998	1998–2008

comparative democratization, I discuss the legacies of the late imperial period in shaping the prospects for post-imperial democracy and party building. I then discuss the conduct of key leaders of politically relevant parties during the initial period of *chaos* that followed imperial collapse, showing that ideologically consistent elites attained greater organizational success in comparison with their more pragmatic rivals. Next I turn my attention to an analysis of the *stalemate* that emerged as a result of the success of competing ideological parties, examining in particular the interactions among the executive and legislative branches in this period. Finally, I analyze the ultimate *crisis and resolution* that ended the period of stalemate in each country, leading either to decisive control over the state by a particular ideological party or, in the case of Russia, to the collapse of all independent political parties and the hegemony of a nonideological president (see Table 3.1).

PART TWO

CASE STUDIES

4

The Founding of the French Third Republic

The story of how France became a consolidated democracy after its defeat and occupation in the Franco-Prussian War of 1870 has received little attention from students of comparative democratization. It is difficult to understand why. The case is of obvious historical significance: the Third Republic was the first stable electoral democracy with universal male suffrage on the European continent, and its example inspired republicans throughout Europe and beyond. From a theoretical point of view, too, the consolidation of French democracy from 1870 through 1940 poses fascinating puzzles: surely one would not ordinarily have predicted the long-term success of democratic institutions in a country emerging from a century of dictatorship and violence, in a geopolitical neighborhood dominated by well-established monarchies, and with powerful economic and social elites staunchly opposed to democratic ideals. Moreover, this period of French history is intrinsically dramatic and fascinating in its own right, filled with unpredictable twists and turns and animated by intense philosophical debates about the most enduring problems of politics.

That the origins of the Third Republic have nevertheless so rarely been subjected to political science analysis may reflect in part the bad reputation of that regime in the wake of its collapse during World War II. Given the rapidity of France's capitulation to Hitler, the burning issue for comparativists was to explain the fragility of French democratic institutions rather than to account for the success of French democracy in the first place. Thus, during the postwar period, scholars tended to portray the Third Republic as a regime marked by perpetual governmental instability, periodic scandals and crises, and disturbing indications of latent fascist cultural sympathies such as those evident in the Dreyfus affair. France's relatively slow economic development in this period, too, appeared to indicate a general loss of social dynamism. In Stanley Hoffmann's memorable phrase, France under the Third Republic could be summed up as a "stalemate society" – a system incapable of making a full breakthrough to dynamic capitalism owing to its dependence on small-scale agriculture combined with its weak executive capacity, inefficient bureaucracy, and pervasive official corruption.[1]

Yet, given France's domestic turmoil and international isolation in the mid-nineteenth century, the fact that the Third Republic managed to maintain genuinely democratic institutions for seven decades seems a nearly miraculous achievement. And while the problems of governmental instability and crisis throughout the Third Republic were indeed serious, the regime was nevertheless able in these years to institutionalize a national system of free, secular public education; to develop a rich artistic tradition in literature, painting, music, and theater; and to establish enduring symbols of French national citizenship that remain at the core of contemporary French democracy.[2] In foreign affairs, democratic France was able to build a powerful colonial empire comparable in scope (and cruelty) to that of Great Britain and ultimately to emerge victorious over Germany in World War I. Indeed, such was the success of the French republican movement of the mid-nineteenth century that the founding of the Third Republic can even be seen as the "natural" culmination of French democratic aspirations dating back to the French Revolution of 1789: as Francois Furet has put it, with the consolidation of republican rule in this period, the French Revolution had finally "come home to port."[3]

Of course, such a teleological assessment of the origins of French democracy has its own intellectual dangers, glossing over the contingencies and turbulence of the early years of the Third Republic in order to proclaim a heroic narrative of inevitable republican victory over various antidemocratic enemies. In fact, close analysis of French politics in these years clearly demonstrates that the ultimate victory of democracy was by no means a sure thing. The most likely political outcome in France during the 1870s was arguably some form of monarchy with at most a limited role for an elected parliament – that is, the sort of regime found in neighboring Germany in the same time period. As Mitchell has argued,

> The republican tradition in France was far from being unified or omnipotent. Both of the republican experiments before 1870 ended in disarray after brief and troubled tenures. Moreover, as Tocqueville among others perceived, French democracy derived strength from an egalitarian surge that also sustained its dictatorial opposite. The Napoleonic mystique was scarcely less potent than the thrust of republicanism. Nor could monarchy be discounted as only a quaint relic of the old regime. Whether in a Bonapartist or a royalist guise, the possibility of a constitutional dynasty remained for France a plausible option.[4]

---

[1] Stanley Hoffmann, "Paradoxes of the French Political Community," in Hoffman et al., *In Search of France* (Cambridge, MA: Harvard University Press, 1963), 1–117. See also Michel Crozier, *La Société Bloquée* (Paris: Éditions de Seuil, 1970).

[2] Philip G. Nord, *The Republican Moment: Struggles for Democracy in Nineteenth Century France* (Cambridge, MA: Harvard University Press, 1995).

[3] François Furet, *Revolutionary France, 1770–1880* (Oxford Cambridge, MA: Blackwell, 1992).

[4] Allan Mitchell, *The German Influence in France after 1870: The Formation of the French Republic* (Chapel Hill: University of North Carolina Press, 1979), p. 3.

What made the crucial difference, I argue, was the clarity and consistency of republican democratic ideology in comparison with the ideologies of its main authoritarian competitors.

To restate the central hypothesis of this book: in periods of high social uncertainty, political elites with clear and consistent definitions of the criteria for membership in their desired polity can potentially generate large-scale networks of party activists that give them a strategic advantage over their more "pragmatic" opponents, by artificially elongating the time horizons of ideological converts. France in the 1870s, provides an excellent test of this argument. From the defeat of Louis Napoleon at Sedan through the final departure of the last Prussian occupying troops in 1873, almost nothing in French politics, economics, or foreign policy could be taken for granted. Indeed, nearly every month seemed to bring a new crisis. In such an environment, groups with radical ideological visions – both democratic and antidemocratic – were able to mobilize grass-roots support far more successfully than political "centrists."

Specifically, liberal Orléanists and moderate Bonapartists, despite their initial advantages in organization and resources, soon found themselves outflanked on the right by ideological legitimists who were passionate advocates of the reestablishment of a divine-right monarchy led by the Bourbon pretender, the Comte de Chambord, and on the left by the "radical" republicans led by Léon Gambetta, who wished to build a secular democratic polity based on "new social strata" previously excluded from French political life.[5] This ideological battle shaped the terrain of political struggle even after the period of initial chaos ended, generating a stalemate that was resolved only with the decisive victory of Gambetta's republicans in the *seize mai* crisis of 1877. In the years that followed, Gambetta's "radical" republicanism was transformed into "opportunism," as the institutions and symbols of the Third Republic were consolidated through thorough purges of both monarchists and Bonapartists in the state administration and the creation of a secular education system designed to inculcate republican values. In sum, ideologically consistent republicans and legitimists built effective networks of party activists, while the ideologically inconsistent Orléanists and Bonapartists failed to do so; this ultimately allowed the victorious republicans to place their distinctive ideological stamp on state institutions – in this case with prodemocratic consequences.

Of course, political parties in the early Third Republic were by no means the sort of highly bureaucratized mass parties developed in Europe in the twentieth century. Instead, as was first emphasized by Duverger, French parties in the mid-nineteenth century began as little more than parliamentary clubs with relatively fluid memberships.[6] By the 1870s, however, party elites were already

---

[5] Marvin L. Brown Jr., *The Comte de Chambord: The Third Republic's Uncompromising King* (Durham, NC: Duke University Press, 1967); J. P. T. Bury, *Gambetta and the Making of the Third Republic* (London: Longman, 1973).

[6] Maurice Duverger, *Political Parties: Their Organization and Activity in the Modern State* (London: Methuen; New York: Wiley, 1954).

beginning to recognize the need to develop effective, disciplined organizations in order to coordinate electoral campaigns and disseminate their messages to the broader electorate – and some parties were able to do these things better than others. In this sense, to study party organization in the incipient phase of a weakly institutionalized party system is actually an advantage for the kind of causal process tracing attempted here, as it allows us to see more clearly how the transition from parliamentary parties to national party organizations first began. With this goal in mind, then, the analysis of this chapter begins with a discussion of the state of both party ideologies and party organizations in the French Second Empire before 1870, to provide a baseline against which we can measure later party development in the post-imperial period.

French Parties in the Second Empire

The popular image of the regime of Louis Napoleon, from his coup d'état of 1851 through his ignominious surrender in 1870, has long been a derisory one. Karl Marx famously characterized the Second Empire's attempt to recapture the glory of the Napoleonic era as history repeating itself – the second time as farce.[7] This image has largely stuck in the popular consciousness. Napoleon III is remembered as a vain and incompetent dictator who launched a series of disastrous foreign policy schemes, such as the invasion of Mexico in 1862 and, ultimately, the catastrophic war with Prussia that destroyed his regime. Reviled by monarchists, liberals, and republicans alike, the Second Empire has had few intellectual defenders.

This popular image of the Second Empire is not entirely inaccurate. Napoleon III consistently relied on large-scale repression and electoral manipulation to maintain his dictatorship, and his foreign policy grew increasingly irresponsible over time. A recent revisionist historiography, however, argues that the Second Empire nevertheless did contribute to France's national development, paving the way for the eventual triumph of modern French democracy. Economically, the Second Empire was a period of significant growth, during which French heavy industry rapidly expanded, the national railway system was constructed, and Paris was (controversially) redesigned as a modern metropolis of broad boulevards and imposing monuments.[8] Politically, as Hazareesingh has emphasized, the regime's consistent promotion of universal male suffrage – albeit in a plebiscitary form tightly controlled by the imperial state – provided French citizens nearly twenty years of experience with at least semicompetitive electoral politics, in a period when nearly every other European power sharply

---

[7] Karl Marx, "The Eighteenth Brumaire of Louis Bonaparte," in David Fernbach, ed., *Karl Marx: Surveys from Exile*, vol. 1 (New York: Random House, 1973), pp. 143–249.

[8] Alain Plessis, *The Rise and Fall of the Second Empire, 1852–1871*, trans. by Jonathan Mandelbaum (Cambridge: Cambridge University Press; Paris: Editions de la Maison des Sciences de l'Homme, 1985); David P. Jordan, *Transforming Paris: The Life and Labors of Baron Haussmann* (New York: Free Press, 1995).

limited the right to vote.[9] Particularly during the regime's later stages, when it began to experiment with greater liberalization, political opposition in the Legislative Corps and in local elected assemblies became increasingly assertive.[10] And although freedom of the press and assembly were tightly restricted throughout the reign of Napoleon III, the regime was hardly totalitarian; beneath the facade of official unity and devotion to the emperor, heated debates raged among competing parties about the future political order of France.

For all of these reasons, the origins of the French party system must be traced back before the founding of the Third Republic. Indeed, all four major parties that emerged after 1870 – the republicans, the legitimists, the Orléanists, and of course the Bonapartists themselves – had already developed reasonably distinct identities and at least rudimentary electoral organizations under the Second Empire. These four parties can also be clearly distinguished in terms of their ideological development in this period, allowing for comparative analysis of ideological and nonideological party formation. Thus, by the time of the Franco-Prussian War, the republicans and the legitimists had both developed clear and specific definitions of the future French polity for which they stood. Orléanist liberals, by contrast, despite their strong financial position and eminent leadership, were unable to develop any consistent ideology in this sense. Finally, by the end of Louis Napoleon's reign, the "Napoleonic ideas" supposedly animating the Second Empire themselves became so vague and confused that Bonapartists after Sedan, despite the substantial support they still maintained among significant sectors of the French electorate, found it nearly impossible to articulate precisely what sort of polity they hoped to reestablish.

Republicans

The central ideological question in mid-nineteenth-century France was how to make sense of the country's turbulent history after the Revolution of 1789. As the Second Empire came to a close, the country had witnessed nearly a century of continuous revolution, war, and dictatorship – with seemingly no end in sight. How could France redefine itself so as to escape this vicious cycle of violent rebellion and reaction? While this intellectual problem bedeviled all French political elites, it was perhaps most immediate for the republicans, who saw themselves as the direct heirs of the original French revolutionaries, and who were therefore compelled to explain why past efforts to achieve secular democracy and universal male citizenship in France had failed so quickly, and so bloodily.

The republican party did not at first have a single primary leader. Prominent intellectuals and politicians such as Jules Simon, Jules Ferry, and Eugène

---

[9] Sudhir Hazareesingh, *From Subject to Citizen: The Second Empire and the Emergence of Modern French Democracy* (Princeton, NJ: Princeton University Press, 1998).

[10] Theodore Zeldin, *The Political System of Napoleon III* (London: Macmillan; New York: St. Martin's Press, 1958); Zeldin, *Émile Ollivier and the Liberal Empire of Napoleon III* (Oxford: Clarendon Press, 1963).

Pelletan all played important roles in mobilizing support for the republican cause.[11] Such a collegial form of leadership fit naturally with the republican ideological emphasis on autonomous citizenship rather than hierarchy. For this reason, however, the republican movement in the 1850s and 1860s also initially displayed a certain degree of ideological fuzziness. While all republicans agreed that monarchy must be replaced with some form of elected government built on the central principles of liberty, equality, and fraternity, they quarreled about the proper philosophical basis upon which the future French republic should be built. Some republicans – especially those of the older generation, such as Jules Simon – based their republicanism on a deist conception of natural religion for which even some liberal Catholics professed sympathy.[12] Among the younger generation, Jules Ferry was influenced by the positivism of Auguste Comte, while Jules Barni was inspired by neo-Kantian philosophy.[13] Along with these varying metaphysical positions, republicans adopted opposing strategies for building a prorepublican social coalition: some saw their cause as allied with liberalism and recoiled from any association with worker radicalism, while others associated with socialists who proposed to reform or even overthrow capitalism. Republicanism in mid-nineteenth-century France had generated a vibrant political culture, but it did not yet constitute a clear and consistent vision of the future French polity.

By the last years of the Second Empire, however, Léon Gambetta, the young lawyer from Marseille, had risen to a clear position of ideological prominence in the republican movement.[14] Gambetta, the son of an Italian immigrant shopkeeper, had moved to Paris in the 1850s to pursue his legal studies – and, incidentally, to enjoy the ambience of the café scene in the Latin Quarter. He became a noted orator, rallying the Parisian crowds with stirring denunciations of noble, imperial, and clerical privilege in all their manifestations. Like other republican activists of his generation, he venerated icons of the movement such as Victor Hugo and Jules Michelet for their intellectual brilliance and personal conviction, but he also saw the failures of the First and Second Republics of 1789 and 1848 as a cautionary tale about the dangers of political romanticism.[15] Gambetta demanded that the republicans henceforth conduct themselves more strategically in political struggle.

---

[11] The literature on the republican movement in the mid-nineteenth century is vast and growing. See especially the recent excellent works of Sudhir Hazareesingh, *Intellectual Founders of the Republic: Five Studies in Nineteenth Century French Republican Political Thought* (Oxford: Oxford University Press, 2001); Nord, *The Republican Moment*; and Judith Stone, *Sons of the Revolution: Radical Democrats in France, 1862–1914* (Baton Rouge: Louisiana State University Press, 1996).

[12] Philip A. Bertocci, *Jules Simon: Republican Anticlericalism and Cultural Politics in France, 1848–1886* (Columbia: University of Missouri Press, 1978).

[13] Hazareesingh, *Intellectual Founders*.

[14] On Gambetta's early career, see J. P. T. Bury, *Gambetta and the National Defence: A Republican Dictatorship in France* (New York: Howard Fertig, 1970).

[15] Nord, *The Republican Moment*.

By 1869 Gambetta had codified his ideological definition of the French polity in a specific program, unveiled as part of his first electoral campaign for the Legislative Corps, purposefully waged against the well-known republican Hippolyte Carnot so as to establish Gambetta's political independence from established republican elites – to the disgust of veterans like Simon.[16] The Belleville Program can be summed up in a few key phrases: unimpeded individual liberty; a system of free, compulsory secular public education; and complete popular sovereignty built on the principles of 1789.[17] The first of these three principles, Gambetta argued, required a complete embrace of universal suffrage with no arbitrary restrictions designed to preserve the influence of established elites. The second principle, free secular education, was necessary in order to inculcate the habits of republican virtue among ordinary French citizens from childhood, so they might resist the political intrigues of kings, priests, and dictators alike. Finally, the new republican France would henceforth be a true exemplar of the universal values first proclaimed in the Declaration of the Rights of Man and Citizen.

With these demands, Gambetta was able to distinguish clearly the radical republican vision of the polity from those proffered by liberals, who wished to restrict voting rights to property holders; by Bonapartists, who manipulated electoral results and tolerated the Catholic Church's influence in education; and by legitimists, who, despite their rhetorical defense of local "liberties," appeared to be staunch allies of the reactionary pope, Pius IX. Gambetta's radical anticlericalism and wholehearted embrace of democracy also separated him from the more cautious older republicans such as Simon. As Gambetta himself put it, the left was now a word with "definite, precise, and restricted meaning; it denotes and defines a political party composed of homogeneous elements, identical in origin and possessed of common principles.... We must organize a Left party exclusively composed of citizens who adhere to the same principles."[18]

Gambetta's clarity and consistency about the new democratic criteria for membership in the French polity proved inspiring to a wide range of social groups with cultural affinities for the republican cause.[19] France's powerful Masonic lodges, despite Napoleon III's initial purges of their overtly republican leadership, were similarly committed to Gambetta's professed values of secularism and universal citizenship; Gambetta himself, like many other leading republicans, was a member of the Grand-Orient. Professional groups, especially lawyers' and doctors' associations, were attracted to the radical republicans' attacks on outmoded feudal obstacles to the revolutionary ideal of "careers

---

[16] Bertocci, *Jules Simon*, p. 149.

[17] The Belleville program is reprinted in Pierre Barral, ed., *Les fondateurs de la Troisième Republique* (Paris: Armand Colin, 1968), pp. 66–69.

[18] Quoted in Bury, *Gambetta and the National Defence*, p. 23.

[19] On grass-roots support for republicanism under the Second Empire, see Nord, *The Republican Moment*.

open to talent." Workers in big cities, too, proved a receptive potential audience for Gambetta's message, although more radical socialist doctrines predominated in some cities and industries. In sum, the radical republicans by 1870 had a clear party leadership structure led by an individual with a remarkably clear and consistent ideological vision, as well as a significant social network that might be mobilized in support of this vision.

Legitimists

At roughly the same time that Gambetta's republicans were building their committed ideological movement, French legitimists were developing another clear, consistent vision of France's future polity. Like the republicans, too, the legitimists based their ideology on a sustained analysis of the failures of French politics since 1789. However, their analysis proceeded according to diametrically opposed philosophical principles, emphasizing hierarchy, fidelity to tradition, and faith over secular individualism and materialism.[20]

The legitimist movement was born out of a simple dynastic claim – namely, that of the line of the Bourbon monarchy that had been deposed first in the French Revolution of 1789 and again, after the post-Napoleonic restoration, by the Orléanist revolution of 1830. The sole male heir of this dynasty, the Comte de Chambord, was born seven months after the assassination of his father the Duc de Berry in 1820; hence, he became known as the *enfant de miracle*.[21] Both during the reign of Louis-Philippe and after the revolution of 1848, legitimism had also become associated with mystical traditions in French Catholicism as well as a bitter rejection of many aspects of French political and social history after 1789. As long as Chambord was still a child, however, legitimism remained more a cultural tendency than a political movement with an official ideology.

By the middle years of the Second Empire, however, Chambord, now living with his wife in exile at Frohsdorf Palace in Austria, began to compose a series of political manifestos that are remarkable for their clarity and consistency.[22] Indeed, Chambord's entire political career, from the 1860s until his death in 1883, shows him to be nearly an ideal-typical ideologue, motivated almost entirely by what he saw as the defense of sacred "principles," even when this cost him significant power and wealth. Chambord's ideological understanding of how one should define "France" can be summed up in three phrases: divine-right monarchy, faithful Catholicism, and reestablishment of the "natural" hierarchical order of society. Yet, while these positions might first appear to imply a simple return to feudalism, Chambord's articulation of legitimism was

---

[20] On French legitimism in this period, see Robert R. Locke, *French Legitimists and the Politics of Moral Order in the Early Third Republic* (Princeton, NJ: Princeton University Press, 1974); Steven D. Kale, *Legitimism and the Reconstruction of French Society, 1852–1883* (Baton Rouge: Louisiana State University Press, 1992).

[21] Brown, *The Comte de Chambord*, p. 10.

[22] Kale, *Legitimism and the Reconstruction of French Society*; Brown, *The Comte de Chambord*.

in fact explicitly designed to respond to the problems of French modernity. Indeed, the distinctiveness of legitimist ideology was precisely its call to return to "God's will" in politics, religion, and society as a remedy for France's century-long political instability, violence, and uncertainty.[23]

Thus, Chambord argued that France's bitter experience of seemingly continuous revolution, war, and occupation since 1789 reflected God's punishment for the sin of regicide during the French Revolution. The moral degradation of the French working class, which had generated such violent radicalism, too, reflected the loss of Christian values of charity and community. Fortunately, at the level of the local commune, far from the perverting influence of Paris, the true Christian France was still alive and healthy. Once France as a nation finally repented its sins of regicide and atheism and embraced the monarchy, Chambord insisted, true liberty and order, based upon a proper social recognition of the divine will, would reign again.

Chambord's ideological consistency proved inspiring not only to the comparatively narrow stratum of nobles directly connected with the Bourbon dynasty but also to broader social networks within rural France. In particular, local Catholic curés and their congregations frequently saw in Chambord's principled rejection of modern French politics and society an inspiring alternative to the seeming materialism and depravity of France's "cabaret culture." Catholic believers within the influential Marian tradition, which throughout the nineteenth century had inspired mass pilgrimages to places where miracles had been observed, such as Lourdes and Chartres, saw Chambord as their natural leader.[24] Thus, while Chambord ordered his followers to abstain from official politics under the Second Empire until God called them later to action, the legitimist movement in the 1860s, like the republican party, had already attained a potentially significant social base.

Orléanists

Compared with both the republicans and the legitimists, Orléanist liberals under the Second Empire never succeeded in producing an authoritative ideological synthesis. This is by no means due to any lack of outstanding individuals who might potentially have emerged as ideological leaders of the liberal party. Indeed, French liberalism had long produced outstanding intellectuals

---

[23] Hazareesingh has argued that legitimist ideology was actually inconsistent, because it advocated simultaneously for local liberty and decentralization and for central monarchical direction of French mores. However, for Chambord and his followers, the return of the divine-right monarchy to France would be possible only as a necessary consequence of the total moral regeneration of French society. Hence, the Bourbon restoration would automatically suffice to eliminate any contradiction between local liberty – understood as the desire to implement God's will in one's own life – and central authority. In other words, Hazareesingh applies a nonlegitimist standard of practicality in assessing the consistency of legitimist ideology. See Hazareesingh, *From Subject to Citizen*, pp. 96–161.

[24] Raymond Jonas, *France and the Cult of the Sacred Heart: An Epic Tale for Modern Times* (Berkeley: University of California Press, 2000).

and politicians of worldwide fame, from Condorcet during the French Revolution, to Benjamin Constant and Alexis de Tocqueville in the early nineteenth century, to Aldophe Thiers and Victor de Broglie, who remained prominent under the Second Empire. Nor did liberalism suffer from any difficulties of a financial sort, backed as it was by some of the wealthiest members of the French bourgeoisie. Over the course of the Second Empire's history, liberalism gradually influenced even the leading figures of the Napoleonic regime; after the 1870 plebiscite approving Emile Ollivier's proposal for a "liberal empire," with expanded scope for legislative power and political competition, liberalism in a certain sense became France's official ruling doctrine.[25]

The biggest problem for French liberals who wished to organize the movement as an effective political party, then, was not administrative or material but ideological: just what would a truly liberal French polity look like? How could its central criteria of membership be defined? Here, making sense of the place of the July Monarchy in French history proved an especially thorny issue. In 1830 liberal admirers of British parliamentarianism could reasonably portray the constitutional monarchy of Louis-Philippe, with its strictly limited suffrage, as an effort to emulate one of the most democratic countries in the world; certainly, the 1830 revolution marked a progressive advance from the reactionary regime of Charles X. By the 1860s, however, with Great Britain and the United States moving toward full universal male suffrage and even the Second Empire promoting mass democracy, albeit in authoritarian guise, the reestablishment of Orléanist constitutional monarchy seemed a step backward for liberal values. The Orléanist princes and their liberal supporters recognized, too, that any effort at monarchical restoration would have to wrestle with the competing dynastic claim of the Comte de Chambord – who would surely lead France in a profoundly antiliberal direction. Yet, at the same time, a complete embrace of universal suffrage would threaten to erode the distinction between liberalism and radical republicanism.

These contradictions in terms of establishing the precise criteria for defining a liberal French regime led most liberal thinkers in the Second Empire to argue for a procedural, pragmatic definition of liberalism: liberals would simply argue for "evolutionary" rather than utopian politics, for "necessary liberties" in politics combined with a prudent defense of "order."[26] But even liberals who sincerely believed in these principles had great difficulty deciding what their specific political implications might be. Some liberals who had long been loyal to the Orléanist cause, such as Thiers, began to distance themselves subtly from the Orléanist princes, flirting with outright republicanism. Others, such as Ollivier, rallied to the empire, arguing that its combination of imperial authority with universal suffrage was the best hope for defending both liberty and order. The Orléanist mainstream, whose leading figure was Albert de Broglie – Victor de Broglie's son – continued to be faithful to the principles of the July Monarchy

[25] Zeldin, *Émile Ollivier.*
[26] Hazareesingh, *From Subject to Citizen*, pp. 162–232.

in the abstract but adopted a studied agnosticism about final questions of regime type. As Broglie put it, "In politics, one must not pursue the impossible while hoping to realize the ideal."[27] This principled rejection of ideologies of all sorts generated an Orléanist movement that, quite unlike legitimism or republicanism, saw openness to political compromise as a virtue. As the Second Empire came crashing down, Orléanist liberals had every reason to believe that their essentially pragmatic politics could be pursued successfully, given their institutional and resource advantages over their more radical competitors on both the right and the left.

Bonapartists

A final political grouping that would emerge as a serious contender in the party competition of the early Third Republic was made up of the Bonapartists themselves. Like the Orléanists, however, the Bonapartists entered the post-Sedan period with no clear, consistent definition of the French polity that might unite party activists. Of course, defining the ideology of an actually existing regime, rather than one that is merely proposed for the future, involves somewhat different intellectual challenges for party elites. The process of governing invariably involves tactical compromises that can erode the clarity and consistency of any ruling ideology. Still, as we will see in the case of Gennadii Ziuganov's Communist Party of the Russian Federation in the post-Soviet case, a relatively successful reformulation of formerly dominant regime ideologies for renewed party building is sometimes possible.

Would-be intellectual defenders of the Second Empire after 1870, however, proved incapable of responding effectively to this ideological challenge. For one thing, while the original Napoleon was a brilliant administrator whose legal and political reforms ultimately reshaped the entire European continent, he essentially built his legitimacy around military charisma rather than articulating any distinct political ideology. This is even more true of his nephew, who, despite strenuous efforts to claim his fidelity to the key "Napoleonic ideas" underlying the First Empire, adopted highly eclectic positions on central issues of French national identity. By the outbreak of the Franco-Prussian War, the Second Empire had been both strongly authoritarian and officially "liberal." It had defended the temporal power of the pope against attack from Italian republicans but had also supported the cause of Italian unification. It had simultaneously embraced the cause of social modernization through its support of French industry and insisted on the legitimacy of traditional dynastic succession. Thus, Bonapartism in the wake of the defeat at Sedan contained within it almost the entire spectrum of ideological views, from "right-wing" supporters of dictatorship such as Paul Cassagnac and Fidus, to "liberal" Bonapartists associated with Emile Ollivier and even supporters of Bonapartist "socialism" such as

---

[27] Albert de Broglie, *Mémoires*, quoted in Alan Grubb, *The Politics of Pessimism: Albert de Broglie and Conservative Politics in the Early Third Republic* (Newark: University of Delaware Press, 1996).

Prince Napoleon. In the middle of this spectrum was a broad group of former imperial officials and bureaucrats who owed their careers to Bonapartism and could be swayed in any ideological direction as circumstances demanded.[28]

Nevertheless, the Bonapartists, like the Orléanists, entered the post-Sedan era with considerable institutional support that might potentially be mobilized for party building. Despite the regime's crushing defeat to Prussia, state officials throughout France might be expected to rally once again to the Bonapartist cause in time. Within the army – and especially among the officer corps – habits of loyalty to the Napoleonic vision of France were still widespread.[29] And the Bonapartists seemed to have mastered the art of manipulating emotional sentiments and mobilizing administrative pressure to produce impressive pro-imperial majorities in the French electorate. It is not surprising, then, that many legitimists, republicans, and liberals alike during the 1870s saw a resurgence of Bonapartism as the main threat to their own alternative visions of the French future.

An unbiased observer of French party politics in the wake of Sedan might well have concluded that either the Orléanist liberals in alliance with the leading figures of the French haute bourgeoisie or, failing that, the political forces arrayed around the exiled Louis Napoleon and his dashing young heir, the Prince Imperial, would likely emerge as the victors in an open partisan struggle. In comparison, the legitimists, for all their support among local clergy and the traditional nobility, professed an ideology of dynastic and Catholic purity seemingly at odds with the entire previous century of French history, and were led by a man who had not set foot in France in more than two decades. The radical republicans under Gambetta, too, were widely viewed as dangerous extremists whose political ascendancy would likely lead to another period of bloody street violence and dictatorship. In short, the collapse of the Second Empire, followed by reasonably free and fair elections with universal male suffrage, provides an excellent first test of the proposition that ideological parties will tend to build national networks of party activists, whereas pragmatic parties will tend to fall apart because of free riding.

Chaos, 1870–1873

It is not difficult to demonstrate that the French defeat at Sedan in September 1870 ushered in a period of massive social uncertainty. The suddenness and thoroughness of France's battlefield collapse came as a shock to most French citizens, who had generally greeted the outbreak of war with Prussia just a few months earlier with patriotic enthusiasm. French parliamentary elites in Paris, pressured by mass demonstrations by ordinary Parisians, quickly proclaimed

---

[28] John Rothney, *Bonapartism after Sedan* (Ithaca, NY: Cornell University Press, 1969).

[29] A survey carried out by one of Gambetta's allies as late as 1875 showed that approximately half of the generals whose opinions were recorded favored Bonapartism. Bury, *Gambetta and the Making of the Third Republic*, p. 372.

a republic on September 4; Gambetta managed to maneuver for himself the powerful position of minister of the interior in the new Government of National Defense.[30] Within weeks, however, the capital was surrounded by Prussian troops. After the failure of Gambetta's desperate last-ditch efforts to stave off defeat, France was forced in January 1871 to accept a long-term German military occupation, to pay five billion francs in war reparations, and to give up the cherished provinces of Alsace and Lorraine to be annexed by the newly unified German state. Partly in rebellion against this outcome, radical Parisian workers declared the Paris Commune and wrested de facto control over the capital for two months in the spring of 1871, before it was brutally suppressed by the new French government led by Adolphe Thiers at the cost of more than twenty thousand lives; another fifty thousand were imprisoned.[31] Efforts to emulate the Commune also led to political turbulence in other major French cities such as Lyons and Marseille. Unsurprisingly, all of this turmoil had devastating effects on the French economy; the Paris Chamber of Commerce reported in February 1871 that "the factories are idle, the shops are for the most part closed, and business entirely suspended."[32] Meanwhile, secessionist movements arose in the provinces of Nice and Savoy, which had been annexed by Napoleon III only a decade before; even Brittany became restive. It is thus unsurprising that 1870–1871 became popularly known as *l'année terrible.*

The chaos of this period, however, did not immediately subside with the suppression of the Commune. As long as Prussian troops continued to occupy much of eastern France and the massive debt to Germany had somehow to be repaid, uncertainty about France's fate as a nation necessarily remained deep and widespread. Meanwhile, the ultimate shape of France's political regime remained utterly unclear: both the legitimists and the Orléanists quickly asserted their rival claims to restore the monarchy; radical republicans pressed for the elimination of all forms of monarchical and imperial privilege; even more radical socialists kept alive the spirit of the Commune among significant sectors of the urban working class; and the exiled Louis Napoleon in England kept in close touch with his key lieutenants to assess the chances for a successful "return from Elba" of his own.

In this context, Adolphe Thiers, seen as a senior statesman who might at least maintain France's diplomatic credibility in postwar negotiations, was accepted by all rival forces as the temporary presidency of France. Thiers, a longtime associate of the Orléanists who now claimed to rule above the competing parties, endeavored to stabilize the situation by eliminating France's war debt.[33] He launched two major bond issues to the French public and

---

[30] Bury, *Gambetta and the National Defence*, pp. 69–71.
[31] R. D. Anderson, *France, 1870–1914: Politics and Society* (London: Routledge and Kegan Paul, 1977), p. 8; J. P. T. Bury and R. P. Tombs, *Thiers, 1797–1877: A Political Life* (London: Allen and Unwin, 1986), p. 208.
[32] Quoted in Mitchell, *The German Influence in France*, p. 23.
[33] Bury and Tombs, *Thiers*, pp. 196–197.

international investors at an approximately 6 percent interest rate per annum –
an extremely generous rate of return by mid-nineteenth-century standards, but
necessary to convince both French and foreign investors to accept the risk of
investing in such a fragile government. Both bond issues were successful, and
by 1873 Thiers was able to negotiate the departure of the last Prussian troops
from the country – except, of course, from Alsace-Lorraine, now formally a
part of Germany. Nevertheless, Thiers's remarkable success in paying off the
German reparations bill came at a serious cost: well over half of the French
budget for 1873 was reserved to pay public debts. As Mitchell notes, "France
was in reality an uncertain nation living far beyond its means with an economy
already heavily mortgaged."[34]

Moreover, ironically, Thiers's success in ending the German occupation
ended the diplomatic crisis that had made him temporarily indispensable even
to right-wing monarchists who opposed his increasingly open embrace of the
republic, and he was ousted by a parliamentary vote on May 24, 1873. The
resulting power vacuum generated another six months of severe political instability, during which the chances of a monarchical restoration appeared to be
excellent. The post-imperial period of chaos finally came to an end in November 1873 with the National Assembly's compromise acceptance of a seven-year
presidential term for Marshal Patrice MacMahon, a hero of the French conquest of Algeria and the Crimean War, who had also commanded a regiment in
the failed war against Prussia and led French troops against the Paris Commune
in 1871.

In an unpredictable political, economic, and social environment of this sort,
instrumentally rational actors should be forced to adopt a series of short-
term compromises as institutional and international incentives shift. Ideological
actors, by contrast, should be easily distinguished by their political consistency
in defense of cherished values. To test this hypothesis, we now examine the
conduct of the leaders of the republican, legitimist, Orléanist, and Bonapartist
leaderships.

Republicans

Napoleon III's defeat at Sedan appeared to confirm the uncompromising opposition of Gambetta's republicans to the entire imperial system. Just as Gambetta
had argued, the supposed "forces of order" had proved incapable of defending
the nation because of their incompetence, corruption, and vanity. The de facto
declaration of the republic on September 4, 1870, put Gambetta, only thirty-
two years old, in a position to demonstrate the superiority of republican virtue
as a basis for French patriotism. He quickly rose to the occasion, taking on
the role of temporary "dictator" of the Government of National Defense, with
the initial support of most Parisians. For the remainder of the war, Gambetta
engaged in a heroic, if futile, effort to rally ordinary French citizens against
the advancing Prussian armies. When it appeared as if the Prussians would

[34] Mitchell, *The German Influence in France*, p. 40.

capture Paris, Gambetta dramatically escaped the capital in a hot-air balloon; he then traveled throughout the French Southwest trying to mobilize citizens' armies wherever he went. By January 1871, however, with Paris exhausted and hungry and the hopelessness of the French cause apparent to almost everyone else, Gambetta's desire somehow to continue the war effort was rejected by the rest of the Government of National Defense, and an armistice was signed.[35]

The end of the war found Gambetta in an unenviable political position. Postwar elections to the new National Assembly in February 1871 produced a strong monarchist majority of 394 out of 644 total seats for the legitimists and Orléanists, who were seen as promoters of peace with Germany; meanwhile, moderate republicans associated with Simon garnered 110 seats, while Gambetta's own radical republicans gained just 40.[36] Gambetta himself went into exile in northern Spain, exhausted and depressed after the French defeat. He had remained true to his patriotic republican principles, refusing to compromise in any way either with the Prussian autocracy or with French moderates and conservatives who hoped to bring an early end to the war, but in early 1871 it might well have seemed that these principles had once again proved disastrous in practice – particularly after the Paris Commune's bloody suppression, which appeared again to tie French republicanism in all its forms to street violence and anarchy. By the spring of 1871, Gambetta's political comeback looked very unlikely. Certainly a more pragmatic politician would have concluded peace with Bismarck much earlier, in order to hold on to his powerful initial position in the post-imperial context.

The end of the Commune, however, opened up new opportunities for Gambetta's radical republican politics. Gambetta himself had remained in Spain during the entire period of the Commune's rise and fall, and so he escaped any blame either for siding with the communards or for acquiescing in their suppression; instead, responsibility for the government's brutality lay with Thiers and his noble-dominated government based in Versailles. In fact, Gambetta had little ideological sympathy with the Commune, with its essentially socialist orientation; his own radical republicanism focused on individual citizenship and secular education rather than socioeconomic revolution. When Gambetta returned to Paris, however, he was once again greeted by his supporters in Belleville with warm enthusiasm, and his leadership of the radical republican movement was never seriously challenged. Special by-elections held on June 2, 1871, to fill vacant seats in the National Assembly demonstrated the extent of Gambetta's comeback: 99 out of 114 contested seats went to the republicans.[37]

Gambetta thus reentered the chaos of post-imperial French politics with three key advantages over most of his competitors. First, because of his selfless efforts to defend the nation against Germany, he now had an unassailable

---

[35] For a more detailed account of this period, see Bury, *Gambetta and the National Defence.*
[36] Jacques Gouault, *Comment la France est devenue républicaine: Les élections générales et partielles à l'Assemblée Nationale, 1870–1875* (Paris: Colin, 1954), p. 73.
[37] Ibid.

record as a passionate promoter of French sovereignty – a crucial asset for a left-wing politician who might otherwise have been depicted by his opponents as a dangerously unpatriotic "internationalist" (even if, as we have seen, Gambetta's ideological emphasis on French patriotism was consistent and long-standing). Second, Gambetta was now known as the most uncompromising republican in a country that had become, de facto if not yet de jure, a republic based on universal suffrage. He could thus persuasively argue that his ideological position was no longer "revolutionary"; it was in fact the various monarchical and imperialist parties that posed a true threat to "social order." Finally, Gambetta's demonstrated value-rational commitment to republican principles gave him credibility as he began to work to mobilize potential supporters to build a disciplined national network of radical republican activists around the "new social strata" (*nouvelles couches sociales*), which, in a famous speech in Grenoble in 1872, he claimed would henceforth dominate French political life.[38]

In 1872 and 1873, the task of party organization and social mobilization occupied most of Gambetta's time. Working with close collaborators such as Barni, he set up a central committee to coordinate republican party strategy for recruiting supporters throughout France. This central committee worked closely with allied organizations such as the Ligue d'Enseignement and the Société d'Instruction Républicaine, which promoted the cause of free secular education.[39] The party newspaper, *La République Francaişe*, founded in 1872, promoted the party's ideological positions in cities and towns all over the country; when the paper was suppressed by the censors, its articles were read aloud in newly established republican clubs set up in most French cities. In a period of enormous uncertainty, this focused, consistent effort to disseminate radical republican ideology convinced growing numbers of party activists to commit themselves to the cause. Previous strongholds such as the Masonic Lodges and professional associations, naturally, once again proved fertile grounds for republican party recruitment.[40] But perhaps more surprisingly, so too did social groups that had previously appeared resistant to Gambetta's message, including liberal intellectuals, who were alienated by the often reactionary rhetoric of the monarchists; radical urban workers, who had become disillusioned with socialism after the fall of the Commune; and even peasants, who feared the possible restoration of feudal rights by the extreme right.[41] As a result of these successful organizational efforts, radical republicans from 1872 until 1874 continued to win a series of by-elections held to fill empty seats in the National Assembly – deeply unsettling the conservative interests still, for the moment, dominant therein.

---

[38] Bury, *Gambetta and the Making of the Third Republic*, pp. 111–116.
[39] For more details on Jules Barni and his role in the republican movement, see Hazareesingh, *Intellectual Founders*, pp. 227–280.
[40] For details, see Nord, *The Republican Moment*.
[41] An excellent treatment of the slow conversion of previous uncommitted social groups to republicanism in the provincial context is given in Stone, *Sons of the Revolution*.

Legitimists

France's defeat in the Franco-Prussian War was seen by the Comte de Chambord, as well as by his loyal followers in France, as a clear punishment from God for the sins of the country since 1789. Indeed, in terms of the ideological framework forcefully articulated by Chambord during the Second Empire, France's sudden collapse seemed almost prophetically to confirm the legitimist analysis of the nation's moral decay. Moreover, Chambord's instructions to abstain from political life under Napoleon III allowed legitimist elites now to present themselves as uniquely unsullied by the corruption and materialism of the Second Empire. As ordinary French citizens struggled to reorient themselves in these turbulent years, a resurgence of interest in the mystical Catholicism associated with Chambord emerged throughout the country.[42] As the chaos of the post-Sedan era continued, the legitimists only became more convinced that the return of Chambord as the divinely ordained ruler of France was the only hope to restore peace and prosperity.

Naturally, the legitimists had no sympathy for Gambetta's Government of National Defense, and his fall appeared to open the political field for Chambord's imminent restoration. Even as hostilities with Prussia continued, the legitimists proved capable of significant social mobilization, as their careful preparations for the February 1871 elections to the National Assembly show. Traditional historiography portrays the remarkable success of promonarchical candidates in these elections as a simple vote for peace in the wake of Gambetta's defeat, and no doubt at the level of the mass electorate, there is much truth in this view.[43] However, for the legitimists to capitalize on this sentiment among French voters, they had to coordinate their electoral campaign effectively enough to emphasize consistently the message of "order and stability"; after all, there was no a priori reason for French voters to associate monarchical restoration with peace. As Locke has shown, the evidence of the legitimists' partisan coordination in this period was long obscured because of the gaps in central Parisian archival records during the chaos of the Franco-Prussian War. Provincial archives throughout France, however, demonstrate that the legitimist party leadership kept in close touch with its regional candidates in the run-up to February 1871, carefully coordinating its activities with the Orléanists in order to ensure the election of a dominant monarchist bloc.[44] In the end, 180 legitimists were elected along with 214 Orléanists.[45] This was a remarkable performance by the former party, given that the Orléanist leaders had far greater public prominence (including among their ranks Thiers, the president of the republic himself – at least for the time being).

Having secured their position in parliament, the legitimists never wavered in their clear articulation of their vision of the new French polity. Chambord himself clarified his uncompromising stance in a manifesto issued in July 1871,

[42] Jonas, *France and the Cult of the Sacred Heart.*
[43] For example, see Anderson, *France, 1870–1914*, pp. 6–7.
[44] Locke, *French Legitimists*, pp. 17–28.
[45] Gouault, *Comment la France.*

issued upon his (brief) return to France from exile, in which he declared that
he would rule under the white flag emblazoned with the fleur-de-lis of the
Bourbon dynasty: "I have received it as a sacred bequest from the old King,
my ancestor, dying in exile; it floated over my cradle, and I want it draped
on my tomb."[46] Some perspicacious observers at the time could foresee that
such a stand would ultimately make it impossible for Chambord to court
even potential allies among the moderate monarchist factions in the National
Assembly, making a legitimist restoration impossible. Thiers himself noted
wryly that Chambord would "go down in history as the French Washington –
the founder of the Republic."[47] For the time being, however, Chambord's
manifesto did nothing to damage his growing popularity and influence; on the
contrary, Chambord's fidelity to his principles made him a hero to conservatives
and Catholic traditionalists throughout France. Within the National Assembly
itself, about half of the legitimist faction belonged to the *chevau-légers* group
that was willing to follow Chambord's orders unquestioningly; even the more
"liberal" legitimists eagerly anticipated a Bourbon restoration.[48] Given this
relative partisan unity and broad social base, the legitimists exerted an influence
in parliament disproportionate to their numbers. From 1871 to 1873 they
agitated successfully for a national effort to "atone" for the sins that had
caused defeat in the Franco-Prussian War by building the massive new Basilica
de Sacre-Coeur on the hill of Montmartre – not coincidentally, in the very
heart of a Parisian neighborhood that had historically been strongly supportive
of radical republicanism and the Commune. This movement was bolstered by
several well-coordinated pilgrimages of the faithful to France's holy sites, where
legitimist political rhetoric was freely interspersed with traditional Catholic
and ultramontane themes.[49] Legitimism even had appeal among the youth;
during this period, the thirty-year-old legitimist Count Albert de Mun saw
his movement to spread Catholic charitable organizations among the working
class – the *cercles d'ouvriers* – achieve remarkable success; between 1872 and
1875, the *cercles* spread both in historically conservative areas of France such
as the Vendée and Brittany and in northern industrial regions, increasing to
150 clubs with eighteen thousand members.[50]

Like the republicans, then, the legitimist party not only survived the initial period of post-imperial chaos but even gained in strength. By 1873 when
the last German troops began to withdraw from France, seemingly the only
serious obstacle to Bourbon restoration was the continuing power and popularity of Thiers – whom the legitimists detested for his efforts to augment his
personal power and for his increasing flirtation with outright republicanism.

---

[46] Quoted in Brown, *The Comte de Chambord*, p. 91.
[47] Bury and Tombs, *Thiers*, p. 210.
[48] Kale, *Legitimism and the Reconstruction of French Society*, pp. 263–293.
[49] Jonas, *France and the Sacred Heart*.
[50] Benjamin F. Martin, *Count Albert de Mun: Paladin of the Third Republic* (Chapel Hill: University of North Carolina Press, 1978), p. 19.

When the conservative Orléanist faction led by Albert de Broglie finally also broke formally with Thiers in May 1873, the legitimists voted as a bloc for his dismissal as president. Chambord's triumphant return to Paris to be crowned as "Henri V" now appeared imminent. All that was necessary was some agreement with the Orléanist princes and their parliamentary supporters that might ensure an Orléanist succession to the throne after Chambord's death. Because Chambord was childless and in his fifties, and the Orléanist pretender, the Comte de Paris, was willing to wait his turn, arranging such a "fusion" (as the Orléanists called it) or "reconciliation" (as Chambord preferred) between the two monarchist parties did not appear to be an insuperable problem.

It is worth pausing to reflect on this remarkable situation, which provides nearly an ideal-typical case of the power of ideology in times of political chaos. Chambord was essentially invited to be the ruler of France, forty-three years after the fall of the last Bourbon king, despite his complete lack of political experience and his longtime residence in Austria, and political positions that might well have seemed hopelessly anachronistic to a dispassionate observer. His only real political asset was his clarity and consistency about the sort of France he wished to reestablish – but this asset alone had provided him by 1873 with the most powerful political party in France. Key nobles, parliamentarians, religious leaders, and conservative intellectuals had converted to Chambord's ideological values. Hundreds of thousands of ordinary French citizens, too, had embraced his mystical vision of French rebirth because of its emotional appeal in the turbulent aftermath of the Franco-Prussian War. By the summer of 1873, even the most pragmatic politicians of the French right were angling to secure a place in what seemed very likely to be the new Bourbon, Catholic France.

The only outstanding issue was the problem of the French flag. Chambord continued to insist on the white flag with the fleur-de-lis, while the Orléanists, Bonapartists, and republicans alike pledged their loyalty to the tricolor flag under which France had fought for most of the past century. So did the entire French officer corps; President MacMahon warned that the troops would immediately rebel against any government that forced them to serve under the white flag of the royalists.[51] Given these realities, most French politicians – including most of the legitimists themselves – were sure that Chambord would soon find a way gracefully to back down from his position in the flag controversy. In the years after his initial manifesto on the flag issue in July 1781, several leading legitimists visited the pretender in exile at Frohsdorf, trying desperately to change his mind. One of them creatively suggested a new French flag in which a white cross with a lily would be superimposed on the tricolor, showing how the former symbolism had transcended the latter. But Chambord would not budge on this issue, even after the Comte de Paris himself made a pilgrimage to Frohsdorf in August 1873 to try to reach formal agreement on the

---

[51] Brown, *The Comte de Chambord*, p. 119.

"fusion" of the Bourbon and Orléanist lines.[52] Finally, in October, Chambord issued another manifesto in which his position on the flag controversy was set in stone. Accepting the tricolor flag, he averred, would hopelessly compromise the key moral principles for which he stood:

I have conserved intact during forty-three years the sacred trust of our traditions and our liberties. . . . My person is nothing; my principle is all. France will see the end of her troubles when she is willing to understand this. I am the necessary pilot, the only one capable of guiding the ship to port, because I have the mission and the authority for this.[53]

In despair, the Orléanists gave up all hope of monarchical restoration for the foreseeable future, and Chambord's chance to rule France in essence evaporated.

Both contemporaries and later historians have branded Chambord a fool for his uncompromising conduct in this period. Even Chambord's staunch ally Pope Pius IX apparently could not understand his decision, as was clear from the message to the legitimists he relayed through an intermediary: "The color of a flag is not of great importance. It was with the tricolor that the French restored me in Rome. You see that with this flag one is able to do good things. But the Comte of Chambord has not wanted to believe me."[54] In most standard historical treatments, Chambord is portrayed as a pathetic figure, hopelessly out of touch with French political and social realities. Such analyses, however, miss the crucial point: had Chambord not been the sort of consistent ideologue who would insist on a central question of French national identity, he would never have been in a position to rule France in the first place. Indeed, Chambord's argument that his acceptance of the tricolor would make him merely the "legitimate king of the revolution," and that this untenable position would soon erode his institutional position and generate yet another cycle of violence and rebellion, was arguably quite perspicacious.[55] It is certainly unclear at the time, at least, how long a hybrid regime of divine-right monarchy with symbols imposed by a parliamentary majority would have endured in the France of the 1870s. By remaining ideologically consistent even at the cost of the French throne, too, Chambord retained the support of his most loyal partisan followers. Many *chevau-légers* and conservative Catholics applauded Chambord's faith in his vision and unwillingness to make tawdry political deals and continued along with Chambord himself to wait for the day when God would fulfill his plan for a truly regenerated Christian France. As we shall see, the commitment of these networks – diminished though they were by defections

---

[52] Ibid., p. 109.
[53] Quoted in ibid., p. 130.
[54] Quoted in ibid., p. 115. A more dramatic version of the pope's reaction, probably apocryphal, has him asking in exasperation why, if Paris was "well worth a mass" to Henri IV, France wasn't worth even a "napkin" (*serviette*) to Henri V!
[55] A similar argument is made in Kale, *Legitimism and the Reconstruction of French Society*, p. 276.

from more instrumentally rational politicians after 1873 – continued to be an important factor in French politics as the 1870s unfolded.

Orléanists

Unlike the radical republicans and legitimists, who were perceived in the late stages of the Second Empire as "extremists" of the left and right, respectively, the Orléanists entered the Third Republic in an enviable political position. With the collapse of the empire, Orléanist liberalism constituted in many respects the core of the French political establishment. The Orléanists also emerged as the most numerous group in the National Assembly in the February 1871 elections, with 214 deputies. Finally, President Thiers himself was known as a prominent Orléanist, having served as a minister in Louis-Philippe's government; at least at first, most supporters of constitutional monarchy assumed that Thiers was an ally. By the end of 1873, however, the Orléanist party had suffered a series of factional splits, gravely hampering its effectiveness and social influence. The key problem was that while all the leading Orléanist politicians promoted political "gradualism" and "prudence" as an antidote to France's history of revolution and instability, they could not agree on the precise institutional definition of the "liberal France" they hoped to establish. As a result, various Orléanist deputies interpreted their partisan commitments quite differently as the chaotic transformations of French politics in this period unfolded.

The first and most significant split came with Thiers's own rejection of the cause of monarchical restoration in favor of what he called the "conservative republic" – that is, a republican form of government with various institutional safeguards against radicalism, in particular, a strong presidency and appointed senate, along with unspecified restrictions on the suffrage.[56] Thiers's new political stance was hardly ideological in nature; rather, he merely saw the republic as "that form of government which divides us least," and therefore as the only safeguard against new forms of revolutionary upheaval that might erupt in the event of either a monarchical restoration or a radical republican victory.[57] No doubt Thiers's political ambition and vanity played a role as well in his argument for replacing a king with a strong executive branch under his direction. His middle-class social background, too, may have led him to feel out of place among the nobility and wealthy bourgeoisie who made up the majority of the Orléanist establishment.

It is important to emphasize, however, that Thiers's formal embrace of the republic was neither immediate nor expected, and thus it came as a serious blow to many leading Orléanists. One faction of parliamentary liberals, the "center left," ultimately followed Thiers's lead in embracing the republic. Another, the

---

[56] Thiers moved gradually to this position over the course of 1871–1872, fully embracing the republic in a speech to the National Assembly in November 1972. See Grubb, *The Politics of Pessimism*, p. 91.

[57] Thiers first uttered this famous phrase in February 1850 in defending the Loi Falloux. See Bury and Tombs, *Thiers*, p. 123.

"center right" under the leadership of Albert de Broglie, remained true to the cause of constitutional monarchy. The bitterness of this split was evident in de Broglie's machinations to subordinate Thiers's power to that of parliament and, ultimately, his drive to dismiss him as president in May 1873. In these battles, the center right was forced to ally with the legitimists – and the Orléanist party gradually lost what remained of its reputation for "liberalism" as a result.[58] De Broglie himself emerged as the formal leader of the National Assembly, the president of the council, but he found himself personally detested by much of the parliament – by the legitimists, for his history of "liberal Catholicism" and his skepticism about Chambord; by the republicans, for his continuing defense of noble privilege and evident disdain for "the masses"; and by the center left, for his intrigues against Thiers.

Nevertheless, it fell to de Broglie to pick up the pieces after the fiasco of the white flag controversy in November 1873, and his response was to propose that new president Marshal MacMahon be granted a seven-year term – the septennate – that would give monarchists and conservative liberals alike a chance to regroup.[59] The "temporary" nature of MacMahon's presidency would serve many political purposes at once: it would place a popular ally of conservatism and Catholicism in the highest office of the land; it would defer any final decision about the precise institutional form of the new French regime; and it would provide a potential last-ditch alternative to radical republicanism in case its social power could not otherwise be checked. What the septennate explicitly could not do, however, was resolve France's identity crisis. Indeed, the whole raison d'être of the new "government of moral order" was, in a sense, to extend that identity crisis for the time being, so as to find some pragmatic way to stave off the threat from Gambetta and defend the interests of conservatives – even if the precise conceptions of "moral order" desired by legitimists, monarchists, and Bonapartists continued to be very different. As we shall see, de Broglie's pragmatic strategy to preserve the facade of conservative unity by evading the issue of regime type proved wholly inadequate to defeat the radical republican challenge.

Bonapartists

Napoleon III's ignominious military defeat in 1870, followed by his exile to England, left the Bonapartists in temporary disarray, and during the chaotic first three years of the Third Republic, the party's influence was slight. Certainly the Bonapartists did very poorly in the February 1871 elections, gaining only nineteen seats in the National Assembly.[60] These electoral results can be partly attributed simply to French citizens' general revulsion against Bonapartism in the wake of the French collapse, which temporarily promoted the political popularity of the empire's main partisan competitors.

---

[58] This thesis is developed in detail by Grubb, *The Politics of Pessimism*.
[59] Ibid., pp. 167–211.
[60] Rothney, *Bonapartism after Sedan*, p. 12.

But the failure of post-Sedan Bonapartism was not only organizational; it was also ideological. The wide range of views on the proper definition of France within Bonapartist circles by 1870 has already been noted; the early years of the Third Republic did not bring any additional clarity in this respect. The party's main slogan, *l'appel au peuple* – which was also the name taken by its parliamentary faction – remained purposefully vague. The Bonapartists, in short, would be the party that asked the "French people" to choose the ultimate form of the regime. The party leadership assumed that a plebiscite on this issue would once again produce an overwhelming demand for empire, as it had in 1852, but declared (as a later party pamphlet put it) that "whatever the outcome, they [would] obey the sovereign will of the nation."[61] Unlike Chambord's manifestos or Gambetta's programs, this vague message contained no clear and specific ideological principles that might inspire renewed commitment by converts to the Bonapartist cause.

Nevertheless, the exiled Napoleon III kept in close touch with his friends and allies in France, above all Eugène Rouher, eagerly anticipating the possibility that he might somehow make a successful comeback. Indeed, the series of crises in French politics and society in 1871 and 1872 did lead to a renewed interest in Bonapartism in various regions of France, especially where local imperial notables had remained generally popular, as in the Southwest. But when Napoleon III died in January 1873 after surgery – precisely as the campaign to restore the Comte de Chambord was gaining steam – the chances for a Bonapartist restoration under the Prince Imperial appeared dim.

Stalemate, 1874–1877

The Third Republic entered the middle part of its first decade having weathered the worst of its post-imperial crises. With the Prussian troops now departed, war reparations paid off, and diplomatic recognition of the new French regime by the leading European powers secured, France's ultimate viability as a nation-state was no longer in question. The French economy, too, had recovered from its immediate postwar disruption. Socially, the upheavals of the period of the Commune had now receded, and a growing acceptance of the new regime on the part of French workers and peasants was evident.

Yet defining France's regime type remained as problematic as ever. The competing ideological proposals of legitimists and radical republicans, as before, were the only two clear and consistent definitions of France on the political playing field – and they remained utterly antithetical. The more pragmatic politicians associated with Orléanist liberalism and Bonapartism were forced to navigate within a political landscape in which committed party activists generally gravitated either toward Chambord or Gambetta – and increasingly, after the defeat of the monarchical campaign of 1873, it was Gambetta's partisan

---

[61] *Guide to the Bonapartist Voter*, 1875, quoted in ibid., p. 70.

network that was gaining social momentum. This unsettled political landscape appeared to open the door to all sorts of possible outcomes, including some sort of Bonapartist resurgence – a prospect that seemed particularly threatening as the example of the destruction of the Second Republic after 1848 remained fresh in everyone's minds. As both Gambettists and Bonapartists began increasingly to win important parliamentary by-elections, the parliamentary center right and center left alike began to work in earnest to establish a new French constitution that might somehow guarantee the "conservative" nature of the Third Republic against any future revolutions.

To design a formal constitution that might be acceptable to a parliamentary majority, however, would require a renewed effort to wrestle with the definition of the new French regime. Given the strength of the monarchical factions in the National Assembly, any explicit reference to the "republic" in the text of the document might be seen as an unacceptable betrayal of principle – certainly for the legitimists and for many conservative Orléanists as well. On the other hand, the growing faction of republicans in parliament might insist on nothing less than a full constitutional promotion of republican ideals. The first to fall victim to these crosscurrents was de Broglie, whose efforts to find common ground among the rival partisan groupings only united the legitimists, republicans, and even many of the left center deputies against him; he was dismissed from his ministry in May 1874. Negotiations to produce a constitution with a strong presidency and a partially appointed Senate continued for the rest of the year, but without success. Finally in February 1875, the left center deputy Henri Wallon introduced a compromise by which the second article of the constitution would simply state the duties of the "president of the republic" – thus mentioning the previously taboo word only in passing, so as to mollify moderate monarchists. The Wallon amendment was passed by a single vote, with de Broglie's right center hopelessly divided.[62]

The new constitution did not end France's political stalemate, however. The fragility of the constitutional compromise raised the hopes of diehard monarchists and Bonapartists alike that an eventual Bourbon, Orléanist, or imperial restoration might still be possible. MacMahon's septennate still had nearly six years to run, and the newly codified constitutional right of the president to dissolve the Chamber of Deputies might be utilized to fend off further political advances by the Gambettists. Finally, the 1876 parliamentary elections to the Chamber of Deputies and, indirectly, the Senate would test the social strength of the four rival French political parties in ways that might quickly overturn the tiny minority that had accepted the Wallon amendment and reopen the question of regime definition. Indeed, had someone predicted in early 1875 that the new constitution of the Third Republic would become the most enduring basic law in France's modern history, most leading French politicians would have laughed. This outcome, I argue, can be attributed directly to the decisive

---

[62] Grubb, *The Politics of Pessimism*, pp. 233–235.

political victory just a few years later of an ideological party that was deeply committed to republican principles, rather than seeing them as merely a distasteful temporary compromise.

Republicans

Gambetta's political strategy during the stalemate period in the early Third Republic was nothing short of masterful, as nearly every historian of the period has acknowledged.[63] By 1874 Gambetta commanded a remarkably disciplined national activist network committed to key republican values of secularism, universal primary education, and democracy. Now Gambetta recognized that his most important task was to convince respectable French elites that his "radical republicans" could be trusted to defend peace and prosperity once in power. For this reason, Gambetta instructed his supporters to approve the constitutional compromise of 1875, despite the fact that the document's potentially strong presidency and partially unelected senate were Orléanist inventions that appeared to contradict key republican political demands. The constitutional compromise, Gambetta reasoned, would codify France's status as a republic – in effect turning all monarchists and Bonapartists into de facto revolutionaries and enshrining the republican party as the true "conservative" one. It would also ensure that elections to the Chamber of Deputies would take place according to universal male suffrage in the immediate future, as the republicans desired. Moreover, because according to the constitution much of the Senate would be elected by local assemblies that were themselves to be elected through universal male suffrage, while MacMahon's presidential term would come to an end no later than 1881, the republicans might hope in time to gain control over these "conservative" institutions of the republic as well.

Gambetta also took advantage of another key feature of France's ideological stalemate – the hatred of the legitimists for de Broglie and the other Orléanists, whom they blamed for the failure of Chambord's campaign for Bourbon restoration. Thus, the republicans voted with the legitimists in May 1874 to dismiss de Broglie's ministry, depriving the center right of its most effective parliamentary leader. Even more remarkably, a small group of legitimists was so bitter about its "betrayal" at the hands of the liberals that Gambetta, in secret negotiations, managed to persuade eleven of them to vote in December 1875 to appoint a slate of republicans for the unelected seats in the Senate; in turn, the Gambettists supported the senatorial bids of a handful of staunch legitimists. Thus, to the shock and horror of de Broglie and his allies, even the upper house of parliament, designed to be a bulwark of conservatism, ended up with a strong minority contingent of republicans.

But Gambetta's greatest success of all was his organization of the republican campaign for the 1876 elections to the Chamber of Deputies.[64] As election day approached, he personally devoted nearly every waking hour to strategy

---

[63] The best single account remains Bury, *Gambetta and the Making of the Third Republic.*
[64] Stone, *Sons of the Revolution.*

sessions with leading republicans and the composition and dissemination of republican party propaganda. Consistent with Gambetta's Belleville Program of 1869, his heroic defense of France in the late stages of the Franco-Prussian War, and his promise to incorporate the "new social strata" of France into the future political order, republican party pamphlets and speeches hammered home the themes of universal citizenship and equality as the basis for the greatness of the French nation. Simultaneously, Gambetta and his colleagues portrayed the Bonapartists as corrupt power seekers aiming only to manipulate the voters, and the monarchists as dangerous reactionaries whose defense of the pope would likely lead to renewed war with Protestant Germany. The results of this national campaign were brilliant: the republicans received 4,028,000 votes to the conservatives' total of 3,202,000; the republicans now claimed 340 of a total of 533 deputies in the new Chamber of Deputies – 98 of whom were dedicated followers of Gambetta.[65]

Gambetta's conduct in this period has been interpreted by many analysts as highly pragmatic rather than ideological; indeed, it was in these years that Gambetta's faction began to be known as the "opportunists" rather than the "extreme left." Such analysis is mistaken. The ideological consistency of any political leader, as has been stressed throughout this book, can be judged only in terms of the political ideals he or she has actually adopted and articulated. And none of Gambetta's strategic maneuvers in the mid-1870s forced him to abandon or modify his core principles. If legitimist bitterness could be utilized against the Orléanist center for republican purposes, why should one not take advantage of this? If a supposedly "conservative" constitution might afford opportunities for advancing the republican cause, why not support its adoption? The Gambettists only appeared to be "opportunists" after 1876 because their genuinely radical program had succeeded in redefining the very nature of the regime. But this success could never have been achieved without the prior commitment of Gambetta and his colleagues to principles that had been seen as marginal and dangerous by the majority of the French political and economic elite only a few years earlier.

Legitimists

Historians generally discuss Chambord's movement after 1873 as a sad tale of a group of die-hard reactionaries fated to fade into irrelevance.[66] In hindsight, of course, it is easy to see that 1873 marked the end of the legitimists' serious chance to attain political power; many politicians and analysts at the time also saw this fact clearly enough. For genuine converts to legitimist ideology, however, the future prospects of Chambord's movement could not be discarded so quickly. After all, God had already nearly miraculously placed the throne in Bourbon hands; surely his divine will would not be thwarted again when the proper time for France's spiritual regeneration had come. This was at least

---

[65] Figures given in Anderson, *France, 1870–1914*, p. 164.
[66] See, for instance, Kale, *Legitimism and the Reconstruction of French Society*, pp. 292–294.

the position taken by Chambord himself, who counseled his followers to wait patiently for their next opportunity. And there is evidence that for at least a core group of political activists, the principles of Catholic and monarchical purity remained as inspiring as ever.[67]

Within the parliament, the legitimists continued to vote in a relatively disciplined manner for favored policies, such as steps to ensure Catholic influence over the educational system.[68] A majority of them voted in May 1874 to oust de Broglie, eliminating a man who, in the legitimists' view, was a traitor to the cause of monarchical restoration.[69] And despite the votes of the eleven disgruntled legitimists to help elect Gambetta's republicans as life senators, a strong majority among the *chevau-légers* held firm on this issue, formally expelling the eleven defectors from the group shortly thereafter.[70] As the 1876 elections approached, the legitimists could still boast of a strong presence in the local press, funded by regional notables who remained loyal to the restorationist cause, as well as the continuing support of most local curés. In the cities, de Mun's *cercles* remained active, providing another platform for legitimist propaganda.[71] While the 1876 elections were generally disastrous for the royalists, given the huge majority won by the republicans, this national network of activists helped the legitimist party salvage at least some continuing legislative representation. In the indirect elections to the Senate, the legitimists attained forty-five seats; even in the general elections to the new Chamber of Deputies, twenty-four staunch supporters of the Bourbon dynasty were elected.[72] Convinced ideological legitimists could and did believe that the decline in their political fortunes was only temporary and would soon be reversed once the nation realized the true costs of radical republicanism.

Orléanists

If the stalemate period saw a serious erosion of support for the legitimists, it was an outright disaster for the Orléanist party. Despite the fact that MacMahon's septennate was originally de Broglie's idea, the temporary presidential regime did nothing to alleviate the deep factionalization of the Orléanist deputies. The failure of "fusion" with Chambord made it difficult to imagine any realistic path that might lead to the installation of the Comte de Paris as king – and, unlike the legitimists, the Orléanists were not given to mystical beliefs about potential future miracles. De Broglie himself continued to pursue a cautious, pragmatic policy designed to check republicanism rather than to advocate

---

[67] Thus, the legitimist Comte Le Serrac de Kervily could even in 1874 compare the coming restoration to "the reunion of a 'regiment...dispersed, in disarray,' that all at once 'catches a glimpse of the flag' and 'rallies to it and masses itself around [the king] against the enemy.'" Quoted in Kale, *Legitimism and the Reconstruction of French Society*, p. 279.

[68] Locke, *French Legitimists*, pp. 205–206.

[69] Ibid., p. 227.

[70] Ibid., p. 229.

[71] Martin, *Count Albert de Mun*, pp. 21–28.

[72] Locke, *French Legitimists*, p. 260; Gouault, *Comment La France*.

any explicit alternative vision of conservative France; his conception of "moral order" remained purposefully vague, a phrase chosen precisely because it could be accepted by the entire spectrum of the French right, from legitimists to conservative republicans.[73] As a result, however, almost no one felt any passionate commitment to the Orléanist cause itself – an important factor in de Broglie's fall just a year after his victory of Thiers.

With the disintegration of Orléanism, however, came a parallel collapse of French liberalism, because the two labels had been so closely identified for so long. This can be clearly seen in the deep divides among former Orléanists concerning the 1875 constitution, which with its de jure embrace of the republic, partially unelected Senate, and potentially strong presidency seemed to reflect the original institutional preferences of Thiers – whom most Orléanists had helped to oust just two years before. Supporters of constitutional monarchy thus saw the constitution as a betrayal of the Orléanist dynasty; ironically, the constitution's adoption by one vote could take place only with the support of the Gambettists whose influence the document was supposedly designed to check.

Given this deep factional division, it is unsurprising that the 1876 elections to the Chamber of Deputies were an utter disaster for the party. Indeed, de Broglie's focus as party leader had always been more on parliamentary maneuvering than mass electoral politics; the Orléanists possessed no partisan network at the grass roots parallel to those of the republicans and legitimists, relying entirely on the influence of local notables affiliated with the movement. This left them vulnerable to purely parliamentary intrigues, such as the bargain between Gambetta, the legitimists, and the Bonapartists to deny them seats on the newly formed Senate in 1875 – the result of which was that only three avowed Orléanists were elected to that body, which de Broglie himself had worked so hard to create.[74] In the 1876 elections to the new Chamber of Deputies, the Orléanists split into two factions: the old center right, which gradually merged with the rest of the monarchists, and the so-called Constitutionnels, who ran on a platform of acceptance of the 1875 constitutional compromise.[75] As the stalemate period came to an end, the future of the Orléanist party as a coherent political force was in serious question.

Bonapartists

The stalemate period also ultimately destroyed the coherence of the Bonapartist party – a result that is particularly interesting, given the fact that it was precisely between 1874 and 1877 that contemporaries most feared a restoration of the empire.[76] Certainly an opportunity for a Bonapartist comeback did exist

---

[73] Grubb, *The Politics of Pessimism*, p. 112.
[74] Rothney, *Bonapartists after Sedan*, pp. 147–148.
[75] Anderson, *France, 1870–1914*, p. 165.
[76] Rothney, *Bonapartism after Sedan*. The following section relies heavily on Rothney's account.

after the failure of the monarchical campaign of 1873. The death of Napoleon III tended to delink the party from direct associations with the defeat at Sedan, and the Prince Imperial, while still in his late teenage years and thus too young to rule, cut a dashing figure who raised Bonapartist hopes about their prospects in the not-too-distant future. The three years of political and social chaos from the fall of 1870 through the fall of 1873 made the Second Empire seem, in retrospect, far more attractive. Within the army, disgust at France's reduced international status might be mobilized on behalf of imperial restoration, while in the countryside, peasants who feared a Bourbon restoration might potentially be persuaded to vote once again for a Bonaparte as their best defense against feudalism. Finally, in the National Assembly itself, at least some former monarchists might, after the failure of fusion, be convinced that the only feasible restoration would come through the Bonapartist line.

As Rothney has meticulously shown, however, the threat of Bonapartism that so worried contemporaries in the middle of the 1870s was more apparent than real – to a large extent, precisely because of the party's internal ideological divisions, which prevented it from articulating a vision capable of generating principled grass-roots support.[77] While Bonapartist victories in by-elections after 1871 gradually increased the party's influence in the National Assembly, the faction's tendency to vote along with other advocates of "moral order" eroded any ideological distinction between them and the other monarchical factions. The Bonapartists voted with de Broglie to oust Thiers, for example, but received almost no specific partisan advantages in return. In the vote on the septennate – which, by prolonging MacMahon's presidency through the end of the decade, made the organization of a pro-imperial plebiscite far more difficult – a large group of Bonapartist deputies ignored Rouher's explicit instructions and supported the conservative majority.

The tendency for Bonapartist deputies to vote alongside legitimists and conservative Orléanists in this period inhibited efforts by party leaders to mobilize support at the grass roots. The Bonapartists had previously been a party proudly committed in principle to universal suffrage and citizenship; now they appeared to be siding with feudal and bourgeois skeptics about democracy. Subscriptions to the party's main newspaper rapidly declined in this period – precisely as the circulation of Gambetta's *La République Française* was burgeoning. Donations to the Bonapartist party fell off as well, leaving Rouher perilously short of funds as the 1876 parliamentary campaign approached. Outside a few regions where individual Bonapartists had maintained local political machines that had managed to survive the chaos period – particularly in the Southwest – the party was forced to rely on candidates who could pay for their own campaigns.[78] Naturally, this made it impossible to insist on any clear and consistent *profession de foi* that all Bonapartists must defend; the campaign materials that

---

[77] Ibid., pp. 104–158.
[78] The best-organized and best-funded local Bonapartist party organization was that of Baron Eugène Eschasseriaux in the Charente-Inférieure. Ibid., pp. 173–229.

were distributed to local districts were derided for their vagueness, and many candidates refused to use them.

Thus, while superficially the performance of the Bonapartists in the 1876 elections looked reasonably good, with seventy-five seats gained, the situation under the surface was far less promising. Few of the newly elected "Bonapartists" could be counted on to accept party discipline, so no consistent parliamentary strategy was possible. As in the National Assembly, the Bonapartist faction in the Chamber of Deputies tended to vote alongside the legitimists and Orléanists against the "threat" of Gambetta's radical republicanism, blending into the overall coalition for "moral order" – a coalition whose ideological identity, in the end, depended on a grass-roots network of nobles, priests, and conservative Catholics that still identified much more closely with Chambord and the pope than with MacMahon, Rouher, or de Broglie. In this environment, the political prospects for a restoration of the Prince Imperial after 1876 were essentially nil.

Crisis and Resolution

With the convening of the new Chamber of Deputies in 1876, the stage was set for a final showdown concerning France's regime type. The electoral triumph of the republicans, and the particular success of Gambetta's radical faction, seemed to indicate the positive verdict of the nation on the new republican constitution of 1875; not only urban workers, professionals, and intellectuals but even a growing number of peasants had expressed their support for the republican cause. At the same time, the defenders of moral order still had a few major trump cards in their hands. Fear of republican radicalism of the sort that had generated the Paris Commune was still a potent factor inclining many French officials and wealthy capitalists toward the conservatives. The avowed anticlericalism of Gambetta and his colleagues could be mobilized to inspire local resistance to republican politics in regions where the church remained a powerful force. Most importantly, the conservatives still held on to the presidency of Marshal MacMahon, whose own political inclinations – while hardly ideological in nature – tended toward legitimism and conservative Catholicism.[79]

By this point, however, the collapse in essence of both Orléanism and Bonapartism as separate partisan identities led to the merger of all "conservatives" into a single, antirepublican bloc – one that by its very nature could not arrive at any unified ideological position. As the final crisis of the 1870s unfolded, then, the ideologically consistent Gambettist movement now faced an alliance of notables united only by their distaste for republicanism and their instrumental

---

[79] As MacMahon once declared to the German ambassador to France: "Believe me, I am Legitimist in my soul. I began my military career in the service of good King Charles X. My family has always been Legitimist. I have not forgotten. But difficulties, political necessities! We have to proceed with the greatest care." Quoted in Brown, *The Comte de Chambord*, p. 148.

interest in preserving their traditional power. Once again, even against daunting odds, the ideologically committed party was able to overcome collective action problems in mobilizing local activists; once again, the nonideological coalition failed to coordinate successfully.

For the first year after the 1876 elections, Marshal MacMahon and his advisers initially chose to respect parliamentary norms by approving a republican government. Some of MacMahon's advisers, including de Broglie, insisted that the republicans in power would quickly discredit themselves by their "radicalism"; at some point in the future, then, the president's right to dissolve the lower house could be utilized with some meaningful degree of popular support. Nevertheless, MacMahon and his advisers chose the conservative republican Jules Simon as president of the council, in effect undercutting the strategy of letting Gambetta manifest his political "extremism." Simon, now in his seventies, had long been a bitter opponent of Gambetta, particularly objecting to the latter's fiery anticlericalism. Yet, while Simon valiantly struggled to placate both the parliamentary left and the right during his time in office, his ultimate fidelity to the republican cause led him to support legislation reducing Catholic influence in French universities at a time when Pope Pius IX was promoting an extremist antiliberal theology. During the parliamentary debate on this issue, Gambetta's own rhetoric became increasingly heated, famously declaring at one point, "le clericalisme – voilà l'ennemi!"[80] Terrified that the last vestiges of French tradition and faith would soon be wiped out by the ascendant radical republicans, MacMahon dismissed Simon on May 16, 1877, replacing him with de Broglie and a cabinet of legitimists, Orléanists, and right-wing Bonapartists. The resulting *seize mai* crisis would mean a struggle to the death between conservatives and republicans to define France's ultimate regime type.

But Gambetta and his movement were well positioned for such a struggle. For MacMahon's dismissal of the Simon ministry, followed by his dissolution of the Chamber of Deputies, raised central questions about the constitution of 1875. While the text of that document did allow the president to dissolve the chamber, the circumstances under which he might do so were not spelled out; hence, to accept MacMahon's decision to overturn the will of the voters meant to elevate the power of the presidency above that of the parliamentary majority. In this context, Gambetta could easily portray MacMahon's decision as a dangerous revolutionary step that would once again thrust France back into political chaos; again, Gambetta's own "radical republicanism" could now be framed as simple fidelity to constitutional norms. With the coming republican victory, Gambetta declared, it would be necessary for the president to "submit or resign" (*se soumettre ou se démettre*).[81]

[80] Bertocci, *Jules Simon*, p. 190.
[81] Gambetta did not use the name of the president explicitly in his speech, but this did not prevent the government from prosecuting him later for "insulting the President of the Republic" – thus handing Gambetta more free positive publicity. Bury, *Gambetta and the Making of the Third Republic*, pp. 421–422.

Such an argument proved convincing even to many conservative liberals. Thiers, for example, now emerged as Gambetta's most stalwart defender; although no doubt this in part reflected his desire to turn the tables on MacMahon and retake the presidency himself, at the same time it confirmed Gambetta's own newly preeminent position in French politics. When Thiers died unexpectedly in September 1877, Gambetta took the opportunity to organize a mass civil ceremony for his funeral in Paris – cementing the symbolic unification of radical republicanism and "respectable" liberalism.[82] As the new election date of November 1877 approached, Gambetta once again took over the direction of the republican campaign, mobilizing all of the party's affiliated newspapers, clubs, worker organizations, and professional associations to distribute republican propaganda and get out the vote throughout the country.[83] Gambetta's key theme: a victory for MacMahon would mean the restoration of the most reactionary clerical and feudal elites in France, who would soon unleash war with Germany and Italy over the status of the pope's temporal power.[84]

On one level, of course, Gambetta's campaign rhetoric was hyperbolic and misleading: the forces of "moral order" were hardly unified around ultramontanist or legitimist themes.[85] At the same time, there was an important kernel of truth to Gambetta's charges that made the republican propaganda in the *seize mai* crisis seem credible: of all the conservative forces supporting MacMahon, only the legitimists possessed any clear and consistent vision of the French polity, backed by a network of committed supporters at the grass roots. Thus, as the struggle deepened, even the most pragmatic conservatives would be forced to make common cause with their allies on the extreme right, despite its negative effects on the conservative campaign.

This dynamic was evident in the first days after Simon's dismissal, when de Broglie – now officially again the leader of the conservative campaign – clashed with more radical right-wing Catholics such as Félix Dupanloup and extremist Bonapartists such as Cassagnac on how to carry out the campaign against Gambetta.[86] The former, hoping to portray the *seize mai* as a defense

---

[82] As Jules Ferry described the scene: "From the Rue Lepeletier to Père Lachaise, a million men, drawn up in serried ranks along the route of the funeral cortege, standing bare-headed, contemplative, an immortelle in the button-hold, saluted the carriage – covered with mountains of flowers... with one single cry... rolling, grave, resolute, formidable: Vive la République!" Quoted in Nord, *Republican Moment*, p. 200.

[83] Hazareesingh, *Intellectual Founders*.

[84] Mitchell shows that Bismarck aided and abetted this propaganda campaign, having become convinced that the republicans under Gambetta posed less of a long-term threat to Germany than the conservative forces – which Bismarck saw as dangerously tied to clericalism. See *The German Influence in France after 1870*, pp. 159–170.

[85] This point is emphasized by Grubb, *The Politics of Pessimism*, against earlier prorepublican histories of this period that accepted Gambetta's propagandistic characterization of the right as universally monarchist and ultramontane. See, for example, Fresnette Pisani-Ferry, *Le Coup d'État Manqué du 16 Mai 1877* (Paris: Robert Laffont, 1965).

[86] Grubb, *Politics of Pessimism*, pp. 259–261.

of legality and order against the threat of radicalism, remained committed to constitutional procedures; the latter, seeing the crisis as a fight to the death for conservative France, argued for an immediate dismissal of parliament followed by the declaration of a presidential regime. Given MacMahon's own personal aversion to "revolutionary" action, de Broglie's position was adopted; the Chamber of Deputies was dismissed only after returning from its scheduled break, in order to preserve at least the appearance of constitutionality, and new elections were scheduled for the fall. This time, de Broglie promised, the crippling divisions of the right into three competing factions would be overcome, and all the administrative pressure of the French state would be utilized to stop Gambetta. But this was not to be.

A central problem for the campaign was that de Broglie's odd mixture of legal proceduralism and undemocratic dirty tricks made no coherent ideological sense. Unable to orient the campaign toward conservative liberalism, toward Catholicism, toward monarchism, or toward empire, de Broglie and his colleagues were forced simply to run as defenders of President MacMahon. MacMahon's picture on horseback, recalling his glorious days in the Crimean War, was distributed by the thousands in every French province; the new prefects appointed by de Broglie were given clear instructions to censor opposition campaign materials and to turn out the vote for the president.[87] At the same time, de Broglie discouraged all efforts by local conservatives to inject monarchical or religious themes into the campaign, realizing that to do so would play into Gambetta's hands. Nevertheless, bishops and curés throughout France rallied the faithful for the upcoming electoral struggle. Prominent legitimists like de Mun, still in close touch with an approving Chambord, continued to link the defense of Catholicism with the restoration of the Bourbon dynasty.[88] Gambetta thus sounded entirely credible when he insisted to the electorate that under the formal surface of nonideological French "conservatism" lurked an organized, reactionary "clericalism."

In the end, the French electorate in 1877 was presented with a clear choice of regime types: either a right-wing presidential regime with no definite program of its own but under the strong influence of ideologically legitimist and conservative Catholic forces or a parliamentary republic devoted to universal citizenship and secular education. Given these options – and swayed by effective propaganda from the disciplined network of republican activists who painted MacMahon's cause in the most terrifying possible terms – the French electorate resoundingly reaffirmed its support for republicanism. The final tally was 4,367,000 votes for the republicans, and 3,577,000 for the conservatives.[89]

Central to Gambetta's victory in 1877 was his ability to persuade key socioeconomic groups to commit themselves to his cause. The textile and luxury manufacturers and merchants in the Union Nationale du Commerce et de l'Industrie

[87] Ibid., pp. 299–304; Stone, *Sons of the Revolution*.
[88] Martin, *Count Albert de Mun*, p. 34.
[89] Anderson, *France, 1870–1814*, p. 165.

(UNCI), who had previously sided with Thiers or with the moderate republican Simon, began to fear that after *seize mai* President MacMahon's regime might turn in a reactionary anticapitalist direction. After MacMahon at first tried to ignore the results of the October elections, appointing an even more authoritarian Orléanist General Gaëtan de Rochebouët to head the government, the UNCI mobilized a demonstration of eighteen hundred businessmen in Paris in protest. MacMahon's refusal even to meet with UNCI leaders sparked further business protests against the Rochebouët ministry, and by December 6 petitions from small shopkeepers all over the country began to pour in.[90] Combined with the remarkable success of the republican electoral campaign among independent peasants in rural regions, this pressure from organized social interests was too great to ignore.[91] On December 13, a fully republican government was finally installed.

With the end of the *seize mai* crisis, the future shape of the French political regime was determined for nearly seven decades. Gambetta wasted no time in declaring that the "forces of the future" had triumphed over those of the past. The prefecture, civil service, and judiciary were purged of rightist elements and replaced by loyal republicans who could demonstrate long-standing fidelity to the cause. As Gambetta had predicted in 1875, new elections to the Senate in the more favorable circumstances of 1879 produced a slim republican majority even in the upper house of the French parliament. Given these unpalatable changes in French politics, President MacMahon chose to step down from his post two years before the expiration of the septennate; he was replaced by the veteran republican Jules Grévy.

The victorious republicans quickly solidified their political success by reorienting French political culture to reflect the key principles of republican ideology. In 1879 the *Marseillaise* was declared to be the French national anthem and the fourteenth of July became the most important national holiday. Already by 1880, new education minister Jules Ferry introduced legislation to mandate universal secular public education throughout France – as had been demanded by radical republicans since the Belleville Program of 1869. The Jesuit order was dissolved, and thousands of monks and nuns were forced out of the classroom.[92] The content of schooling in the new free public education

---

[90] This account follows Nord, *The Republican Moment*, pp. 58–61.

[91] For a graphic illustration of the extent of republican gains in the countryside in 1876 and 1877, see the regional election maps presented in Gouault, *Comment la France*. Sanford Elwitt's Marxist argument that the consolidation of the Third Republic under an ideology of universal citizenship was driven by the political ascendancy of the French "bourgeoisie" relies on a functionalist logic that drastically overstates the degree to which Gambetta's narrow victory was predetermined by class structure. See Elwitt, *The Making of the Third Republic, Class and Politics in France, 1868–1884* (Baton Rouge: Louisiana State University Press, 1975).

[92] This was only the start of a whole series of laws designed to achieve a full separation of church and state, including the forbidding of public prayers, the restoration of divorce in the civil code, and the dismissal of army chaplains. Public prayers were forbidden, and divorce became part of the civil code. Brown, *The Comte de Chambord*, pp. 170–171. For an excellent analysis of

system naturally also reinforced republican ideology in mass culture. Along with the emphasis on positivism, citizenship, and democracy came a noticeable effort to indoctrinate youth into a distinctive republican conception of French nationalism meant to erode earlier regional loyalties inherited from the feudal past. Indeed, the process of turning "peasants into Frenchman" that was famously analyzed by Eugene Weber arguably owed less to processes of social modernization and more to the explicit ideological design of French republican schooling in this period.[93]

The clear and consistent principles of radical republican ideology, it should be noted, also help to account for what from a contemporary perspective must be seen as the early Third Republic's key democratic failures. For example, the regime took a clear stand against political equality for women, basing its policies on the works of republican philosophers dating back to Rousseau who had consistently proclaimed women's primary duty to the state as the raising of the next generation of republican (male) citizens.[94] Jules Ferry and other leading republicans also promoted and glorified France's continued imperial expansion in North Africa and Indochina. Since Gambetta's last-ditch defense of France against the Prussians, top republican leaders had been united in their desire to further the "universal" principles of 1789 by making France a global great power.[95]

Of course, the history of French politics did not come to an end in 1879. In fact, the consolidation of France's new republican democracy coincided with the beginning of a severe depression that lasted through the next decade. Stagnation in French industry, an increasing trade deficit with Germany, and a severe agricultural crisis worsened by the devastating impact of the phylloxeria disease that destroyed much of France's wine industry combined to generate substantial social discontent with the rule of Opportunist Republicans – as the ruling faction of Gambetta and Ferry was now universally known. Not surprisingly, under these conditions, the 1880s saw the rapid growth of radical new parties of both right and left. Within the republican movement itself, the new Radical party led by Georges Clemenceau promised both an expansion of employment opportunities for the less fortunate and a more aggressive foreign policy vis-à-vis the hated German Empire aimed at retaking the lost territories of Alsace-Lorraine. At the same time, Jules Guesde and Karl Marx's son-in-law Paul Lafargue cofounded France's first orthodox Marxist party, the Party of

the role of anticlericalism in the development of later French democracy, see Andrew Gould, *Origins of Liberal Dominance: State, Church, and Party in Nineteenth-Century Europe* (Ann Arbor: University of Michigan Press, 1999), pp. 45–64. An interesting comparative analysis of France's "active secularism" as compared to the American and Turkish variants is provided in Ahmet Kuru, *Secularism and State Policies toward Religion: The United States, France, and Turkey* (Cambridge: Cambridge University Press, 2009).

93 Eugene Weber, *Peasants into Frenchmen: The Modernization of Rural France, 1870–1914* (Stanford, CA: Stanford University Press, 1976).

94 Jean-Jacques Rousseau, *Emile or, On Education* (New York: Basic Books, 1979).

95 Bury, *Gambetta and the Making of the Third Republic*, pp. 356–370.

French Workers. By the time of the 1885 elections, too, the three defeated strains of French monarchism had regrouped and finally united, attaining significant victories at the ballot box for the first time since the early 1870s. This new French right ultimately generated a whole series of antisystem parties over the course of the Third Republic's history, ranging from the Boulanger movement of the late 1880s to later anti-Semitic movements of an increasingly fascist variety.[96]

Thus, the first half of the 1880s saw the early signs of long-term political tensions that would generate a whole series of government scandals and crises in the later history of the Third Republic. Yet what is more remarkable, in retrospect, is that the new party formations on both the left and the right would henceforth generally agree to compete within the context of the 1875 constitutional compromise, rather than try to overthrow that constitution. The victory of Gambetta's radical republicans in 1877, followed by the consolidation of democracy in the years afterward, thus created the first durable framework for channeling French social interests into a consensual regime framework since the Revolution of 1789. In key respects, the clear and consistent ideological principles for defining membership in the French polity originally espoused by Gambetta in the Second Empire had become the core features of France's new institutional order.

---

[96] See William D. Irvine, *The Boulanger Affair Reconsidered: Royalism, Boulangism, and the Origins of the Radical Right in France* (New York: Oxford University Press, 1989); Zeev Sternhell, *Neither Right nor Left: Fascist Ideology in France* (Berkeley: University of California Press, 1986).

5

The Rise and Fall of the Weimar Republic

Unlike the case of the early French Third Republic, the rise and fall of the Weimar Republic in Germany has long been at the very center of theoretical attention among comparative-historical analysts of democratization. The reasons are clear. First, the fact that German democracy failed despite the country's high degree of economic, social, and cultural development has long struck observers as theoretically puzzling.[1] Second, the history of the fifteen years of Weimar democracy is undeniably dramatic, including multiple coup attempts and uprisings led by both the extreme right and left, economic challenges ranging from hyperinflation to stubbornly persistent unemployment, and a long series of international crises with direct implications for the future of the German state. Indeed, that the Weimar constitution managed to survive so many early storms and to produce a seemingly stable democratic order by the late 1920s makes its ultimate failure even more tragic. Finally, no scholar can forget that the fall of Weimar Germany generated a genocidal Nazi Party dictatorship responsible for the deaths of tens of millions of people in the Holocaust and World War II.[2] Understanding why Weimar failed is thus inextricably connected to debates about how humanity might prevent another Hitler from coming to power.

Perhaps unsurprisingly, given the unusually high stakes involved in this debate, scholars have yet to reach a consensus about the main causes of Weimar's collapse. Initially, in the wake of World War II when the full horror of the Nazi regime had come to light, scholars tended to assume that some deep, underlying flaw in German history and culture must be to blame. Theorists of the German *Sonderweg* – or special path – saw German authoritarianism as more or less a continuous and central feature of the country's political life from

---

[1] Juan Linz and Alfred Stepan, eds., *The Breakdown of Democratic Regimes* (Baltimore: Johns Hopkins University Press, 1978).

[2] Charles Maier, *The Unmasterable Past: History, Holocaust, and German National Identity* (Cambridge, MA: Harvard University Press, 1988).

feudalism through the Nazi period; from this perspective, Weimar democracy was but a short interlude during which authoritarian tendencies in German society were never really overcome.[3] In a similar vein, modernization theorists such as Ralf Dahrendorf emphasized that despite Germany's rapid economic development in the latter part of the nineteenth century, fundamentally traditional social groups continued to maintain significant influence.[4] Much of the country's eastern territory continued to be dominated by large feudal estates ruled by reactionary Junkers, while even its industrial sector remained closely tied to the authoritarian state. The result was a widespread cultural orientation toward hierarchical obedience that undermined pluralist democratic politics in the early twentieth century. The basic argument that German culture was distinctly conducive to genocidal outcomes has been restated forcefully in recent years by Daniel Goldhagen, who claimed that Nazism emerged directly from a unique form of "eliminationist anti-Semitism" that had penetrated nearly every major social group in German society during the nineteenth and early twentieth centuries.[5]

Other scholars, however, have called the *Sonderweg* thesis into question. As Blackbourn and Eley pointed out, while Germany during the nineteenth century certainly did remain an authoritarian regime with important social groups hostile to liberal market institutions, the same can be said of nearly every other European country in that period.[6] As we have already seen, France was the only continental European country to institute full democratic male suffrage by 1870; elsewhere, constitutionalism was combined with monarchical forms of rule combined with suffrage restrictions of various types. Even in Great Britain, the supposed paragon of liberal capitalism, legal restrictions on working-class suffrage and labor organization blocked full democratic representation until the end of the nineteenth century. Nor was the demand for protection from the free market by threatened artisans, shopkeepers, or agrarian interests a uniquely German phenomenon; on the contrary, anticapitalist revolts by such groups were an endemic feature of European politics well into the twentieth century. Sadly, virulent anti-Semitism has also been a remarkably common feature of modern European political culture – arguably no less prevalent in France, Poland, or Russia than in Germany itself. The enormity of the Nazis' crimes against humanity, then, could not easily have been foreseen simply by examining the main features of prior German history.

A second theoretical approach to explaining the failure of Weimar democracy focuses not on supposed flaws in Germany's distinct model of

3 Hans Ulrich Wehler, *The German Empire, 1871–1918* (Dover: Berg, 1985).
4 Ralf Dahrendorf, *Society and Democracy in Germany* (New York: Norton, 1967).
5 Daniel Goldhagen, *Hitler's Willing Executioners: Ordinary Germans and the Holocaust* (New York: Knopf, 1996).
6 David Blackbourn and Geoff Eley, *The Peculiarities of German History: Bourgeais Society and Politics in Nineteenth-Century Germany* (Oxford: Oxford University Press 1984); Blackbourn, *The Long Nineteenth Century: A History of Germany, 1780–1918* (New York: Oxford University Press, 1998).

modernization but rather on more general structural forces that appeared to prevent a full breakthrough to bourgeois democracy in the period – not only in Germany but also in most of Europe in the early twentieth century. Writing during World War II, for example, Karl Polanyi argued that fascism could be seen as a logical (if reprehensible) form of social resistance in European late developers to the imposition of a global "market society" in which land, labor, and money must all be simultaneously turned into commodities, regardless of the social dislocation this process produces.[7] Marxist analyses of the Nazi regime argued that Nazism was a predictable response by the German bourgeoisie to the threat of communist revolution during the Great Depression – explaining why (non-Jewish) business interests were promoted under Hitler's regime before the Second World War.[8] Barrington Moore's well-known neo-Marxist theory provided a more general set of hypotheses about how particular class formations typically generate the regime types of democracy, fascism, and communism. In Moore's view, both Japanese and German fascism emerged because of the absence of any revolutionary breakthrough to commercialized agriculture in these countries, which in turn enabled an alliance between the state-dependent bourgeoisie and feudal agricultural elites to repress labor through an embrace of reactionary authoritarianism.[9]

These structuralist explanations of fascism have clearly made an important contribution to our understanding of the general social causes of antiliberal movements in societies undergoing severe economic crises in the capitalist global economy. More recent scholarship, however, calls into question the degree to which quite general causal hypotheses of a Marxist or neo-Marxist variety can account for the specific trajectories of new democracies facing similar historical and geographic contexts. As Capoccia points out, many other democracies in interwar Europe faced parallel structural constraints to those of Weimar Germany, but several nevertheless managed to escape fascism until it was imposed by the Nazis through armed intervention. Some sort of "agent-based" explanation, then, seems necessary to account for the variance among successes like Czechoslovakia and failures like Germany.[10] Surely, too, attention must be paid to the particular features of institutional design that may have contributed to Weimar Germany's chronic governmental instability and its eventual devolution into authoritarian presidentialism, such as its extreme form of proportional representation and the dangerously broad emergency powers granted to the Reich president in the infamous Article 48 of the Weimar

[7] Karl Polanyi, *The Great Transformation* (Boston: Beacon Press, 1944).

[8] See, for example, Franz L. Neumann, *Behemoth: The Structure and Practice of National Socialism, 1933–1944* (New York: Octagon Books, 1963).

[9] Barrington Moore, *Social Origins of Dictatorship and Democracy: Lord and Peasant in the Making of the Modern World* (Boston: Beacon Press, 1966). See also Gregory Luebbert, *Liberalism, Fascism, or Social Democracy: Social Classes and the Political Origins of Regimes in Interwar Europe* (New York: Oxford University Press, 1991).

[10] Giovanni Capoccia, *Defending Democracy: Reactions to Extremism in Interwar Europe* (Baltimore: Johns Hopkins University Press, 2005).

Constitution.[11] Recent works of comparative historical analysis thus sensitize us to potential counterfactual causes that might have worked to reduce or even eliminate the probability of a Nazi outcome in the 1930s.

In tandem with these developments in the social sciences, recent historiography increasingly treats the decade and a half of Weimar democracy as a distinct historical period, during which many potential paths of future development were potentially available – notwithstanding the cultural and structural obstacles to democratic consolidation Germany inherited from the period of the Second Reich.[12] Scholars continue to debate, for example, whether a Keynesian policy of "pump priming" after 1929, rather than the deflationary course chosen by Chancellor Heinrich Brüning, might have helped to win greater social support for the Weimar Republic.[13] Even at the height of the Great Depression, Hitler's rise to power was by no means inevitable; on the contrary, both the organizational cohesion and social support of the Nazi Party were visibly waning by the end of 1932. If so, Hitler's appointment as German chancellor in January 1933 was the tragic, wholly unnecessary result of desperate political schemes hatched up by reactionary circles around President Paul von Hindenburg.[14]

These trends in the social scientific and historical analysis of Weimar Germany fit well with the theoretical approach adopted in this book, which classifies the Weimar case along with the early French Third Republic as a "post-imperial democracy." As in France in 1870, German democracy emerged from total defeat in an unexpected war, accompanied by the humiliating twin burdens of military occupation and reparation payments. Like the Third Republic, the Weimar Republic had no international support from any reliable foreign allies. Both countries suffered through a prolonged period of social and institutional chaos in the immediate postwar period. Yet, as we have seen, the success of Gambetta's radical republicanism in welding together a network

---

[11] Several excellent books examining the institutions of Weimar Germany in comparative historical perspective have recently appeared. See in particular Michael Bernhard, *Institutions and the Fate of Democracy: Germany and Poland in the Twentieth Century* (Pittsburgh: University of Pittsburgh Press, 2005); Cindy Skach, *Borrowing Constitutional Designs: Constitutional Law in Weimar Germany and the French Fifth Republic* (Princeton, NJ: Princeton University Press, 2005); and Marcus Kreuzer, *Institutions and Innovation: Voters, Parties, and Interest Groups in the Consolidation of Democracy: France and Germany, 1870–1939* (Ann Arbor: University of Michigan Press, 2001).

[12] See, for example, Detlev J. K. Peukert, *The Weimar Republic: The Crisis of Classical Modernity* (New York: Hill and Wang, 1989); Larry Eugene Jones, *German Liberalism and the Dissolution of the Weimar Party System, 1918–1933* (Chapel Hill: University of North Carolina Press, 1988); and Hans Mommsen, *The Rise and Fall of Weimar Democracy*, trans. Elborg Forster and Larry Eugene Jones (Chapel Hill: University of North Carolina Press, 1996).

[13] See, for example, the essays contained in Ian Kershaw, ed., *Weimar: Why Did German Democracy Fail?* (London: Weidenfeld and Nicolson, 1990).

[14] Henry Ashby Turner, *Hitler's Thirty Days to Power: January 1933* (Reading, MA: Addison-Wesley, 1996). See also Dietrich Orlow, *A History of the Nazi Party, 1918–1933* (Pittsburgh: University of Pittsburgh Press, 1969).

of prodemocratic party activists forged a consolidated democracy even under such conditions. Germany's post-imperial democracy, too, was marked by profound political, economic, and cultural uncertainties that might in principle have resulted in a wide range of potential institutional outcomes. If so, burdensome institutional legacies of the past cannot account by themselves for Germany's descent into fascism.[15]

In this chapter I argue that the failure of German democracy in the 1920s – like the success of French democracy in the 1870s – can be traced in large part to the role of ideology in shaping the Weimar party system.[16] In the chaotic wake of defeat in World War I, antirepublican political elites managed to define clear and consistent conceptions of the principles of membership that would guide the future reconstruction of the German polity with far greater success than prodemocratic politicians. Specifically, both the German National People's Party (DNVP) and the National Socialist German Workers' Party (NSDAP, or Nazis) on the right, as well as the Social Democratic Party of Germany (SPD) and the Communist Party of Germany (KPD) on the left, managed to articulate clear party ideologies in the initial post-imperial period; as a result, they were able to preserve and extend their initial activist core through the five years of intense turbulence in German society from the German Revolution of November 1918 until the arrest of Hitler and stabilization of the mark in late 1923. By contrast, the Independent Social Democratic Party (USPD), along with the two major liberal parties – the left-center German Democratic Party (DDP) and the right-center German People's Party (DVP) – found it impossible to articulate any clear ideological principles. By 1923 the USPD had disintegrated, and the liberal parties had both seen their ability to mobilize party activists in electoral struggles erode significantly.

Thus, by the mid-1920s the stage was set for a prolonged and bitter political stalemate, as Weimar's four major ideological parties struggled to redefine the German polity and society along communist, socialist, monarchist, or racialist lines – while the two liberal parties continued to lose their organizational cohesion, despite the stabilization of the German economy in this period. By the time the Great Depression hit Germany in the fall of 1929, the German parliamentary system was already in serious trouble. The short-circuiting of parliamentary authority by President Hindenburg and Chancellor Brüning after 1930 merely forced the struggle over competing regime types out of the Reichstag and into extraparliamentary venues. In that context, the parties that had particularly specialized in mobilizing gang violence – the KPD and the Nazis – had a decisive advantage.

---

[15] Stephen E. Hanson and Jeffrey S. Kopstein, "The Weimar/Russia Comparison," *Post-Soviet Affairs* 13(3, July–September 1997): 252–283. See also Sheri Berman, "Civil Society and the Collapse of the Weimar Republic," *World Politics* 49(3, April 1997): 401–429.

[16] In this respect, the argument here can be seen as providing microfoundations for Sartori's classic analysis of Weimar's "polarized pluralism." See Giovanni Sartori, *Parties and Party Systems: A Framework for Analysis* (Cambridge: Cambridge University Press, 1976).

I should also note here that the Catholic Center Party represents an anomalous case for my theoretical argument. Unable to articulate its political ideology with any consistency in the wake of the collapse of the Reich, the Center was indeed constantly riven by factional splits – as my main hypothesis would predict. The Center Party nevertheless managed to maintain its organizational capacity relatively successfully throughout the 1920s. I argue that this disconfirming result can be explained by the lack of viable alternative party affiliations for most Catholics in the highly ideologically polarized Weimar polity. Because Social Democratic secularism, communism, Prussian (Protestant) monarchist restoration, and Nazi racial theory were each ideologically incompatible with Catholic identity and interests, individuals in the Center Party's activist network of Catholic priests, landowners, union organizers, and intellectuals saw no personal advantage in defection to rival parties. As a result, however, Center Party activism could be maintained only in connection with the handful of issues where these disparate social groups shared consensual goals – in particular, the defense of religious education and relations with the papacy. Given its lack of a positive vision of the polity for which it stood, the Center remained a fragile coalition that disintegrated almost instantaneously when confronted with new selective incentives imposed by the Nazis after Hitler's rise to power.

Because the roots of the Weimar party system can be traced back to their origins in the Second Reich, this chapter begins with a brief discussion of the four main party groupings in the imperial Reichstag to show how splits in these groupings before and during World War I shaped the ideological foundations of German political parties in the Weimar period. I then analyze the relative success or failure of each of the eight main parties in the Weimar system in solving the collective action problem of building a national network of party activists, first in the period of post-imperial chaos from 1918 to 1923, then in the period of stalemate from 1924 to 1929. Finally, I examine how Weimar's polarized party system interacted with the structural crisis of the Great Depression to generate the conditions in which Hitler's rise to power could become possible.

Parties in Imperial Germany

Like France under the Second Empire, Germany under the Second Reich after unification in 1871 was an odd mix of authoritarianism and semidemocratic constitutionalism, of dynamic industrial capitalists and reactionary aristocrats, of centralized state power and localism – or, as Wolfgang Mommsen puts it, a "system of skirted decisions" about basic questions of regime type.[17] As in France under Louis Napoleon, universal male suffrage in Reich elections together with the nontrivial role for the Reichstag in passing legislation led to the formation of genuinely competitive and representative political

---

[17] Wolfgang J. Mommsen, *Imperial Germany, 1867–1918: Politics, Culture, and Society in an Authoritarian State*, trans. Richard Deveson (London: Arnold Press, 1995), pp. 1–19.

parties – even if at first these parties began as essentially clubs of notables (or in Max Weber's terms, *Honoratiorenparteien*), which adapted to modern techniques of mass mobilization with varying degrees of success.[18] In particular, four major party groupings played the central role in parliamentary competition in this period: the social democrats, the liberals, the conservatives, and the Catholic Center. Elements of these four groups ultimately formed the core of the Weimar party system. The degree of party system transformation after Germany's defeat in World War I, however, was rather greater than in France after Sedan.

Social Democrats

Although socialism of various strands existed in every part of Europe in the nineteenth century, there is no question that the German Social Democratic Party was the most powerful and influential of its kind. At first, however, the SPD was not particularly consistent in ideological terms. The SPD's founding congress in Gotha in 1875 forged a party program that mixed elements of Marxism with ideologically incompatible ideas from rival socialist theoretician Ferdinand Lassalle, who emphasized the role of the state in creating equality among various social classes.[19] Otto von Bismarck's efforts to crush the fledgling party through the antisocialist laws of 1878–1890 – under which socialist leaders were prosecuted, socialist meetings were banned, party publications were censored, and independent trade unions suppressed – did much to discredit Lassallean statism among SPD activists and to confirm instead the views of Marx and Engels about the inevitable intensification of class struggle under advanced capitalism.[20]

Indeed, the SPD's ability not only to survive in this period but to grow in both organizational power and popular support owed a great deal to the increasing ideological and strategic consistency of the party leadership. After Marx's death in 1883, the chief theoretician of the SPD, Karl Kautsky – in close collaboration with Engels himself – began to produce popular, easily readable interpretations of the key tenets of Marxist theory, which were later translated and distributed to socialists all over Europe. In 1891 Kautsky and Eduard Bernstein co-wrote the new SPD Erfurt Party Program, which officially codified Marx's theory of class struggle as the sole theoretical basis of future party activity. The Erfurt Program confidently predicted the ultimate demise of capitalism in the foreseeable future as a result of its internal contradictions and proclaimed as the SPD's primary mission the preparation of the new proletarian

---

[18] Max Weber, "Politics as a Vocation," in Hans Gerth and C. Wright Mills, eds., *From Max Weber: Essays in Sociology* (New York: Oxford, 1946), pp. 77–128.

[19] Marx's own reaction to the ideological incoherence of this program was famously vituperative. See Marx, "Critique of the Gotha Program," in Robert C. Tucker, ed., *The Marx-Engels Reader* (New York: Norton, 1978), pp. 525–541.

[20] W. L. Guttsman, *The German Social Democratic Party, 1875–1933: From Ghetto to Government* (London: George Allen and Unwin, 1981).

society through a campaign of disciplined agitation and education among the working class. The SPD also took the lead role in the formation of the Second International to coordinate the activities of Marxist parties on a global scale.

Accompanying the SPD's ideological embrace of what came to be known as "orthodox Marxism" was a new strategy for tying the party's working-class base more closely to the party elite by building systematic organizational linkages between them. In order to get around the antisocialist laws, the party leadership under August Bebel worked tirelessly to build and institutionalize a wide range of socialist civil society groups that were ostensibly independent of the SPD itself and thus more difficult to shut down under the laws of the Reich. These included socialist sports clubs, choirs, and reading circles and, most importantly, socialist trade unions – although the latter maintained comparatively greater independence from the SPD organization.[21] The remarkable success of this strategy resulted in the formation of a sort of parallel society for industrial workers in imperial Germany, within which Marxism became a sort of secular religion lived out in daily life both in the workplace and in private life.[22] This strategy also helped to ensure the growing success of the SPD at the polls. During the 1890s, the SPD regularly attained about a quarter of the German vote; by 1912 it had become the single largest party in the Reichstag with 34.8 percent of the vote and 27.7 percent of the parliamentary deputies.[23] Indeed, in the early twentieth century, the SPD was the largest political party in the world, with more than a million members.[24] Observers of the period began to describe the SPD as the "elective fatherland of the German working class."[25]

The very success of the Social Democratic Party, however, generated new sources of ideological tension within the movement from both "right" and "left" perspectives.[26] In the latter half of the 1890s, Bernstein rocked the SPD with a series of articles calling for a rejection of Marxist orthodoxy about the inevitability of communist revolution in favor of an explicit strategy of promoting working-class interests in an evolutionary manner, within the context of existing German democratic institutions – a strategy that, he argued, had already in effect become the practice of the party. Shortly thereafter, in

---

[21] David W. Morgan, *The Socialist Left and the German Revolution: A History of the German Independent Social Democratic Party, 1917–1922* (Ithaca, NY: Cornell University Press, 1975), p. 22.

[22] Guenther Roth, *The Social Democrats in Imperial Germany: A Study in Working-Class Isolation and National Integration* (Totowa, NJ: Bedminster Press, 1963).

[23] Edgar J. Feuchtwanger, *Imperial Germany, 1850–1918* (London: Routledge, 2001), p. 202.

[24] David W. Morgan, *The Socialist Left and the German Revolution: A History of the German Independent Social Democratic Party, 1917–1922* (Ithaca, NY: Cornell University Press, 1975), p. 20.

[25] Guttsman, *The German Social Democratic Party*, p. 3.

[26] These ideological splits are analyzed in greater detail in Stephen E. Hanson, *Time and Revolution: Marxism and the Design of Soviet Institutions* (Chapel Hill: University of North Carolina Press, 1997).

direct contradiction to Bernstein's "revisionism," Rosa Luxemburg argued that the SPD had become far too complacent and bureaucratic. Instead of focusing on minor "reforms" of capitalism, she argued, the party should promote immediate proletarian revolution through such mechanisms as mass strikes. In defending party orthodoxy against these two critiques, Kautsky found himself in a personally as well as theoretically awkward position, given the fact that he had long been a close friend of Bernstein, while his wife was one of Luxemburg's best friends. Nevertheless, Kautsky and the SPD leadership officially denounced both "right" and "left" revisionism, arguing that Marxism must always maintain a simultaneous focus on a scientific analysis of contemporary social realities and a clear commitment to the ultimate goal of communism. In the contemporary period of booming German capitalism, Kautsky argued, the SPD would thus be a "revolutionary but not a revolution-making party."[27]

The onset of World War I brought these internal battles into the open, splitting the party into three separate parts. The initial popularity of the war among the party's working-class constituency forced the party leadership to choose between defending its long-standing anti-imperialist principles and holding on to its current privileged position within the political establishment of the Reich. Despite decades of propaganda within the SPD and the Second International promising immediate mobilization against efforts to begin an "imperialist war," the SPD voted overwhelmingly in support of war credits to the Reich – as did all the other major socialist parties of Europe with respect to their own national governments. The SPD left wing, led by Luxemburg and soon joined by Karl Liebknecht, denounced their erstwhile comrades as traitors to the working class and mounted a radical opposition to the Reich that resulted quickly in their arrest and imprisonment. By January 1917, as the war continued to drag on with ever greater losses, another section of the SPD – including not only Bernstein but also Kautsky himself – broke with the party center and formed the Independent Social Democratic Party (USPD), which called for an immediate peace without annexations.[28] The majority Social Democrats, however, maintained their support for the Reich government until battlefield losses and garrison mutinies in the fall of 1918 had generated a revolutionary situation.

Liberals

Theorists of the *Sonderweg* have typically argued that German liberalism in the nineteenth and early twentieth centuries was a comparatively weak and ineffective political movement. The failure of the 1848 revolution to generate full constitutional democracy, the tendency of so many leading German philosophers (beginning with Hegel) to justify monarchy and nationalism as historically progressive, and the willingness of prominent German liberals to

[27] Kautsky, quoted in Guttsman, *The German Social Democratic Party*, p. 288.
[28] Formally, the left-wing Spartacist group chose to join the USPD, but their relationship between the left and the USPD leadership was fraught with tension from the start, and the two factions split in December 1918. See Morgan, *The Socialist Left*, pp. 62–63.

lend their support to Bismarck's authoritarian government are all cited as evidence of this weakness.[29] The comparative perspective tends to cast doubt on the assumption that German liberalism was somehow fatally flawed from the outset. After all, the democratic revolutions of 1848 failed in every European country; liberalism was allied with nationalism and opposed to "radical democracy" in England and France as well as in Germany.[30] Increasingly, historians are establishing that liberalism was in fact a robust and dynamic political and social movement in the years of the Wilhelmine Reich, with a strong social base among civil servants, small businessmen, and educated city dwellers more generally.[31]

There is no doubt, however, that attitudes toward Bismarck played a decisive role in shaping the key ideological disputes among German liberals in the Second Reich. The Iron Chancellor's explicit bargain with liberal politicians – inclusion in the Prussian establishment in return for their support of the three wars that led to German unification in 1871 (with Schleswig-Holstein, Austria, and France) – was certainly very hard for the majority to turn down, and not only for obvious reasons of self-interest. The founders of the pro-Bismarck National Liberal Party could reason with some justification that, despite his close personal ties to the monarchy and the Junkers, Bismarck was accomplishing many of the goals they themselves had long advocated: the elimination of feudal barriers to free trade, the rapid industrialization of the country, and the formation of a powerful German national state. Even Bismarck's repression of domestic socialists and Catholics could be justified to the extent that one saw Marxism and Catholicism as twin threats to the "freedom of the individual," as most liberals did. The end result of this series of bargains with Bismarck, however, was to render the National Liberal Party a reliable ally of the authoritarian state – even after the Iron Chancellor himself turned away from liberal trade policies toward protectionism and support for the welfare state in the 1880s.

Another sector of German liberalism more consistently opposed Bismarck and his policies, seeing them as a direct betrayal of the ideals of 1848. The Prussian Progressive Party, founded in 1861 by liberals who objected to Kaiser Wilhelm I's decision to remove Prussia's military budget from the control of parliament, soon found themselves increasingly marginalized as the newly appointed chancellor utilized the Prussian army to build a new German Empire. Even after German unification in 1871, the Progressives continued in opposition, providing at least some degree of resistance to the authoritarian policies of the Kulturkampf (although the party was split on the issue) and the

---

[29] Dahrendorf, *Society and Democracy in Germany*; William L. Shirer, *The Rise and Fall of the Third Reich: A History of Nazi Germany* (New York: Simon and Schuster, 1960).

[30] Blackbourn and Eley, *Peculiarities of German History*.

[31] Dieter Langewiesche, *Liberalism in Germany*, trans. Christiane Banerji (Princeton, NJ: Princeton University Press, 2000); Jennifer Jenkins, *Provincial Modernity: Local Culture and Liberal Politics in fin-de-siècle Hamburg* (Ithaca, NY: Cornell University Press, 2003).

antisocialist laws.[32] They also agitated for the abolition of outdated restrictions on universal suffrage – in particular, Prussia's three-tier system of voting, which guaranteed greater parliamentary representation for feudal elites while drastically undercounting the working-class vote. In none of these causes, however, did the Progressives manage to effect meaningful political reform.

The split between the two main German liberal parties was to have important long-term consequences. Multiple efforts were made to reunify the liberal movement, but all of them ultimately failed. In 1884, for example, the new Freisinn Party united Progressives and former National Liberals who had objected to Bismarck's turn to the right, but the party fared poorly at the polls and soon split up again. At the turn of the century, the Young Liberals movement, which was associated with the National Liberal Party, tried to generate a mass base for what had been a primarily old-style party of notables; in this context, Young Liberal activists called for increased cooperation with the Progressives. Also at this time, the left liberal Friedrich Naumann developed a philosophy of "social liberalism" that combined the defense of individual rights with an increased emphasis on social solidarity among various German social classes; politically, Naumann called for an alliance of all the German left parties "from Bassermann to Bebel" – that is, from the National Liberals to the SPD. Yet despite such olive branches proffered by moderate wings in both parties, their party organizations remained entirely separate. The results could be seen clearly in the 1912 Reichstag elections, when the new Progressive People's Party (founded in 1910 from a merger of all the previous left liberal factions) nearly equaled the electoral performance of the National Liberals, with 12.3 percent of the vote for the former and 13.6 percent for the latter.[33]

Ironically, despite their frequent battles over matters of principle, neither the National Liberals nor the Progressives managed to articulate clear party ideologies detailing their precise views about the sort of polity they hoped to establish – albeit for different reasons. By the end of the Bismarck era, the National Liberals had abandoned so many basic philosophical principles of classical liberalism that they had become in effect a "party of power," willing to support Kaiser Wilhelm II and his government against all forms of political opposition. Yet the precise political content of left liberalism remained equally vague. Most progressives considered themselves supporters of what they termed a "people's community" (*Volksgemeinschaft*) that would somehow unify Germans of all social backgrounds – but this word meant different things to different factions. Thus, the People's Progressive Party combined dedicated constitutional monarchists, romantic liberal idealists, and imperialists

---

[32] For example, the law disbanding the Society of Jesus in Germany and exiling the Jesuits, which was passed overwhelming by the Reichstag in July 1872, was opposed by eleven members of the Progressive Party's Reichstag delegation, while nine voted in favor and fifteen abstained. Ellen Lovell Evans, *The German Center Party, 1870–1933: A Study in Political Catholicism* (Carbondale: Southern Illinois University Press, 1981), p. 61.

[33] Feuchtwanger, *Imperial Germany, 1850–1871*, p. 202.

who saw the defense of German national interests as the foundation for effective citizenship. Indeed, both the Progressives and the National Liberals quickly joined in the initial general patriotic enthusiasm for World War I. And while many leading Progressives did become disillusioned with the trajectory of the German military's performance over the course of the war, few were any more prepared than their National Liberal counterparts for the total collapse of the Reich in the fall of 1918.

Conservatives

Like the liberals, imperial Germany's conservatives were split into two rival factions – and once again, the primary source of the dispute was attitudes toward Bismarck. The Old Conservatives in Prussia before German unification were made up of monarchists, evangelical Protestants, and traditional agrarian elites – the so-called Junkers – who stubbornly resisted modernization in any form. Given the direct control by the Junkers over vast estates in East Prussia with thousands of peasants, along with the three-tier system of voting, they managed to translate their economic and social power into a significant degree of representation in the Prussian parliament. But while the Conservatives were naturally staunch supporters of the Hohenzollern dynasty, they also objected in principle to bureaucratic forms of state centralization that might limit Prussian autonomy along with that of the various smaller kingdoms that made up the German Confederation. Thus, as Bismarck began to build the new unified German Reich through the use of modern techniques of military organization and social mobilization, the majority of Conservatives went into opposition. Conservative concern about the effects of Bismarck's policies increased further toward the end of the Kulturkampf, as evangelical Lutherans began to fear that the state's attacks on the Catholic Church could ultimately have pernicious effects on Protestantism as well. And while the Conservatives uniformly detested and feared social democracy, Bismarck's willingness during the 1880s to promote an extensive welfare state in order to defang worker opposition appeared to many of them to be another dangerous departure from noble German traditions of the past.

A smaller group of conservatives – the so-called Free Conservatives – rallied to Bismarck's side, arguing that the Iron Chancellor's promotion of German state interests in a hostile international environment should be supported, even if this required a certain degree of compromise with traditional conservative principles. Many Free Conservatives were leaders of industries that had received substantial state support during Bismarck's industrialization drive. Not surprisingly, after 1871 the Free Conservatives frequently collaborated in the Reichstag with the National Liberals, forming a reliable pro-Bismarck coalition.

After Wilhelm II's accession to the throne in 1888 and the dismissal of Bismarck in 1890, the conservative movement began to metamorphose.[34]

---

[34] For a detailed discussion, see Geoff Eley, *Reshaping the German Right: Radical Nationalism and Political Change after Bismarck* (New Haven: Yale University Press, 1980).

The movement now saw an infusion into its ranks of lower-middle-class arti-sans and farmers who sought protection from Germany's increasingly capital-ist economy. At the same time, the conservatives' message became increasingly mixed with new ideological forms of anti-Semitism and extreme nationalism. "Patriotic" clubs such as the Eastern Marches league and the Pan-German Asso-ciation agitated for German annexation of huge new swaths of territory in Cen-tral Europe to advance the interests of the "German race" in the "Darwinian struggle" against foreign and domestic enemies. Attitudes of this sort pene-trated into the highest reaches of the German High Command. During World War I, such thinking played an important role in influencing General Erich Ludendorff and Field Marshal Paul von Hindenburg to reject the increasing calls for an end to World War I without annexations, as the Allies demanded, and generated the impulse to create the German Fatherland Party, which ral-lied millions of nationalists against the supposedly defeatist policies of the SPD, Zentrum, and left liberals in the Reichstag.

The Center

The Center Party was the first Catholic party in Europe with a genuine mass base. Yet it was formed almost by accident. The party's origins can be traced to 1858, when a small group of deputies in the Prussian parliament decided to organize a separate Catholic fraction. The new party was dubbed the Zentrum because of a dispute among the founders about whether the word "Catholi-cism" should appear explicitly in the party's name; some wished to establish a more ecumenical Christian party, while others felt that without a direct asso-ciation with Catholic identity, the party would have less electoral appeal to its key constituencies.[35]

Still, the party was nevertheless remarkably successful in forging a national network of loyal activists. One reason was that its most important early leader, Ludwig Windthorst, was a highly effective orator and parliamentarian who courageously organized Catholic resistance to the Kulturkampf by positioning the Center as a reliable promoter of tolerance for all German citizens. Affec-tive ties to Windthorst among his followers were an important glue in the early, vulnerable years of the Center Party's history; support for Windthorst and the Center then grew dramatically as the Kulturkampf was rolled back. Overall, the experience of severe state repression had the effect of cementing German Catholic loyalty to the Zentrum in a way that parallels the effect of the antisocialist laws for supporters of the SPD.

The Center also maintained its cohesion simply because every other major political force in Germany was unpalatable to most Catholic politicians. The Social Democrats had by 1891 adopted an orthodox Marxism which portrayed religion in all its forms as the "opiate of the people." The National Liberals enthusiastically supported the Kulturkampf, and the National Liberals and

---

[35] For a comprehensive history of the German Center Party, see Evans, *The German Center Party, 1870–1933*.

Progressives alike favored a secular education system. While some Catholic landowners supported the old Conservative party because of its firm stand in favor of political decentralization, the party's close association with evangelical Lutheranism rendered it, too, an uncomfortable home at best for the vast majority of German Catholics. Thus, the Zentrum maintained a fairly consistent level of representation in the Reichstag throughout the history of the German Reich, World War I, and into the Weimar period.

Chaos, 1918–1923

The level of disruption in the German polity, economy, and society in the immediate aftermath of the country's unexpected total defeat in World War I can scarcely be overstated. In the five years between the abdication of Kaiser Wilhelm II in November 1918 and the arrest of Hitler after his beer hall putsch in November 1923, Germany experienced an almost unbelievable number of political and economic crises: a democratic revolution that brought down the German monarchy; several attempts to foment a socialist revolution in the months after that; secessionist movements in Bavaria and the Rhineland that flared up throughout the postwar period; a paralyzing internal debate over the terms of the Versailles Treaty of June 1919; the failed Kapp Putsch by disgruntled military officers in March 1920; the assassinations by right-wing radicals of Matthias Erzberger in August 1921 and Walter Rathenau in June 1922; the invasion of the Ruhr by the French army in January 1923; a year of disastrous hyperinflation stemming from Germany's policy of "passive resistance" to the French occupation; and, finally, several new uprisings by both the communist left and the nationalist right. Even the end of hyperinflation and the suppression of revolutionary threats by the end of 1923 was achieved only through a partial suspension of parliamentary sovereignty and a policy of economic stabilization that generated serious unemployment among industrial workers – flaws that came back to haunt the Weimar Republic as a new global economic crisis erupted in the fall of 1929.

Indeed, each of these crises led to serious internal debates within each of Weimar's political parties. Thus, the chaotic early years of the Weimar Republic provide another excellent test of the ability of party leaders to overcome collective action problems in maintaining activist loyalty in a period of high uncertainty. Again, we should expect to find that rational political actors in these early years of the Weimar Republic would be forced to make a whole series of short-term compromises with their professed principles in order to cope with rapidly changing circumstances. Against this background, genuine ideologues should stand out for their consistency concerning their vision of Germany's future regime type.

Analyzing the formation of the Weimar party system from this theoretical vantage point allows us to analyze its origins in rather different terms from those conventionally used by previous historians and political scientists. First, while it is obviously true that most Weimar parties were founded on the basis of the inherited organizational networks of the Social Democrats, National Liberals, Progressives, and Conservatives of the Imperial Reichstag, taking seriously the problem of collective action under high uncertainty in the immediate postwar period forces us to explain precisely how these inherited networks were maintained despite the obvious short-run incentives for individual defection facing party activists in such a turbulent environment. Looking more closely at the microfoundations of Weimar party organizations, too, reveals that the degree of continuity between the Reich party system and that of Weimar has frequently been overstated. It is true that the results of the elections for the new National Assembly in January 1919 could be divided into percentages for socialists, liberals, conservatives, and the Center that roughly resembled those achieved by these broad groupings in the last Reichstag election of 1912.[36] However, the parties that competed for these slices of the German electorate were in many cases now organized around quite different principles compared to those of their prewar predecessors. Moreover, an emphasis on party system continuity fails to explain how two entirely new extremist parties formed after 1918 – the Communists and National Socialists – ultimately outstripped all their competitors, making democratic consolidation in Germany impossible.

We analyze first the German parties that managed to maintain or redefine clear ideological principles in the immediate postwar period – the SPD, the Communist Party of Germany (KPD), the German National People's Party (DNVP), and the National Socialist German Workers' Party (NSDAP or Nazis) – showing how all four of these parties managed to maintain collective action among their core group of activists. We then examine the four major parties that failed to arrive at clear, consistent definitions of the principles of political membership they hoped to establish in Germany's future – the Independent Social Democratic Party (USPD), the German Democratic Party (DDP), the German People's Party (DVP), and the Center Party. The USPD failed to survive the chaos period, while the DDP and DVP both suffered serious defections among their original core activists, leaving the two liberal party organizations fatally weakened by the end of 1923. The Zentrum, too, was badly split, but it managed to maintain its organizational cohesion because of the continuing lack of acceptable partisan options for sincere Catholics.

Social Democrats

The literature on the role of the Social Democratic Party and the fate of the Weimar Republic is vast and contentious – unsurprisingly, given that for most of this period the SPD was the largest party in the German parliament and the one most closely associated with the republic's foundation. At the core of the scholarly debate about the SPD's role in either hindering or advancing the cause of democracy in the 1920s is the question of SPD ideology. On the one

---

[36] Peukert, for example, writes: "Apart from some changes at the margins, these results display a considerable degree of electoral continuity between the monarchy and the Republic." *The Weimar Republic*, p. 33.

hand, Marxists have criticized the Social Democrats for not taking Marxist ideology seriously enough. From this point of view – first articulated by former party member Robert Michels before World War I – the SPD had become an essentially bureaucratic organization, divorced from its original ideals.[37] Those who accept this argument see the SPD leadership as too skeptical of the genuine revolutionary impulses of the German working class after the fall of the Reich; too willing to make common cause with reactionary forces to put down worker uprisings by force; too quick to abandon even basic social achievements of the 1918 revolution, such as the eight-hour day; and too spineless to mount an effective social resistance to the rise of fascism during the early 1930s.[38] On the other hand, non-Marxists (including some social democrats) have criticized the SPD leadership from precisely the opposite point of view, accusing it of an overly rigid ideological approach to party politics that prevented it from making the necessary strategic alliances with farmers, white-collar workers, and liberals that might have helped consolidate social support for Weimar democracy.[39]

The definition of ideology adopted in this study forces us to side more closely with the latter point of view. By the end of the Wilhelmine period, the SPD had consolidated around a very clear and explicit definition of the future polity for which it stood – namely, a fully proletarian society in which private property would be abolished and bourgeois exploitation overcome. Under Kautsky's theoretical guidance, the party had clearly defined its role in the "inevitable" historical process that would generate this result: it would not make the revolution actively but rather would help to organize and educate the proletariat to prepare for its eventual hegemony. Such a strategy in effect defined membership in the future socialist polity in rigid class terms. The industrial working class and those intellectuals who saw clearly the future lines of history would inherit the new world; all other classes were destined to disappear, and thus political alliances with them could only be tactical.

The fact that the SPD had succeeded so spectacularly following this ideology and strategy under the Second Reich made it unlikely that the party leadership would easily change course as circumstances changed. Even during World War I, as the radical left and the independent social democrats (USPD) peeled away from the Majority Social Democratic Party (MSPD) in protest over the

---

37 Robert Michels, *Political Parties: A Sociological Study of the Oligarchical Tendencies of Modern Democracy* (New York: Free Press 1966 [1915]).

38 Eric E. Weitz, *Creating German Communism: From Popular Protests to Socialist State* (Princeton, NJ: Princeton University Press, 1997), pp. 84–91.

39 See the illuminating analysis of the SPD in Sheri Berman, *The Social Democratic Moment: Ideas and Politics in the Making of Interwar Europe* (Cambridge, MA: Harvard University Press, 1998). I follow Berman's account closely here. A similar approach is taken by Donna Harsch, *German Social Democracy and the Rise of Nazism* (Chapel Hill: University of North Carolina Press, 1993). Harsch argues that the SPD was ideologically inconsistent but that its "organizational culture" had become doctrinaire in ways that severely limited the party's tactical flexibility. Because Harsch's understanding of organizational culture focuses on issues of community membership and norms, it is fairly close to my own definition of ideology; therefore, there is no real contradiction between Harsch's approach and the present analysis.

latter's support for war budgets, the party leadership under Friedrich Ebert continued to see its primary duty as pressing for long-standing demands within the Reich political system – such as an end to the Prussian three-tier electoral system that inhibited full representation of working-class voters – rather than pursue "revolutionary" goals that would arguably lead only to renewed state repression of the party. The Bolshevik Revolution in Russia in November 1917 further reinforced the MSPD's commitment to Marxist orthodoxy, since Leninism appeared to most mainstream German social democrats as an unjustified form of revolutionary "voluntarism" fundamentally at odds with Marx's teachings.

When General Ludendorff handed power to a coalition of the MSPD, Center, and National Liberals in October 1918 – largely in order to saddle these parties with the onus of presiding officially over Germany's impending defeat – and military mutinies brought down the Reich itself a month later, the MSPD leaders found themselves nearly as surprised as their bourgeois colleagues in the Reichstag. Indeed, Social Democratic deputy Philip Scheidemann's spontaneous announcement of the establishment of the republic to revolutionary crowds in Berlin on November 9 was met with severe disapproval by party leader Ebert, who saw such a move as precipitous. The rapid spread of the *Räte* (council) movement throughout German cities and military units, which appeared to raise the prospect that the revolution could immediately turn "socialist" in the near future, forced the SPD to take a stand on yet another regime-defining issue.

Overall, however, the SPD leadership in this crucial period remained remarkably unified around what it saw as a genuinely socialist strategy to help defend and consolidate Germany's new democratic institutions in the long-term interest of the proletariat. The Social Democrats could, and did, present the events of November 1918 as the culmination of their long-stated Marxist strategy to take power as a result of imperialism's "inner contradictions," rather than risking the party's hard-won influence through an unwise frontal assault on the state. And there were truly significant ideological gains for mainstream Social Democrats to celebrate: the monarchy had disintegrated; the most reactionary officers of the German military had resigned; the three-tier voting system in Prussia was finally abolished (ultimately allowing the SPD to hold power in that crucial state throughout the Weimar period); leading bourgeois politicians now acknowledged the legitimate importance of negotiating economic policy with socialist union representatives; and, by 1919, Ebert himself had been selected by the new National Assembly as the first Reich president of the Weimar Republic.

Thus, it seemed quite ideologically consistent to Ebert, Minister of Defense Gustav Noske, and other top MSPD leaders to do everything in their power to defend these gains against "threats" from left-wing forces that hoped to radicalize the November Revolution. The MSPD saw the *Räte* movement as a potentially dangerous trend that could ultimately generate an outcome similar to that in Soviet Russia; therefore the party leadership did its best to channel the councils toward purely economic goals. The MSPD also condemned the efforts of the USPD to mobilize revolutionary shop stewards and other activists in several German cities to establish a "socialist republic." Finally, the January 1919 uprising of the Spartacists in Berlin led by Luxemburg and Liebknecht to establish an immediate proletarian dictatorship constituted a direct threat to MSPD political supremacy that must be put down at all costs. Such reasoning explains why the MSPD decided to mobilize the so-called Freikorps – militias made up of demobilized soldiers with radical right views – to crush the Spartacist uprising, even if this meant the deaths of thousands of workers and communist activists and the murders of Luxemburg and Liebknecht themselves. The MSPD-Freikorps alliance continued through the spring of 1919, crushing a general strike in Munich in March and the self-proclaimed "Bavarian Soviet Republic" in May, again in each case at the cost of hundreds of lives.

The continued fidelity of the MSPD leadership to its brand of orthodox Marxism – and its consistent, even violent opposition to the sort of "leftism" it had so long opposed – paid immediate political dividends. The vast majority of industrial workers, who had been inculcated in orthodox Marxist ideology for their entire working lives, followed the mainstream Social Democratic leadership rather than joining any radical opposition group. The MSPD maintained its strong electoral support in the January 1919 elections to the Constituent Assembly, attaining 37.9 percent of the vote; the USPD managed only 7.6 percent, while the newly formed KPD chose not to participate.[40] This put the MSPD in a position to exercise major influence over the future shape of the Weimar Republic's constitution – a heady political position for a formerly outlawed party that had adopted its orthodox Marxist party program at Erfurt not three decades earlier.

The superior party discipline of the MSPD sustained its core leadership and activist networks throughout the remaining crises of the early Weimar period. The party was the key political force pushing for a policy of fulfillment of the provisions of the Versailles Treaty, a position it maintained against rather bitter and deep social hostility. It helped to mobilize the mass strikes that undermined the right-wing Kapp Putsch of March 1920. And while the MSPD was temporarily threatened by a surge of electoral support for the USPD in the elections of June 1920, owing to protest voting by workers who objected to the MSPD's role in signing the Versailles Treaty and its failure to push for the nationalization of industry, the mainstream Social Democrats emerged in an even stronger position on the left when the USPD disintegrated a few months later. Even during the hyperinflation of 1923, when most German political parties were suffering serious budgetary problems, SPD finances remained relatively sound due to the party network's continuing ability to raise membership dues from its loyal constituents.

Still, the remarkable success of the SPD in the early years of Weimar concealed a limitation that necessarily accompanied its ideological recommitment

---

[40] See figures in Kershaw, *Weimar: Why Did German Democracy Fail?*, table I, p. 204.

to orthodox Marxism: officially, the party remained wedded to its professed definition of the future German polity as a "workers' state" that would finally triumph when private property disappeared in capitalism's final crisis.[41] Party propaganda spread to socialist unions and clubs throughout the country continued to portray all nonproletarian social classes as either enemies (the aristocracy and bourgeoisie) or anachronisms (the petty bourgeoisie and peasantry). In many respects, the party and its supporters continued to be only "negatively integrated" into the Weimar political system – despite the fact that this system owed its very origins to the MSPD.

The MSPD's orthodox Marxism helps to explain why, having secured a dominant position in the National Assembly in 1919, it nevertheless ceded the leading role in drafting the new German constitution to liberals from the DDP.[42] Ideological orthodoxy also prevented the MSPD from building stable coalitions in order to secure its long-term role in the political establishment. Indeed, throughout this period, the party's local activists remained highly resistant to compromises with the leading liberal parties, let alone the monarchist right – a tendency that was augmented further as a result of the infusion into the SPD of USPD activists after that party's breakup in September 1922. Thus, after serving as a partner in most ruling Weimar government coalitions from 1919 until November 1922 – even joining with the DDP and Center parties to form the so-called Alliance of the Constitutional Middle after the assassination of Rathenau – the SPD chose to withdraw from the government to protest the inclusion of the right-wing liberal German People's Party under Chancellor Wilhelm Cuno in November 1922. After a major internal debate, the SPD rejoined the government of DVP leader Gustav Stresemann in August 1923, only to leave it just three months later to protest its use of police force to oust communist governments in Saxony and Thuringia. Despite the SPD's formative role in shaping the Weimar Republic, it remained in opposition to parliamentary governments for the next five years. The ironic result of this principled unwillingness to collaborate with class enemies, however, was that the SPD ended up in government only during times of defeat and crisis, foregoing the chance to gain credit among voters for subsequent periods of growth and stability.

KPD

Given the initial marginality of the Spartacist movement during World War I, it is surprising that Weimar Germany ended up with not one but two ideologically consistent socialist mass parties. While the mainstream SPD set forth a clear and consistent definition of the criteria for membership in the

---

[41] This goal was reconfirmed in the new MSPD program of 1921 at Goerlitz. See "Programm der Sozialdemokratischen Partei," Goerlitz, 23 September 1921, reprinted in Wolfgang Treue, ed., *Deutsche Parteiprogramme, 1861–1956* (Göttingen: Musterschmidt, 1956), pp. 101–106.

[42] As Michael Bernhard explains, "the constitution did not figure prominently in the demands of the labor movement." Bernhard, *Institutions and the Fate of Democracy*, p. 44.

"socialist polity" by working to build an "electoral fatherland" for the working class in advance of the inevitable collapse of capitalism, left Marxists such as Luxemburg and Liebknecht had remained comparatively vague concerning the precise shape of the future workers' utopia they hoped to establish through immediate revolutionary action. To some extent this vagueness was itself a matter of principle, because left Marxists objected to any attempt by socialist leaders to define communism in advance rather than let it emerge from the spontaneous actions of workers themselves. After the crushing of the Spartacist revolt in January 1919, the new Communist Party of Germany could for a time only limp along with a tiny group of committed members, subject to intense political repression.

The party's future prospects were transformed by the creation in Soviet Russia of the Communist International, or Comintern. The Comintern was founded in March 1919 to replace the Second International, which Lenin saw as hopelessly corrupted by Kautskyan "opportunism." Because the first Comintern Congress was held in Moscow at the height of the Russian Civil War, when the survival of Soviet Russia itself was hardly a sure thing, no immediate material aid to the KPD was forthcoming from the organization at this stage. It is clearly a mistake to think that German Communists in this initial period were in any sense following direct orders from the Kremlin; instead, they continued to mobilize around the indigenous left Marxist traditions of Luxemburg and Liebknecht.[43] Still, by establishing a rival international organization to mobilize socialist support for the Bolshevik cause at this early stage, Lenin managed to give KPD activists both a renewed self-confidence and a special international and domestic status in its competition with its much larger rivals, the MSPD and USPD. By the fall of 1919, KPD leader Paul Levi felt confident enough to initiate a major purge of "syndicalist" elements that were unwilling to accept the sort of centralized direction now considered necessary for a serious revolutionary communist party.

The second Comintern Congress in June–July 1920 can be seen as the true beginning of the KPD as a distinct ideological party. Lenin's twenty-one conditions for joining the Communist International – which included the demands that all member parties immediately remove "reformists" and "opportunists" from their ranks, adopt Bolshevik rules of "democratic centralism" to increase internal discipline, carry out the orders of the Comintern leadership without question, and prioritize the foreign policy interests of the Soviet state above those of their own governments – were consciously designed to ensure that communist parties everywhere would be ideologically and organizationally separate from their "social democratic" competitors. This strategy worked exactly as intended in Germany, reinforcing the connection between the KPD and the Soviet global revolutionary mission, branding the USPD and MSPD as loathsome opportunists, and ultimately splitting the USPD apart. The KPD now clearly and consistently stood for a definition of the German polity as a

---

[43] Weitz, *Creating German Communism*.

future "Soviet republic," organized institutionally along Bolshevik lines – and after absorbing the USPD's left wing, it had its own significant national activist network as well.

From 1920 to 1923, however, the party remained in a state of revolutionary turmoil. The fragility of the Weimar Republic appeared to open up the possibility of successful revolutionary action, and periodic instructions from Comintern leader Grigorii Zinoviev to launch revolutionary uprisings in one or another seemingly promising location made it difficult to preserve organizational discipline among leftists in the party organization. At the same time, the party's increasing subordination to the Comintern led to a whole series of leadership crises. Thus, Luxemburg's former ally Paul Levi was expelled for criticizing Bolshevik strategy in the failed "March action" in Berlin in March 1921; he joined the USPD, and then after the latter party's demise, the SPD. Levi's immediate successor, Ernst Meyer, was in turn purged on the orders of Zinoviev in the fall of 1922, accused of being overly conciliatory toward the SPD in its efforts to organize a general working-class "defense of the republic" after the Rathenau assassination. The same fate befell the next KPD leader, Heinrich Brandler, after the disastrous attempt to launch a proletarian revolution in Saxony in October 1923.

Despite these repeated crises and purges, the subordination of the KPD to the Soviet Union served over time to rid the party of its more independent members – and thus to reshape it more consistently along classic Leninist lines. Even after the debacle of October 1923, the party's connection with the newly declared Union of Soviet Socialist Republics, the world's first avowedly socialist state, made it highly attractive to German left-wing antirepublicans – particularly to the growing ranks of the unemployed, for whom the SPD could plausibly be portrayed as too wedded to the interests of German capitalism. For the inner circle of KPD activists, too, the clear picture of the political future provided by alliance with the USSR provided a degree of confidence that greatly facilitated collective action oriented toward long-term party goals. For these true believers, the party's revolutionary failures in the first few years of the Weimar Republic were nevertheless noble efforts to acquire experience and "hardness" for the inevitable proletarian revolution to come.

DNVP

The central role of the German National People's Party in the rise and fall of Weimar democracy has received comparatively little theoretical attention. Yet the DNVP, and not the NSDAP, was by far the most significant right-wing "anti-system party" during the Weimar Republic's first decade, receiving between 10 and 20 percent of the vote in every national election between 1919 and 1928. Indeed, DNVP leader Alfred Hugenberg's strategic decision to ally with Hitler in 1930, which provided the Nazis invaluable financial and organizational backing, was crucial to Hitler's ultimate success. Thus, understanding the dynamics of DNVP party organization in this period is of unquestionable importance.

Most historians have seen the DNVP as something of an ideological hodgepodge.[44] The party was founded out of the wreckage of the conservative cause in the wake of Germany's defeat in World War I, and included all of the disparate groupings that had become associated with the Conservative Party in the last years of the Reich: the old core elite of Junkers, Old Conservatives, and Free Conservatives; advocates of German imperialism and militarism; big industrialists with a hatred of democracy and socialism; anti-Semitic advocates of German "racial" supremacy; and reactionary elements associated with the Protestant and (to a much lesser extent) Catholic churches. The party's organization, too, remained quite loose by comparison with those of its main competitors. The Old Conservative Party proper under Count Kuno von Westarp joined the DNVP with some reluctance and even maintained its formal organizational autonomy from the DNVP throughout the Weimar period. The various *völkische* clubs and movements that made up much of the party's activist base continued to resist centralized direction. Many big-business backers of the party contributed simply in order to ensure a political counterweight to socialism. It is not surprising, then, that historians have tended to argue that the DNVP's unity was solely negative, centering on the hostility of all of its members to Germany's new republican form of government.[45]

Again, such an interpretation appears unsatisfying once one takes the collective action problem of national party formation seriously. Many Germans hated the Weimar Republic, but far from all of them contributed their personal time and resources to the DNVP; on the contrary, as we have seen, the early Weimar years witnessed a plethora of antisystem parties and movements of both left and right, most of which existed only for a short period. Given the intense political uncertainty facing individual political activists after November 1918, how did the DNVP leadership manage to keep the party's disparate elements together, by and large, in order to build what became Germany's largest right-wing party in the mid-1920s?

I argue here that the key to the DNVP's success was its clarity and consistency about the core of the regime type for which it stood – namely, the restoration of the monarchy.[46] This single ideological principle served to unite the disparate factions of the party around a consensual, specific notion of the political future – one that remained credible as long as not only Kaiser Wilhelm II and the Crown Prince (who had both formally abdicated) but also the former kaiser's many other sons and grandsons remained alive and well in exile. Membership in the restored German monarchy, according to the DNVP leadership, would be organized around the same status hierarchies as in the nineteenth century, with

---

44 See especially the excellent study by Lewis Hertzman, *DNVP: Right-Wing Opposition in the Weimar Republic, 1918–1924* (Lincoln: University of Nebraska Press, 1963).

45 John A. Leopold, for example, writes that "only opposition united [the DNVP]; it was impossible to rally racists, Pan-Germans, Christian Socialists, responsible parliamentarians and rabid radicals behind a specific, positive program." See Leopold, *Alfred Hugenberg: The Radical Nationalist Campaign against the Weimar Republic* (New Haven: Yale University Press, 1977).

46 Walter H. Kaufmann, *Monarchism in the Weimar Republic* (New York: Octagon Books, 1973).

nobles, clergy, and military officers restored to privileged political positions. As long as the monarchical principle remained at the center of the party's program, the DNVP remained a united and successful national force. The moment that principle was questioned at the top levels of the party in 1929, its unity quickly disintegrated.

Admittedly, the ideal of a Hohenzollern restoration could be, and was, interpreted in very different ways by different DNVP factions. In comparison to the ideology of legitimism worked out by the Comte de Chambord in nineteenth-century France, monarchism in the Weimar Republic was undeniably less philosophically elaborate and comparatively more reliant on affect for the symbols and personages of the departed Kaiserreich. DNVP supporters were united, for example, in their demand that the imperial black-white-red flag be restored in place of the black-red-gold of the republic. Many of them also participated avidly in the growing "Bismarck cult," which centered around celebrations of the Iron Chancellor's birthday and ritual pilgrimages to his former home in Friedrichsruh.[47]

Still, there is ample evidence that for DNVP activists from a variety of the party's associated factions, the myth of monarchical return possessed a value rational as well as an emotional quality. To declare one's undying faith in the principle of monarchy – even if it could be realized only in the distant future – marked one as an irreconcilable opponent of the democracy and socialism, the twin philosophies that for most of the German right threatened to undermine the nation's heroic spirit and leave it defenseless against foreign and domestic enemies. As DNVP leader Count Posadowski-Wehner told the Weimar National Assembly,

We have always been loyal and devoted servants of our dynasties, with whom the German people . . . seemed inseparably united. We have always regarded the emperor-dom, which once upon a time originated as the realization of a centuries-old longing of the German people, as the culmination of and the safest bond for the unity of our fatherland. . . . Now we shall cooperate conscientiously and objectively to rebuild our country. This, however, does not mean that monarchy is not the best form of government conceivable, especially for Germany.[48]

This commitment to a positive regime alternative to replace the hated Weimar Republic allowed the diverse factions in the DNVP to cooperate over the long run, even if many individual party leaders admitted privately that they had no particular notion of precisely how Hohenzollern restoration was to take place. Thus, the proposal by party leader Oskar Hergt in September 1919 to associate the DNVP with a "program of order" in which the principle of monarchy was missing met with severe disapproval from his party colleagues; the final party platform approved in April 1920 – never altered until the party's

---

[47] For details on the Bismarck cult, see Richard E. Frankel, *Bismarck's Shadow: The Cult of Leadership and the Transformation of the German Right, 1898–1945* (Oxford: Berg, 2005).
[48] Quoted in Kaufmann, *Monarchism in the Weimar Republic*, p. 62.

final dissolution in 1933 – stated clearly that "in the Reich we are striving for a renewal of the monarchy erected by the Hohenzollerns."[49] Efforts by radical *völkische* elements within the DNVP to elevate anti-Semitism above monarchy as a party principle were also consistently rebuffed; after Rathenau's murder, when public opinion turned strongly against rightist extremism, the most committed anti-Semites left the DNVP to found the short-lived German Racial Freedom Party.[50]

Armed with this consensus on political principles, the DNVP provided the most consistent opposition to the Weimar coalition in the early days of the republic. The party voted as a bloc to reject the terms of the Versailles Treaty and remained intransigent enemies of the policy of "fulfillment" of its terms pursued by the SPD, DDP, and Center. Many of the DNVP's leaders were closely associated with the Kapp Putsch in 1920, and none of them openly criticized it.[51] Despite several overtures from DVP leader Stresemann and pressure from some of its big-business supporters, the party refused to join any governing coalitions in Weimar's chaotic first years. This stand of uncompromising opposition brought significant rewards at the ballot box: the DNVP received 10.3 percent of the vote in the January 1919 elections to the National Assembly, 15.1 percent in the June 1920 elections to the Reichstag, and 19.5 percent of the vote in the elections of May 1924.[52]

The Nazi Party

The literature on the Nazi Party is, for obvious reasons, far too vast to summarize briefly here. In its broadest outlines, however, the central debate about Nazism's origins has revolved around the extent to which its initial appeal and later rise to power can be explained as the result of "irrational" or rational causes. The early postwar literature on Hitler's rise to power tended to emphasize the importance of psychological factors accounting for conversion to Nazism, such as Hitler's personal charisma and the longing for a strong leader in Germany's disrupted society.[53] More recently, scholars have

---

49 "Grundsätze der Deutschnationalen Volkspartei, 1920," in Treue, *Deutsche Patreiprogramme*, p. 111. Hertzman argues that this passage was ambiguous enough to allow for the possibility of a non-Hohenzollern restoration, thus satisfying those Nationalists who felt that Kaiser Wilhelm's defeat and his conduct in exile had irretrievably sullied his reputation and that of his family. Nevertheless, in comparison to the official programs of all other Weimar parties, the DNVP's embrace of monarchy was remarkably clear and consistent through 1928. See Hertzman, *DNVP*, p. 87.

50 This is not to deny, of course, that the DNVP leadership was itself generally deeply anti-Semitic. Hertzman, *DNVP*, pp. 141–164.

51 The DNVP's failure to condemn the putsch and its increasing indulgence of anti-Semitic and racist rhetoric did lead Free Conservatives such as Siegfried von Kardoff to leave the party and join the DVP. Because Kardoff was also opposed to monarchism, however, this split tends to provide further evidence in favor of my thesis. See ibid., pp. 116–119.

52 Kershaw, *Weimar: Why Did German Democracy Fail?*, table I, p. 204.

53 Alan Bullock, *Hitler: A Study in Tyranny* (New York: Harper and Row, 1962); Hannah Arendt, *The Origins of Totalitarianism* (New York: Harcourt, Brace, and World, 1966).

questioned this assumption, pointing out that the Nazis' economic programs had substantial appeal, and important sectors of German society may have chosen to join or vote for the party for entirely rational, self-interested reasons.[54]

The Weberian theory of ideology presented in this book suggests that both points of view contain elements of truth. The situation of extreme social uncertainty facing most Germans after World War I clearly did increase the emotional appeal of radical nationalist movements, especially for such marginalized groups as demobilized soldiers, disaffected youth, and failed academics. An emphasis on social dislocation alone, however, cannot explain why Hitler's NSDAP rather than any number of competing *völkische* groups emerged in the end as the strongest antisystem party in Weimar Germany. Brustein is clearly right to insist that there must have also been instrumentally rational reasons for individuals to choose to ally with Hitler in particular. But because his study and dataset on party membership begin only in 1925, he cannot explain the rational basis of the choices of Hitler's earliest converts to remain loyal to the party in the face of serious individual temptations to defect for self-interested reasons.

A close examination of Nazi Party history from its foundation in 1919 shows that Hitler's relatively clear and consistent ideology played a central role in its successful mobilization of collective action. When the German Workers' Party was founded in January 1919 by Anton Drexler and Karl Herrer, it was indeed just one of a myriad of regional racist groupings with similar anti-Semitic, antirepublican platforms. Hitler joined the party in September and became its propaganda chief by the end of the year, arguing that it make as its explicit goal the ultimate seizure of political power. By the spring of 1920, the newly renamed National Socialist German Workers' Party began to grow dynamically – first of all in Bavaria but increasingly on a national scale as well. By the beginning of 1921, the NSDAP had about three thousand members.[55] To some extent the success of Nazi recruitment in these early years was due simply to the emotional effects of Hitler's frequent speeches at party gatherings. At the same time, however, utilizing his control over the party newspaper, the *Völkische Beobachter*, Hitler began to outline a picture of Germany's political future that stood out for its clarity and consistency in comparison with competing ultranationalist programs. Three principles above all underlay Hitler's speeches and writings in this period: an uncompromising Social Darwinist theory of racial "struggle" as the motor of history; the ideal of rebirth of the German Reich as a result of the conquest of new "living space" (*Lebensraum*) in Eastern Europe and Russia; and the leader principle (*Führerprinzip*).

The first of these principles, Social Darwinism, was a widespread tenet of nationalist thinking throughout early twentieth-century Europe. The claim that

---

54 Richard F. Hamilton, *Who Voted for Hitler?* (Princeton, NJ: Princeton University Press, 1982); William Brustein, *The Logic of Evil: Social Origins of the Nazi Party, 1925–1933* (New Haven: Yale University Press, 1996).

55 Orlow, *History of the Nazi Party*, p. 25.

defeat in World War I had been due to a "stab in the back" by disloyal, antinational elements – in particular, the Social Democrats and the Jewish conspiracy
that supposedly controlled them – could be heard not only among partisans
of all of Weimar's nationalist movements but also in respectable salons and
academic lecture halls throughout the country. Still, Hitler's elaborate fantasy
that one could explain all of world history through a systematic examination
of the "bloodlines" that animated one or another regime type stood out for
its quasi-intellectual sweep and ambition. Similarly, Hitler's particular conception of Germans as descendants of the superior Aryan race, along with his
pathological depiction of Jews as "subhuman" parasites who could live only
by sucking the blood of the German "*Volk*," was notable not so much for
its originality but instead for the monomaniacal consistency and passion with
which he continually expounded this theme.

The notion of *Lebensraum* as the ultimate goal of German foreign policy
stemmed directly from Hitler's theory of race struggle. As Turner has shown,
Hitler's vision of Aryan rule in a new Third Reich was built around a vision
of a new agrarian society in which the German *Volk* would be freed of urban
corruption and returned to a "healthy" relationship with the soil.[56] Hitler continually argued that Germany's defeat in World War I had been the direct result
of the weakening of national will due to the corrupting effects of impersonal
urban life, and thus only conquest of vast territories to the east could serve
to renew the German heroic spirit. Here, too, there were many precedents for
Hitler's thinking, including not only the annexationist goals of the Fatherland
Party but also the concept of a German-dominated Mitteleuropa advocated
by liberals such as Naumann. Yet no other German ideologue so consistently
envisioned Germany's role as the leader of a struggle against enemies of the
"Aryan race" that would be fought on a genuinely global scale.

The third key element of Hitler's ideology, the leader principle, provided
not only the mechanism through which he promised to achieve victory in the
struggle for *Lebensraum* but also one of Hitler's key criteria for membership
in the future Nazi polity. From an early age, Hitler saw himself as fulfilling
a historic destiny to rebuild the German nation by imposing unquestioning,
disciplined obedience on the entire citizenry. Such discipline would begin with
total subordination to the leader within the Nazi Party itself; once the party had
attained full power over the state, the leader principle could then be extended
to all other organizations within the polity, economy, and culture. As early
as the summer of 1921 Hitler insisted on such strict obedience to his party
leadership, threatening to resign if this policy were not adopted.

Combined, these three principles defined quite clearly just who would be
considered the core members of a new Nazi polity: namely, racially "pure"
Aryans willing to obey the leader without question in a violent battle for
control of the entire planet. Setting out the key principles of Hitler's ideology

---

[56] Henry Ashby Turner, "Fascism and Modernization: Utopian Anti-Modernism," *World Politics*
24(4, July 1972): 547–562.

also helps to clarify what was not central to it – in particular, economic policy. While Hitler did evince a consistent disdain for what he saw as the weakness and materialism of the German big bourgeoisie, he had no interest in imposing state ownership over the means of production. The "socialism" in National Socialism, he insisted from the beginning, signified only the collective, unified willpower that would emerge in a truly Aryan Reich. As Hitler put it in 1922,

Every truly national principle is in the final analysis social, that is: whoever is prepared to devote himself so completely to his Volk that he recognizes no higher idea than the welfare of his Volk, whoever understands our great anthem "Deutschland, Deutschland über Alles" to mean that nothing in this world is more important to him than this Germany, Volk and land, land and Volk, he is a socialist.[57]

Hitler's vagueness about the economic policy goals of the Nazi Party allowed him to adapt the party's propaganda to different target audiences in order to attract members, donors, and voters from a wide variety of social strata. Concerning the core principles of Nazi ideology outlined here, however, Hitler remained clear and consistent throughout his career.[58]

By 1923 Hitler had managed to attract a loyal group of activists who would remain influential in the Nazi Party for many years to come, including such figures as Rudolf Hess, Heinrich Himmler, Hermann Göring, Wilhelm Frick, Alfred Rosenberg, Joseph Göbbels, and Ernst Röhm. Former Freikorps members, too, had flocked to the party in droves after the formal disbandment following Rathenau's assassination, forming the core of Hitler's Storm Troopers (SA). By the fall of 1923, the Nazi Party boasted some fifty-five thousand members; the SA alone had about fifteen thousand men.[59] The NSDAP had by this time also become the core of a national network of revolutionary ultranationalist paramilitary groups, the Kampfbund. Overall, the NSDAP had become nationally influential enough that Hitler began to harbor dreams of an immediate political coup.

As is well known, Hitler's plan to realize these dreams through the amateurish "beer hall putsch" in Munich in November led instead to his arrest and the temporary disbanding of the NSDAP. Hitler now began to reevaluate his strategy for taking power through an alliance with disgruntled elements

[57] Adolf Hitler, quoted in Turner, *German Big Business and the Rise of Hitler* (New York: Oxford University Press, 1985), p. 77.

[58] The frequent claim that Hitler's message was ideologically inconsistent and incoherent, and that his appeal was due solely to his histrionic speaking style, appears to stem from a lack of differentiation between core ideological concepts – in particular, the three outlined here – and rhetoric designed to appeal tactically to one or another of Hitler's audiences. To refute the claim that Hitler's ideology was clear and consistent, one would need to find examples of speeches claiming, for instance, that an integration of diverse races into a single Germany might be possible; that Germany might ultimately achieve some way to live within internationally sanctioned borders; or that some degree of democratic debate might be necessary for the rebirth of the German nation.

[59] Otis C. Mitchell, *Hitler Over Germany: The Establishment of the Nazi Dictatorship, 1918–1934* (Philadelphia: Institute for the Study of Human Issues, 1983), p. 94.

within the German military, realizing that he needed much broader national support in order to overthrow the Weimar system. Yet his core ideological commitments – viciously anti-Semitic Social Darwinism, the goal of German *Lebensraum*, and an insistence on the miraculous power of his own leadership – remained unchanged. Indeed, the tedious consistency with which Hitler propounded these themes is obvious to anyone who suffers through a complete reading of his 1924 prison memoir, *Mein Kampf*.[60]

USPD

At first glance, it might seem odd to label the Independent Social Democratic Party a "nonideological" organization. After all, the USPD owed its very existence to its principled rejection of the Majority Social Democrats' support for the German war effort in World War I, and during its brief existence it attracted to its ranks many of the more idealistic German believers in the future socialist utopia. Adopting the definition of ideology utilized in this book, however, highlights the USPD's lack of any consensus about the sort of regime it hoped to establish. Morgan succinctly notes that: "the leaders, at least, of the parties on either flank of the Independents, the SPD and the KPD, knew what they wanted; the USPD did not."[61] The debilitating effects of struggles over the question of regime identity help to explain why the party failed to sustain its substantial initial political support in the early Weimar years – disintegrating entirely just over two years after receiving 17.9 percent of the popular vote in the June 1920 Reichstag elections.[62]

The USPD entered into the German Revolution in 1918 with about 100,000 members – a figure which nearly tripled by January 1919 as workers became radicalized and demobilized soldiers returned home.[63] These seemingly impressive numbers, however, concealed the continuing deep split between the party's left wing, which was sympathetic to Spartacist and Bolshevik ideals, and its right wing, which considered its primary objections to the MSPD to be merely tactical ones. Given that the two wings of the USPD had been united primarily by their common struggle for peace, Germany's final defeat was bound to bring this internal fissure into the open. Thus, after the declaration of the republic on November 8, the right wing of the USPD began to argue for cooperation with the MSPD to realize long-cherished goals of full political democracy, whereas the left wing began to mobilize revolutionary workers for the immediate establishment of a full "socialist republic."

The two wings of the USPD leadership were reunited again by the beginning of 1919, as a result of their common opposition to the MSPD's support of a new Constituent Assembly, which appeared likely to end all hopes of realizing a thoroughgoing socialist transformation of Germany for the foreseeable future,

[60] Adolf Hitler, *Mein Kampf* (Boston: Houghton Mifflin, 1943).
[61] Morgan, *The Socialist Left*, pp. 245–246.
[62] Kershaw, *Weimar: Why Did German Democracy Fail?*, table I, p. 204.
[63] Morgan, *The Socialist Left*, p. 179.

and their bitter disgust at Ebert's and Noske's alliance with the Freikorps in brutally crushing revolutionary uprisings of radical workers. The USPD now declared itself to be the home of all genuinely revolutionary left-wing forces in the country. Despite the failure of the attempt to establish a Soviet Republic in Bavaria and the gradual disintegration of the council movement in the spring, this image propelled the party toward even greater levels of popular support. By October 1919 the USPD numbered perhaps 750,000 members. The party played a significant role in mobilizing the general strike that brought the Kapp Putsch in March 1920 to an end and was rewarded by its best-ever showing at the polls in the June Reichstag elections.

However, the same factor that provided a clear and consistent regime ideology to the previously marginal KPD proved to be the undoing of the initially more powerful USPD: the establishment of the Comintern in Soviet Russia. Lenin and the rest of the Soviet leadership had a deep distrust for the USPD; the presence therein of such reviled figures as Kautsky and Bernstein convinced the Bolsheviks that the Independents were just a minor variant of the "rotten" social democracy of the Second International. From the founding of the Comintern in March 1919, the Soviet leadership hoped to integrate German communism into its orbit by forcing the USPD left to unite with the KPD. In the summer of 1920, as we have seen, the KPD leadership quickly accepted Lenin's twenty-one conditions for Comintern membership. The USPD, by contrast, was divided almost precisely in two on this question; indeed, the USPD delegation to the Second Comintern Congress included two members who favored acceptance of Lenin's terms and two who opposed it. At the Halle Congress of the USPD in October, the USPD formally split, with its left wing voting to join the Comintern – and, in essence, to join the KPD – and the right wing voting to reorganize the USPD on a non-Leninist basis. This "rump" USPD managed to survive nearly two more years, receiving a fresh infusion of support when Paul Levi and his followers were expelled from the KPD in June 1921, but ultimately merged into the old SPD after Rathenau's assassination pushed the Majority Social Democrats in a left-wing direction.

DDP

There is a strong consensus among historians that the German Democratic Party lacked any clear and consistent political ideology and also that its ideological vagueness played a significant role in the party's eventual downfall.[64] Too frequently, however, the DDP's poor performance has been attributed simply to the supposed long-term weakness of the German liberal tradition.[65] As we have seen, more recent historiography has exposed this idea as a

[64] See especially the seminal work of Jones, *German Liberalism and the Dissolution of the Weimar Party System*. See also Bruce B. Frye, *Liberal Democrats in the Weimar Republic: The History of the German Democratic Party and the German State Party* (Carbondale: Southern Illinois University Press, 1985).

[65] Dahrendorf, *Society and Democracy in Germany*, p. 375.

myth: liberalism was in fact one of the most powerful political creeds of the Wilhelmine period. Although the divisions between the Progressive People's Party and National Liberals were certainly serious ones, similar divisions also plagued the conservative and socialist movements – yet these latter groupings ultimately developed very powerful mass parties in the Weimar period. In the fall of 1918, it initially seemed very likely that German liberalism would finally be united into a single powerful party able to build on the strong performance of both the Progressives and National Liberals in the Reichstag elections of 1912. That this project failed has to be explained not in terms of preexisting social structures, but instead through an examination of the specific collective action problems facing would-be liberal party builders in the first months of the German Revolution. Our focus on the problem of defining coherent principles of the future polity helps to illustrate more clearly the causal link between the DDP's ideological and organizational failings.

In essence, the DDP leadership chose explicitly to build its new pan-liberal party around the ideal of the *Volksgemeinschaft* rather than around a clear and consistent defense of key liberal principles of political membership, such as individualism, proceduralism, and the defense of private property. The decision to broaden the party's political message in part reflected the philosophical influence of Naumann and his followers, who felt that a true "social liberalism" must find ways to include the entirety of the German citizenry rather than focus solely on the middle classes. Philosophical ecumenicalism, as well as the political vagueness that inevitably accompanied it, was also in part a result of the continuing debates among key DDP leaders around questions of foreign and economic policy. Naumann had been a strong advocate of aggressive German expansionism, while left liberals such as Alfred Weber and Theodor Wolff were closely associated with antimilitarist, internationalist views. On the economic dimension, meanwhile, Naumann's sympathy for a greatly expanded welfare state clashed directly with the more mainstream economic liberalism of those National Liberals who had joined the DDP in its early months. DDP leaders were also divided on the question of federalism, with important figures such as Otto Preuss arguing for the creation of a highly centralized state and others vehemently opposing this idea.

The decision to build the DDP as a party to represent all Germans, however, merely papered over all of these political differences without really resolving them. As Frye points out, the result was that "in both the founding *Aufruf* [proclamation] of the DDP and the principal election statement of 14 December, the party made sweeping and specious generalizations intended to win supporters and to avoid serious division within the party's electorate."[66] In short, DDP election propaganda promised all things to all people: protection for workers from unbridled capitalism, help for the German peasantry, and state support for artisans, small businessmen, and civil servants. Given this

---

[66] Frye, *Liberal Democrats*, p. 59.

broad and often incoherent message, individuals tended to provide financial and organizational support for the DDP not because of any deep commitment to its ideals but simply because of a desire to realize specific instrumental goals. Thus, big business provided huge sums to support the Democrats in the January 1919 elections to the National Assembly despite its deep distrust of the left-wing elements of the DDP with their plans for the "socialization" of monopolies, solely because of its desire to keep the hated Social Democrats from dominating the new regime. Even at this early stage, several businessmen agreed to provide the party with crucial funding only if they or their allies were given prominent slots on DDP electoral lists. The institutionalization of this practice, however, naturally led to the rapid disillusionment of those young people, intellectuals, journalists, and feminists who had joined the party for reasons of political principle.

The party's great success in the January 1919 elections, when it received 18.6 percent of the vote, placed it in a strong position to define the institutional shape of the future Weimar Republic. Prominent DDP intellectuals such as Preuss and Max Weber played crucial roles in the constitutional drafting process. Yet, on basic questions of regime type, these eminent figures pursued political compromises that badly damaged the end product. Thus, to satisfy monarchist elements within the broad liberal movement, DDP leader Erich Koch proposed to maintain the label "Reich" for the new democratic Germany, inserting as Article 1 of the Weimar Constitution the uninspiring mixed formula: "The German Reich is a republic."[67] Max Weber, meanwhile, feared that a purely rational-legal parliamentary system might lack sufficient legitimacy to survive in a Germany accustomed to authoritarian leadership and insisted on the creation of a strong "plebiscitarian" presidency in order to infuse the Weimar Republic with "charismatic" meaning; this was the source of the infamous Article 48, which gave the president emergency powers to rule by decree with no effective parliamentary check.[68] Remarkably, in July 1919 the DDP faction in the National Assembly – enraged by the terms of the Versailles Treaty – even rejected the symbolic change of the German national flag from the imperial

---

[67] Ibid., p. 81.

[68] Here I am in the odd position of using my refinement of Weber's sociological theory to criticize Weber's own application of it during the Weimar constitutional debate. My view is that Weber's mistaken tendency to conflate charismatic legitimacy with personal affect, owing to his incomplete presentation of the theoretical links between his four types of individual social action and his three types of legitimate domination, led him at this crucial juncture to overemphasize the importance of presidential leadership and to underemphasize the importance of "value-rational principle" as a charismatic force. I would like to think, however, that Weber himself would concur with this critique were he somehow able to read it – because, after all, Weber knew clearly that every contribution to social science, no matter how brilliant, is destined ultimately to be superseded. Certainly the critique of Weber's conduct in the Constitutional Committee I make here has nothing at all in common with Wolfgang Mommsen's highly misleading argument that Weber paved the way to the rise of Hitler by calling for the institutionalization of a new German "*Führer*" See Wolfgang J. Mommsen, *Max Weber and German Politics, 1890–1920* (Chicago, University of Chicago Press, 1984), also Bernhard, *Institutions and the Fate of Democracy*.

black-white-red to the new republican black-red-gold, by a vote of forty-three to fourteen.[69]

As Germany lurched from one crisis to the next in the months and years after the November Revolution, the DDP's lack of any clear ideological core, its effort not to offend its diverse constituencies, and the untimely deaths of key founders such as Naumann and Max Weber inevitably resulted in strategic incoherence. The party's decision to leave the government in protest against the SPD leadership's decision to fulfill the terms of Versailles was meant to demonstrate the DDP's nationalist credentials, but the decision to try to rejoin the SPD-led government just a few months later in order to influence its economic policies undercut this stance.[70] The party's efforts to woo businessmen compelled it to take strong rhetorical stands in favor of low taxes and private property, but its need to maintain its relations with the ruling SPD forced it to vote in favor of both higher taxes and an expanded welfare state. Unsurprisingly, given these internal contradictions, the DDP's attempt to create a grass-roots network of party activists through the Young Democratic Organization utterly failed; from twenty thousand members in 1919, membership dropped to only a few thousand by the mid-twenties.[71]

Indeed, maintaining collective action among even the core groups initially supporting the DDP became increasingly difficult over time. The Democrats' support for the mass strike that brought down the Kapp Putsch led dozens of conservative DDP leaders and several prominent business executives to switch their allegiance to the DVP; the resulting inability of the DDP to raise sufficient campaign funds played a major role in its disastrous performance in the Reichstag elections of June 1920, when the party received just 8.3 percent of the vote. By 1921 both the *Deutsche Bauerbund*, which represented small businesses, and the German Peasants' League, which represented independent farmers, had begun to reconsider their alliances with the DDP in protest against the party's failure to represent their members' interests. All of these defections, combined with the Democrats' lack of a network of devoted party activists, meant that the effects of the inflation in 1922–1923 on the party organization would be particularly devastating.[72]

DVP

While the failure of the German Democratic Party to develop a coherent ideology reflected the party leadership's philosophical ecumenicalism, the right liberal German People's Party was nonideological by the explicit choice of its leader, Gustav Stresemann. Stresemann's role in the Weimar Republic has

---

[69] Frye, *Liberal Democrats*, p. 86.
[70] Jones, *German Liberalism*, p. 56.
[71] Frye, *Liberal Democrats*, p. 94.
[72] Jones notes that an effort by the DDP to raise membership dues in 1923 should have produced more than ten million marks, given the party's official membership of 209,530 at the end of 1922. In reality, fewer than one million marks were ever forwarded to the party's national headquarters that year. Jones, *German Liberalism*, p. 189.

long been a controversial one given the multiple allegiances he proclaimed over time – from staunch monarchist and extreme annexationist in 1918 to the single most skillful diplomatic defender of the republic by the mid- to late 1920s. The weight of the evidence, however, points to a relatively simple explanation for Stresemann's political flexibility: he was a consummate pragmatist for whom questions of "regime type" were always secondary to short-term strategic considerations. The same pragmatism that so effectively furthered Stresemann's personal career, however, over time played a key role in undermining the national organization of the party he led.

Thus, Stresemann's personal ambition was one major factor in the failure of German liberalism to unite under DDP auspices in the early months of the republic. Unwilling to commit himself and those National Liberals who remained loyal to him to a left liberal party program, Stresemann continued to negotiate with the DDP leadership for a united liberal party within which he and his followers would have an effectively coequal leadership role. At a time when most of German big business and much of the regional party organizations of both the Progressive People's Party and the National Liberal Party appeared to be moving to the DDP's side, however, the Democrats saw no reason to cede so much power to Stresemann. The new German People's Party was thus founded largely as a vehicle for Stresemann's continuing political ambitions. As a result of the DDP-DVP split, many local branches of the old National Liberal Party were divided and ceased to function effectively. In the January 1919 National Assembly elections, the DVP polled just 4.4 percent of the vote.

The political principles of the DVP were also remarkably vague.[73] At first, Stresemann came out in open opposition to the Weimar Republic and the Versailles Treaty. But as the unabashedly monarchist DNVP gained in political strength, it became difficult to see the need for two parties with essentially the same platform, and many of Stresemann's big-business supporters strongly pressured him to join the DNVP in a unified right opposition. To resist this, Stresemann now began to emphasize the DVP's desire to be a "constructive opposition" to the government. Unsurprisingly, given this background, the party program accepted at the DVP party congress of October 1919 was, as Jones puts it, "a masterpiece of political compromise, reconciling the divergent views within the party on one major issue after another."[74]

The questionable ideological commitment of the DVP, and of Stresemann himself, to the Weimar Republic was glaringly illustrated by the party leadership's equivocal conduct during the Kapp Putsch. On March 13, 1920, the DVP issued a declaration that basically accepted the Kapp government as a fait accompli and denounced the national strike against it. Stresemann began to

[73] As DVP deputy Kahl tellingly declared in the National Assembly, the party stood "true to the past and uncommitted toward the future." Quoted in Kaufman, *Monarchism in the Weimar Republic*, p. 56.

[74] Jones, *German Liberalism*, p. 53. The DVP program is reprinted in condensed form in Treue, *Deutsche Parteiprogramme*, pp. 110–117.

qualify his support only on the third day of the putsch when its future began to look dim. On March 18, the DVP now proclaimed that it was a "loyal defender of the Weimar Constitution, whose commitment to the principle of organic development precluded any accommodation with the putschists."[75]

Despite this rather sorry record, the DVP nevertheless grew quickly, benefiting from the growing dissatisfaction with the DDP among right-wing liberals and business interests. The result was a dramatic improvement in the party's fortunes in the June 1920 Reichstag elections, when the DVP received 13.9 percent of the vote – more than tripling its performance in January 1919. This performance led to the DVP's inclusion in the new governing coalition of Center Party chancellor Konstantin Fehrenbach. Yet, from the start, the party's participation in government forced it into uncomfortable compromises. Leading industrialists in the party such as coal magnate Hugo Stinnes vented their continued hostility to the policy of fulfillment of the Versailles Treaty, while the DVP Reichstag delegation was forced to uphold this same policy as part of its duty to the governing coalition. By the end of 1920, the party had split into three factions: a left wing that sought to collaborate with the republican government, a right wing that remained deeply hostile to the Weimar system and pushed for collaboration with the DNVP, and a faction of industrialists who "viewed politics in essentially economic terms and whose loyalty to the Weimar Republic was predicated on the extent to which it allowed them to pursue their economic self-interest."[76]

Such internal tensions continued to bedevil the party as Germany's domestic and international crises continued. The DVP Reichstag delegation split over the decision to accept the terms of the London Ultimatum of May 1921 demanding immediate German acceptance of the Allies' schedule for reparations, with a substantial minority voting to reject the DNVP's uncompromising nationalism and to pursue a more realistic foreign policy. Even after the DVP withdrew from the government to protest President Ebert's designation of left-wing Center Party leader Joseph Wirth to head a government to fulfill the terms of the London Ultimatum, Stresemann refused to support a DNVP-sponsored motion of no confidence in the Wirth government; indeed, the DVP collaborated with Wirth to help push Germany's tax policies in a probusiness direction. By the time DVP rejoined the nationalist government of Wilhelm Cuno in November 1922, Stresemann's ambition to take the chancellorship for himself – and his willingness to compromise his former nationalist and monarchist principles in order to do so – was evident to everyone.

By the time Stresemann was finally named chancellor of Germany in August 1923, the Cuno government's policy of "passive resistance" to French occupation of the Ruhr had become an obvious failure and hyperinflation had reached astronomical levels. Stresemann was thus forced immediately to discard any remaining scruples he may have had about working in partnership

---

[75] Jones, *German Liberalism*, pp. 63–64.
[76] Ibid., p. 90.

with the SPD to defend the Weimar system or to lose all hope of gaining control over the disastrous situation. Characteristically, he chose the former, pragmatic course. In just three months in office, Stresemann managed to end passive resistance and begin direct negotiations with the Allies to hammer out acceptable terms for Germany's reparation payment schedule, to prepare the introduction of a new currency that finally brought an end to Germany's hyperinflation, and to put down communist rebellions in Saxony and Thuringia as well as the Hitler putsch in Bavaria. In many ways, the relative stabilization of the Weimar Republic in its middle years was the work of one great statesman who had managed to move beyond his initial intransigence to work for Germany's national interests.

Yet the effect of these undeniably pragmatic policies on the DVP's activist base was nevertheless extremely damaging. Stresemann's decision to end passive resistance to the French occupation was so at odds with the DVP's prior reputation for uncompromising nationalism that the party's right wing turned decisively against the chancellor, and local party activists resigned from the party in droves.[77] Industrialists like Stinnes now began to plot with DNVP and Reichswehr leaders to replace Stresemann with a military dictatorship to be led by General Hans von Seeckt. But Stresemann won no loyal friends on the left in this period, either. Indeed, Stresemann fell in November 1923 not because of right-wing opposition but because of the SPD's decision to withdraw from his government to protest his actions in Saxony and Thuringia. Ironically, Stresemann's very success in practical action had left the DVP organizationally weakened and politically isolated.

Zentrum

The Catholic Center Party entered into the postwar era with an organizational and confessional identity closely tied to that of its predecessor in the Kaiserreich. Close examination of the refounding of the Zentrum in the fall of 1918, however, demonstrates that the party continued to lack any clear, consistent definition of the sort of polity it preferred. In fact, the Center Party leadership spanned nearly the entire range of German political opinion. The party's left wing included intellectuals and Catholic union leaders who were inspired by the *Rerum Novarum* papal encyclical of 1891, which called for social welfare to mitigate the harshness of modern capitalism; thus they stood fairly close to the SPD on economic policy. The party's right wing was made up of Catholic monarchists who shared many of the antidemocratic and antisocialist prejudices of the DNVP. This divergence of views could not easily be bridged. Indeed, the very decision to continue using the noncommittal title of "Center" in the party's name reflects the inability of the party elite to arrive at any satisfactory new definition of its political orientation in the wake of the German Revolution.[78]

---

[77] Ibid., p. 199.
[78] Evans, *The German Center Party*, p. 224.

As we might expect, ideological fuzziness of the Center Party led to splits in the party organization in the early chaotic years of the Weimar Republic. The majority of the party elite did support the decision to cooperate with the SPD and the DDP in the Weimar coalition in order to secure a constitutional order in which freedom of religious practice could be legally guaranteed, as Windthorst had long dreamed. But this strategy implicitly also committed the Center to support both republicanism and prolabor policies, to the dismay of the right. Right Centrist Martin Spahn, for example, objecting to the second sentence of the new Weimar Constitution, which derived the "supreme power of the state" from the German people rather than from God, left the Center in 1919 to establish a "Catholic committee" within the DNVP.[79] In 1920 the Bavarian branch of the Center Party, which was dominated by monarchists and rejected the Center leadership's efforts to centralize the Reich's finance and taxation policies, seceded to form the new Bavarian People's Party (BVP). Indeed, the BVP initially hoped to compete with the Center in elections throughout Germany. But while its limited organizational base prevented it from realizing this ambitious goal, and the BVP and Center ultimately agreed to cooperate in the Reichstag on issues of common concern, the two parties remained formally split throughout the Weimar period.

One factor prevented the intense factionalism within the Center Party from tearing the organization apart entirely in this period: the continuing inability of most disgruntled activists to find any acceptable alternative political home. Right Centrists strenuously objected to the heavy taxes on industry and land introduced by ministers from the Catholic left such as Martin Erzberger and his protégé Joseph Wirth – but few were interested in joining either the DVP, with its liberal secularism, or the DNVP, which consistently promoted a vision of Hohenzollern restoration dominated by conservative Lutheranism. Later, after Wirth's government fell and the more conservative Cuno ministry was established, left Centrists became equally disillusioned with the new course of their party. But they, in turn, could not find a congenial home within such staunchly secular parties as the SPD or the (already greatly weakened) German Democratic Party.

The anomalous result was that the Catholic Center Party's national network of party activists largely held together through the chaos period in Weimar's history – but on the relatively fragile basis of shared cultural values rather than shared political ideology. On the one hand, the unique role of the Center in protecting Catholic interests secured the party a stable electorate; remarkably, the Zentrum received between 11 and 16 percent of the vote in every national election between January 1919 and March 1933.[80] The Center's lack of ideology also allowed it to form coalitions with parties across the Weimar political spectrum, and as a result the party was included in every governing coalition during the years of the republic without exception. On the other hand, bitter

[79] Ibid., p. 231.
[80] Kershaw, *Weimar: Why Did German Democracy Fail?*, table I, p. 204.

disputes between leftists and rightists in the Center Party leadership continued to bedevil the organization, and by the end of the 1920s it could fundamentally unite around only two issues of core concern to its electorate: the defense of Catholic education and German relations with the papacy. This made the Center highly vulnerable to strategic defection once an alternative ideological regime under Hitler drastically changed the selective incentives facing party activists.

Stalemate, 1924–1929

From 1924 through 1929, Weimar Germany entered into five years of relative calm and stability. Politically, the new Weimar constitutional system had managed to survive an almost unbelievable series of crises, and now appeared at last to be the established order of the land. Economically, hyperinflation had come to an end, and while the high unemployment that accompanied Stresemann's stabilization measures remained a persistent problem, relatively strong rates of GDP growth in the latter 1920s seemed to herald continuing progress on this front as well. Internationally, the Dawes Plan of 1924 and the Locarno Agreement of 1925 appeared to reintegrate Germany successfully into the European family of nations.

Yet underneath the surface of this apparent calm, troubling signs of weakness in Weimar's party system remained. Government instability remained extremely high, with six separate cabinets formed between 1924 and 1929 – four of them representing only a minority of the German electorate.[81] The vote shares of Germany's two liberal parties, the DDP and DVP, continued their steady decline. By 1928 they polled just 13.6 percent of the electorate; by 1930 their combined vote share had declined to a pitiful 8.5 percent. An increasing number of votes and Reichstag seats meanwhile went to various splinter parties representing specific economic interests; by 1928 these parties had managed to attain the support of nearly 14 percent of the electorate.[82]

The middle years of the Weimar Republic can be seen as parallel in many ways to the period between 1873 and 1877 in the early French Third Republic, when electoral democracy under a contested constitution concealed a sharp struggle among competing parties to define the future nature of the regime. Whereas the struggle in France was a relatively straightforward one between defenders and opponents of the radical republican definition of the polity, Weimar's "polarized pluralism" involved no less than four radically different ideological visions of the future: the proletarian fatherland defended by the SPD, the "Soviet Germany" advocated by the KPD, the monarchical restoration longed for by the DNVP, and the Aryan Third Reich demanded by Hitler's Nazi Party. All four of these parties had managed to maintain strong networks of dedicated activists through the period of chaos, in large part because party

---

[81] Ibid., table II, pp. 206–207.
[82] Ibid., table I, p. 204.

loyalists had remained united around the various long-run visions of the German future while competing parties – in particular, those most closely associated with liberalism – succumbed to self-interested free riding. Now, despite the
stabilization of Germany's domestic and international political environments,
the SPD, KPD, DNVP, and NSDAP alike continued to nurture the dreams of
their activist bases – with disastrous long-term effects on Weimar democracy.

SPD

The SPD entered the Weimar Republic's period of relative stability after 1923
with enviable political advantages. Despite the challenges it had faced from the
extreme left, the party had emerged at the end of the republic's chaotic first five
years with its prewar organization almost entirely intact. The SPD remained
the largest party in Germany, with approximately a million members, and its
activist network of union leaders, socialist intellectuals, and explicitly social-
democratic civil society organizations was unparalleled. With the disappearance of the USPD and the banning of the KPD in the wake of the events in
Saxony and Thuringia in 1923, the SPD now monopolized the socialist niche
of the German political establishment. These advantages combined to provide
the SPD with continuing power at the ballot box. The party's share of the vote
steadily increased in this period, from 20.5 percent in May 1924, to 26 percent
in December 1924, to a decisive plurality of 29.8 percent of the electorate in
May 1928.

Nevertheless, the SPD was unable in this period to break out of its ideological
orthodoxy in order to fully embrace alliances with nonproletarian parties and
interests – in large part because the party's activists continued to define their
interests in terms of the long-term goal of achieving a fully proletarian society.
Thus, the new Reichsbanner militia, which was formed in 1924 at the initiative
of social-democratic activists in Saxony and Munich – the two regions most
threatened by radical coup attempts by the extreme left and right – remained
almost exclusively tied to the SPD, even though its formal mission was to unite
all parties that supported the republic. Of its three million members, approximately 90 percent voted for the Social Democrats.[83] The new party program
adopted at Heidelberg in 1925, too, continued to insist that "the democratic
republic is the most favorable soil for the liberation struggle of the working
class and thus for the implementation of socialism"; it insisted, as before, that
the "middle strata" of German society between the proletariat and the bourgeoisie were destined inexorably to disappear.[84] The Free Trade Unions, despite
their continuing formal independence from the SPD, maintained close informal contacts with the party; in fact, trade-union officials made up more than
one-fourth of the SPD's Reichstag delegation.[85] Finally, the vast network of

---

[83] Ibid., p. 21.
[84] "Programm der Vereinigten Sozialdemokratischen Partei," September 18, 1925, excerpted in
Treue, *Deutsche Parteiprogramme*, pp. 106–110.
[85] Harsch, *German Social Democracy*, p. 20.

leisure organizations affiliated with the Social Democrats – chess clubs, choirs, sports associations, and so on – continued to resist cooperation with similarly oriented "bourgeois" associations. SPD-sponsored cultural events continued to be oriented toward the goal of "awaken[ing] the socialist cultural conscious-ness of the masses" – and even if most of these events centered on simple entertainment rather than Marxist theory, SPD propaganda nevertheless con-tinued to reinforce the idea of opposition to the "bourgeois" order, and rarely emphasized the values of democratic governance for its own sake.[86]

It is easy in hindsight to criticize the SPD leadership in the mid-1920s for not breaking free entirely of the "socialist ghetto" to which it had been consigned by the repressive laws of the Kaiserreich. At the time, however, there were few if any reasons for the SPD to reconsider its Marxist ideological orthodoxy. Indeed, the party continued to grow in popularity and influence in these years. Its support for Stresemann's foreign policies was crucial in allowing the foreign minister to negotiate the Dawes Plan and the Locarno Treaty. In 1926 its campaign to expropriate the lands of the German princes – although it failed in the end – brought valuable national exposure and was very popular among the party's key constituencies. By 1927 it cooperated with the "bourgeois" government of Hans Luther to pass a law providing generous unemployment insurance to the German citizenry. The Social Democrats continued throughout this period as the main governing party in several German states, including Prussia itself. With its electoral breakthrough in May 1928, the SPD under Herman Müller was in a position to form its own government for the first time since the early years of the republic. All of these indicators seemed once again to confirm the correctness of the party's orthodox course as a "revolutionary, but not revolution-making," organization.

KPD

The failure of the communist uprisings of November 1923 put an end, for the time being, to plans for an immediate KPD conquest of political power in Germany. That the party continued to be oriented clearly and consistently toward the eventual establishment of a Soviet Germany, however, was never in doubt. Indeed, the party emerged from its tumultuous early years more dependent than ever on the Comintern and the Soviet Union. And while subor-dination to Moscow continued to trouble KPD leftists, the growing importance of the Soviet Union in world politics – including in this period secret cooper-ation with the Reichswehr in evading the restrictions on weapons production and military exercises imposed by the Versailles Treaty – guaranteed that the German Communists, too, would henceforth be a force to be reckoned with.

The electoral strength of the KPD was reinforced at the same time by the growth of unemployment in this period. The unemployment rate increased to

---

[86] Ibid., pp. 20–21; Guttsman, *The German Social Democratic Party*, pp. 167–215; Sheri Berman, "Civil Society and the Collapse of the Weimar Republic," *World Politics* 49(3, April 1997): 401–429.

4.9 percent of the workforce in 1924 and, after a brief decline to 3.4 percent in 1925, shot up to 10 percent – more than two million people – by 1926.[87] Partly because of its appeal among newly unemployed workers, the party recovered from the disasters in Saxony and Thuringia remarkably quickly, receiving an impressive 12.4 percent of the vote in the Reichstag elections of May 1924. The KPD also moved to organize this new mass base for ideological struggle, creating the new paramilitary organization, the Red League of Front Fighters (Rotfrontkämpferbund, or RFB), to defend communist gatherings against police harassment.

The ideological orientation of the KPD was also directly affected by the struggle for power in the USSR after Lenin's death in 1924. Zinoviev, who had strongly backed the KPD uprisings of November 1923 as the prelude to a full "proletarian revolution" in Germany, now increasingly came under attack by Stalin and Nikolai Bukharin, who called for a new strategy of building "socialism in one country" rather than relying on help from revolutions abroad. One of the earliest supporters of Stalin's line in the KPD was Ernst Thälmann from Hamburg, who stood out in the party for his particularly slavish devotion to Moscow. As Stalin's influence in the Communist Party of the Soviet Union grew, so did Thälmann's in the KPD. In the presidential elections of spring 1925, the KPD rejected Zinoviev's advice to cooperate with the SPD against the monarchical candidate Hindenburg, nominating Thälmann in both the first and second rounds. Thälmann received 7 percent of the vote in the first round, and 6.4 percent in the second – the latter total enough to deprive prorepublican candidate Wilhelm Marx from a victory over Hindenburg.

By the end of 1925, Zinoviev and his allies had largely been stripped of their power in Moscow – and so had Zinoviev's allies in the KPD associated with Brandler. Thälmann soon emerged as party leader, defeating a "leftist" faction of Ruth Fischer and Arkadi Maslow, who continued to refuse absolute deference to Moscow's orders. When leadership of the Communist International passed from Zinoviev to Bukharin in 1926, Thälmann began to pursue a line of relative accommodation with the Social Democrats, uniting with the SPD, for example, to promote the national referendum on dispossessing princely estates in 1927. By the winter of 1928–1929, however, Stalin had turned decisively against his former ally Bukharin, whom he now labeled a "right deviationist" in league with the bourgeoisie and rich peasants. The KPD and all the other parties of the Comintern were instructed that a new wave of social revolution was on the rise and that any and all collaboration with the "revisionists and opportunists" of Social Democracy must immediately cease so as to prepare the working class for militant struggle. The SPD, in particular, was labeled a party of "social fascists" – supposedly more harmful to the cause of proletarian solidarity, because of its support for Germany's integration with "imperialist" France and Britain, than the Nazi Party itself. Propaganda denouncing "social

---

[87] Kershaw, *Weimar: Why Did German Democracy Fail?*, table III(e), p. 211.

fascism" was relayed through the KPD party organization and the RFB to the rank-and-file membership, with fateful consequences in the years to come.

DNVP

Like the SPD and KPD, the German National People's Party entered into the Weimar Republic's era of stabilization with a clear ideological identity and a strong network of activists throughout the country. The DNVP continued to reap the rewards of its consistent opposition to the Weimar system and to the policy of fulfillment of the Versailles Treaty. The party received nearly 20 percent of the vote in the May Reichstag elections of 1924, coming in second only to the SPD. While the DNVP did not possess a paramilitary organization with direct links to the party organization such as the Reichsbanner or RFB, it did maintain close links with the Stalhelm, an association of German war veterans and nationalist sympathizers numbering over 300,000 members, with strong monarchist sympathies and an increasingly *völkische* orientation. Members of the Stalhelm were also very active in the Bismarck cult, marching in formation under the imperial black-white-red flag on key holidays, such as the Iron Chancellor's birthday.[88]

Ironically, however, the DNVP's ideological consistency began to unravel at the very height of the party's success. An early sign of trouble came during the vote in parliament on the terms of the Dawes Plan in August 1924, when the party split nearly down the middle as a result of pressure in favor of acceptance from the industrialists who funded party activities. Party leader Oskar Hergt was forced to resign his position; he was replaced by the old Conservative Party leader Count Kuno von Westarp. Nevertheless, the party publicly repudiated the forty-eight deputies who joined the government in this instance, and once again its campaign in December 1924 presented the party as one of uncompromising opposition to the Weimar system. Again, too, the results of this strategy were excellent; the DNVP's vote share increased to 20.5 percent, the best performance in its history. As of January 1925, the party decided to join the government for the first time, hoping in this way to keep the SPD from claiming ministries for itself. To convince President Ebert to appoint a government with DNVP representatives, Westarp was forced to make a public declaration of support for the Weimar Constitution; he did so, but added that the DNVP would continue "to enlighten the people about the deficiencies of the democratic-parliamentaristic system" and "to continue agitating for the idea that the reconstruction of the Reich can only be accomplished in closest connection with our historically proven tradition."[89]

What finally brought the ideological unity of the DNVP to an end was the election campaign for Field Marshal Paul von Hindenburg in the spring of 1925. Monarchists within the party were overjoyed when their proposal after

---

[88] Frankel, *Bismarck's Shadow*, pp. 110–111; Peter Fritzsche, *Rehearsals for Fascism: Populism and Political Mobilization in Weimar Germany* (New York: Oxford University Press, 1990).
[89] Westarp, quoted in Kaufmann, *Monarchism in the Weimar Republic*, p. 137.

the inconclusive first round of elections to nominate this loyal friend of the Hohenzollerns to the highest office in the republic met with such remarkable success. Although the DNVP sent explicit instructions to its party activists not to mention the question of monarchy during the campaign itself, many of them nevertheless expected the victorious Hindenburg immediately to invite the Hohenzollern dynasty back to Germany to reestablish its rule. President Hindenburg's refusal to overturn the Weimar Constitution, however, presented the DNVP with a severe dilemma. If the party turned its back on Hindenburg and pushed for a more actively monarchist stance, it risked alienating its expanded electorate; however, if it embraced Hindenburg and joined the Weimar governing coalition, it would inevitably become part of the parliamentary order it had ideologically rejected for so many years.

Under these circumstances, the party chose the latter course – and was soon forced into painful ideological compromises as a result. True, the DNVP continued to represent its activist base by promoting wider use of the imperial German flag, vehemently opposing the SPD and KPD referendum on dispossession of the royal estates, and continuing to denounce Stresemann's foreign policy "concessions" to the Allies. But after rejoining the government in 1927, the DNVP felt compelled to vote in favor of an extension of the 1922 Law on the Defense of the Republic, which had been adopted after Rathenau's assassination and initially designed to extend for only five years. Because this law included an explicit provision preventing the return of Kaiser Wilhelm II to Germany, the DNVP's support for the legislation directly contradicted the party's monarchical platform.

Deprived of ideological coherence, the party's election campaign in the May 1928 Reichstag elections was poorly organized and uninspiring. The party suffered a disastrous decline, receiving only 14.2 percent of the vote. Shortly after this defeat, prominent DNVP leaders began to call for the formal abandonment of the monarchical principle in the party program. Walter Lambach, head of the DNVP-affiliated German National Union of Commercial Employees and previously a staunch monarchist, now published an article that essentially sounded the death knell of monarchical ideology:

If, after Ebert's death, Jarres or Marx or Thälmann had become Reich President, we would have today in Germany a vital movement for the restoration of the monarchy. But because the monarchistic part of our nation elected Hindenburg to the Presidency, the monarchic idea in Germany has been buried. Or does any intelligent and politically alert person actually believe that there exists in Germany today yet – except for certain unimportant traces in Bavaria – an active and a determined monarchism? Maybe so in Hungary, but certainly not in Germany.[90]

[90] Quoted in ibid., p. 182. Lambach went on to note that the youth would never again be attracted to the monarchical cause: "Kings and emperors are to our growing generation no longer sacrosanct and venerable persons or institutions. They have been degraded in the eyes of our youth to figures of the stage and of the screen. The fad for beauty queens ... has further precipitated a devaluation of the concept of kingdom." Ibid., p. 184.

For telling the truth, Lambach was drummed out of the DNVP – but not before precipitating an open split in the party that soon led it into an open alliance with Hitler.

The Nazi Party

After the failure of the "beer hall putsch," Hitler and the Nazi Party appeared to be politically finished. To be sure, Hitler took advantage of the publicity surrounding his trial in February 1924 to rant and rave as usual about the perfidy of the government of "traitors" in Berlin, and his prison term of five years – with eligibility for parole in just six months – was extraordinarily lenient. While Hitler was in prison, however, the Weimar Republic began at last to stabilize, undercutting any immediate hopes of another opportunity for right-wing revolution. The Nazi Party, too, began to lose its less committed activists, who drifted off to competing nationalist formations.[91] Ernst Röhm's efforts to maintain the SA, meanwhile, met with some success, but only at the cost of watering down the organization's links with the NSDAP. After his release from prison in December 1924, Hitler faced long odds indeed in his effort to make a political comeback.

The dynamics through which Hitler nevertheless managed to weld together one of the most powerful national party organizations in Weimar Germany – precisely during its years of greatest political and economic stability – can be understood only in connection with Hitler's continuing ideological consistency. For those core supporters who had embraced Hitler's theory of German rebirth as a global empire through racial struggle led by an infallible *Führer*, the events of November 1923 in Munich only demonstrated Hitler's "unshakable will" and devotion to the nation. Having decided to pursue a path to power through the use of legal means, Hitler now patiently rebuilt the Nazi organization by building on the collective action of those who continued to demonstrate fidelity to his long-term vision of Germany's future. As Orlow has pointed out, Hitler's decision to instruct his party loyalists to back General Ludendorff rather than the mainstream right-wing candidate Karl Jarres in the first round of the 1925 presidential elections played a key role in separating out "true believers" from mere fellow travelers:

Above all, the Ludendorff-for-President movement forced every NSDAP member to choose between loyalty to the larger movement and loyalty and obedience to Hitler…Many Nazi followers remained true to the larger *völkisch* movement and refused to follow Hitler. Those who supported Hitler paid a heavy price: after the election Hitler deliberately isolated the small band of his followers from the *völkisch* movement. A directive of May 1925 prohibited further organizational cooperation between NSDAP locals and their counterparts from other *völkisch* political units even though in the runoff elections Hitler had rejoined the *völkisch* movement and supported the victorious candidate, Field Marshal von Hindenburg.[92]

[91] Mitchell, *Hitler Over Germany*, p. 97.
[92] Orlow, *History of the Nazi Party*, p. 61.

Having found a way in effect to purge the Nazi Party of ideologically impure elements, Hitler and his inner circle proceeded to establish a remarkably well-organized bureaucratic hierarchy throughout Germany. In 1925 Hitler established a new personal security service – the *Schutzstaffel*, or SS – thus creating a more fully "Aryan" paramilitary to rein in the more unpredictable elements within the SA. The NSDAP itself was reorganized as well. Long-standing Nazi party officials were given positions as *Gauleiters* – district leaders – each forced to swear absolute loyalty to Hitler. Their further progress to the top ranks of the party then depended directly on their ability to raise money, sign up new members, and win votes in elections. Hitler rewarded successful *Gauleiters*, too, by showing up in person in their districts to give speeches to rouse the faithful and open their pocketbooks. At the same time, the NSDAP forged a whole series of party-affiliated civil society associations of their own to compete directly with those sponsored by the KPD, SPD, and DNVP. The most successful of these was the Hitler Youth, which managed to attract an increasing number of students who found the ideological messages of the monarchists and Social Democrats to be anachronistic. By 1929 NSDAP membership had risen to 175,000 – more than three times its size in 1923.[93]

Clearly, those who joined the Nazi Party in the years between 1925 and 1929 did so not solely because of Hitler's personal charisma. In a party of this size, few new members would have had much opportunity to interact with the leader personally. It is also true that NSDAP propaganda in this period generally played down its more extreme anti-Semitic beliefs, aiming to win new adherents among the peasantry, the threatened middle classes, and youth. It is nevertheless a mistake to conclude, with Brustein, that Hitler's success in recruiting new Nazi Party members can be understood solely in terms of the instrumentally rational decision making of ordinary Germans.[94] The party's elite core of activists, after all, had shown its loyalty to Hitler for many years, over a period when any individual "payoffs" from such behavior would have appeared plausible only to genuine ideological fanatics. Hitler's willingness to further reduce, rather than expand, NSDAP party membership in 1925 in order to ensure the absolute loyalty among activists, and the willingness of thousands of committed Nazis to sever ties with mainstream conservative parties in response to Hitler's orders, are also hard to explain by looking only at short-term instrumental calculations. Finally, as Brustein himself emphasizes, the Nazi Party in the period of Weimar's stabilization remained very much a fringe movement in electoral politics, attaining just 2.6 percent of the vote in the March 1928 Reichstag elections; thus, it is hard to explain why any purely instrumental Germans would have seen the NSDAP as a promising vehicle for realizing their material ambitions at this stage.

In fact, the Nazis' use of instrumentally chosen economic themes to mobilize new converts at the grass roots signified no departure from their core

93 Mitchell, *Hitler Over Germany*, p. 103.
94 Brustein, *The Logic of Evil*.

ideological principles of race struggle, *Lebensraum*, and the *Führerprinzip*. All three remained consistent and central themes in internal party propaganda, even if they temporarily became less prominent in election pamphlets – and the higher one climbed in the Nazi Party ranks, the more openly such ideas were discussed. A nonideological Hitler surely would not have taken several months out of his busy schedule of speeches and rallies in 1927 to write yet another sprawling, two-hundred-page book outlining Germany's future foreign policy goals in Eastern Europe and concluding with several pages of the vilest imaginable anti-Semitism.[95] Overall, the evidence suggests that the Nazi Party, like the SPD, KPD, and DNVP, was able to overcome the collective action problem in mobilizing a national network of activists because a sufficient number of ideological converts accepted Hitler's long-run vision of the Third Reich as a credible picture of the future German state.

DDP and DVP

One might have thought that, with the Weimar Republic's recovery after 1923, its two liberal parties would have been in an ideal position to capitalize on this success. Instead, exactly the opposite occurred. Both the DDP and the DVP continued to suffer from internal splits and organizational defections, generating increasingly disappointing results at the polls. In May 1924 the DDP and DVP together attained just 15.2 percent of the vote – a decline of 8 percent compared to June 1920. After a very slight rebound in December 1924, the process of liberal disintegration accelerated again; by May 1928 the combined vote share of the two liberal parties was down to just 13.6 percent. Why didn't the German Democrats and the People's Party benefit more from the stabilization of a republic they had both, in different ways, done so much to create?

The answer is that by 1924, the national party organizations of the DDP and DVP alike were already in a severely weakened state. Big-business associations that had initially backed the German Democrats had by this point almost completely ceased to support the party, which had chronic funding problems as a result. The party had flip-flopped on so many issues of vital importance to key constituents that recruiting new, loyal activists was essentially impossible. The DDP's dwindling Reichstag delegation entered the latter half of 1924 deeply split between a left wing under Erich Koch-Weser, which opposed any cooperation with a government that included the DNVP, and a right wing that saw compromise on this issue – at a minimum, the retention of DDP minister of defense Otto Gessler in the cabinet – as crucial to maintaining some modicum of political influence. Koch-Weser's ability to rally the majority of

---

95 See Gerhard L. Weinberg, ed., *Hitler's Second Book: The Unpublished Sequel to Mein Kampf*, trans. Krista Smith (New York: Enigma Books, 2003). Hitler's second book is persuasively analyzed, and related to Hitler's ultimate ideological goals, in Eberhard Jäckel, *Hitler's World View: A Blueprint for Power*, trans. Herbert Arnold (Cambridge, MA: Harvard University Press, 1981).

the DDP Reichstag delegation behind him led to the resignations of several prominent DDP rightists in October 1924; they then joined with industrialist Carl Friedrich von Siemens to found the "Liberal Association," a technically nonpartisan group aiming to reestablish the unity of all German liberals but which served in practice only to divide them even further.

These developments might have benefited the DVP, but that party faced its own ideological problems. Despite Stresemann's remarkable success in countering the international and domestic threats to German democracy in his hundred days as chancellor, his conciliatory policy toward the Allies appeared to be directly at odds with the DVP's initial image as an antirepublican party with monarchical leanings. Right-wingers now increasingly gravitated toward the surging DNVP – forcing Stresemann to work very hard to convince the Nationalists to join a new coalition government, despite their vehement opposition to his foreign policy strategy. Meanwhile, pragmatic business elites continued to support the DVP only in return for specific favors in the Reichstag.

At the same time, both liberal parties were losing the support of key interest groups among the German middle classes. Already in the May 1924 Reichstag elections, middle-class splinter parties running against the DDP and DVP won 15 percent of the vote. The largest of these, the Business Party of the German Middle Class (Wirtschaftpartei des deutschen mittelstandes, or WP), originally founded in 1920, now allied with the Bavarian Peasants' League to attain nearly 700,000 votes and ten Reichstag seats.[96] The appeal of splinter parties was furthered by the unwillingness of either the DDP or the DVP to adopt a populist position on the issue of compensation for German investors who had lost their fortunes during the hyperinflation of 1923. The powerful Mortgagees and Savers' Protective Association thus withheld its endorsement of either liberal party, supporting instead the DNVP and the newly formed *völkische* alliance, the National Socialist Freedom Movement. Both the DDP and DVP did slightly increase their vote shares in the December 1924 Reichstag elections – but so too did the DNVP, the SPD, and a range of new parties that competed directly with the liberals to represent various special interest groups. The WP, meanwhile, increased its vote share to more than one million and its Reichstag delegation to seventeen.[97]

As the 1920s progressed, the DDP and DVP continued to lose support to various middle-class parties organized to defend particular economic interests. In 1926 the People's Justice Party organized to provide a more effective defense of small investors dispossessed by the hyperinflation. In 1928 the mounting crisis in German agriculture and the final severing of ties between the German Peasants' League and the DDP led to the founding of the German Peasants' Party. Together, the WP, the People's Justice Party, and the German Peasants' Party polled more than three million votes in the March 1928 elections – much

[96] Jones, *German Liberalism*, p. 257.
[97] Ibid., p. 257.

of this support coming directly at the expense of the previous DDP and DVP electorate. As Jones summarizes,

The two liberal parties were severely hampered in their efforts to develop an effective response to this situation by the fact that they continued to conceive of themselves . . . as parties that sought to represent the German nation in all of its sociological heterogeneity and therefore refused to give primacy to the interests of any particular group. . . . In the final analysis, it was precisely this sort of ideological ambiguity that left the two liberal parties so vulnerable to the agitation of special interest parties that sought to mobilize the more disgruntled elements of the German middle class by promising the more effective representation than either the DDP or DVP was capable of providing.[98]

Zentrum

The Catholic Center party emerged into the post-chaos years in a paradoxical situation. On the one hand, it remained one of Germany's most important and successful political parties, with an activist network incorporating diverse social strata, including local clergy, Catholic unionists, youth groups associated with the Windthorstbund, and supporters of the rights of Catholic regions against the dominance of Protestant Prussia. On the other hand, the party's lack of ideological consensus made it increasingly difficult to say clearly just what the Center stood for. As Evans summarizes,

The Center party in the Weimar republic was a more highly structured organization than the prewar confederation of state and provincial parties, and it had a large and loyal electorate, but this surface vigor concealed a declining state of health which was all too evident to the party leadership. The postwar Center lacked the integrating forces which had bound the old party together in spite of its loose formal structure. The prewar party had had just as heterogeneous a composition as the postwar, but it has possessed a much more clearly defined platform and a much more strongly felt sense of mission. Of that platform, little remained.[99]

The Center's nonideological stand was personified in this period by party leader Wilhelm Marx, a man who proudly declared himself to be "a man of the middle in the party of the middle."[100] The same theme was proudly proclaimed in the party's electoral propaganda in 1924, when voters were exhorted to "Strengthen the Middle! Strengthen, above all, the heart of any healthy Middle, the German Center Party!"[101] But while such slogans worked well enough in maintaining the Zentrum's traditional electorate, Marx's lack of consistent ideology proved far more problematic when he was chosen to be the prorepublican candidate against Hindenburg in the second round of the 1925 elections for the Reich presidency. Right-wing Catholic activists saw Marx as too willing to compromise with Social Democrats and other secularists in the Weimar parliament. Leftists feared the election to the highest office in the land

[98] Ibid., pp. 252–253.
[99] Evans, *The German Center Party*, p. 262.
[100] Ibid., p. 245.
[101] Ibid., p. 294.

of a deeply religious man who headed up the Catholic School Organization. Liberal Protestants who might have otherwise supported a republican candidate feared Marx both for his "socialism" and for his "clericalism." When even the nominal ally of the Center, the Bavarian People's Party, chose to back Hindenburg, Marx's defeat as presidential candidate was sealed.[102]

After Marx's defeat in May 1925, the party leadership found itself deeply divided on its future strategic direction. The Center's left wing, led by Joseph Wirth, hoped to steer the party back toward its stand in the early Weimar period in favor of socialist labor legislation and strict opposition to the DNVP. The right wing, meanwhile, saw opportunities for collaboration with the Nationalists on areas of common interest, such as the law to ban "trashy and filthy writings" in November 1926. Ultimately, the various factions within the Center found it could unite in the Reichstag solely around narrowly tailored legislation targeted directly toward the party's main constituency on two familiar issues: closer ties between German states and the papacy, and the expansion of Catholic schooling. Failure to achieve significant results even in these areas, combined with the continuing wounds from the disputes between the Center's left and right factions, led the party in May 1928 to its worst performance in the Weimar period to date, with just 12 percent of the vote.

Crisis and Resolution, 1929–1933

As we have seen, by 1929 the Weimar party system was already in deep trouble, notwithstanding Germany's previous five years of relative stability. Thus, the shock of the Great Depression that developed after the United States stock market crash in October – as horrendous as it was – did not by itself cause the final destruction of German democracy. Instead, the structural impact of Germany's economic crisis and massive unemployment interacted with the political landscape generated by the Weimar party stalemate to produce ultimately disastrous results.

To begin with, the Great Depression finished off what little prospect remained for a resurgence of Germany's two liberal parties. The DDP leadership endeavored to respond to the nightmarish new situation by augmenting its credentials as a nationalist, centralizing party, rechristening it as the German State Party. This reformulation was entirely lacking in ideological credibility, given the party's past history; by 1930 the party had become itself no more than a liberal splinter group. The somewhat stronger DVP, meanwhile, was decimated when its longtime leader Stresemann died suddenly of a heart attack in October 1929 – ironically just after his efforts at negotiation with the Allies had finally produced an agreement for a full and final French withdrawal from the Rhineland. Unsurprisingly, given the leader-based nature of the DVP, it too suffered massive defections of its remaining supporters; by 1930 it had become hopelessly marginalized in German national politics.

[102] Ibid., pp. 298–300.

In essence, Weimar Germany entered into its final crisis in 1929 with five effective national parties. Four of these – the DNVP, the SPD, the KPD, and the NSDAP – were ideologically committed to irreconcilably different conceptions of Germany's future regime type, symbolized graphically by the four different flags to which they swore allegiance: the imperial black-white-red of the Kaiserreich, the republican black-red-gold, the red flag of communism, and the swastika flag of Hitler. The fifth, the Catholic Center Party, had no consistent principles concerning the future of the German polity, and thus never used its pivotal political position to mount a principled defense of the Weimar Constitution. Standing above all of these parties was President Hindenburg, now in his eighties and increasingly influenced by the opinions of a small circle of reactionary advisers. The final destruction of the Weimar Republic can be understood as the step-by-step discrediting of all partisan alternatives to the Nazis in this political and socioeconomic structural context.

The first party to self-destruct was the DNVP. Lambach's devastating and well-publicized break with monarchism, which preceded the onset of the depression by only a few months, had the effect of reopening the collective action problem for party activists that common allegiance to the ideal of Hohenzollern restoration had initially solved. Lambach had unwittingly forced every party member to confront the need to find an alternative regime principle around which to organize for the long term – or to defect in favor of some more promising short-term political affiliation. In this context, the decision by new party leader Alfred Hugenburg to reorient the DNVP explicitly toward Pan-German *völkische* nationalism was strategically disastrous. Hugenburg essentially brought his party into ideological alignment with Hitler – but with a message far fuzzier and less convincing, given the party's previous cooperation in the Weimar parliament, than that conveyed in Nazi Party propaganda. Hugenburg's willingness to collaborate with the NSDAP in a nationwide referendum against the Young Plan to reschedule Germany's remaining reparations payments compounded his initial error, providing Hitler with priceless national exposure through the Hugenburg media empire just as the Great Depression was dawning. The failure of the referendum on the Young Plan thus simultaneously discredited Hugenburg while promoting Hitler overnight into the leading ranks of German politicians. Unsurprisingly, the DNVP began to crumble quickly after 1930, as disillusioned loyal monarchists under Westarp founded their own Conservative People's Party, while previously loyal activist networks such as the Stalhelm gravitated toward the Nazis and the SA.

None of this might have mattered had it not been for a similarly self-destructive strategy by the ideologically orthodox SPD. After all, the SPD controlled the government during the onset of the depression, and it was still by far the largest party in Germany. Yet, in order to form any sort of stable governing coalition in the new conditions of deep economic crisis, the party had to compromise on key provisions of its social policy – in particular, to contain the skyrocketing costs of the unemployment insurance that the party had so recently been able to pass. The party leadership under Müller proved entirely inflexible on this matter. In part, this was due to the enormous pressure on the SPD leadership of party activists and trade-union leaders throughout the country, who had long been steeped in Social Democratic propaganda warning against any compromise of workers' interests to cooperate with "nonproletarian classes." The SPD's inflexibility was further reinforced by the Marxist orthodoxy of top party officials such as Rudolf Hilferding, who saw the Great Depression as confirming Marx's predictions of capitalism's inevitable downfall and the rise of a new form of political economy that would be controlled by the central state – and who thus had little interest in preserving the "inherently unsustainable" status quo. Only such ideological considerations can explain the SPD leaders' remarkably inopportune decision to bring down their own government in early 1930, rather than compromise on levels of unemployment insurance. The SPD was now forced to tolerate the deflationary policies of the new government of Heinrich Brüning – despite their painful effects on the working class – for fear that failure to do so would cause the Center to abandon the SPD in its last remaining political stronghold, the Prussian government of Otto Braun. And after the September Reichstag elections produced a vote of 18.3 percent for the Nazis and 13.1 percent for the KPD, while the SPD's own vote share was cut by a sixth, the Social Democrats found themselves in an incomparably weaker political position.

The disintegration of the Nationalists and the weakening of Social Democracy could not help but please the Marxist-Leninist leadership of the Communist Party of Germany, which reacted to the Great Depression with its own characteristic form of ideological rigidity. Thälmann and his colleagues naturally saw the new global crisis of capitalism as fresh proof of the genius of Joseph Stalin, who had after all "predicted" a new turn toward world revolution at the beginning of 1929. The Comintern line that painted the SPD "revisionists" as "social fascists" and the number one enemy of the proletariat was therefore only strengthened – even after the Nazi Party electoral breakthrough of 1930. Hitler's movement was seen as merely a front for "reactionary imperialist circles" within the German bourgeoisie that would be easily defeated by the unified KPD and German proletariat, once the Social Democratic "traitors" to the working class had been exposed and eliminated. The RFB escalated its street fighting against SPD party activists and their supporters in the Reichsbanner; the latter organization, in response, itself became more directly oriented than before toward the mobilization of street violence. Thus, while plenty of RFB battles with SA gangs in German cities certainly also took place in this period, the KPD had opened up a paramilitary "second front" against the SPD that made any combined left-wing defense of the republic unthinkable. Meanwhile, German unemployment continued to worsen, swelling the ranks of the KPD at the expense of the SPD. By July 1932 the party received fully 14.5 percent of the national vote; by November of that year, the KPD electorate had increased to 16.9 percent. That same year, Stalin had announced the early successful completion of the first Five-Year Plan to industrialize the Soviet Union in record time. Against the backdrop of the devastating crisis in the capitalist

West, communist dreams of a new wave of proletarian revolution hardly seemed unrealistic. As the 1930s progressed, the KPD leadership could reasonably argue that fidelity to Comintern strategy was paying off handsomely.

Of course, it was not the KPD but Hitler's Nazi Party that finally managed to impose its ideological will on Germany – and eventually most of Europe. Uniquely among Weimar parties, the NSDAP entered the depression not only with a remarkably strong national organization that trumpeted a consistent nationalist message about Germany's "victimization" by Jews, Masons, foreigners, and other assorted enemies but also with an economic platform promising a "pump-priming" strategy of state stimulus designed to appeal to nearly every sector of German society. At the same time, Hitler's consistent pledge to observe "legality" in his pursuit of party aims – even if party leaders often openly declared that such legal means were only tactical – allowed mainstream public opinion to ignore the revolutionary threat posed by the Nazi's radical statements on foreign policy and the growing extremism of the SA. By July 1932 the Nazi bandwagon had become so powerful that the party attained nearly a third of the German vote. As sociological analysis has conclusively demonstrated, the Nazi electorate was drawn from nearly every social stratum – not only the lower middle classes but also landowners, peasants, civil servants, youth, and even the industrial working class.[103]

The final ingredient in the toxic recipe that allowed Hitler to come to power, however, was the complicity of President Hindenburg and the Center Party in dismantling the parliamentary institutions that might have blocked the final establishment of an ideologically antiliberal regime. Brüning's willingness to implement a deflationary strategy for dealing with the depression by collaborating with Hindenburg to invoke the Weimar Constitution's Article 48, which allowed for rule by decree in states of emergency, in effect deprived the Reichstag of any meaningful role in the outcome of Weimar's final crisis. Persuaded that under the circumstances it was better to have one of their own in command rather than go into opposition, the rest of the Center Party chose instrumentally to go along with this strategy. Indeed, the general radicalization of Weimar society by this point had generated substantial support for a new dictatorship even among the Center's core electorate. The Windthorstbund, for example, now began to reorient itself from the defense of religious liberty toward support for Brüning himself, who was portrayed as the "*Führer*" who could rescue Germany from its trials.[104] Still, Brüning's authority ultimately did not depend on society but rather on the continued support of the president – and as the depression deepened further, Hindenburg's inner circle became increasingly restless about this. The Zentrum's loyal support for Hindenburg's presidential campaign in April 1932 against the surging Hitler

[103] See Thomas Childers, *The Nazi Voter: The Social Foundations of Fascism in Germany, 1919–1933* (Chapel Hill: University of North Carolina Press, 1983); Hamilton, *Who Voted for Hitler?*

[104] Evans, *The German Center Party*, p. 372.

was not repaid in kind: soon after Hindenburg's reelection, Franz von Papen, a Catholic monarchist who came from the Center's extreme right, was named chancellor. But while the Center Party refused to support von Papen's government, once the July 1932 elections produced a Reichstag with an explicit majority for revolutionary parties of the left and right, its influence over the situation was minimal.

For many Germans, the choice by the fall of 1932 seemed to be clear: either a communist takeover or a Nazi government. When this viewpoint became dominant among the leadership of the German military and the Junker elite who made up Hindenburg's camarilla, and Hitler was finally named chancellor on January 30, 1933, Germany's fate was sealed. And while Turner is certainly correct to insist that the German business elite on the whole did not support Hitler, and indeed tried to utilize whatever influence they had with Hindenburg to prevent his appointment, there is nevertheless no doubt that its willingness to go along in the end with the National Socialist agenda had a great deal to do with their fear that the ideological alternative would be Soviet communism.[105]

As in the case of the Gambettists during the French Third Republic, the institutions imposed and the policies pursued by Hitler and his followers after taking power reflected the Nazis' initial ideological convictions quite faithfully. The "leader principle" quickly became the guiding norm of all political life: utilizing the pretext of the Reichstag fire in February, Hitler banned the KPD, arresting the party's leaders en masse; in March, the Center Party was cowed into voting for the enabling law that legalized Hitler's dictatorship and was soon after dissolved along with the SPD; and the unruly elements in the SA were brought under control after the assassination of Ernst Röhm and other top SA officials in 1934. The struggle for *Lebensraum* soon became the guiding principle of German foreign policy, beginning with Hitler's rapid expansion of the military and arms production, and soon extending to a policy of territorial annexation that eventually encompassed most of Europe. Finally, Hitler's theory of "race struggle" between Aryans and "subhumans" led to the construction of an increasingly segregated and repressive society – culminating in the murder of more than six million Jews in the Holocaust.

---

[105] Turner, *German Big Business and the Rise of Hitler.*

6

Post-Soviet Russia

In examining the sixteen years from the formal establishment of the Russian Federation in 1992 through the election of Dmitrii Medvedev as the presidential successor to Vladimir Putin in early 2008, we obviously cannot yet rely on the sort of comprehensive, detailed historiography of the period that exists for the early French Third Republic or Weimar Germany. Fortunately, where a few historians are now just beginning to tread, a whole team of intrepid political scientists – both in Russia and the West – has over these years collectively generated a remarkably detailed account of the rise and fall of post-Soviet democracy. Indeed, our documentation of the formative years of the Russian Federation, at the levels of both elite politics and mass public opinion, is among the best that exists for any newly democratizing regime. We owe a great debt to those scholars who braved substantial professional and popular disinterest in postcommunist Russian studies, often working in challenging conditions, to obtain and analyze these data.

Despite the abundance of empirical evidence, however, how to account for Russia's political trajectory – from the collapse of the Soviet Union, through Russia's troubled experiment with representative rule in the 1990s, to its increasing authoritarianism of the early twenty-first century – remains theoretically contentious. Taken as a whole, these developments appear to have confounded the expectations of nearly all early analysts of Russian politics. Russia's experience does not fit the widespread idea that democracy is rooted in sociocultural modernization that generates a "civil society" and thus emerges primarily from the "bottom up." Nor is it easy to explain the dynamics of post-Soviet politics utilizing the rival theory that successful democracy reflects the imposition of institutional rules from the "top down."[1] As emphasized by a

---

[1] For an intriguing argument that U.S. elites tend to see democracy as coming from the bottom up, while European policy makers tend to adopt a "top-down" view, see Jeffrey Kopstein, "The Transatlantic Divide over Democracy Promotion," *Washington Quarterly* 29(2, Spring 2006): 87–98.

third school of thought, Russia's turbulent politics do owe a great deal to the country's unfavorable past legacies as well as to its unfavorable geographic position – but such contextual factors cannot fully explain why the country's leaders launched Russia's experiment in multiparty democracy in the first place. The most successful analyses of Russia's failed postcommunist democratization emphasize the revolutionary nature of this transformation and the pervasive social and institutional uncertainty that it necessarily generated – making it exceedingly difficult for Russian politicians to build stable state institutions of either the democratic or authoritarian type. I examine each of these schools of thought in turn.

The "bottom up" view of democratization is rooted in the dominant social science paradigm in the United States from World War II through the 1970s – modernization theory. According to this viewpoint, democracy in its modern form – involving an emphasis on individual political liberties, procedurally fair elections, and impersonal legal institutions that enforce both majority rule and minority rights – is possible only after a prolonged prior process of social modernization.[2] Urbanization, education, and the spread of new technologies of mass communication, according to this view, all tend over time to uproot people from parochial, agricultural communities and to shatter their traditional stereotypes, allowing them to develop new identities as individual citizens inter-acting with others in a tolerant and pluralist spirit. Thus, the development of a democratic civic culture generated by such processes of modernization is seen as a prerequisite for effective democratic institutions.[3] Elections in societies still tied to traditional notions of communal loyalty, modernization theorists argue, will result only in a zero-sum struggle between opposing clans, sects, or tribes; efforts to establish the impersonal rule of law in traditional societies will run aground as state officials increasingly rely on patron-client relationships rather than formal bureaucratic procedures. Conversely, when a society has become sufficiently modernized through economic and technological development, the demand for modern democracy becomes overwhelming and irresistible, and outmoded personalistic dictatorships quickly crumble.[4]

Recent statistical analysis of the relationship between economic development and democratization, however, casts this simple hypothesis into some doubt. For one thing, economic growth seems to stabilize dictatorships – especially, it seems, the most ruthless ones – as much as it does democratic regimes.[5] Rapid

---

[2] For classic works in this tradition, see Seymour Martin Lipset, *Political Man: The Social Bases of Politics* (Garden City, NY: Doubleday, 1960), and Robert A. Dahl, *Polyarchy: Participation and Opposition* (New Haven: Yale University Press, 1971).

[3] Gabriel A. Almond and Sidney Verba, *The Civic Culture: Political Attitudes and Democracy in Five Nations* (Princeton, NJ: Princeton University Press, 1963).

[4] Many of these assumptions lie behind the excellent comparative research of Larry Diamond. See, for example, Larry Jay Diamond, *Developing Democracy: Toward Consolidation* (Baltimore: Johns Hopkins University Press, 1999).

[5] Adam Przeworski and Fernando Limongi, "Modernization: Theories and Facts," *World Politics* 49(2, January 1997): 155–183; Alex Hadenius and Jan Teorell, "Cultural and Economic Pre-requisites of Democracy: Reassessing Recent Evidence," *Studies in Comparative International Development* 39(4, Winter 2005): 87–106.

growth in the Soviet Union from Stalin through the early Brezhnev period, involving both rapid urbanization and mass education, clearly heightened the Soviet communist dictatorship's popular appeal. A similar process continued in the People's Republic of China for nearly three decades after the introduction of Deng Xiao-Ping's reforms. Some scholars insist that in the longer term, economic growth still tends to make democratic change more likely, but even they admit that the long-run causal link between social modernization and democratic institutional outcomes is poorly understood.[6] We have no grounds, then, for assuming in any particular country or historical period that booming economic growth will necessarily promote democracy.

In the case of Russia, a modernization theoretic analysis of democratization and its reversal under Putin appears to fail us completely. The Soviet Union under Mikhail Gorbachev was a highly urbanized and educated society: more than 80 percent of its population lived in cities, and literacy was nearly universal. Per capita GDP in 1990 in the USSR was about $3,700, well above the levels found in most developing nations in that period.[7] Not surprisingly, many modernization theorists argued that Gorbachev's reforms indeed reflected the emergence of a "civic culture" among modernized Soviet citizens and predicted a successful democratic outcome as a consequence of this.[8] Yet Gorbachev's efforts at political liberalization led not to stable democracy in the USSR as a whole but rather to the breakup of the Soviet Union along the lines of its constituent ethnic republics.

Modernization theory logically generated optimistic predictions about the prospects for democracy in the post-Soviet Russian Federation under Boris Yeltsin, too. After all, Russia inherited not only a highly modern society but also a relatively homogeneous one, with about 80 percent of its population ethnically Russian, which greatly reduced another putative social cause of democratic breakdown, ethnolinguistic fractionalization. Yet Russian democracy under Yeltsin lurched from crisis to crisis, including a near civil war between supporters of the president and of the parliament in October 1993; a flawed and falsified constitutional referendum in December 1993; a disputed electoral victory by Yeltsin over the communist leader Gennadii Ziuganov in July 1996; extreme and growing levels of political corruption throughout the 1990s; a civil society marked by personal infighting and dependence on foreign funding sources; and, finally, a carefully managed transfer of executive power to Yeltsin's designated "successor" in 2000. Even more troubling for modernization theory, Russia's experiment with democratic institutions was ultimately curtailed under Putin precisely at the time Russian economic growth resumed. Far from generating mass demands for political liberalization, Russia's economic

---

[6] Carles Boix and Susan Stokes, "Endogenous Democratization," *World Politics* 55(4, July 2003): 517–549.

[7] M. Steven Fish, "Stronger Legislatures, Stronger Democracies," *Journal of Democracy* 17(1, January 2006): 14.

[8] Moshe Lewin, *The Gorbachev Phenomenon: A Historical Interpretation* (Berkeley: University of California Press, 1988).

rebound greatly increased Russian support for the Putin regime's recentralization of state authority.[9]

Confronted with this history, some modernization theorists have reverted
to a rather less dynamic view of Russian culture – namely, that such a culture
is the product of deeper "civilizational" forces rooted in Orthodoxy and the
Mongol conquest, leading ordinary Russians to reject liberal individualism
in favor of the "strong hand" of the state.[10] Such stereotypes, however, do
nothing to explain why both Gorbachev and then Yeltsin endeavored for so
long to decentralize Russian politics, with the support of significant sectors of
Russian society. It is worth remembering that static "cultural" theorists have
also predicted the impossibility of civic culture in Catholic Europe after World
War II; the infeasibility of economic growth in "Confucian" societies like
China; and the likely failure of democracy in postcommunist Eastern Europe
after the collapse of the Soviet Union. Like a broken clock that is right twice a
day, "civilizational" theories are bound to look good when democratic prospects in non-Western countries look bleakest.

Frustrated with the inadequacies of modernization theory for explaining
and predicting the pattern of global democratization over the past century
and a half, many political scientists have abandoned the notion of "social
prerequisites" for democracy altogether, focusing instead on the opportunities
for "crafting" democratic outcomes through political creativity and careful
institutional design – even in the seemingly most unlikely places. Democratic
leadership, according to this school of thought, involves an ability to forge compromises with moderate members of the political opposition in order to generate "pacts" that guarantee the rules of free political competition and access for
both former autocratic elites and emerging social groups.[11] Equally important,
from this perspective, is the design of formal constitutional rules that ensure
the continuing decentralization of power after the democratic "transition" is
over. In particular, the majority of top-down analysts of democracy have come
to the conclusion that parliamentary rule is vastly preferable to presidentialism
for democracy's future prospects. The concentration of power in the hands of
a president, especially in the context of a new democracy with typically weak
legislative and judicial institutions, makes autocratic behavior too tempting to
resist; conversely, the dispersion of power among multiple competing parties

---

9 Public support in Russia for "our system of government" remained under 40 percent in public
   opinion polls from 1992 through 2000, but shot up to 65 percent by 2004 before falling back in
   2005. See Richard Rose, William Mishler, and Neil Munro, *Russia Transformed: Developing
   Support for a New Regime* (Cambridge: Cambridge University Press, 2006), fig. 5.1, p. 90.

10 Richard Pipes, "Flight from Freedom: What Russians Think and Want," *Foreign Affairs* 83(3,
    May–June 2004): 9–15; Samuel P. Huntington, *The Clash of Civilizations and the Remaking
    of World Order* (New York: Simon and Schuster, 1996).

11 Classic works in this tradition include Guillermo O'Donnell and Phillippe Schmitter, *Transitions
    from Authoritarian Rule: Tentative Conclusions about Uncertain Democracies* (Baltimore:
    Johns Hopkins University Press, 1986), and Guiseppe Di Palma, *To Craft Democracies: An
    Essay on Democratic Transitions* (Berkeley: University of California Press, 1990).

in a pure parliamentary system helps to forestall undemocratic moves toward political recentralization.[12]

Recent democratic reversals in the Middle East, Latin America, and Africa as well as in the former Soviet region, however, have led to increasing disillusionment with the optimistic predictions of theorists of elite-led democratization. As Thomas Carothers has argued, the "transition paradigm" gives us no way to explain the long-term persistence of corrupt semidemocratic regimes with very limited social accountability or legitimacy.[13] Far from being "on the road" toward democratic consolidation, such personalistic semidemocracies and "competitive authoritarian regimes" seem to have a remarkable staying power of their own.[14] Moreover, while statistical studies have cast into doubt the simple correlation of economic development and democracy postulated by early modernization theory, it is nevertheless clear that both legacies of past institutions and sociological conditions do matter for the prospects of stable democratic institution building.[15] Most strikingly in the postcommunist context, democracy has been much more successful in East-Central Europe and the Baltic States than in the non-Baltic former USSR, where Leninist political and economic institutions were imposed much longer and enforced more rigidly. And while it is true that parliamentary systems are ubiquitous in the successful new European democracies, whereas presidential systems are typical in the former Soviet republics, theories of institutional design alone cannot explain why the distribution of regime types itself so closely parallels historical and geographic factors.[16] Apparently, one cannot simply "design democracy" from above in any country one chooses, whenever one wishes.

The history of Russian democratization since the Gorbachev era also casts doubt on the utility of the top-down approach. Few politicians, after all, could match Gorbachev in his ability to "craft" democratic compromises with opposition figures, even under conditions of enormous political strain; yet all of Gorbachev's carefully negotiated pacts with Yeltsin and the other leaders of Soviet republics fell apart instantaneously after the August coup.[17] Yeltsin, too, came to power after negotiating a compromise with the freely elected Russian Congress of People's Deputies, according to which his presidential "emergency

[12] Juan Linz, "The Perils of Presidentialism," *Journal of Democracy* 1(1, Winter 1990): 51–69; Fish, "Stronger Legislatures, Stronger Democracies."

[13] Thomas Carothers, "The End of the Transition Paradigm?" *Journal of Democracy* 13(1, January 2002): 13–19.

[14] Steven Levitsky and Lucan Way, "The Rise of Competitive Authoritarianism," *Journal of Democracy* 13(2, April 2002): 51–63.

[15] Ken Jowitt, "The Leninist Legacy," in *New World Disorder: The Leninist Extinction* (Berkeley: University of California Press, 1992), pp. 284–305; Marc Morjé Howard, *The Weakness of Civil Society in Post-Communist Europe* (Cambridge: Cambridge University Press, 2003); Grzegorz Ekiert and Stephen E. Hanson, eds., *Capitalism and Democracy in Eastern and Central Europe: Assessing the Legacy of Communist Rule* (Cambridge: Cambridge University Press, 2003).

[16] Gerald Easter, "Preference for Presidentialism: Postcommunist Regime Change in Russia and the NIS," *World Politics* 49(2, January 1997): 184–211.

[17] Archie Brown, *The Gorbachev Factor* (Oxford: Oxford University Press, 1996).

powers" to introduce economic reform would expire after one year, thus establishing a constitutional parliamentary regime. This compromise broke down because of the intensity of the post-Soviet economic crisis in the country, which hardened ideological positions on both sides and led ultimately to a zero-sum battle between Yeltsin and the Congress for political supremacy.[18] The establishment of Yeltsin's more fully presidential regime, then, was not the cause of Russia's democratic breakdown in 1993 but its effect. And while the "superpresidential" constitution adopted in December 1993 has arguably played a negative role in the further development of democratic checks and balances in the Russian Federation, it is worth noting that during the Yeltsin era, many scholars saw the weakness of the state, not the strength of the executive, as the major problem for Russian democracy.[19] Indeed, many analysts initially greeted President Putin's own drive to "rebuild the Russian state" as at least potentially salutary for democratic consolidation, arguing that establishing the rule of law under chaotic post-Soviet Russian conditions might initially require a strong push from the executive branch.[20] That Putin's policies have so quickly generated autocratic results constitutes something of a "third strike" for theories of democratization from the top down in the Russian context.

Both "bottom-up" and "top-down" theories of democratic change seem to have led us astray, in the postcommunist milieu and elsewhere. Recently, scholars have begun to argue that our major mistake in this respect has been to focus on individual states and societies without reference to their temporal and spatial context. Advocates of "comparative-historical analysis" emphasize that the "path-dependent" effects of previous institutions may endure even as political regimes on a given territory rise and fall.[21] Thus, it is logical that particular institutional legacies will position new democracies in more or less advantageous ways, with distinct effects on their future probabilities of democratic consolidation.

[18] Michael McFaul, *Russia's Unfinished Revolution: Political Change from Gorbachev to Putin* (Ithaca, NY: Cornell University Press, 2001), pp. 121–203.

[19] On the deleterious consequences of superpresidentialism, see M. Steven Fish, *Democracy Derailed in Russia: The Failure of Open Politics* (Cambridge: Cambridge University Press, 2005); for earlier arguments about Russian state weakness, see Stephen Holmes, "What Russia Teaches Us Now: How Weak States Threaten Freedom," *American Prospect*, no. 33 (July–August 1997): 30–39, and the essays collected in Valerie Sperling, ed., *Rebuilding the Russian State: Institutional Crisis and the Quest for Democratic Governance* (Boulder, CO: Westview, 2000).

[20] Richard Sakwa, *Putin: Russia's Choice* (New York: Routledge, 2004); M. Steven Fish, "Putin's Path," *Journal of Democracy* 12(4, October 2001): 71–78; Marcia Weigle, *Russia's Liberal Project: State-Society Relations in the Transition from Communism* (University Park: Pennsylvania State University Press, 2000).

[21] James Mahoney and Dietrich Rueschemeyer, eds., *Comparative Historical Analysis in the Social Sciences* (Cambridge: Cambridge University Press, 2003); Paul Pierson, *Politics in Time: History, Institutions, and Social Analysis* (Princeton, NJ: Princeton University Press, 2004); Kathleen Thelen, *How Institutions Evolve: The Political Economy of Skills in Germany, Britain, the United States, and Japan* (Cambridge: Cambridge University Press, 2004).

A comparative-historical approach to democratization appears to fit the empirical record better than either a simple modernization-theoretic approach or one emphasizing the importance of elite pacts. Democracy, after all, has tended to spread in distinct geographic and temporal "waves," from its geographic origins in Europe and North America to countries such as Germany and Japan after World War II, to many parts of Latin America and Southeast Asia in the 1980s, to Eastern Europe and sub-Saharan Africa in the 1990s; it is now at least on the political agenda in much of Northern Africa and the Middle East.[22] De-democratization, too, has proceeded in a wavelike pattern, resulting in the collapse of most continental European democracies in the interwar period, retrenchment in much of the developing world in the 1960s and 1970s, and now a growing autocratic trend in much of the former Soviet Union. If so, our attention to specific social circumstances or elite institutions in individual countries may have blinded us to more fundamental features of the international environment thanks to which both successful democratic leadership and the emergence of vibrant civil societies tend to emerge in several societies more or less simultaneously.

Recent statistical studies have shown, for example, that placement in a "democratic neighborhood" has a significant impact on a country's prospects for democracy; conversely, establishing democracy in a country surrounded by autocracies is extremely difficult.[23] The impact of international factors appears to be much greater, too, not simply when it is the result of "leverage" over the domestic politics of autocracies exerted by democratic global powers, but rather when multiple forms of political, economic, and social "linkage" tie the fates of citizens in democratic and nondemocratic countries together in concrete ways.[24] Proximity to other successful, established democracies also provides models for institutional emulation that can profoundly influence the worldviews and everyday conduct of both elites and citizens in newly established democracies; such emulation has been a key factor in the remarkably successful integration of much of postcommunist Eastern and Central Europe into the European Union.[25] The international environment also accounts for an important factor promoting autocratic politics over the past century: namely,

---

[22] Samuel Huntington, *The Third Wave: Democratization in the Late 20th Century* (Norman: University of Oklahoma Press); Mark R. Beissinger, "Structure and Example in Modular Political Phenomena: The Diffusion of Bulldozer/Rose/Orange/Tulip Revolutions," *Perspectives on Politics* 5(2, June, 2007): 259–276.

[23] Jeffrey Kopstein and David Reilly, "Geographic Diffusion and the Transformation of the Postcommunist World," *World Politics* 53(1, October 2000): 1–35.

[24] Steven Levitsky and Lucan Way, "International Linkage and Democratization," *Journal of Democracy* 16(3, July 2005): 20–34.

[25] On the importance of norm diffusion in European Union expansion, see Jeffrey Checkel, "International Institutions and Socialization in Europe: Introduction and Framework," *International Organization* 59(2005): 801–826. On the success of EU expansion, see Milada Vachudova, *Europe Undivided: Democracy, Leverage, and Integration after Communism* (Oxford: Oxford University Press, 2005).

the possession of easily exportable energy resources. In a global capitalist economy that remains highly dependent on scarce fossil fuels, elites who control substantial oil and gas reserves can quickly amass enough money to hire well-trained security forces, buy off opposition politicians, and even pay for expensive public relations campaigns to influence public opinion in major democratic trading partners. It is not surprising that large oil and gas reserves play a statistically significant role in inhibiting democratization, both globally and in the post-Soviet context.[26]

This third perspective on the causes of democratization and de-democratization, in contrast to the "bottom-up" and "top-down" theories analyzed earlier, does help to explain Russia's turn toward autocracy under Putin. Clearly, Russia has inherited some of the most disadvantageous institutional legacies from the failed Soviet experiment. Like the other non-Baltic former Soviet republics, and unlike the new democracies of East-Central Europe, the Russian Federation lived under Leninist one-party rule for more than seven decades – long enough to preclude active political participation in postcommunist reconstruction by individuals with any direct memory of the pre-Leninist past. Like the rest of the former USSR, too, Russia inherited a socioeconomic system based on near-total state control over both industry and agriculture, with enterprises built around outdated technology and collective farms that were notoriously stagnant and inefficient. As the core of the former Soviet empire, Russia has also confronted a special obstacle to democratic consolidation – namely, the pervasive cultural association of "democracy" itself with a catastrophic loss of international status.

Not only did Russia have to overcome especially burdensome institutional legacies, but Russia's geographic placement and historical inheritance has also put democratic activists there in a very disadvantageous position. Most of Russia's neighbors, including North Korea, China, Kazakhstan, Azerbaijan, and Belarus, are led by committed dictators; its more democratic neighbors, such as Georgia, Ukraine, and the Baltic States, are comparatively small or politically fragile. Russia is simply too big and too far away from Western markets and flows of people to experience much direct "linkage" with established democratic societies; as a result, Western attempts at exerting "leverage" over Russian domestic politics have generally been ineffective. Russia's population, while highly urbanized and educated, is still only weakly linked on a personal level to the citizens of successful democratic societies, allowing stereotypes about Western "conspiracies" to destroy Russia to fester and spread. Western efforts to foster democratic civil society from the outside, however important and well intentioned, thus generated a dependent community of nongovernmental organizations (NGOs) focused on pleasing Western funders, with only

---

[26] M. Steven Fish, *Democracy Derailed in Russia: The Failure of Open Politics* (Cambridge: Cambridge University Press, 2005), pp. 114–138.

fragile support among the general public.[27] Russia under Putin was the second largest oil exporter in the world and possessed the greatest global reserves of natural gas, allowing the Kremlin to amass hundreds of billions of dollars in foreign currency reserves. Decentralization and state weakness in the Yeltsin era, from this point of view, was an anomaly caused in part by the unprecedented decline in global energy prices during the 1990s. It is hardly surprising that Putin has tended to rely on raw material exports rather than the promotion of efficient markets to fund his regime – unfortunately generating a zero-sum political struggle for the control of strategic exportable assets that is inimical to democratic compromise.[28] If we take all these contextual factors into account, Russia's democratic failure seems in retrospect not only predictable but perhaps even inevitable.

Yet however powerful, such "structural" approaches to post-Soviet Russia face one central problem: they cannot explain why Russian elites endeavored for a full decade to build genuinely competitive democratic institutions, against all the historical and geographic odds. During the 1990s, for the first time in Russian history, relatively free and fair elections were held repeatedly, for every major political office, from the presidency to local legislatures. President Boris Yeltsin, despite several opportunities to rule dictatorially, continued to tolerate serious electoral challenges to his rule. By the time of the financial crisis of August 1998, the Russian Constitution had become authoritative enough to serve as the framework for a legal transfer of government power to a coalition led by some of Yeltsin's leading political opponents. Indeed, by the turn of the century, it seemed to many leading specialists that the main theoretical task was to explain the remarkable stabilization of the imperfect but genuine democratic system created by the 1993 Russian Constitution – not to account for its failure.[29] In short, Russian democratization in the 1990s succeeded too well to be explained by structuralist theories – but then failed too dramatically in the first decade of the twenty-first century to be explained by modernization or institutionalist theories.

We are left, then, with a final, relatively persuasive approach for understanding the first decade and a half of Russia's postcommunist history: one

---

[27] Sarah Henderson, *Building Democracy in Contemporary Russia: Western Support for Grassroots Organizations* (Ithaca, NY: Cornell University Press, 2003). In response to Henderson's trenchant criticisms of Western democratization assistance efforts, however, it should be noted that a weak and dependent NGO sector is still better for democratization than no NGO sector at all.

[28] Andrew Barnes, *Owning Russia: The Struggle for Factories, Farms, and Power* (Ithaca, NY: Cornell University Press, 2006); Anders Aslund, *Russia's Capitalist Revolution: Why Market Reform Succeeded and Democracy Failed* (Cambridge: Cambridge University Press, 2007).

[29] McFaul, *Russia's Unfinished Revolution*; Steven S. Smith and Thomas F. Remington, *The Politics of Institutional Choice: The Formation of the Russian State Duma* (Princeton, NJ: Princeton University Press, 2001); Thomas Remington, *The Russian Parliament: Institutional Evolution in a Transitional Regime, 1989–1999* (New Haven: Yale University Press, 2001).

that emphasizes above all the truly revolutionary nature of Leninism's collapse and aftermath and, connected with this, the remarkably high level of social and political uncertainty in the post-Soviet context. As Offe pointed out early on, the postcommunist "triple transition" forced elites to wrestle simultaneously with fundamental rules governing politics, economics, and national identity – and nowhere were these overlapping issues more daunting than in Russia, the core of the former Soviet bloc.[30] Bunce and Csanadi, similarly, saw the unprecedented level of uncertainty about institutional rules as the key factor invalidating comparisons between postcommunist transformations and "democratic transitions" elsewhere in the world.[31] Building on these insights, McFaul has insisted that political change in Russia be studied in the context of theories of revolution, rather than theories of democratic transition alone; thus Russia's simultaneous lack of clarity about fundamental questions of political identity and high uncertainty about the political balance of power have predictably led to repeated regime crises.[32] Such approaches to Russian politics do help to explain both why such dramatic institutional changes were possible in a few short years after communism's collapse – and why liberalizing reforms were nevertheless later reversed under the combined pressure of elite and social resistance in an unfavorable structural setting.

What the "revolutionary" approach to theorizing about post-Soviet Russia lacks, however, is an appropriate set of comparative reference points by which to evaluate Russia's prospects for democracy or dictatorship. Analogies to "great social revolutions," such as the French Revolution of 1789, the Russian Revolution of 1917, or the Chinese Revolution of 1911–1949 – although helpful in highlighting their similarly high levels of institutional and social uncertainty – are of limited utility for analysis of the Russian Federation under Yeltsin and Putin, given the absence of any extended period of electoral democracy in these prior revolutions. The role of electoral parties in postrevolutionary institutional design, in particular, was naturally very limited given the replacement of parliaments with revolutionary dictatorships under the Jacobins, Bolsheviks, and Maoists. Including the Russian Federation among such revolutionary regimes inevitably biases the analyst toward very pessimistic conclusions about Russia's democratic potential. On the other hand, the inclusion of Russia as a case comparable to other postcommunist transformations

---

[30] Claus Offe, "Capitalism by Democratic Design? Democratic Theory Facing the Triple Transition in East-Central Europe," *Social Research* 58(4, Winter 1991): 865–892.

[31] Valerie Bunce and Maria Csanadi, "Uncertainty in the Transition: Post-Communist in Hungary," *East European Politics and Societies* 7(2, Spring 1993): 240–275. See also Mary McAuley, *Russia's Politics of Uncertainty* (Cambridge: Cambridge University Press, 1997).

[32] McFaul, *Russia's Unfinished Revolution*. See also Vladimir Mau and Irina Starodubroksaya, *The Challenge of Revolution: Contemporary Russia in Comparative Perspective* (Oxford: Oxford University Press, 2001); Gordon M. Hahn, *Russia's Revolution from Above, 1985–2000: Reform, Transition, and Revolution in the Fall of the Soviet Regime* (New Brunswick, NJ: Transaction Publishers, 2002); and Marc Garcelon, *Revolutionary Passage: From Soviet to Post-Soviet Russia, 1985–2000* (Philadelphia: Temple University Press, 2005).

in East-Central Europe – as in the early works of Offe as well as Bunce and Csanadi – tends to overstate the degree of uncertainty in states immediately bordering the European Union and fails to isolate the distinctive situation of Russia as the core of the former Soviet bloc. We should compare post-Soviet Russia, instead, to other cases where sudden regime collapse was followed by a sufficiently long period of reasonably competitive elections to gauge precisely what is similar and what is distinctive about Russian party formation and regime choice in a turbulent social milieu – and to assess whether Russia might, given different choices by key actors, have managed after all to attain a more consolidated democratic system.

My purpose in this chapter, therefore, is not to introduce new facts about the dynamics of post-Soviet democratization and de-democratization, but rather to bring to bear a Weberian comparative-historical approach to the Yeltsin and Putin eras, building on the analysis already presented in this book. I try to show that the history of these dramatic sixteen years has remarkable parallels to the dynamics of post-imperial democracy we have examined before. Once again, the collapse of empire led to institutional and social chaos, in which levels of individual uncertainty were abnormally high; again, this chaotic period greatly augmented the collective action problems facing would-be builders of new Russian political parties with a "centrist" or "pragmatic" orientation. By the time comparative stability had returned to Russia in 1994, the only parties with effective national networks of activists were the Communist Party of the Russian Federation under Gennadii Ziuganov and the Liberal Democratic Party of Russia under Vladimir Zhirinovskii – the two party organizations, I argue, with relatively clear and consistent ideological definitions of the future Russian polity for which they stood. From 1994 to 1999, however, the rival and incompatible visions of the Russian future held by Ziuganov, Zhirinovskii, and the first post-Soviet president Boris Yeltsin, generated a prolonged stalemate about Russia's regime type that prevented any consolidation of constitutional democracy.

However, while the "synchronic" comparison of relevant parties in post-Soviet Russia once again shows how ideological party builders triumphed over their more "pragmatic" competitors, a "diachronic" comparison with the ideological parties that formed in the early French Third Republic and Weimar Germany shows that even the more successful Russian political parties remained organizationally weak.[33] The relative weakness of Russian parties, I argue, reflects the relatively limited popular appeal of communist, fascist, and liberal ideologies alike in the wake of the Soviet Union's collapse. The effect of seven decades of failed ideological indoctrination appears to have been the

---

[33] Failure to distinguish between these two types of comparative analysis of Russian parties can quickly lead to analytic confusion. The argument that Russia's ideological parties were stronger in the 1990s than their nonideological competitors should not be understood as contradicting the larger point that Russia's party system overall remained weak and inchoate by comparison with other, more consolidated democracies. Both points are true, and important.

creation of a society largely allergic to ideological appeals of any sort. Thus, even after the severe political crisis generated by the Russian financial collapse of August 1998, none of the parties represented in the Duma possessed sufficient institutional and social power to impose its favored regime type. Unlike the situation in France or Germany, where Presidents MacMahon and Hindenburg were ultimately subordinated to well-disciplined ideological party organizations, President Vladimir Putin triumphed over all independent parties; he then proceeded to build a compliant and nonideological "party of power" from the top down. The result was the institutionalization of a personalistic form of quasi-constitutional authoritarian rule that lacked any coherent ideological legitimation. Instead of democratic consolidation as in the French case or fascist consolidation as in the German case, Russia's regime can be characterized a highly personalistic form of weak state authoritarianism.

The Origin of Parties in the Late Soviet Period

As in the cases of the French Third Republic and Weimar Germany, we must trace the origins of the newly competitive political parties of the Russian Federation back to their origins in the previous empire. That the USSR can be understood as an "empire," despite its socialist and officially "anti-imperialist" ideology, is, by now, widely accepted among scholars.[34] Of course, the Soviet Union differed from previous empires in significant respects. No other empire in history so fully centralized authority through a one-party state and secret police apparatus that attempted to control nearly every aspect of daily life down to the local level. Nor does the planned economy, with its imposing bureaucracy, massive citadels of heavy industry, gulag labor, and brutal imposition of collective farming, have any counterpart in the imperial regimes of the past. Finally, the influence of official Marxism-Leninism shaped imperial relationships in the USSR in distinctive ways.

However, after Stalin's death in 1953, growing popular skepticism about Marx's original vision of communism as a practical guide for state policy, combined with the pervasive corruption of the Soviet bureaucracy, produced a palpable disconnect between the official ideology of the Soviet regime and the everyday lives of millions of Soviet citizens. The end of Stalinist mass terror allowed room for the tentative emergence of political alternatives to Soviet orthodoxy, ranging from the democratic "evolutionary socialism" of reformers like Andrei Sakharov to the Slavic nationalism of Aleksandr Solzhenitsyn. As

---

[34] For an early debate about the utility of the term, see Ronald Grigor Suny, "Ambiguous Categories: States, Empires, and Nations," and Mark Beissinger, "The Persisting Ambiguity of Empire," *Post-Soviet Affairs* 11(2, April–June 1995): 149–196. For recent comparative analyses of the USSR and other examples of imperial collapse, see Alexander J. Motyl, *Imperial Ends: The Decay, Collapse, and Revival of Empires* (New York: Columbia University Press, 2001), and Hendrik Spruyt, *Ending Empire: Contested Sovereignty and Territorial Partition* (Ithaca, NY: Cornell University Press, 2005).

long as the Brezhnev leadership continued to crack down on any signs of open dissent, of course, such figures remained marginalized and largely powerless. But widespread informal opposition to Soviet ideology and policy – ranging from pilfering and foot-dragging by workers at state enterprises to ubiquitous jokes about the Brezhnev leadership retold in kitchens throughout the country – became a central part of Soviet mass culture in the 1970s.[35] As the Brezhnev leadership entered senescence and the Soviet Union began to face serious international and domestic crises in the 1980s, there was a growing sense among both Soviet elites and ordinary citizens that serious reforms were becoming indispensable.

The growing ideological vacuum created by the discrediting of Marxism-Leninism also generated powerful new forms of nationalist opposition to Soviet authorities in every part of the Soviet bloc. In part, the growth of nationalism was the inadvertent effect of Soviet official nationalities policy. On the one hand, Soviet authorities since Stalin had proscribed "bourgeois nationalism" and crushed even the most tentative movements toward independence. On the other hand, the CPSU leadership inadvertently encouraged new forms of national sentiment by setting up separate administrative hierarchies in all of the non-Russian Soviet Socialist republics (SSRs), inscribing national identity on the mandatory passports of Soviet citizens, and even promoting – within strict ideological boundaries, of course – the study of the languages, cultures, and intellectual traditions of the Soviet peoples.[36] Even this relatively limited opportunity to study the lives and works of great "national" figures became a cultural refuge from the boredom of official Marxism-Leninism for a growing number of intellectuals, both in the non-Russian republics and in the Russian Soviet Federative Socialist Republic (RSFSR) itself.[37]

Thus, while it stretches the point too far to suggest that the USSR in the Brezhnev era resembled Louis Napoleon's Second Empire or the Wilhelmine Reich in its lack of clarity about regime definition – indeed, the Soviet Union continued to defend a rather rigid conception of communist ideology throughout this period – the social milieu of the late Soviet era nevertheless had important elements in common with these earlier regimes. All three regimes

[35] Vladimir Shlapentokh, *A Normal Totalitarian Society: How the USSR Functioned and How it Collapsed* (Armonk, NY: M. E. Sharpe, 2001).

[36] There is by now a large body of literature on this theme. See, for example, Victor Zaslavsky, *The Neo-Stalinist State: Class, Ethnicity, and Consensus in Soviet Society* (Armonk, NY: M. E. Sharpe, 1982); Ronald Suny, *Revenge of the Past: Nationalism, Revolution, and the Collapse of the Soviet Union* (Stanford, CA: Stanford University Press, 1993); Yuri Slezkine, "The USSR as a Communal Apartment, or How a Socialist State Promoted Ethnic Particularism," *Slavic Review* 53(2, Summer 1994): 414–453; Rogers Brubaker, *Nationalism Reframed: Nationhood and the National Question in the New Europe* (Cambridge: Cambridge University Press, 1996); and Terry Martin, *Affirmative Action Empire: Nations and Nationalism in the Soviet Union, 1923–1939* (Ithaca, NY: Cornell University Press, 2001).

[37] Georgi Derluguian, *Bourdieu's Secret Admirer in the Caucasus: A World System Biography* (Chicago: University of Chicago Press, 2005).

combined an emphasis on rapid industrialization and socioeconomic modernization designed to bolster the military might and international status of the state, generating genuine pride among significant social groups. At the same time, all three regimes found themselves struggling to legitimate state repression, elite privilege, and censorship in the context of increasing social pressures for democratic reform. Ultimately, the French Second Empire, Wilhelmine Germany, and the late Soviet Union alike responded to these pressures by allowing the emergence of more genuinely competitive parliaments – which subsequently generated even more powerful forms of democratic and reactionary opposition to the status quo.

To be sure, when Mikhail Gorbachev was elected general secretary of the Soviet Union in March 1985 with a clear party mandate to introduce "radical reform," he had no intention whatsoever of undermining Soviet socialism. On the contrary, the evidence suggests that Gorbachev held fast to a remarkably naive version of romantic Marxism-Leninism through most if not all of his tenure in office.[38] Believing that Soviet society had "matured" as a result of its decades of experience under Leninism, he concentrated his efforts on dismantling the corrupt bureaucracy built up during the Brezhnev "era of stagnation," assuming that the decentralization of power would by itself spur ordinary Soviet citizens to engage voluntarily in heroic work on behalf of the socialist cause. By January 1987 Gorbachev's full-scale launch of his program of perestroika, or restructuring, sparked the beginnings of genuine political pluralism in the USSR.

Gorbachev's conception of perestroika was built around three key elements, each of which quickly developed in a truly radical direction.[39] First, Gorbachev's conception of glasnost', or openness, evolved quickly from an initially tentative toleration of public criticism of Soviet policies to an increasingly all-encompassing freedom of speech. Second, Gorbachev's proposals for "new thinking" in foreign policy began as standard propaganda designed to paint the Reagan administration as the main threat to world peace, but within two years they spurred official calls by Gorbachev's spokesmen for an end to the "Brezhnev doctrine" of Soviet military intervention to crush threats to socialism within the Soviet bloc – a policy that ultimately led to the peaceful collapse of communism in East-Central Europe in the fall of 1989.[40] Finally, Gorbachev's concept of democratization was initially designed to increase the

[38] I first made this argument a year before the collapse of the USSR. See Stephen E. Hanson, "Gorbachev: The Last True Leninist Believer?" in Daniel Chirot, ed., *The Crisis of Leninism and the Decline of the Left* (Seattle: University of Washington Press, 1991), pp. 33–59.

[39] Excellent accounts are given in Archie Brown, *The Gorbachev Factor* (Oxford: Oxford University Press, 1996); George W. Breslauer, *Gorbachev and Yeltsin as Leaders* (Cambridge: Cambridge University Press, 2002). Gorbachev's own reflections are presented in his autobiography, *Zhizn' i Reformy* (Moscow: Novosti, 1995).

[40] Mikhail S. Gorbachev, *Perestroika: New Thinking for Our Country and the World* (New York: Harper and Row, 1987); Jacques Lévesque, *The Enigma of 1989: The USSR and the Liberation of Eastern Europe* (Berkeley: University of California Press, 1997).

power of the soviets – the local councils of Soviet citizens which had been decisively subordinated to the party since 1919 – and thus to put pressure on "conservative" party bureaucrats. By the Nineteenth Party Conference in June 1988, however, Gorbachev had decided that the power of the hidebound CPSU apparatus could be dislodged only through competitive elections to a new USSR Congress of People's Deputies.

The spring 1989 elections to the USSR Congress of People's Deputies were carried out under rules that were hardly democratic by Western liberal standards.[41] The Communist Party of the Soviet Union remained, at this point, the only legal political party in the country. One-third of the seats in the new 2,250 person assembly were reserved in advance for "public organizations" designated by Gorbachev's elite – including the CPSU itself. A registration process controlled by local nomenklatura representatives sufficed to eliminate competition in a majority of the remaining open seats. Nevertheless, many seats for the Congress were contested in genuinely competitive elections, and several prominent conservative Leninists were defeated by "reformist" candidates. Most importantly, these elections enabled the stunning political comeback of Boris Yeltsin, who had been ousted from Gorbachev's Politburo the year before for violating party discipline with his open criticisms of conservative Leninists such as Deputy General Secretary Yegor Ligachev. Yeltsin, whose political future had been written off by knowledgeable observers, defeated his rival in Moscow District Number 1 – Yevgenii Brakov, the manager of the ZIL automobile factory – attaining a remarkable 89 percent of the votes cast.[42] By June 1988, when the Congress met for the first time, Yeltsin had allied himself with dissident Andrei Sakharov and other "democrats" in the new Interregional Group of Deputies, which at the height of its popularity claimed 17 percent of the parliamentary seats.[43] Of course, Gorbachev still firmly controlled the Congress's majority, and he had no problem convincing it to elect him to the newly created post of president of the USSR. Nevertheless, the emergence in the Congress of a genuine political opposition to Gorbachev led by the charismatic Yeltsin, whose open criticisms of the Soviet leadership were televised to enthralled audiences throughout the Soviet Union, was a dramatic political turning point.

Despite growing conservative CPSU opposition, mounting economic problems, and the collapse of the Soviet bloc, Gorbachev's democratization program continued to intensify in 1990 with elections for republican parliaments in each of the fifteen Soviet republics. Unlike the elections for the USSR Congress of

[41] Michael Urban with Viacheslav Igrunov and Sergei Mitrokhin, *The Rebirth of Politics in Russia* (Cambridge: Cambridge University Press, 1997); Remington, *The Russian Parliament*, pp. 20–46; McFaul, *Russia's Unfinished Revolution*, pp. 33–60.

[42] For Yeltsin's premature political obituary, see Seweryn Bialer, "The Yeltsin Affair: The Dilemma of the Left in Gorbachev's Revolution," in Bialer, ed., *Politics, Society, and Nationality Inside Gorbachev's Russia* (Boulder, CO: Westview, 1989), pp. 91–119. On Yeltsin's victory over Brakov, see Timothy J. Colton, *Yeltsin: A Life* (New York: Basic Books, 2008), pp. 165–166.

[43] McFaul, *Russia's Unfinished Revolution*, p. 73.

People's Deputies, however, Gorbachev's team paid little attention to managing these latter contests, apparently believing them to be politically insignificant given the historic dominance of all-union institutions over republican ones.[44] The republican Soviet elections, in fact, were largely free and fair, with no seats reserved for "public organizations" and greater freedom for opposition candidates to campaign – especially after March 1990, when the Soviet Constitution was formally amended to drop the Brezhnev-era provision that the CPSU should be guaranteed a "leading role" in Soviet society. In the wake of the revolutions of 1989 in East-Central Europe and the rebirth of nationalist ideology in most of the SSRs, the republican parliamentary elections would inevitably provide a powerful political impetus to movements in each republic demanding greater "sovereignty" from the Soviet center.[45]

Increasingly this was true within the RSFSR itself. In fact, the beginnings of Russia's multiparty system can be traced directly to the elections for the Russian Congress of People's Deputies in March 1990, which saw sharp divisions between "democrats" calling for much greater political liberalization than that envisioned by Gorbachev and conservatives terrified that the Soviet system was on the verge of total collapse. In this context, Yeltsin's decision to run for a seat in the Russian CPD proved to be extremely perspicacious. Upon his election, Yeltsin was immediately acknowledged as the leader of the democratic faction in the Congress, and in May he managed to get elected as its chairman by a close vote of 535 to 467 – just four votes above the required absolute majority of deputies.[46] From this point on, Yeltsin's demands for Russian "sovereignty" logically also implied the elevation of his own political authority over that of Gorbachev.

Gorbachev's last-ditch efforts in late 1990 and early 1991 to save the Soviet center by relying on a new coalition of KGB, Interior Ministry, and military hard-liners – culminating in the January 1991 coup attempts in the Baltic states that led to the deaths of dozens of Baltic protestors – only served further to increase Yeltsin's popularity. Gorbachev's tactical victory in the March 1991 referendum on preserving the USSR, in which more than 70 percent of Soviet voters appeared to support the union state, was undermined by the ambiguous wording of the resolution, the nonparticipation of several Soviet republics, and the simultaneous support of Russian voters for a new, elected Russian presidency. In June 1991 Yeltsin became the first elected president in Russia's history, with an overwhelming margin of 59 percent to 18 percent over the second-place finisher, Gorbachev's preferred candidate Premier Nikolai Ryzhkov.[47] It was difficult now not to notice that Gorbachev himself had never

[44] Ibid., p. 78.
[45] Mark R. Beissinger, *Nationalist Mobilization and the Collapse of the Soviet State* (Cambridge: Cambridge University Press, 2002); Edward W. Walker, *Dissolution: Sovereignty and the Breakup of the Soviet Union* (Lanham, MD: Rowman and Littlefield, 2003).
[46] Remington, *The Russian Parliament*, p. 91.
[47] Colton, *Yeltsin: A Life*, p. 193.

subjected his authority to a popular vote. Indeed, Yeltsin's ascendancy over Gorbachev, along with the impending signing of the Novo-Ogareva agreement to create a "Union of Sovereign States" to replace the USSR, were key factors motivating the hard-line coup attempt by the leaders of the military, Interior Ministry, and KGB on August 19, 1991. When the August coup imploded in three days, Yeltsin became the de facto leader of Russia. Four months later, when the republican leaders of Russia, Belarus, and Ukraine and soon the other non-Baltic republics signed the Belovezh Forest accords to dissolve the USSR, Yeltsin's authority over the new Russian state became de jure as well.

The dynamics of the collapse of the Soviet Union deeply affected the formulation of new, postcommunist ideologies and parties in the 1990s. For communists, ethnic nationalists, and democrats alike, making sense of Russia's new political identity in the wake of such dramatic and disorienting institutional and cultural changes proved to be a serious intellectual challenge. I examine each of these ideological groupings in turn.

Communists

The fact that Gorbachev legitimated his perestroika reform program by claiming it to be fully consistent with the ideals of original Leninism was of inestimable importance for the subsequent evolution of communist ideology in the post-Soviet period. Had Gorbachev simply called for the straightforward "liberalization" of Soviet institutions, communist "true believers" could easily have positioned themselves as the defenders of the Soviet status quo – and given widespread discontent with Gorbachev's leadership after 1989, party conservatives might then well have succeed in overthrowing Gorbachev, as they did with Khrushchev before him. It was incomparably more difficult, however, to craft a coherent Leninist ideological response to a CPSU general secretary who as late as December 1989 declared himself to be a "convinced communist" and who consistently argued that dismantling the central institutions of one-party rule would lead somehow to "more socialism" in Soviet society.[48] Gorbachev's adoption of this policy line ensured that lower-level apparatchiki would be forced to destroy Leninism no matter what they did: if they disobeyed the direct orders of the general secretary, they would clearly be violating Leninist norms of absolute obedience to the party leadership, but if they obeyed, they would inevitably open up political space for increasingly powerful anti-Leninist movements.[49] This paradoxical situation ensured that opposition to Gorbachev

---

[48] Gorbachev's famous declaration of communist conviction is quoted in Breslauer, *Gorbachev and Yeltsin as Leaders*, p. 136.

[49] This no-win situation can be illustrated by a personal experience of the author. In the summer of 1988, I traveled on an official Intourist tour of Russia that included stops in Moscow, Leningrad, and the Caucasus. In Moscow, while touring Red Square, our tour group watched in horror as a small demonstration of Crimean Tatars demanding the return of their ancestral lands was quickly and brutally broken up by the KGB. When the mostly pro-Gorbachev Americans and British citizens on our tour bus asked our tour guide how this could happen under perestroika, she took the microphone to reply: "Those were not legitimate protestors! Those people were hooligans!" A week later, however, while we were on a bus ride through the mountains of

within the framework of the CPSU would remain highly fragmented among several competing camps: nostalgic Stalinists such as Leningrad schoolteacher Nina Andreeva; "reformers" who continued to believe in Gorbachev's vision of socialism; socialist liberals (including Politburo member Aleksandr Yakovlev) who hoped to transform perestroika into a full-fledged embrace of European-style social democracy; and a growing number of political opportunists who began to take advantage of institutional chaos to convert their party positions into personal wealth.[50]

Under these circumstances, it soon became clear to Gorbachev's hard-line critics that a coherent communist challenge to perestroika required an alternative institutional base to the CPSU itself. For this reason, the movement to found a new, distinctive Russian Communist Party soon became the single most powerful ideological faction within the communist opposition. The call to create a separate RCP emerged as early as 1987, when Russian communists called their attention to what they saw as the injustice of Soviet federal design, in which every Soviet Republic other than the RSFSR was given its own separate party bureaucracy, KGB, and Academy of Sciences. Ironically, this institutional setup merely reflected the unconscious way in which the early CPSU leadership assumed the dominance of Russia within the Soviet Union. Given the control by ethnic Russians (and to a lesser extent Ukrainians) over every major Soviet institution, creating a separate party hierarchy for the RSFSR had hardly seemed necessary to the early Bolshevik leadership.[51]

Over the course of the post-Stalin era, however, a new form of resentful Russian nationalism emerged that blamed the "internationalism" of Marxism-Leninism for perceived discrimination by Soviet authorities against the Russians themselves.[52] Such nationalists criticized CPSU policies such as the destruction of the Russian countryside through collectivization and rapid industrialization; the proposal to divert Siberian rivers to flow to Central Asia for irrigation purposes; and the invasion of Afghanistan in 1979, which was portrayed as a purely ideological decision with no relationship to "Russian" national interests. In the Brezhnev era, because of the intervention of sympathetic, highly placed Soviet officials, resentful Russian nationalists found an institutional home in journals such as *Molodaia Gvardia* and *Nash Sovremennik* and party organizations

---

Georgia, without warning she turned on the microphone again to report: "I wanted to let you all know that I was wrong about those Crimean Tatars you saw in Moscow. They had every right to demonstrate! This is democracy!" One can only imagine the psychological tension of our dutiful tour guide, trying to uphold what was surely to her an incomprehensible new party line. But similar tensions confronted every member of the CPSU apparatus at this time.

[50] On the conversion of party assets into wealth, see Steven Lee Solnick, *Stealing the State: Control and Collapse in Soviet Institutions* (Cambridge, MA: Harvard University Press, 1998).

[51] Seweryn Bialer, *Stalin's Successors: Leadership, Stability, and Change in the Soviet Union* (Cambridge: Cambridge University Press, 1980).

[52] The history of Russian nationalism in the post-Soviet era has been exceptionally well documented by Yitzhak Brudny, *Reinventing Russia: Russian Nationalism and the Soviet State, 1953–1991* (Cambridge, MA: Harvard University Press, 1998). See also John B. Dunlop, *The Rise of Russia and the Fall of the Soviet Empire* (Princeton, NJ: Princeton University Press, 1993).

such as the RSFSR Writers' Union. The CPSU also repeatedly awarded coveted Lenin and USSR state prizes for literature to nationalist "village prose" writers such as Valentin Rasputin and Vasilii Belov.[53] Many Brezhnev-era Russian nationalists adopted quasi-fascist conspiracy theories, tracing the supposedly anti-Russian policies of the CPSU to Jewish elements within the Bolshevik elite, explaining Western hostility to Russia as the product of a global conspiracy of Jews and Masons, and circulating the well-known anti-Semitic forgery of the late tsarist era, the *Protocols of the Elders of Zion*. For Russian nationalists of this sort, Gorbachev's perestroika was anathema, destined to lead to the full-scale destruction of the Russian *derzhava* (great power) in the service of "cosmopolitan" – that is, Jewish – ideals of antinational democratic socialism. By June 1990 CPSU conservatives such as Ivan Polozkov could portray the call to found a separate Russian Communist Party in June 1990 as a crucial step in organizing Russian "patriotic" resistance to Western schemes to destroy the country. Initiating a seemingly unlikely alliance between former atheists and their supposed adversaries, Polozkov also openly called for close cooperation between defenders of communism and the Russian Orthodox Church.

It was in this ideological and institutional context that the future leader of the Communist Party of the Russian Federation, Gennadii Ziuganov, first came to political prominence. Ziuganov, a longtime CPSU functionary working on ideological issues, was evidently inspired by the example of Slobodan Milosevic in Serbia to believe that only by welding nationalism and communism together could the future of the Soviet state be secured.[54] He took to this task with genuine enthusiasm, organizing the conservative communist campaign for the Russian Congress of People's Deputies in March 1990. In December 1990 he spoke at the Seventh Congress of the RSFSR Writer's Union, arguing that only such an embrace of Russian nationalism could unite the disparate opponents of Gorbachev's reforms. In February 1991 he organized a conference of leading Russian nationalist organizations under the rubric: "For a Great, United Russia!" By the summer, Ziuganov had helped to coordinate leading nationalist intellectuals and communist hard-liners into an organized movement which openly called for a coup against Gorbachev; their manifesto "A Word to the People" was published in the hard-line journal *Sovetskaia Rossiia* in July 1991, and it has widely been seen as the inspiration for the August coup a month later. Contrary to widespread assumptions, Ziuganov's embrace of communist nationalism cannot be attributed to simple political opportunism in the post-Soviet context; on the contrary, this has been his consistent credo from nearly the beginning of his political career.[55]

[53] Brudny, *Reinventing Russia*, pp. 105–106.
[54] Ibid., p. 255.
[55] At the same time, it should be noted that Ziuganov from the beginning showed far more flexibility on questions of economic policy than many of his associates within the emerging communist-nationalist "patriotic left"; here he was willing from the outset to embrace the idea of a mixed economy in which state, collective, and even private property could coexist and supplement one another.

Ethnic Nationalists

A second ideological tendency that emerged in the late Gorbachev era was the defense of ethnic Russian nationalism – a position that in many cases shaded over into an implicit embrace of fascism. Russian fascism, however, faced ideological obstacles even greater than those confronting orthodox communists. To begin with, the widespread identification among Russians of the word *fashist* with the Nazis, whose invasion of the Soviet Union had cost twenty-five million lives, made it almost impossible even for the most extreme Russian rightists to embrace this term openly.[56] The relatively powerful movement to fuse Soviet communism and Russian nationalism also made the task of articulating an anticommunist Russian nationalist ideology much more complicated: such a position would seem to require the "patriotic" rejection of a Soviet regime, which, after all, had placed Russia at the very center of world geopolitics. Finally, whereas in East-Central Europe and the Baltic states anticommunist nationalist politicians could credibly claim to be returning to the "normal European" path of development of the interwar period, in Russia the fact that the Soviet regime had lasted more than seven decades made calls for restoration of pre-Soviet Russian institutions and traditions relatively implausible.[57]

For these reasons, even such a consistent Russian nationalist ideologue as Aleksandr Solzhenitsyn had difficulty mobilizing significant numbers of people in the late Soviet era. After nearly two decades of exile in the United States, Solzhenitsyn's pleas to his countrymen to return to Russian traditions of *sobornost'* (spiritual communalism) and fidelity to God, combined with his geopolitical schemes to reincorporate Belarus, Ukraine, and Northern Kazakhstan into a new unified Slavic Russia, struck most Russians as anachronistic and far-fetched.[58] Meanwhile, Russian nationalists on the extreme anti-Semitic right found some early success mobilizing under the auspices of the so-called *Pamiat'* (Memory) movement. But the leadership of Pamiat' quarreled constantly, almost from the start, and its collection of would-be *Führers* of Russian fascism such as Dmitrii Vasiliev, Aleksandr Barkashov, and Aleksandr Dugin quickly went their separate ways, founding rival nationalist organizations that remained at odds throughout the Yeltsin era.[59]

Thus, the most successful and consistent articulation of nationalist ideology before 1991 was one that managed from the outset to distinguish itself from both communism and traditional fascism and, indeed, from every other

[56] Public opinion polls consistently show that "fascists" are by far the least-liked social group among ordinary Russians. See James Gibson, "Putting up with Fellow Russians: An Analysis of Political Tolerance in the Fledgling Russian Democracy," *Political Science Quarterly* 51(1, March 1998): 37–68.

[57] Stephen E. Hanson, "Defining Democratic Consolidation," in Richard Anderson et al., *Postcommunism and the Theory of Democracy* (Princeton, NJ: Princeton University Press, 2001).

[58] Aleksandr I. Solzhenitsyn, *Kak Nam Obustroit' Rossiu: Posil'nye Soobrazheniia* (Parizh: YMCA-Press, 1990).

[59] Stephen Shenfield, *Russian Fascism: Traditions, Tendencies, Movements* (Armonk, NY: M. E. Sharpe, 2001).

ideology of the twentieth century: the theatrical hypernationalism of Vladimir Zhirinovskii. Zhirinovskii's ideological stance has been widely misinterpreted both in Russia and the West. Some commentators argue that behind Zhirinovskii's buffoonery is a sincere and dangerous fascist threat; others retort that behind Zhirinovskii's fascist rhetoric is simple buffoonery and opportunism. Both sides miss Zhirinovskii's remarkable innovation – namely, to articulate a "joke fascism" that transcends the normal distinction between parody of and commitment to radical nationalist values.[60] From the outset of his political career, Zhirinovskii has consistently articulated all the typical fascist ideological themes: deep-seated xenophobia; a call for centralized, personal authority to counteract social disorder; complex conspiracy theories to "explain" Russia's catastrophic loss of global status; and a grand strategy for geopolitical expansion.[61] But Zhirinovskii has always been careful to leaven his fascism with humor. His threat, issued shortly after the August coup, to bring the Baltic states to their knees by placing giant fans on their borders to blow radioactive waste toward them, for example, was simultaneously a terrifying expression of the desire for geopolitical revenge and an ironic, silly commentary on the chaotic state of Russia's poorly guarded nuclear weapons facilities. Zhirinovskii's openly sexual rhetoric, too, constitutes both an expression of machismo and a call to have a good time in a world where "anything goes." In this sense, Zhirinovskii's reliable cooperation with highly placed supporters in the secret police and the Kremlin, from the Soviet era through the Putin administration, also has a double meaning: it earns him money to support his political network and simultaneously works to demonstrate the farcical nature of Kremlin efforts to build "democracy."

From the theoretical perspective adopted in this book, however, we must classify Zhirinovskii's vision of the Russian polity as ideological rather than pragmatic. The central features of his political creed – including their ironic elements – have been remarkably clear and consistent since nearly the beginning of his career as a public politician in the late Soviet period. Zhirinovskii did cooperate for a short period in 1990 – no doubt with KGB encouragement – with the avowed liberal Vladimir Bogachev, and the first party program of the Liberal Democratic Party of the Soviet Union published in March 1991 was largely written by an unaffiliated academic who was hired to produce the document as quickly as possible.[62] After Zhirinovskii gained full control over his party in fall 1990, however, his own statements and writings

---

[60] I myself missed the importance of the ironic aspects of Zhirinovskii's ideology in my first published analysis of his politics. See Stephen E. Hanson, "Ideology, Uncertainty, and the Rise of Anti-System Parties in Post-Communist Russia," *Journal of Communist Studies and Transition Politics* 14(1–2, March–June 1998): 98–127.

[61] See, for example, Vladimir Zhirinovskii's 1990 interview in Michael McFaul and Sergei Markov, *The Troubled Birth of Russian Democracy: Parties, Personalities, Programs* (Stanford, CA: Hoover Institution Press, 1993).

[62] Andreas Umland, "Vladimir Zhirinovskii in Russian Politics: Three Approaches to the Emergence of the Liberal-Democratic Party of Russia, 1990–1993" (Ph. D. diss., Free University of

consistently reiterated the same basic demands: the elimination of separate ethnically designated regions of the Russian Federation; a reorientation of Russian
foreign policy away from the West toward the Turkic and Islamic "South";
the final destruction of the Communist Party and the introduction of a statist
market economy; and, above all, the introduction of a presidential dictatorship designed to introduce "order" into Russian politics and society. Privileged
membership in the future Zhirinovskii-led polity would thus belong to tough
guys asserting the superiority of the Russian state and Russian ethnicity – and
willing to obey orders. Zhirinovskii adopted this explicit picture of Russia's
political future at a time when it was hardly expedient to do so. His notoriety
and bombast did help him place third in the RSFSR presidential elections of
June 1991, with 8 percent of the vote, but after the failure of the August coup,
such rhetoric quickly placed him at the fringes of Russian politics. Far from
being a simple opportunist, then, Zhirinovskii's willingness to defend initially
unpopular beliefs has arguably played a significant role in shaping the Russian
polity along the lines of his original vision. Indeed, examining the main points
of Zhirinovskii's creed, it is striking to see the extent to which Zhirinovskii's
ideological principles have been implemented in Russia under Putin.

Democrats

As with communists and nationalists, the unraveling of Soviet power also
posed complex ideological difficulties for those hoping to bring Russia quickly
into alignment with the West. To be sure, the Russian "democrats" – as they
described themselves and soon became universally known – did have several
advantages over their ideological competitors. First, they possessed a clear
empirical reference point for the kinds of political change they hoped to introduce: namely, the existing liberal capitalist democracies of Europe and North
America. In the wake of the "return to Europe" of nearly every country in the
former Soviet bloc, and given the increasingly pro-European stance of nationalist leaders in the Baltic states, the Caucasus, and Ukraine, Russian democrats
could also feel they were riding with the tide of history, rather than trying
to turn it back. Finally, with the emergence of Boris Yeltsin as the universally
acknowledged standard-bearer for the movement, Russian democrats were able
to mobilize crowds of hundreds of thousands at crucial turning points in the
battle against the decaying Soviet center.

Yet liberal democracy in the context of late Soviet history was also forced to
grapple with a range of uncomfortable institutional and social questions. First
and foremost, whereas for every other former Soviet republic "liberalism" and
"nationalism" could be easily reconciled as allies in the struggle against Kremlin
"totalitarianism," in Russia the "democrats" appeared to be working toward
the destruction of Russian control over territories that had taken centuries to

Berlin, 1997), p. 127. Western researchers attempting to demonstrate Zhirinovskii's ideological inconsistency frequently quote this source. See, for example, Derek S. Hutcheson, *Political
Parties in the Russian Regions* (London: RoutledgeCurzon, 2003), p. 22.

conquer.[63] Second, calls for the rapid introduction of a "market economy," however appealing initially to a Russian population facing increasingly empty store shelves that exacerbated an already-obvious gap between Soviet and Western living standards, ran up against the reality that more than 90 percent of the property in the USSR under Gorbachev was still officially state owned.[64] Not only was the task of destroying the "command-administrative system" of economic planning especially daunting in the Russian context, but such a centralized economy also made it impossible for leaders of Russia's democratic opposition to raise funds from sources truly independent of the state. Such constraints ensured that the earliest full-fledged democratic opposition movements under perestroika – such as Valeriia Novodvorskaia's Democratic Union, founded in May 1988 – would remain tiny intellectual clubs with little or no direct political influence.[65]

This marginalization changed dramatically after the formation of the Interregional Group of Deputies in the USSR Supreme Soviet, and especially after Boris Yeltsin had been elected as chairman of the Russian Supreme Soviet in May 1990. Such crucial footholds within the state inspired the creation of the pro-Yeltsin umbrella organization Democratic Russia, which for a time united most of Russia's otherwise fractious democratic activist community. Despite its ability to organize impressive popular demonstrations against Gorbachev and for Yeltsin, however, Democratic Russia found its unity more in the common struggle against communism than in any shared ideological vision of a new post-Soviet Russian polity. As Fish has argued, Russian democrats – allergic after decades of communist tyranny to the very idea of a "political party" – tended now to reject the need for any organizational discipline whatsoever. The result was the formation among Russian democrats of a kind of utopian "movement society" in which local activists ignored practical planning in favor of endless discussions of their principles.[66] Democratic utopianism also encouraged a kind of binary thinking, in which the task of destroying the USSR was seen as automatically generating Westernization. This enthusiasm for "creative destruction" was, in fact, shared to a significant degree by Yeltsin himself.[67]

It is telling in this connection that what would become the most significant split in post-Soviet Russian liberalism emerged out of a competition between two economists who both pledged to destroy the Soviet planned economy in record time, Grigorii Yavlinskii and Yegor Gaidar. Yavlinskii came to

[63] Stephen E. Hanson, "Ideology, Interests, and Identity: Comparing the Soviet and Russian Secession Crises," in Mikhail Alexseev, ed., *Center-Periphery Conflict in Post-Soviet Russia: A Federation Imperiled* (New York: St. Martin's Press, 1999), pp. 15–46.

[64] Anders Aslund, *Gorbachev's Struggle for Economic Reform, The Soviet Reform Process, 1985–1988* (Ithaca, NY: Cornell University Press, 1989).

[65] M. Steven Fish, *Democracy from Scratch: Opposition and Regime in the New Russian Revolution* (Princeton, NJ: Princeton University Press, 1995).

[66] Ibid.

[67] Alexander Lukin, *The Political Culture of the Russian "Democrats"* (Oxford: Oxford University Press, 2000).

public prominence as the author of the "500-days plan" for the introduction of a market economy in the Soviet Union – a timetable that appeared more politically symbolic than institutionally practical. Yet it suited the prevailing utopian mood among Russia's democrats, as well as helping Yeltsin score points against the vacillating Gorbachev, who ultimately proposed in the fall of 1990 to "synthesize" Yavlinskii's plan with the more statist approach of Prime Minister Ryzhkov. Now Yeltsin appeared to be the only leader with a clear plan for addressing the USSR's spiraling economic crisis. But Yavlinskii had explicitly designed the 500-days plan for implementation on a Soviet-wide scale, and Yeltsin's movement for Russian "sovereignty" logically precluded such direct control over the economic policies of other Soviet republics. Thus, after the failure of the August coup, Yeltsin abandoned Yavlinskii and promoted Yegor Gaidar, a rival economist who was perfectly willing to launch rapid liberal reforms at once, even if this could only be introduced in the territory of the Russian Federation. From Yavlinskii's perspective, such a plan would necessarily result in the catastrophic breakdown of organic economic links between the fifteen former Soviet republics. From Gaidar's perspective, Yavlinskii's reluctance to implement reforms within the borders of the newly independent Russian Federation showed him to be unwilling to shoulder political responsibility at a critical historical turning point. Such charges and countercharges remained at the core of the rivalry between the two men and their respective liberal parties for the next sixteen years.[68]

The overall result, however, was that no prominent Russian democrat – including Yeltsin himself – developed a clear and consistent ideological vision of the future Russian polity before the Soviet Union's final collapse. Indeed, the majority of Russian democratic activists explicitly abjured "ideology" altogether, proclaiming their goal simply to be a return to "normal life" by destroying the communist "experiment" as quickly as possible. Yavlinskii's vision of how to do so depended on the maintenance of the Soviet Union in some form; as a result, he did not clearly articulate any separate political vision for Russia alone before December 1991. Gaidar, meanwhile, argued that the urgency of the economic crisis demanded an immediate prioritization of market reform over political reform.[69] As in Weimar Germany, then – but for very different reasons – post-Soviet Russia would end up with two rival liberal parties, neither of which managed to articulate a clear, consistent definition of the Russian polity.

Chaos, 1992–1993

As in the cases of the early French Third Republic and the Weimar Republic, the first years after the collapse of the Soviet empire were ones of unprecedented

---

[68] This point is argued persuasively in David White, *The Russian Democratic Party Yabloko: Opposition in a Managed Democracy* (Burlington, VT: Ashgate, 2006).

[69] McFaul, *Russia's Unfinished Revolution*, p. 146. For Gaidar's own account, see Yegor T. Gaidar, *Days of Defeat and Victory* (Seattle: University of Washington Press, 1999).

institutional and social turbulence. The so-called shock therapy reforms of Yegor Gaidar introduced in January 1992 – the immediate freeing of prices for most consumer goods and the elimination of the Soviet state's monopoly on foreign trade, along with the announcement of near-term plans to build up a separate Russian central bank pursuing sound macroeconomic policies and to privatize as much state property as possible – were designed to concentrate the pain of economic restructuring in a short period, so as to allow for a relatively rapid recovery under market institutions. Unfortunately, these policies were followed instead by several years of near hyperinflation accompanied by catas-trophic declines in GDP. The rapid decline in the value of the ruble wiped out the savings of countless Russian citizens, forcing millions to survive by selling household items on the street and by relying on the gardens of family dachas. The breakdown of the Soviet command-administrative system – as Yavlinskii had predicted – led to the sudden disappearance of raw materials for produc-tion previously obtained from other former Soviet republics; entire sectors of industry such as textile production in the Ivanovo region were nearly wiped out, and unemployment rates in such places approached staggering levels.

The privatization program carried out by Gaidar's close ally Anatolii Chubais beginning in the fall of 1992 exacerbated the general feeling of social confusion, as the privatization "vouchers" distributed to every Russian man, woman, and child were siphoned away by the directors of fraudulent investment funds or corralled by existing Soviet enterprise managers, many of whom then made huge personal profits by stripping enterprise assets for private sale. Meanwhile, a handful of well-connected businessman who had already amassed huge property holdings through asset grabs in the late Gorbachev period took advantage of the continuing chaos to gain title to many of Russia's largest mineral and energy concerns. The Chubais plan became widely derided as *prikhvatizatsiia* rather than *privatizatsiia* – "grabification" instead of priva-tization – and the feeling that Russia's national wealth had been handed over to unscrupulous bandits left long-lasting social scars.[70]

In retrospect, it is clear that most of these painful results were due not to the new Russian government's economic policies – which did at least have the virtue of generating market incentives for the production and delivery of goods to nearly empty urban store shelves – but rather to the structural aftereffects of the final collapse of the Soviet system. The statist, evolutionary economic policies advocated by most of Gaidar's domestic and foreign critics were, in fact, unreal-istic in a situation of institutional disintegration such as that facing the Russian Federation in the early post-Soviet period.[71] Nevertheless, ordinary Russians experienced a degree of economic uncertainty in the first years of the post-Soviet period that is hard to overstate. It is certainly understandable – especially

[70] Timothy Frye, "Original Sin, Good Works, and Property Rights in Russia," *World Politics* 58(4, July 2006): 479–504.
[71] Stephen E. Hanson, "Analyzing Postcommunist Economic Change: A Review Essay," *East European Politics and Societies* 12(1, Spring 1998): 145–170; Gaidar, *Days of Defeat and Victory*.

given misguided public predictions by Yeltsin and some of his more optimistic advisers in the fall of 1991 of an economic turnaround within less than a year – that increasing numbers of them began to associate their personal misfortunes with Gaidar's policies and not with the burdensome legacy of the Soviet planned economy.[72]

The immediate effect of the worsening economic situation was a concomitant polarization of Russian politics. Adopting the views of both domestic and foreign economic advisers, Yeltsin had been persuaded in the fall of 1991 that the rapid imposition of capitalist markets should take priority over purely political tasks such as the drafting of a new constitution or the holding of new parliamentary elections. The Russian Congress of People's Deputies and its chairman Ruslan Khasbulatov had, after all, been Yeltsin's staunch allies in the battle against Gorbachev. To force them out of office, so soon after standing on a tank in their defense during the August coup, would have alienated many of Yeltsin's initial supporters. When the post-Soviet economic crisis turned out to be so much longer and deeper than originally expected, however, the absence of prior constitutional reforms inevitably exacerbated the mounting tension between the president and the parliament. Khasbulatov, along with Yeltsin's vice president Aleksandr Rutskoi, now declared themselves to be not only bitter opponents of Gaidar's economic program but also – despite their own recent support for Russia's "sovereignty" from the USSR – defenders of the rights of the twenty-five million ethnic Russians now living in Russia's so-called near abroad. After Yeltsin's emergency powers to implement economic reform expired in November 1992, the Congress leadership successfully demanded that Gaidar step down as prime minister in favor of the stolid former head of the Soviet gas monopoly, Viktor Chernomyrdin. By the spring of 1993, Yeltsin and his opponents in the Congress were working on separate drafts for a new Russian constitution. Not surprisingly, Yeltsin's favored draft dramatically strengthened the power of the executive branch, whereas the Congress's draft reasserted the sovereignty of the soviets.

On top of all these dizzying political and economic changes came an escalating challenge to the territorial integrity of the Russian state. During Yeltsin's political battle with Gorbachev, both sides had tried to woo the support of subnational regional politicians by promising them greater local autonomy. At one point Yeltsin had gone so far as to proclaim: "Take as much sovereignty as you can swallow."[73] Now, in the context of post-Soviet social chaos, an increasing

---

[72] In a televised address at the end of 1991, Yeltsin declared about economic reform: "I have said more than once and want to say it again: it will be tough for us, but this period will not be long. We are talking about 6–8 months." Quoted in McFaul, *Russia's Unfinished Revolution*, p. 144. For 1995 public opinion data showing a majority of 60 percent agreeing with the proposition that "the West is pursuing the goal of weakening Russia with its economic advice," see Jerry Hough, Evelyn Davidheiser, and Susan Goodrich Lehmann, *The 1996 Russian Presidential Election* (Washington, DC: Brookings Institution Press, 1996), p. 41.

[73] The phrase is from Yeltsin's speech at Kazan State University in Tatarstan on August 5, 1990. Quoted in Timothy Colton, *Yeltsin: A Life*, p. 186.

number of non-Russian ethnic regions, and also some Russian ones, began to reject their subordination to the Moscow government – or even, as in the case of Chechnya, to declare their outright independence. Given the zero-sum battle between Yeltsin and Khasbulatov, Moscow was in no position to crack down on these increasingly brazen regional challenges to central authority, especially because, once again, each rival hoped to woo uncommitted regional politicians to his side. By the summer of 1993, however, the "parade of sovereignties" appeared to be leading the Russian Federation toward the same fate as the Soviet Union two years earlier.

A final factor that should be mentioned in this description of the chaotic first two years of post-Soviet Russian politics and society was the relative absence of any coherent Western policy toward the new Russian state. The administration of George H. W. Bush appeared at first to be caught off guard by the Soviet Union's collapse. As late as July 1991, President Bush pleaded with Ukrainians in Kiev to avoid "suicidal nationalism" and support Gorbachev.[74] Even after the August coup, most Western leaders continued to prefer Gorbachev, whom they knew and trusted, to the upstart Yeltsin with his reputation for drunkenness and capricious decision making. Then in 1992, with the collapse of the USSR a fait accompli, the United States was focused on a highly competitive presidential campaign in which the weak domestic economy was the main theme; in this context, arguing for increased foreign aid to Russia was hardly a vote winner. As a result, no comprehensive international aid program to back up Gaidar's economic reforms was agreed upon. As in France in 1871 and in Germany in 1918, at a time of intense national crisis, the outside world seemed to most Russians to be either indifferent or actively hostile.

The economic, political, and foreign policy struggles that engulfed Russia in this period of chaos ultimately came to a head in September 1993. Yeltsin, having reached the conclusion that compromise with the opposition was impossible, decreed the dissolution of the Congress to be followed by elections for a new parliament, the State Duma, in December. The Congress responded by declaring Yeltsin's authority invalid, promoting Rutskoi to the presidency, and installing Khasbulatov as prime minister. The members of the Supreme Soviet remained holed up in the "White House," as the parliamentary building was known; they were soon joined there by a variety of nationalist and revolutionary communist militias. Negotiations between the two sides failed. On October 3, radical anti-Yeltsin forces, led by figures such as the neofascist Barkashov and the neo-Leninist Viktor Anpilov, attempted to storm the Ostankino television tower and to occupy the Moscow mayor's office. Yeltsin responded by ordering an all-out artillery assault on the White House in which hundreds were killed. Yeltsin emerged as the political victor, with his favored constitutional draft now scheduled to be approved in a referendum, along with

---

[74] For an excellent account of Western policy in this period, see Jack F. Matlock Jr., *Autopsy on an Empire: The American Ambassador's Account of the Collapse of the Soviet Union* (New York: Random House, 1995).

elections for the new parliament, on December 13 – but only at the cost of enormous and irreversible damage to his previous reputation as the undisputed leader of Russia's "democrats."[75]

Such an environment of pervasive uncertainty logically had the effect of making most Russians' individual time horizons exceedingly short. For would-be builders of new Russian political parties, the results were precisely those predicted by the hypothesis advanced in this book. The relatively consistent ideologues Ziuganov and Zhirinovskii each managed to weld together a core group of party activists, catalyzing what would become the two most powerful party organizations in the first decade of the Russian Federation – the Communist Party of the Russian Federation and the Liberal Democratic Party of Russia. The nonideological liberals associated with Democratic Russia, in contrast, split into myriad competing factions, ultimately generating rival liberal parties distinguished primarily not by their positive visions for the Russian future but by their opposing attitudes toward the Yeltsin regime. Meanwhile, various attempts to organize "centrist" coalitions were undermined because of free riding by their transparently instrumentally rational leaderships.

One important difference between the Russian Federation and the early Third Republic or Weimar Germany should be noted, however: in the Russian case, there were no parliamentary elections until the very end of the chaos period. As a result, it is more difficult to identify the "relevant parties" in Sartori's sense during these years, because we cannot utilize the results of initial elections to discern which parties had enough popular support to join government coalitions or to blackmail the authorities with antisystem rhetoric. In the analysis that follows, therefore, I continue to examine the same three broad groupings described in the Gorbachev era, showing how Ziuganov's and Zhirinovskii's relatively clear and consistent definitions of the future Russian polity enabled them to overcome the collective action problems facing would-be party builders more successfully than their communist, nationalist, democratic, and centrist competitors.

The Origins of the Communist Party of the Russian Federation

There is an overwhelming scholarly consensus that the Communist Party of the Russian Federation was by far the strongest political party organization in Russia during the Yeltsin era. However, analysts also commonly make the mistaken assumption that CPRF strength simply reflects the maintenance of the organizational assets of the old CPSU into the post-Soviet era.[76] This thesis drastically underestimates the collective action problems that faced the

---

[75] For a highly critical appraisal of Yeltsin's decision making in this period, see Peter Reddaway and Dmitri Glinsky, *The Tragedy of Russia's Reforms: Market Bolshevism against Democracy* (Washington, DC: United States Institute of Peace Press, 2001).

[76] See, for example, Smith and Remington's analysis: "The Communists had inherited much of the CPSU's organizational network, including, for better or worse, name recognition." Smith and Remington, *The Politics of Institutional Choice*, p. 123.

would-be leaders of a new, reinvigorated Communist Party in the chaotic environment generated by the Soviet Union's collapse. As we have seen in the case of the Bonapartists in France and the National Liberals in Germany, even the strongest preexisting party organizations can disintegrate quickly when instrumental politicians are forced to reevaluate their partisan commitments in conditions of extreme institutional and social turbulence. Indeed, in the early post-Soviet period, at least six distinct leadership groups in Russia laid claim to the organizational assets of the former CPSU. As a result of these internal divisions, there was no unified communist opposition during the period of Yeltsin's struggle with Khasbulatov; indeed, only 67 deputies of some 1,050 members of the Russian CPD remained publicly committed to communism.[77] The emergence of a powerful, disciplined CPRF by the end of 1993, then, was hardly inevitable. For analysts who take the collective action problem of national party formation seriously, it is a puzzle demanding theoretical explanation.

The immediate problem facing would-be reorganizers of the Communist Party was Yeltsin's decree shortly after the August coup banning the CPSU as a "criminal organization." This decree – coupled with Gorbachev's resignation as general secretary, the voluntary disbanding of the USSR Congress of People's Deputies, and the defection of much of the old CPSU elite to join with either Yeltsin or his primary opponents in the Russian Congress – called into question both the legality and future viability of the Russian Communist Party as well. RCP leaders such as Valentin Kuptsov immediately challenged Yeltsin's decree in the Russian Constitutional Court, which, given the rough balance of power between Yeltsin and Khasbulatov at the time, was relatively free to debate the legal merits of this case without political interference. However, the case took nearly a year to decide, during which time the competition among competing factions in the RCP only intensified.

Ziuganov's key advantage over his communist rivals in this crucial phase was his clarity and consistency about the definition of the polity he wished to establish: namely, an antiliberal soviet regime based not on Marxist-Leninist internationalism but on Russian great-power nationalism. This distinctive ideological position – which, as we have seen, he had already clearly articulated in the Gorbachev era – led Ziuganov to concentrate his political efforts in 1992 on building bridges with prominent Russian nationalist intellectuals and activists. He further deepened his long-standing ties with the nationalist publicists Aleksandr Prokhanov, coauthor of the Word to the People manifesto and an editor of *Sovietskaia Rossiia* and the far-right *Den'*; both newspapers became reliable channels for the dissemination of Ziuganov's ideology. He also spearheaded efforts to mobilize a united opposition to Yeltsin of the "left and right" – that is, of national communists and straightforward Russian ethnic nationalists. In January 1992 Ziuganov became chairman of the coordinating council of the People's Patriotic Forces of Russia; in June he attended the first

[77] Joan Barth Urban and V. D. Solovei, *Russia's Communists at the Crossroads* (Boulder, CO: Westview Press, 1997), p. 47.

congress of Aleksandr Sterligov's Russian National Assembly; and in October he cofounded the National Salvation Front, working with stridently antiliberal figures such as General Al'bert Makashov.[78]

In comparison, Ziuganov's main rivals for supremacy within the communist movement found it exceedingly difficult to articulate clear and consistent definitions of what sort of polity they hoped to establish in the new context of the Russian Federation. A first group of communists, including dissident author Roy Medvedev and Russian CPD deputy Ivan Rybkin, organized the Socialist Labor Party (SLP), which was dedicated to social democratic principles and opposed the resurrection of the Soviet Union. By January 1993 the SLP had attracted an estimated 100,000 members.[79] But in the context of the increasing political polarization between President Yeltsin and Russian CPD speaker Khasbulatov, the SLP's calls for a more moderate opposition to "shock therapy" only alienated both "democrats" and the radicalized communist rank and file. After the founding in February of the new CPRF – which also rejected the idea of reestablishing the old CPSU, but for nationalist reasons – the SLP was decimated by mass defections.

A second group of communists attempted to reorganize on the basis of "pure" Marxism-Leninism, which they saw as having been abandoned at some point in the history of the USSR. Ironically, however, the readoption of Marxist-Leninist "principles" hardly constituted a clear ideological position in the context of post-1991 Russia. What, exactly, would a newly revitalized Marxism-Leninism in the Russian Federation look like politically? One faction mobilized around Aleksei Prigarin's Union of Communists, calling for a return to the idealized "workers' democracy" its founders imagined existing in the very early years of the Bolshevik Revolution. Another faction, led by Anatolii Kriuchkov, organized the Russian Party of Communists, which argued for a return to Lenin's New Economic Policy and saw positive elements in both Khrushchev's and Gorbachev's reforms. Neither group could explain clearly just how, in the wake of the Soviet collapse, one could practically establish a new polity based on discarded reform programs of the Soviet era. As in the case of the SLP, after the establishment of the CPRF, both parties saw their memberships rapidly dwindle.

A final group of communists was indeed quite clear about the sort of polity it hoped to establish, calling simply and consistently for the restoration of the USSR itself. However, this faction, too, was split. Nina Andreeva's All-Union Communist Party of Bolsheviks frankly idealized Stalinism, holding up North Korea under Kim Il-Sung as a model for emulation.[80] The larger and more significant Russian Communist Workers' Party led by Viktor Tiulkin and Viktor Anpilov called for the reestablishment of Leninism through a new "proletarian revolution" against Russian capitalism, actively recruiting blue-collar

---

[78] Ibid., pp. 47–48.
[79] Ibid., p. 22.
[80] Ibid., p. 24.

workers for the upcoming struggle against Yeltsin. Such parties did possess clear and consistent visions of Russia's political future – but only at the cost of subordinating Russian nationalism to a resurrection of the Soviet Union under its old "internationalist" ideology.

Thus, by November 1992, when the Constitutional Court finally issued its ruling preserving Yeltsin's ban on the central organs of the CPSU but allowing local branches of the Communist Party to reform under new political leadership, Ziuganov had clearly staked out a unique and particularly advantageous ideological position. On the one hand, more "reformist" rivals hoping to refound the Communist Party on a social-democratic basis found themselves discredited by their associations with Gorbachev and out of sync with the sentiments of the regional party rank and file. On the other hand, communists such as Andreeva, Tiulkin, and Prigarin, who had explicitly called for the restoration of the CPSU, were forced by the court ruling into an openly unconstitutional, revolutionary position. Ziuganov's ideology alone appealed both to supporters of a legal, evolutionary approach to rebuilding the Communist Party and to angry rank-and-file communists who hoped to rebuild a future Soviet Russia.

Ziuganov's advantageous position became manifest at the crucial "revival-unification congress" of the CPRF on February 13–14, 1993. The 805 delegates to the congress represented a wide diversity of political views, testifying to the deep factionalization of the communist movement. Kuptsov led off the debate by declaring that the new CPRF should be the linear successor to the Russian Communist Party of 1991 – and that those who hoped to reestablish the CPSU and the Soviet Union were "either fools or adventurers."[81] Tiulkin, Prigarin, and other neo-Leninists naturally objected to this phrasing, calling instead for a wholesale rejection of Gorbachev-style "revisionism." Then Ziuganov took the podium, calling directly for the "revival of Russia" as the CPRF's main strategic task; this position was subsequently backed up by several of Ziuganov's close political allies. The end result of these debates was that both ideologically orthodox Marxist-Leninists and European-style social democrats found themselves marginalized in the new party. Moreover, key radicals who supported Ziuganov's national-communist line, such as Makashov, now demanded that the moderate Kuptsov step down from the leadership in favor of Ziuganov himself. Ziuganov was elected to the top party post by an overwhelming majority – a position he would hold throughout Yeltsin's and Putin's presidencies.

To be sure, the entire CPRF membership did not instantaneously convert to national-communism as a result of Ziuganov's victory. Many unreconstructed Marxist-Leninists, and even some social democrats, chose to remain within the CPRF after its founding congress, hoping to influence the party line from within. The relatively moderate Kuptsov gracefully accepted the number-two post and became the CPRF's main day-to-day organizational boss, working from that point forward without any apparent tension with Ziuganov. It is analytically

---

[81] Quoted in ibid., p. 50.

unhelpful, however, to see the CPRF after February 1993 as somehow ideologically split among communist-nationalist, orthodox Leninist, and Marxist reformist factions.[82] The heterogeneous positions of rank-and-file membership after February 1993 never generated any serious schisms within the party leadership about the CPRF's public ideology; here Ziuganov's leadership was unchallenged. Indeed, Ziuganov's clear and consistent insistence that the CPRF stood for the revival of Russia's great-power status through the restoration of "soviet" legal principles was a key factor in the growing confidence among CPRF activists throughout the country that their movement was destined for future success.

Nor was Ziuganov's careful conduct during the crisis in the fall of 1993, when he stood aloof from Yeltsin and the Congress opposition alike, a sign of ideological inconsistency. Despite his general sympathy for the position of the opposition, Ziuganov understandably had no interest in collaborating with erstwhile Yeltsin supporters such as Rutskoi and Khasbulatov; both, after all, had directly opposed Ziuganov's activities in the last years of the USSR. Nor was Ziuganov interested in aligning his party with Leninist radicals such as Anpilov during the Moscow street fighting of early October – having only recently defeated them in the struggle for leadership over the mainstream communist movement. Instead, as he had in criticizing the "illegal" decision to break up the USSR, Ziuganov consistently emphasized his party's fidelity to (Soviet) legal principles, and thus his opposition to the revolutionary tactics of pro-Congress hard-liners.

The apparent sincerity of this stance helped Ziuganov reverse Yeltsin's initial ban on the CPRF after the shelling of the White House, allowing the party to compete as one of the thirteen legally registered electoral organizations on the ballot for the State Duma elections in December 1993. The CPRF was rewarded with a third-place party list vote of 12.4 percent, plus an additional sixteen seats in single-member constituencies. When combined with the strong electoral support for the CPRF's close ally, the Agrarian Party, the communists now controlled 18 percent of the total seats in the new Duma.[83] For a party that had been illegal just a year before, such results appeared to be a near-miraculous confirmation of Ziuganov's ideological line.

Zhirinovskii and the Liberal Democratic Party of Russia
For advocates of the common view that Zhirinovskii was a simple opportunist, his consistent anti-Yeltsin line in the fall of 1991 is hard to explain. Not only was Zhirinovskii an early and vocal defender of the coup plotters' State Committee for the Emergency Situation, but he also stuck to that position

[82] This is the categorization given by Urban and Solovei, *Russia's Communists at the Crossroads*, and taken up as well by Luke March, *The Communist Party in Post-Soviet Russia* (Manchester: Manchester University Press, 2002).

[83] Stephen White, Richard Rose, and Ian McAllister, *How Russia Votes* (Chatham, NJ: Chatham House, 1997), p. 123.

at a time when more pragmatic politicians – including nominally nationalist ones – were hedging their bets by supporting Yeltsin against Gorbachev. Thus, Zhirinovskii, unlike Khasbulatov and Rutskoi, called openly for the freeing of the August coup plotters from prison. He also immediately and vehemently rejected the Belovezh accords that formally dissolved the USSR.[84]

Such clarity of conviction, along with Zhirinovskii's colorful personality, were important assets as he struggled to reorganize the LDPSU as the new Liberal Democratic Party of Russia (LDPR). His initial converts to the cause were drawn from the radical fringe of Russian political life, including the openly fascist rock musicians Andrei Arkhipov and Sergei Zharikov, as well as the notorious Russian exile author Eduard Limonov. With their help, he founded the LDPR newspapers *Sokol Zhirinovskogo* (Zhirinovskii's Falcon) and *Liberal*. He also courted leading figures of the European "new right" such as Jean-Marie Le Pen and Gerhard Frey. Zhirinovskii continued to receive financing from shadowy businesses with apparent ties to the security services.

Quite remarkably, Zhirinovskii failed to join any of the major radical nationalist blocs that formed in the first post-Soviet years – partly by design, in order to keep strict personal control over the LDPR and its message, and partly because of the distaste of other Russian nationalists for Zhirinovskii's peculiar political approach. Indeed, it soon became abundantly clear that Zhirinovskii – consistent with his demand for strict presidential dictatorship – brooked no disobedience whatsoever from his LDRP subordinates. As a result, by 1993 more spontaneous nationalists, such as Arkhipov, Zharikov, and Limonov, had all split bitterly from Zhirinovskii. Others, however, remained within the LDPR's core leadership group for many years to come, including activists Aleksandr Vengerovskii, who managed party ties with the military-industrial complex, and Aleksei Mitrofanov, who became the party's specialist on "geopolitics." A final group within the leadership should be mentioned, whose importance grew steadily over time: Zhirinovskii's own relatives, especially his son Igor Lebedev. This relatively disciplined and loyal elite spearheaded a major drive to recruit LDPR activists among radical youth, disaffected military and former KGB officers, and various riffraff from the criminal underworld. By the fall of 1993, the LDPR proudly claimed a membership of more than 100,000 drawn from throughout the country.[85] This figure was surely exaggerated, including individuals signed up in local recruitment campaigns who never actually engaged in partisan activities; 40,000 was probably a more reasonable estimate of LDPR membership.[86] Still, independent research demonstrates that

---

[84] Umland, "Vladimir Zhirinovskii in Russian Politics," p. 188. I am indebted here to Umland's meticulous research into the party's early history.

[85] Evelyn Davidheiser, "Right and Left in the Hard Opposition," in Timothy J. Colton and Jerry F. Hough, eds., *Growing Pains: Russian Democracy and the Election of 1993* (Washington, DC: Brookings Institution Press, 1998), p. 189.

[86] Umland, "Vladimir Zhirinovskii in Russian Politics," p. 168.

the party had indeed developed a remarkable organizational capacity in many of Russia's regions.[87]

Zhirinovskii also mobilized the LDPR's national organization to distribute copies of his famous autobiography *Last Dash to the South*, which was first published in September 1993. The book, which, unlike some later ghostwritten LDPR pamphlets, is clearly the work of Zhirinovskii himself, provided the clearest and most elaborate statement of the LDPR leader's distinctive "joke fascism." Like Hitler, whose Austrian birth predisposed him toward belief in a "Greater Germany," Zhirinovskii emphasized his origins in Alma-Ata (Almaty) to play skillfully on Russian resentments about current internationally recognized boundaries: "I was born in Russia among Russians," he declared.[88] Indeed, according to Zhirinovskii, "Russia" should be formally and consistently defined as encompassing not just the Russian Federation, not just the Slavic republics, not just the former USSR, but the whole of Eurasia: "The USSR was an artificial name, and the CIS is even more artificial. The state has its own proper [*sobstvennoe*] name – Russia. It is an historical name; it is a geographical concept. It doesn't at all signify a state just for ethnic Russians [*dl'a russkikh*]. It is the Eurasian continent."[89] In the absence of imperial expansion, Zhirinovskii perceived a deadly threat to Russian statehood and culture, prophesying an invasion by "Turks" and "Muslims": "Pan-Turkism threatens Russia, for in Russia there are a large number of Turkish-speaking people, of Muslims, of Farsi-speakers – and all of this is a comfortable soil, a good enticement for Afghanistan, Iran and Turkey to rise upwards, to the north, creating a greater Afghanistan, a greater Iran, a greater Turkey."[90]

Vehement anti-Turkic racism, then, played the same role in Zhirinovskii's ideology that anti-Semitism did in Hitler's Nazism, providing both an explanation for Russia's current humiliation and a target for future revenge and expansion: "*Nothing will happen to the world even if the entire Turkic nation perishes*, although I don't wish this."[91] Despite Zhirinovskii's demurral here, his periodic statements that to "cleanse these scabs, this filth that has accumulated during the twentieth century" will "sometimes... call for blood" were hardly reassuring.[92]

Ultimately, Zhirinovskii insisted, the world would be administered according to a general global partition in which the "advanced northern" countries would divide the "corrupt southern" ones into four spheres of influence: the United States ruling over the Americas, Europe dominating Africa, Japan and

---

[87] See the chapters on various regional campaigns for the December 1993 Duma elections in Colton and Hough, *Growing Pains*, which almost uniformly report the relatively successful organization of LDPR offices in each region while disparaging the organizational efforts of "reformist" parties such as Russia's Choice and Yabloko.

[88] Vladimir Zhirinovskii, *Poslednii Brosok Na Iug* (Moscow: LDP, 1993), p. 6.

[89] Ibid., pp. 93–94.

[90] Ibid, p. 130.

[91] Ibid. (Zhirinovskii's emphasis).

[92] Ibid., p. 117.

China taking Southeast Asia and Australia, and, of course, Russia controlling the Middle East.[93] Wherever Russia has not succeeded historically in controlling the "South," Zhirinovskii claimed, civil war, immorality, and corruption have spread – as was proved by developments in post-Soviet Tajikistan, Azerbaijan, Afghanistan, Kurdistan, and, of course, Chechnya.[94] Continuing this theme in a rather sillier vein, Zhirinovskii argued that the Soviet Union itself was fatally corrupted by two Georgians: Stalin, who initially allowed "southern bandits" to run rampant in Russian territory, and Shevardnadze, who gave away Russia's European empire and let the Caucasian "mafia" take over Moscow.[95]

Indeed, as this last passage shows, many sections of *Last Dash to the South* have the distinct ring of parody. Zhirinovskii's picture of a "pacified" South in which Russian Orthodox churches and sanatoria for Russian vacationers and pensioners would be built on the shores of the Indian Ocean, while the Russian language and the ruble would be introduced throughout newly conquered territory, read like a farcical post-Soviet update of Hitler's vision of German *Lebensraum*. Zhirinovskii's insistence that such plans would not meet with substantial resistance on the part of the other major world powers – because they, too, would like to see the threat of "Islamic extremism" eradicated, no matter how or by whom – was equally hard to take seriously. This oddly reassuring combination of ideological extremism and humorous hyperbole can be seen as well in Zhirinovskii's warning to the United States, if it were for some reason to try to prevent the Russians from carrying out Zhirinovskii's plan to divide the globe into separate spheres of influence:

We say to the Americans: stop yourself in time... America will also soon begin to collapse.... In front of you is your perestroika, your sickness, your degradation. And we Russians will not gloat when certain states begin to break away, when your factories come to a halt, when you don't have enough food or medicine, when people begin to leave America for Europe, Russia, Japan, the United Arab Republic, Australia. We won't gloat when California secedes to Mexico, when a Negro republic is formed in Miami, when the Russians return Alaska to themselves.... Therefore, mind that you don't fall into your own trap; don't spit in the well from which you will yourself be forced to drink.[96]

For displaced Russians living through the chaotic collapse of their familiar social world, yet too cynical to embrace the straightforward ethnic nationalist ideology of figures such as Vasiliev or Barkashov, Zhirinovskii's willingness to propound such far-fetched yet emotionally satisfying scenarios made him enormously popular.

As in the case of Ziuganov, Zhirinovskii's ideological and organizational distance from both Yeltsin and his opponents during the fall of 1993 helped the LDPR emerge after the crisis with no serious damage. Also, as in the case of

[93] Ibid., pp. 71–72.
[94] Ibid., pp. 76–77.
[95] Ibid., pp. 69, 132.
[96] Ibid., pp. 118–119.

Ziuganov, Zhirinovskii's tepid support for Yeltsin against Khasbulatov as "the lesser of two evils" in October 1993, along with his more fervent support for Yeltsin's new presidential constitution, was by no means ideologically inconsistent: not only did Zhirinovskii wish to see the presidency vastly strengthened in any case, but Khasbulatov was an ethnic Chechen, and thus in his view unfit for rule over Russia. No doubt Zhirinovskii's support for the Kremlin at this crucial juncture accounts for the fact that his party was the sole representative of extreme nationalism registered to compete in the December Duma elections. It does not follow from this, however, that the LDPR at this early stage was merely a Kremlin "project" explicitly designed to siphon away support for more "radical" nationalist groupings.[97] As we have seen, Zhirinovskii's political associations in the chaotic first years of the Russian Federation were quite consistently and seriously neofascist ones, even if his bombastic style for expressing these ideological convictions was unique. In fact, the remarkable electoral performance of the LDPR in the December 1993 elections – receiving fully 23 percent of the party list vote, plus an additional five single-member district seats, to become the second-largest party in the Duma – came as a profound shock, not only to the West but also to Yeltsin's entourage.[98]

Yavlinskii and "Yabloko"

Grigorii Yavlinskii's essentially pragmatic political strategy after the collapse of the USSR stands in stark contrast to Ziuganov's and Zhirinovskii's ideological strategies of party building. Indeed, until very shortly before the end of the chaotic first two years of the post-Soviet crisis, Yavlinskii was not involved in party building at all. While Ziuganov and Zhirinovskii worked on setting up party newspapers, recruiting extremist nationalists into their inner circles, and building party organizations in Russia's far-flung regions, Yavlinskii's first step in 1992 was to retreat to the Center for Economic and Political Research (*EPITsentr*), an independent think tank he had set up in January 1991 to promote his distinctive "evolutionary" approach to market reform. By May 1992 he had published *Diagnoz*, a pamphlet that roundly criticized Gaidar's monetarist strategy for macroeconomic stabilization. He also volunteered to serve as an economic adviser to Governor Boris Nemtsov in Nizhny Novgorod, Russia's third-largest city. The relative early success of the Nizhny Novgorod reforms earned Yavlinskii good national and international publicity, giving him a reputation as a practical man of action with hands-on experience in economic reform.

Concerning the question of how to define the future of "Russia," however, Yavlinskii remained vague and rather disengaged. From the beginning, he faced

---

[97] Andrew Wilson, *Virtual Politics: Faking Democracy in the Post-Soviet World* (New Haven: Yale University Press, 2005).

[98] See the account presented in Iu. M. Baturin et al., *Epokha El'tsina: Ocherki Politicheskoi Istorii* (Moscow: Vagrius, 2001).

a central dilemma. His opposition to Gaidar's "shock therapy" approach had initially centered on his insistence that economic reform be carried out throughout the entire territory of the USSR. Now that the Soviet Union had collapsed, this position became anachronistic. If Yavlinskii were to call openly for the restoration of the USSR, he would undercut his image as a pro-Western market reformer. But if he gave up entirely on his critique of the breakup of the old planned economy along republican lines, he risked sounding identical to Gaidar. In practice, Yavlinskii tended to split the difference, calling on the one hand for a more robustly pro-Western model of development and on the other hand for the restoration of "economic links" with the other former Soviet republics.

Yavlinskii's pragmatic effort to mix liberalism with an implicit, fuzzy nationalism can also been seen in his choice of key allies in building an electoral association as parliamentary elections approached in the latter half of 1993. Whereas the party's number-two man, Yurii Boldyrev, was a democratic activist and anticorruption activist with a sterling reputation among members of Democratic Russia, Vladimir Lukin, the first post-Soviet Russian ambassador to the United States, had made a number of notably aggressive statements about Western foreign policy, speaking frequently about the need to defend the twenty-five million Russians living in the "near abroad." The party's very name – Yabloko, or "Apple," with represented the initials of Yavlinskii, Boldyrev, and Lukin – thus concretized its ideological ambiguity, associating it permanently with an entirely apolitical symbol.

Beyond a handful of longtime Yavlinskii associates such as Viacheslav Igrunov and Sergei Mitrokhin, Yabloko therefore relied organizationally not on sustained efforts to build support among regional activists but on instrumentally rational defections by disenchanted or marginalized "democrats" who saw no hope for a political career in Gaidar's "party of power."[99] This strategic instrumentalism can be seen in the autumn 1993 debates among the constituent parties of the rapidly disintegrating Democratic Russia movement, such as the Republican Party of Russia (RPR) and the Social Democratic Party of Russia (SDPR), on whether to join Yabloko on the December 1993 Duma ballot. In the end, the RPR split over this issue, with thirty-three regional organizations joining Yabloko and twenty joining Gaidar's party.[100] Moreover, neither the RPR nor the SDPR chose to give up its independent party identity – hedging its bets in case Yabloko turned in a poor performance.

Thus, Yabloko entered into the fall 1993 campaign for the State Duma with no clear ideology in the sense described in this book, and with an organizational base heavily tilted toward Moscow and St. Petersburg, built on the comparatively fragile basis of temporary self-interest. Its campaign, accordingly,

---

[99] This point is made by Vladimir Gel'man, quoted in White, *The Russian Democratic Party Yabloko*, p. 53.
[100] Ibid., p. 56.

was notably low profile, partly because Yavlinskii could not trust the loyalty of many of the party's own regional candidates.[101] Yabloko's electoral appeal thus depended on the national reputation of its leader, especially among Russian liberal voters who wished to protest against the policies of Yeltsin and Gaidar. These factors did suffice to produce a decent electoral showing in December 1993: Yabloko attained 7.9 percent of the party-list vote and three single-member district seats. The party's organizational weakness, however, would continue to bedevil its efforts in later years to expand beyond this initial electoral niche.

Party of Power I: Russia's Choice

The second major political party to emerge from the breakup of the Democratic Russia movement, Russia's Choice, also consciously rejected the need to articulate a clear ideological definition of the nature of the Russian polity. Like Yabloko, Russia's Choice was initially designed as a pragmatic vehicle to organize supporters of liberalism for upcoming parliamentary elections; unlike Yabloko, of course, Russia's Choice stood strongly in favor of Yeltsin's government. Quite explicitly, party builders such as Gennadii Burbulis chose to build the new pro-Kremlin organization from scratch rather than rely on the activists of the Democratic Russia movement, which was seen as too idealistic, too fragmented, and not always sufficiently supportive of Yeltsin's policies to serve as a reliable foundation for a new "party of power." Democratic Russia was ultimately invited to join Russia's Choice as a bloc, but of the individuals selected for the party's federal list, sixteen of the nineteen were former or current government officials, and none were leaders of Democratic Russia.[102] Yeltsin himself, meanwhile, remained aloof from Gaidar's party, preferring to rule "above parties" altogether – again, for instrumentally rational reasons, to hedge against the possibility of electoral defeat.

The very choice of Gaidar to lead Russia's Choice cemented the party's public image as a pro-Kremlin grouping. As has been described, Gaidar had never been very interested in issues of political ideology. As he himself later admitted, "The role of a democracy movement leader was remarkably uncomfortable for me; it didn't feel right. I was well aware of my weaknesses as a public politician, a person called upon to campaign, to explain, to win elections."[103] Gaidar did possess clear value-rational principles about the superiority of market economics to any form of economic statism, but beyond the desire to disentangle the Russian Federation from Soviet economic institutions linking it to the other Soviet republics, he did not promulgate any worked-out ideas about how to define Russia's new postcommunist polity.

---

[101] Michael McFaul, Nikolai Petrov, et al., *Previewing Russia's 1995 Parliamentary Elections* (Moscow: Carnegie Endowment, 1995).

[102] Michael McFaul, "Russia's Choice: The Perils of Revolutionary Democracy," in Hough and Colton, *Growing Pains*, p. 118.

[103] Gaidar, *Days of Defeat and Victory*, p. 261.

Thus, while Russia's Choice entered into the 1993 Duma campaign brimming with confidence, its obviously instrumental foundation left it grappling with severe organizational problems. For one thing, several ambitious politicians who had hoped for higher placement on the Russia's Choice list, or who feared association with the increasingly unpopular Gaidar, decided instead to create their own, equally instrumental "liberal" parties – most significantly, Sergei Shakhrai, whose Party of Russian Unity and Accord took nearly 7 percent of the party-list vote. For another, the absence of any party ideology underlying Russia's Choice undermined its electoral campaign, depriving it of any coherent message; much of the party's television time was "squandered... on long, monotonous, and academic discussions about the macroeconomics of financial stabilization or on overproduced, empty jingles."[104] Finally, the heavy representation of state officials on the Russia's Choice list alienated many Democratic Russia activists, leading them in many cases to run as independents opposed to the party's approved candidates. The end result was an electoral performance that was widely seen as disastrous, especially given the overwhelming financial and organizational backing given to Russia's Choice by the Yeltsin administration: the party attained just 15.5 percent of the proportional representation vote and only thirty seats in single-member districts. The resulting seventy seats for Russia's Choice in the new State Duma did make it the largest party in the parliament, ahead of the LDPR by six seats. But the widespread feeling among both "democrats" and their opponents was that liberalism in Russia had suffered a critical electoral defeat. Moreover, Yeltsin was profoundly disillusioned as well, further reinforcing his desire to avoid partisan affiliations of his own.

Stalemate, 1994–1998

The years between the adoption of the new Russian Constitution in December 1993 and Putin's rise to power have been depicted by leading political scientists as a period of relative stabilization for Russian democratic institutions. During these years, the new State Duma began to develop consensual procedures for organizing parliamentary "fractions," and its legislative work became increasingly professionalized.[105] Elections for governors and regional assemblies in the Russian Federation, too, became a regularized part of the political scene, in which long-standing incumbents were frequently defeated and replaced.[106] Through the representation of governors in the upper house of parliament, the Federation Council, Russian federalism arguably became

---

[104] Ibid., p. 130.

[105] Remington, *The Russian Parliament*; Remington and Smith, *The Politics of Institutional Change*.

[106] Andrew Konitzer, *Voting for Russia's Governors: Regional Elections and Accountability under Yeltsin and Putin* (Washington, DC: Woodrow Wilson Center Press; Baltimore: Johns Hopkins University Press, 2005).

more predictable and institutionalized; as the central government found ways to co-opt the most secessionist regional leaders, the "parade of sovereignties" that once threatened the country with disintegration subsided.[107] Voters began to calculate their decisions at the ballot box in terms largely consistent with their social background, and something like an identifiable left-right spectrum emerged in both the mass electorate and the Duma – with the CPRF on the left and the various liberal parties on the right.[108] Most importantly, Yeltsin's executive power itself was renewed in 1996 not through the cancellation of elections, as had been feared, but through a genuinely competitive (if flawed) electoral process.[109] Such signs of stabilization led Michael McFaul in 2001 to conclude that the "third Russian republic," unlike the failed democratic projects launched under Gorbachev and again in the early Yeltsin years, had developed relative staying power.[110]

Despite the rollback of Russian democracy in the first decade of the twenty-first century, these analyses still contain a great deal of insight. Contrary to the assumptions of cynical Western analysts of Russian affairs who have derided the importance of Russian democratic institutions under Yeltsin, calling the regime a mere "façade democracy," elections in the late 1990s really did matter.[111] Indeed, Putin himself would never have risen to the presidency had it not been for his genuine popular support in the 1999–2000 electoral cycle. Still, in retrospect, it is clear that the more optimistic assessments of Russian democratic stabilization under Yeltsin were premature.

The comparison of post-Soviet Russia with the other two cases of post-imperial democracy in this book helps to explain why, despite six years of repeated, reasonably free and fair elections, Russian democratic institutions remained unconsolidated in the latter part of the 1990s. As in Third Republic France between 1873 and 1877 or Weimar Germany between 1923 and 1929, Russia's post-Soviet democracy, despite emerging from the chaos period with a relatively stable constitutional order, still lacked any clear and consistent ideological identity. President Yeltsin, continuing to rule "above parties," gradually abandoned his initially idealistic embrace of immediate Westernization, but he could not articulate any clear alternative conception of Russian national identity to replace it; meanwhile, serious health problems quickly eroded his

---

[107] Daniel Treisman, *After the Deluge: Regional Crises and Political Consolidation in Russia* (Ann Arbor: University of Michigan Press, 1999).

[108] Timothy J. Colton, *Transitional Citizens: Voters and What Influences Them in the New Russia* (Cambridge, MA: Harvard University Press, 2000); Remington and Smith, *The Politics of Institutional Change*.

[109] Michael McFaul, *Russia's 1996 Presidential Election: The End of Polarized Politics* (Stanford, CA: Hoover Institution Press, 1997).

[110] McFaul, *Russia's Unfinished Revolution*.

[111] Vladimir Brovkin, "The Emperor's New Clothes: Continuity of Soviet Political Culture in Contemporary Russia," *Problems of Post-Communism* 43(2, March–April 1996); Stephen F. Cohen, *Failed Crusade: America and the Tragedy of Post-Communist Russia* (New York: W. W. Norton, 2001).

political influence. The largest parties in the Duma, the CPRF and LDPR, even as they continued to accommodate themselves to the Yeltsin regime, remained rhetorically committed to the destruction of the new liberal democratic order. In comparison, those parties which claimed to uphold liberalism or centrism had relatively weak national organizations. Russia's socioeconomic situation, while improving somewhat after the chaos of the early post-Soviet period, remained bleak overall, with marginal or negative growth, continuing high inflation, massive capital flight, and growing unemployment in the distressed industrial sector.[112] Finally, Russia remained internationally isolated, unable to join the most important Western international clubs such as NATO and the European Union, but also lacking any reliable Asian great-power allies. In this situation, the long-term future definition of the Russian polity remained fuzzy and uncertain – leading instrumentally rational politicians to forgo potentially risky commitments to existing institutions or party organizations. The result was a vicious cycle of uncertainty, in which widespread short-term decision making only made the long-term political future even hazier.[113]

The Communist Party of the Russian Federation

The relatively cooperative conduct of the CPRF in the new State Duma after the December 1993 elections has been interpreted by some analysts as indicating a reconciliation of the party with Yeltsin's constitutional order. As we have seen, however, Ziuganov's adherence to "soviet legality" was a consistent element of his ideological vision, one that separated him from "revolutionary" Marxist-Leninists such as Tiulkin and Anpilov. Ziuganov saw participation in the parliament as an ideal opportunity to strengthen the party's national organization and to disseminate its message of antiliberal communist nationalism, while awaiting the moment when the rebuilding of soviet great power would once again be possible. The party's first act in the State Duma – cooperating with the LDPR to declare amnesty for the August coup plotters and the defenders of the White House in October 1993 – was chosen to symbolize the party's fidelity to the discarded Soviet constitutional order, while reinforcing the parliamentary powers granted to the Duma by the new Yeltsin constitution. In many respects, the CPRF can be compared to the DNVP in the first years of the Weimar Republic or the legitimists in the early Third Republic: all three parties set forth clear ideologies that advocated a future restoration of the ancien regime, while accepting the need to work within existing democratic institutions for the time being.

Indeed, Ziuganov and Kuptsov did capitalize very successfully on the CPRF foothold in the Duma to further strengthen its national organization of activists.

---

[112] Clifford G. Gaddy and Barry William Ickes, *Russia's Virtual Economy* (Washington, DC: Brookings Institution Press, 2002).

[113] Stephen E. Hanson, "Breaking the Vicious Cycle of Uncertainty in Post-Communist Russia," Program on New Approaches to Russian Security (PONARS) Policy Memo No. 40 (Washington, DC: Center for Strategic and International Studies, 1998).

Now that the problem of collective action involved in reestablishing a unified "Communist Party" in the Russian Federation had been solved, local communist officials throughout the country who had been displaced and marginalized in the new Yeltsin regime were happy to commit their energies and resources to the cause. Joining the CPRF provided such regional party activists with central resources to help mobilize social groups such as pensioners, blue-collar workers, and collective farmers for battles with newly ascendant "democrats" and local "oligarchs," as well as the prospect of moving up the party list to gain a seat in the Duma. Moreover, continued value-rational commitment to the cause of communism also played a role in the CPRF's successful regional recruitment of activists. In one regional survey, for example, just under 70 percent of CPRF members surveyed claimed that their primary motive for joining the party was the "construction of a more just society."[114] These ideal and material incentives helped the Communist Party claim more than 500,000 members by 1993 – making it by far the largest party in Russia.[115] In many regions of Russia, in fact, the CPRF was in effect the only effective "civil society" organization, whose activities included distributing charity, preserving historical monuments, and mobilizing protests against Yeltsin's Westernization program.[116] Within the State Duma, too, the CPRF demonstrated remarkable internal party discipline.[117]

Meanwhile, Ziuganov tirelessly explained to his party colleagues the precise new ideological basis on which the refounded CPRF was built. The party leader's output of ideological pamphlets in the mid-1990s was nothing short of prodigious – all of them marked by the same emphasis on Russian great-power nationalism that had been his credo since the Gorbachev era. Indeed, Ziuganov's writings in this period contained many of the same themes emphasized in Solzhenitsyn's political works: the destruction of Russian spiritual values by Westernization, the need for a renewed embrace of the Orthodox Church, and, of course, the artificiality of the current boundaries of the Russian Federation. However, Ziuganov not surprisingly disagreed with Solzhenitsyn's uncompromising anticommunism, arguing that the Soviet Union – especially after 1939, when Stalin began to compromise with the Orthodox Church and incorporate Russian patriotic themes in public speeches – was the true historical continuation of the Russian imperial tradition. Despite the early Bolsheviks' attempts to destroy Russian cultural tradition, over time, Ziuganov argued, Soviet Communism had gradually been merging organically with the Russian "great power" tradition: "In the middle of the 1980s a situation objectively

114 Hutcheson, *Political Parties in the Russian Regions*, table 5.4, p. 93.
115 March, *The Communist Party in Post-Soviet Russia*, p. 137.
116 For a fascinating example of this, see Ivan Kurilla, "Uryupinsk: Civil Activism without NGOs; The Communist Party as a Civil Society Substitute," Program on New Approaches to Russian Security (PONARS) Policy Memo No. 222 (Washington, DC: Center for Strategic and International Studies, January 25, 2002).
117 Smith and Remington, *Politics of Institutional Choice*, pp. 124–131.

developed in the party in which a 'change of generations,' which would naturally have taken place in the nearest future, would inevitably have brought to power politicians of a new orientation, attracted to historical continuities and the ideals of great power nationalism."[118] This did not occur, Ziuganov continued, only because Western "agents of influence" – that is, Gorbachev and Yeltsin – betrayed the Russian fatherland in order to augment their own personal power and wealth.

Reestablishing Russia as a "great power," Ziuganov insisted, would thus constitute the resurrection of Moscow once again as the "Third Rome."[119] Otherwise, Russia would be decisively subordinated to a world conspiracy led by a "transnational cosmopolitan ruling class."[120] Such organizations as the United Nations and the International Monetary Fund, Ziuganov insisted, were mere tools of this "cosmopolitan" elite, which was striving to dominate the entire world through the establishment of modern bureaucratic structures: "The direction of humanity from a single center is impossible without the utmost unification and standardization of this process. Striving to guarantee the greatest effectiveness in this area necessarily reduces to a minimum the local particularities of means of governing."[121] The desire of those implementing the "New World Order" of total standardization, then, was to wipe out every type of cultural distinctiveness that stood in the way of "rational" proceduralism. This essentially genocidal policy, Ziuganov continued, could be implemented "without any concentration camps or gas chambers necessary": "In Russia, in any case, for two years running the population has decreased, and this is a concrete example of how it is possible to regulate demographic processes by means of economic 'reforms.'"[122]

The CPRF's combination of ideological clarity and organizational strength placed it in an exceptionally strong position as the December 1995 elections for the Duma approached. The party's campaign materials continued to underline Ziuganov's favored ideological themes – vehement criticism of Yeltsin, Chubais, and Gaidar; calls to rebuild Russia as a "revolutionary democratic" great power; tolerance of "diverse forms of property" including state, collective, and private property; and conspiracy theories about who was responsible for the destruction of the USSR.[123] Despite Ziuganov's eschewal of television advertising, the CPRF organizational apparatus was by now well developed enough to ensure high voter turnout among those social groups receptive to the communist message. The result was a triumphant electoral performance:

[118] Gennadii Ziuganov, *Derzhava* (Moscow: Informpechat', 1994), p. 37.
[119] Ibid.
[120] Ibid, p. 40.
[121] Ibid.
[122] Ibid.
[123] *Programma Kommunisticheksoi Partii Rossiiskii Federatsii, Priniata III S"ezdom KPRF*, 22 *Ianvaria 1995 Goda* (Moscow, 1995); Laura Belin and Robert W. Orttung, with Ralph S. Clem and Peter R. Craumer, *The Russian Parliamentary Elections of 1995* (Armonk, NY: M. E. Sharpe, 1997), pp. 75–83.

22.3 percent of the PR party-list vote along with fifty-eight single-member district seats. An additional 20 single-member district seats went to the CPRF ally the Agrarian Party, giving Ziuganov's group control over 39.3 percent of the Duma.[124]

By the winter of 1996, many knowledgeable observers had concluded that Ziuganov would very likely be the next leader of Russia.[125] With the first round of presidential elections just months away, Yeltsin's popularity rating was in the single digits, while Ziuganov was supported by nearly a quarter of the population.[126] The CPRF's relatively strong party organization ensured that Ziuganov's campaign message would be delivered faithfully at meetings and rallies throughout the country. Yeltsin's advisers began to debate openly whether to cancel elections entirely so as to prevent what appeared to be a sure communist victory.

That Yeltsin nevertheless managed to get reelected at the polls in July 1996, defeating Ziuganov in the runoff by 54 percent to 40 percent, with 5 percent voting "against both," surely constitutes a major puzzle for economic theories of voting behavior. True, Yeltsin's eventual victory owed much to Kremlin manipulation of the democratic process, including the illegitimate use of billions of dollars of campaign funds from Russian business interests and sympathetic foreign funders, overwhelming media bias against Ziuganov, and outright manipulation of the vote count in at least a few Russian regions.[127] Nevertheless, given Yeltsin's eventual comfortable margin of victory, it seems very likely that Yeltsin would have defeated Ziuganov even in a fully free and fair vote.

As McFaul has argued, one key reason for Yeltsin's triumph was the successful framing of the election as a choice of regimes rather than simply a choice of presidents.[128] Kremlin spin doctors presented Ziuganov as an unreconstructed Stalinist who would bring back the gulag, ban rock music, and isolate Russia from the West. Contrary to purely economic theories of voting behavior, McFaul concludes, the conduct of the 1996 campaign on both sides really mattered. What McFaul's analysis leaves out, however, is any explanation of why, at key turning points, Ziuganov himself kept reinforcing the Kremlin's desired framing of the election. In March 1996 the CPRF pushed through a Duma vote to declare the illegality of the Belovezh Forest accords that formally

---

[124] White, Rose, and McAllister, *How Russia Votes*, table 11.2, p. 224.

[125] See, for example, the judgment of Hough, Davidheiser, and Lehmann in early 1996: "On the surface it is easier to imagine how Zyuganov might win a landslide against Yeltsin than how he might lose." Jerry F. Hough, Evelyn Davidheiser, and Susan Goodrich Lehmann, *The 1996 Russian Presidential Election* (Washington, DC: Brookings Institution Press, 1996), p. 99.

[126] White, Rose, and McAllister, *How Russia Votes*, p. 257.

[127] Daniel Treisman, "Why Yeltsin Won," *Foreign Affairs* 75(5, September–October 1996): 64–77; Dmitry Glinsky and Peter Reddaway, *The Tragedy of Russia's Reforms* (Washington, DC: U.S. Institute of Peace Press, 2001).

[128] Michael McFaul, *Russia's 1996 Presidential Election: The End of Polarized Politics* (Stanford, CA: Hoover Institution Press, 1997).

dissolved the USSR – thus raising the specter of geopolitical revanchism in the event of a Ziuganov presidency. On the campaign trail, Ziuganov proudly told a reporter that he considered Stalin to be a great Russian national hero.[129] And despite Ziuganov's efforts on the campaign trail to outdo Yeltsin in displays of vigorous dancing, his appeals to youth were undercut by his wooden television appearances and frequent complaints by high-ranking party comrades about the number of Jews and foreign soap operas in the Russian media.[130] While certainly many Russian voters did dislike Western cultural influences, approve of Stalin, and wish to reassert Russia's power over its post-Soviet neighbors, taken together Ziuganov's vocal and consistent assertion of all of these themes made it easy for Yeltsin's campaign advisers to paint him as a dangerous reactionary.

The theory of ideology and party formation offered here helps to explain Ziuganov's otherwise puzzling failure to move to the political center during the 1996 presidential campaign. As is clear from this analysis, Ziuganov's campaign platform in 1996 simply reiterated the key points of established CPRF ideology. The Duma declaration of the invalidity of the Commonwealth of Independent States (CIS) expressed the party leader's long-standing claim that the breakup of the USSR was a violation of the soviet constitutional order. Ziuganov's praise of Stalin was no surprise to readers of his speeches and writings since the late Soviet era. His embrace of the Orthodox Church, which struck some observers as glaringly inconsistent with Ziuganov's professed communism, was in fact a major theme of Russian Communist Party propaganda since the RCP's founding under Polozkov. Nor could Ziuganov in 1996 simply reject his long-held value-rational principles in order to win the campaign against Yeltsin. To do so would have undercut the ideological clarity and consistency that had propelled Ziuganov into a leading political role in the first place. Indeed, had he been this sort of instrumentally rational politician, he would never have been in a position to weld the CPRF back together in order to challenge Yeltsin for power.

Ziuganov's ideological sincerity also helps to explain a final puzzle of the 1996 election – namely, the CPRF's notable passivity during the last days of the campaign, when the party appeared to acquiesce in a tainted Yeltsin electoral victory without serious protest, even failing to publicize the fact that Yeltsin suffered a serious heart attack just days before the second round of voting. As March points out, however, the CPRF's unwillingness to engage the mainstream media in order to sway undecided voters in the heat of electoral struggle, along with its continuing efforts to mobilize the party's hard-core support base, had been a consistent feature of CPRF strategy since the party's founding.[131] Ziuganov's defeat in July 1996 was certainly a bitter pill for the CPRF to swallow, but in the broader context of CPRF organizational success in

---

[129] Ibid., p. 43.
[130] March, *The Communist Party in Post-Soviet Russia*, p. 192.
[131] Ibid., p. 197.

the early years of the Russian Federation it could be explained away as a short-term setback in the inevitable disintegration of the Yeltsin regime. Yeltsin's continuing incapacity for much of his second term in office reinforced the CPRF leadership's conviction that history remained on its side. Thus, the CPRF party fraction in the Duma continued to vote in a disciplined manner against proposed market reforms, while party activists in the regions maintained their organizational links with their social base of veterans, pensioners, collective farmers, and former CPSU officials – building, in effect, the social base for future soviet restoration.

Still, there is no denying that the CPRF's strategy of accommodation with the Yeltsin regime in the short run while loudly proclaiming its fidelity to communist restoration in the long run could not help but raise doubts about the depth of the party leadership's commitment to "principled" communist nationalism. As in the case of the DNVP in Weimar Germany, the CPRF began to suffer internal splits between radicals who wished to take a more openly confrontational (and openly anti-Semitic) stance, such as Makashov and Viktor Iliukhin, and moderates who wished to abandon the party's official denunciation of the Yeltsin regime as essentially illegitimate. Ziuganov's synthesis of soviet communism and Russian nationalism sufficed to keep these splits from emerging into open organizational division, but at a cost to the party's reputation for uncompromising opposition to the "regime system."[132]

The Liberal Democratic Party of Russia
The LDPR's strategy during the stalemate period paralleled that of the CPRF in many respects. Like Ziuganov, Zhirinovskii had risen to political prominence by embracing a self-declared "centrist" nationalism distinguished from the more revolutionary, avowedly fascist movements led by such figures as Vasiliev and Barkashov. There was nothing ideologically inconsistent, then, in utilizing the LDPR's newfound parliamentary power to undermine Russian democracy from within. Moreover, Zhirinovskii had pledged support for Yeltsin's 1993 constitution, arguing that its strong presidentialism was a healthy step toward the establishment of a firm dictatorship in Russia – which Zhirinovskii himself, of course, had long advocated. Zhirinovskii further argued that support for Yeltsin was a necessary strategy for blocking any restoration of communism, an ideology that he argued had driven Russia into a historical blind alley.

Thus, the widespread notion both in Russia and in the West that the LDPR and CPRF together constituted a unified "red-brown opposition" to Yeltsin must be rejected. The LDPR did vote alongside the CPRF in rejecting IMF-backed economic reforms and in protesting Yeltsin's pro-Western foreign policy line, but the LDPR voted in support of the Kremlin whenever such a vote was consistent with the party's vision of a renewed Russian empire with a "liberal" market economy. Thus, the party's stances in favor of the Yeltsin

---

[132] Richard Sakwa, "The Regime System in Russia," *Contemporary Politics* 3(1, 1997): 7–26.

constitutional referendum, in favor of amnesty for the August coup plotters, and in favor of Yeltsin's decision to invade Chechnya in 1994 all made logical sense in terms of LDPR ideology. Meanwhile, on issues of less salience to Zhirinovskii and his followers, he took advantage of the opportunity to sell the party's votes to the highest bidder – a practice that had the dual effect of replenishing the party's coffers for further organizational expansion and of reinforcing public skepticism of the parliament as an institution.

Zhirinovskii's remarkable devotion to strengthening the LDPR's national organization in this period – which seems puzzling if one interprets him as a pure opportunist – also makes sense when one takes his ideological commitment to theatrical superimperialism seriously. The party's astounding performance in the December 1993 elections now allowed Zhirinovskii to recruit new activists around the country, particularly among the party's social base of angry former KGB officials, unemployed workers, Russian nationalists in border regions, disaffected youth, and marginalized members of the "subproletariat."[133] LDPR youth camps were set up in party strongholds, and party propaganda was widely distributed.[134] Zhirinovskii continued to write (or, increasingly, to have ghostwritten) a whole series of "joke fascist" pamphlets, following up on the success of *Last Dash to the South* with such inspiring new titles as *Last Wagon to the North* and *Spit on the West*.[135] As the 1995 Duma elections approached, the LDPR had become the clear number-two party to the CPRF in terms of organizational strength, whether measured in terms of party membership or party discipline in the Duma.[136] Indeed, the LDPR actually surpassed the communists in its ability to run candidates in districts covering Russia's vast territory, nominating candidates in 83 percent of Russia's single-member districts as compared to the CPRF's 80 percent.[137]

Given this huge organizational investment, the LDPR's electoral performance in December 1995, attaining only 11 percent of the PR vote and only one single-member district seat, was clearly disappointing to Zhirinovskii and his leadership circle.[138] Nevertheless, the party still had the second-largest fraction in the Duma next to the CPRF. In addition, only two other parties, Our Home Is Russia and Yabloko, had managed to surpass the 5 percent barrier to parliamentary representation. Other competing parties on the nationalist far right had attained only minuscule percentages of the vote. Once again, as in the first Duma, Zhirinovskii could and did argue that, if the threat of communism were eliminated, Zhirinovskii himself would be in a position to succeed the ailing Yeltsin as the presidential *vozhd'* of a new Russian empire.

[133] Davidheiser, "Right and Left in the Hard Opposition."

[134] Vladimir V. Vagin, "Politicheskaia Legitimatsiia LDPR v Pskovskoi Oblastii" (Washington, DC: Kennan Institute for Advanced Russian Studies, 1997).

[135] Vladimir Zhirinovskii, *Poslednii Vagon Na Sever* (Moscow: Conjou Ltd., 1995–1997); Zhirinovskii, *Plevok na Zapad* (Moscow: Liberal'no-Demokraticheskaia Partiia Rossii, 1995).

[136] Hutcheson, *Political Parties in the Russian Regions*, p. 23.

[137] White, Rose, and McAllister, *How Russia Votes*, p. 203.

[138] Ibid., p. 224.

Such rhetoric helped to lessen the sting of Zhirinovskii's poor performance in the 1996 presidential election, in which he attained just 5.7 percent of the vote in the first round before throwing his support to Yeltsin. Indeed, despite these setbacks, the party's future prospects did not look entirely bleak. The election of Yevgenii Mikhailov as the governor of the Pskov region in May 1996 gave the LDPR its first electoral breakthrough in a gubernatorial campaign, and survey research indicated that the party maintained significant support.[139]

As with the CPRF, however, there were obvious signs that the LDPR's ideological cohesion was beginning to ebb during the Second Duma. Key members of the party's inner circle, such as Aleksandr Vengerovskii, found themselves at odds with Zhirinovskii and were soon deprived of political influence. At the same time, the party's increasing reliance on Zhirinovskii family members signified the routinization of the leader's charisma in a traditional, affectual direction. The party's use of its Duma presence to provide parliamentary seats – and thus immunity from criminal prosecution – to well-known figures from the criminal underworld may have earned extra money for Zhirinovskii, but it also undercut the party's efforts to portray itself as tough on crime. LDPR pamphlets under Zhirinovskii's name in the latter 1990s, too, sometimes crossed the fine line separating theatrical "joke fascism" from simple comedy. It is hard to imagine, for example, that many party activists were truly inspired by Zhirinvoskii's call in *Money and Civilization* to utilize new electronic banking technologies to create a paperless national financial system in which no currency touched by foreigners could ever penetrate the Russian economy.[140]

Yabloko

Both the CPRF and the LDPR began to show signs of ideological weakening during the latter 1990s. Yet they still performed relatively better in preserving and expanding their national organizations of party activists than did the more "pragmatic" parties that had attained Duma representation in December 1993. The story of the Yabloko organization in the stalemate period is particularly revealing. The disintegration of Democratic Russia and the continuing decline in popularity of Gaidar's party in the mid-1990s made Yavlinskii and other Yabloko leaders increasingly optimistic about their chances for electoral success in the 1995–1996 cycle. It now seemed as if Yavlinskii was the sole credible pro-Western politician; if he were to run as the consensus candidate of Russian liberalism, he might manage to emerge as one of the top two presidential candidates in the first round – and perhaps even capture the presidency itself.

Such dreams were not to be realized, in large part because Yabloko lacked any clear and consistent ideological vision around which to plan its long-term organizational strategy. First, as the December 1995 elections approached,

---

[139] Richard Rose and Evgeny Tikhomirov, "Russia's Forced-Choice Presidential Election," *Post-Soviet Affairs* 12(4, 1996): 351–379.

[140] Vladimir Zhirinovskii, *Den'gi i Tsivilizatsiia* (Moscow: Liberal'no-Demokraticheskaia Partiia Rossii, 1997).

Yavlinskii made the decision to avoid a merger with the now much-weakened Russia's Democratic Choice. This made short-term tactical sense, because Yabloko support and membership appeared to be growing and much of the Russian electorate had a strong antipathy toward Gaidar and his group – so, according to Yavlinskii, such a merger might well have deflated rather than increased the party's showing at the polls.[141] Yet, in the longer run, Yabloko's failure to absorb Gaidar's group at its weakest moment would come back to haunt the party, preserving the most serious competitor for the Russian "democratic" vote, and reinforcing popular perceptions of Russian liberals as incompetent egoists who could not unite for the good of the country. Yabloko also failed to adopt an energetic plan for recruiting party activists in Russia's regions. Rules for party membership remained remarkably stringent, requiring a six- to twelve-month probationary period for prospective new members to "prove themselves"; in the uncertain environment of the mid-1990s, very few uncommitted citizens would choose to pay such up-front costs.[142] Finally, in the December 1995 elections, the party once again failed to develop any clear campaign themes on issues of national identity, preferring instead to expend party resources on the distribution of massive tomes about Yabloko's macroeconomic policies.[143] The party's television time, too, was largely squandered on nonideological ads, including one famously ineffective depiction of a man sitting under a tree who was hit on the head by a falling apple – prompting him to tell his girlfriend, "I vote for Apple (Yabloko), but it's you I love."[144]

The end result of these decisions was that Yabloko could not capitalize on its temporary advantage over competing liberal groupings: the party's share of the vote in 1995 was nearly identical to what it had attained in 1993. When Yavlinskii's presidential campaign also failed to live up to expectations – attracting only 7.6 percent of the Russian electorate for a fourth-place finish behind Yeltsin, Ziuganov, and the "law and order" candidate Aleksandr Lebed – the party's long-term future viability was once again put into question. After the election cycle, high-ranking party members such as Boldyrev split with Yavlinskii, complaining about the latter's increasing personal control over the organization. Meanwhile, the party's ability to field candidates in districts outside Russia's biggest cities remained extremely limited.[145]

Parties of Power II: Our Home Is Russia

After Gaidar's lamentable electoral performance in December 1993, he belatedly tried to retool the party's image as one of fidelity to uncompromising liberal principle. The party was renamed "Russia's Democratic Choice" in

---

[141] White, *Democratic Party Yabloko*, p. 81.

[142] Ibid., pp. 166–167.

[143] N. A. Orlov, ed., *Reformy dlia Bol'shinstva: Ob"edineniie 'Iabloko'*, (Moscow: Epitsentr, 1995).

[144] White, Rose, and McAllister, *How Russia Votes*, p. 217.

[145] Hutcheson, *Political Parties in the Russian Regions*.

a bid to woo disgruntled members of the now hopelessly fractured camp of Russian "democrats," and Gaidar began increasingly to promote his ties with incorruptible human rights activists like Sergei Kovalev, who was now promoted to number two on the party list. To be sure, these decisions were not simply strategic ones. Gaidar clearly did see himself as a convinced liberal, even if he had eschewed the development of any clear ideology for constructing the future Russian polity. His split with Yeltsin over the latter's decision to invade Chechnya in December 1994, too, was evidently very painful and heartfelt.[146] Unfortunately for the prospects of Gaidar's party, however, his initial decision in 1993 to side with the Kremlin to build a "party of power" ensured that his later professions of value-rational liberal principle would lack credibility. Nor could Russia's Democratic Choice appeal to the short-term instrumental interests of ambitious regional politicians, now that it was disconnected from the state. When Yavlinskii refused to contemplate a merger between his party's and Gaidar's, Russia's Democratic Choice was forced to compete in the December 1995 elections with a skeletal organizational presence at best in most of Russia's electoral districts. The result was a disastrous proportional-representation vote of 3.9 percent, well below the 5 percent threshold for party-list representation. Thus, Gaidar's party was represented in the new Duma only by its nine single-member district seats.[147]

Crisis and Resolution, 1998–2007

By the spring of 1998, Russia's years of political stalemate had generated clear signs of impending crisis. Yeltsin's decision to fire Chernomyrdin in March in favor of the "boy wonder" (*kindersurpriz*) Sergei Kirienko, which had been intended as a way to reignite Russia's transition to capitalism, only eliminated one of the few elements of institutional stability in the Russian state. The global financial crisis set off by the East Asian currency collapses of fall 1997 had led foreign investors to be increasingly wary about other emerging markets. In this context, Russia's record of fiscal mismanagement began to attract increasing international scrutiny. Rates for the short-term government bonds that had been used to finance Russia's growing budget deficit – the so-called GKOs – began to soar, placing Kirienko's government in a serious bind: if it raised interest rates further, Russia's debt to foreign creditors could easily spiral out of control, but if it failed to do so, foreign investors would flee to safer havens and the value of the ruble would plummet – again, making Russia's debt burden unmanageable.

Analysts of the Russian financial collapse of August 1998 have tended understandably to focus on the purely economic causes of the crisis, including weak tax collection, rampant speculation in GKOs by Russian firms and banks, the low price of Russia's major energy and mineral exports, and the corrupt state

[146] See Gaidar, *Days of Defeat and Victory*, p. 283.
[147] White, *How Russia Votes*, p. 224.

bureaucracy that facilitated the flight abroad of billions of dollars in low-interest loans from the International Monetary Fund delivered to Russia just a month before the ruble devaluation. All of these factors clearly did play a role in exacerbating Russia's fiscal and monetary problems.[148] What has been less commonly emphasized, however, are the ways in which these economic issues reflected the unresolved ideological basis of Yeltsin's regime. Had Yeltsin's constitutional order during his second presidential term been supported by committed partisan activists with significant organizational resources across Russian territory, it might have been possible to mobilize Russian social support for liberal democracy as a patriotic duty – despite the painful short-term necessities of higher taxes and budget cuts to unsustainable enterprises and farms. Had the Russian state in the latter 1990s been staffed by reliable bureaucrats committed to the value-rational defense of impersonal legal principles, the state might have been capable of restraining the efforts of Russian business tycoons and corrupt officials to spirit away billions of dollars of capital at the very height of the crisis.[149]

Instead, Yeltsin's weak and corrupted presidential regime was confronted with a parliament whose two largest parties both opposed Western-style liberal capitalism on ideological principle. The CPRF initially protested Kirienko's selection as prime minister, voting to reject the nomination twice – thus delaying the formation of the new government for a crucial six-week period in spring 1998 and deepening investors' uncertainty about Russian economic policy making. To be sure, Kirienko's final confirmation on the third ballot, with most Communist deputies now voting with the majority, was obviously prompted by instrumental calculations that a dissolution of the Duma – as would be constitutionally required in such a case according to the 1993 Russian Constitution – might cost the CPRF its healthy parliamentary majority and ability to distribute perks to its ambitious members. As with past opposition votes to preserve the Yeltsin "system," however, this decision could be justified ideologically as a necessary tactical retreat that in no way implied any deeper acceptance of Kirienko's pro-Western policies. Indeed, throughout the summer of 1998, the CPRF continued to block IMF-sponsored measures to eliminate Russia's growing budget deficit – a crucial factor explaining the failure of Kirienko's stabilization plan.[150] Neither did Zhirinovskii's rhetoric in this period help to inspire confidence among foreign investors in the stability of Russia's institutional order. While the LDPR once again delivered its fraction's votes for Kirienko on the third ballot – and once again was alleged to have been

[148] Andrei Illarionov, "The Roots of the Economic Crisis," *Journal of Democracy* 10(20, 1999): 68–82; Juliet Ellen Johnson, *A Fistful of Rubles: The Rise and Fall of the Russian Banking System* (Ithaca, NY: Cornell University Press, 2000).

[149] That the ruble's weakness in the 1990s should be seen as a corollary of the weakness of the Russian state is a central theme in David Woodruff, *Money Unmade: Barter and the Fate of Russian Capitalism* (Ithaca, NY: Cornell University Press, 2000).

[150] Anders Aslund, "Russia's Collapse," *Foreign Affairs* 78(5, 1999): 64–77.

amply compensated for this – Zhirinovskii's initial description of Kirienko as a "little boy" and a "first-grader" with no business running the state made it clear to the LDPR membership that such instrumentally rational behavior did not signify any deeper ideological embrace of Westernization.[151]

Given the fragility of elite commitment to the Yeltsin regime, Kirienko's sudden announcement on August 17 that the ruble would be devalued and that Russia would default on its debt obligations raised the very real prospect that the constitutional order established in December 1993 would soon collapse altogether. The early signs were clearly ominous: the ruble lost 75 percent of its value within a month; several of Russia's new post-Soviet banks collapsed, wiping out the savings of millions of ordinary Russian citizens for the second time in a decade; and in many of Russia's regions, local politicians sanctioned the hoarding of food and other basic goods.[152] Yeltsin's effort to stem the spiraling crisis by firing Kirienko and nominating Chernomyrdin to return as prime minister smacked of desperation. The Duma majority rejected Chernomyrdin, twice, and this time it was clearly ready to go ahead with a third rejection and face the constitutional showdown that would subsequently ensue. Yavlinskii's proposal of Yevgenii Primakov as a compromise candidate acceptable to all sides – an escape route eagerly embraced by the Kremlin – forestalled this open battle among rival forces for the time being. The formation of a Primakov government within which both the CPRF and LDPR were finally given control over government ministries did not, however, signify any deeper consolidation of the Russian democratic order. Indeed, Primakov's advanced age and lack of any independent organizational base of his own, combined with the renewed uncertainty generated by Russia's latest economic disaster, now encouraged a wide variety of ambitious politicians to position themselves for an impending political struggle for full control over the state.

The temporary nature of Russia's political compromise following the crisis was underscored by the decision of the CPRF leadership in the autumn of 1998 and winter of 1999 to go ahead with a campaign to impeach President Yeltsin for "treason" and failure to fulfill his constitutional duties. Indeed, the Communists' impeachment campaign provides another clear indication of the party's continuing fidelity to its Soviet restorationist ideology, even after nearly a decade of tactical compromise with the Yeltsin regime. Of the five charges Ziuganov and his colleagues leveled against Yeltsin – that he conspired to break up the Soviet Union in 1991, that he unconstitutionally attacked the Russian parliament in October 1993, that he had destroyed the Russian army, that he had committed "genocide" against the Russian people by launching economic "shock therapy," and that he had illegally launched the war in Chechnya in December 1994 – only the last of them actually related to

---

[151] Zhirinovskii quoted in CNN World News, "Yeltsin Nominee Rejected on First Try," April 10, 1998, http://www.cnn.com/WORLD/europe/9804/10/russia.duma.vote/, accessed on November 29, 2008.

[152] See Johnson, *A Fistful of Rubles*.

Yeltsin's performance under the Russian Constitution adopted in December 1993. Yeltsin's role in destroying the USSR, his disbanding of the Russian Congress of People's Deputies, his decision to build a Russian military in place of the old Soviet one, and his early economic reform policies could be considered "unconstitutional" only if one still considered the Brezhnev-era RSFSR Constitution as legally binding, as Ziuganov had been insisting since 1990. Unsurprisingly, then, the remaining Duma party factions would not back up the CPRF on any of these four charges. Only the fifth charge about Yeltsin's bypassing of the Duma to invade Chechnya might plausibly be considered an impeachable offense under Yeltsin's own constitution, and only in this case did at least one other party – namely Yabloko – decide to lend its support to the Communist effort. Zhirinovskii, consistent with his long-standing opposition to CPRF ideological initiatives, argued (not implausibly) that to impeach the president at a time of foreign policy crisis, when the United States was at war with Russia's ally Serbia, would only hasten the collapse of the country.

After Yeltsin's surprise decision to fire Prime Minister Primakov on May 12, 1999, and to replace him with Interior Minister Sergei Stepashin, the future of the Russian constitutional order hung in the balance. The key question was whether the CPRF-Yabloko coalition would produce a vote of 300 or more deputies to impeach Yeltsin on the fifth and final count related to the Chechen war. In the end, only 283 deputies voted for impeachment, while several dozen spoiled their ballots.[153] Cementing Yeltsin's victory, the Duma voted overwhelmingly a few days later to confirm Stepashin as the new prime minister, making it clear that the only political position worth fighting for in post-Soviet Russia was the presidency itself.

With the deeply unpopular Yeltsin still constitutionally mandated to vacate that office at the end of his formal second term in July 2000, however, the question of precisely who would succeed him remained entirely unclear. Indeed, the level of political uncertainty in the second half of 1999 was arguably as high as it had been in the months following the collapse of the Soviet Union. As a result, leading Russian politicians once again scrambled to form instrumental alliances that might secure power and resources in the turbulent transition ahead. In early August, the announcement of the formation of the new Fatherland-All Russia (FAR) partisan alliance, including former Prime Minister Primakov and key regional bosses such as Moscow's Mayor Yurii Luzhkov and Tatarstan's President Mintimer Shaimiev, combined with the news that Chechen rebels Shamil Basaev and Khattab had invaded Chechnya's neighbor Dagestan on the Caspian Sea in order to foment an Islamist rebellion throughout the North Caucasus, shocked the Yeltsin entourage into action. On August 9 Yeltsin announced that the previously obscure Vladimir Putin, head of the Federal Security Service (FSB), would not only replace Stepashin as prime minister, but also serve as the president's "heir" and successor. Remarkably,

---

[153] Colton, *Yeltsin: A Life*, p. 429.

just over six months later, Putin's presidency, backed by a slavishly pro-Kremlin "party of power" with a strong majority in the Duma, was an accomplished fact.

This outcome was due above all to the fact that in the context of the direct threat posed by FAR to Yeltsin's ruling circle, combined with the very real potential for state disintegration generated by the invasion of Dagestan, the Kremlin leadership managed to unify and to deploy overwhelming state resources to promote Putin's political prospects.[154] Unlike in 1993 and 1995, when Yeltsin's efforts to form "parties of power" such as Russia's Choice and Our Home Is Russia were undercut by the simultaneous promotion of competing Kremlin organizational projects, Yeltsin and those close to him remained steadfast in their backing of Putin as presidential successor from August 1999 onward. In short, in place of a clear and consistent ideology that might lower the discount rates of key Russian political actors, the Kremlin put forward Putin's personal leadership as a solution to continuing institutional uncertainty. By September, when mysterious bombings of apartment complexes in various Russian cities that were blamed by the Kremlin on Chechen rebels killed more than three hundred citizens, the equation of Putin with Russia's political future began to take hold in public opinion.[155] By October the announcement of the formation of the new Unity (Edinstvo) Party, whose leaders proudly proclaimed their rejection of any and all ideology other than support for Putin himself, led to an increasing bandwagon effect among those instrumental Russian politicians who had not declared themselves for FAR. Finally, key Russian "oligarchs" such as Boris Berezovskii and Vladimir Gusinskii calculated that they, too, would benefit more from supporting the Putin project than taking their chances with the "leftist" FAR, and they flooded the television stations they controlled with incessant propaganda portraying Putin as the savior of Russia and Primakov as a doddering old fool. By the time of the December 1999 Duma elections, Putin's endorsement of Unity led to a resounding electoral triumph: not two months after its founding, Unity managed to attain 24 percent of the party-list vote along with nine single-member district seats, for a formidable total of seventy-three Duma seats in all.[156] In this context, Yeltsin's surprise resignation as president on New Year's Eve 1999 – thus making Prime Minister Putin the acting president, in accordance with the rules of the 1993 Constitution – put Putin in an overwhelmingly powerful position vis-à-vis his political rivals. The outcome of the formal presidential election campaign in winter 2000 had now suddenly become a foregone conclusion.

---

[154] Timothy J. Colton and Michael McFaul, *Popular Choice and Managed Democracy: The Russian Elections of 1999 and 2000* (Washington, DC: Brookings Institution Press, 2003); Henry Hale, *Why Not Parties in Russia?* (Cambridge: Cambridge University Press, 2006).

[155] In August, 2 percent of Russian voters said they would vote for Putin; by September, this proportion had reached 4 percent; by October, it had reached 21 percent; and by the time of the December 19 Duma elections, this figure reached 51 percent. Colton, *Yeltsin: A Life*, p. 434.

[156] Colton and McFaul, *Popular Choice and Managed Democracy*, p. 8.

Unlike the resolution of analogous political crises in Third Republic France in 1877 or Weimar Germany in 1929, Russia's financial collapse led not to the victory of any ideological party but instead to the reassertion of the nonideological presidential system established by Yeltsin in 1993 – and subsequently, under Putin's presidency, to the gradual elimination of its residual democratic elements. We are now in a position to understand this rather surprising outcome in comparative perspective. To reiterate the main thesis of this book: ideology acts as a causal variable in uncertain institutional environments by artificially extending the time horizons of converts, eventually leading even purely instrumental politicians to rally around ideological parties, and giving ideologues a comparative organizational advantage over more "pragmatic" party builders. This dynamic, as we have seen, fits the Russian case very well, explaining both the comparative organizational success of parties led by initially marginalized extremists and the repeated failure of Kremlin-sponsored "parties of power" in 1993 and 1995. This logic also explains why Russia's formal democratic institutions could not be consolidated as long as powerful antisystem parties continued to call into question the constitutional order, because this generated a zero-sum stalemate among competing ideological visions of the future polity, which perpetuated short-term instrumental action among Russian citizens and foreign investors alike.

However, ideological variables alone cannot fully explain what sort of political regime ultimately emerges once political stalemates are broken. This depends not only on the goals of competing political organizations in periods of regime crisis but also on the broader social environment generated by the interests of the military and police, key economic elites, international actors, and social movements from below. If ideological party organizations are powerful enough – as with Gambetta's Republicans or Hitler's Nazis – they may be able to mobilize collective action on the part of such groups in support of their ideological visions, eventually imposing a political order consistent with their long-standing principles. But there is no guarantee that ideological organizations will always emerge politically triumphant in the end.

Herein lies the most important difference between Russia's post-imperial democracy and those of France after 1870 and Germany after 1918: in diachronic comparative perspective, neither the CPRF nor the LDPR had acquired by 1998 anything like the national organizational capacity, relative to its main competitors, of the French Republicans in 1877 or the German National Socialists in 1933. Indeed, by the latter 1990s the initial charisma of both party leaders and their ideologies had begun to routinize in ways that seriously damaged their mobilizational potential. Nor could Russia's nonideological parties mount any effective resistance to Putin's consolidation of power, because they lacked loyal national activist networks altogether. The unfolding of the resolution of Russia's regime crisis after the failure of the CPRF impeachment effort thus differed from the analogous processes in the Third Republic or Weimar Germany, because the relative weakness of the entire party system allowed the executive branch to compete effectively as an autonomous regime-building actor in its own right.

The CPRF, as we have seen, was still by far the strongest political party in Russia at the close of the 1990s. But the party's repeated tactical compromises with the Kremlin, while ideologically justified in each case as consistent with the long-term goal of restoring a communist-nationalist "great power" in Russia, had nevertheless generated a widespread sense among disaffected Russians that the Communists were now a constituent part of the Yeltsin regime. Indeed, despite the genuinely revolutionary situation facing Russia in 1998–1999 and increasing discontent among the more radical circles of the Communist leadership, Ziuganov, both during and after the impeachment campaign, remained wedded to the strategy of taking power by legal means. To be sure, the Communists did manage to turn in their best electoral performance to date in the December 1999 elections, coming in first in the proportional representation vote with 25 percent and also in the single-member district vote with forty-six mandates.[157] But the CPRF total of 113 deputies hardly looked like a triumph, given that the pro-Putin Unity Party had attained nearly the same proportional representation vote despite being formed less than two months before the election – and would soon be augmented further by defections from FAR and other Duma fractions.

Meanwhile, the LDPR's increasingly open willingness to trade its Duma votes and seats for cash at crucial political turning points, its failure to build on its initial organizational successes to attain significant representation among regional parliaments or governorships, and Zhirinovskii's organizational reliance on close family members instead of like-minded ideological comrades all worked to diminish the party's mobilizational potential. When the Central Electoral Commission decided to deny the LDPR's party registration, charging irregularities in the reporting of the personal assets of individuals on its party list (several of whom were rumored to be bosses in Russia's criminal underworld), Zhirinovskii did little more than issue loud complaints.[158] In the end, he was allowed to reregister the party as the "Zhirinovskii Bloc," but the resulting confusion among LDPR voters led to the party's worst performance to date: just 6 percent of the proportional representation vote and no single-member district seats, for a total of 17 seats in the 450-member Duma.[159]

Russia's nonideological parties, based as they were on instrumentally rational calculations by leading Russian politicians, faced even more serious organizational problems. The quick decline of FAR, which had looked to be unbeatable in August, is a striking illustration of this point. As the Kremlin's project to promote Putin and to undermine Primakov began to gather steam, previously uncommitted politicians signed up to support Unity, while those who had

---

[157] Ibid.
[158] Hale, *Why Not Parties?*, p. 70.
[159] Colton and McFaul, *Popular Choice and Managed Democracy*, p. 8.

initially sided with FAR began to hedge their bets. After FAR gained a disappointing 14 percent of the proportional representation votes in December, the party quickly unraveled completely. Primakov withdrew his candidacy for the presidency, and FAR leaders began to open negotiations with Unity to unite in support of the Kremlin. By 2001 the two rival parties of power had merged into a single pro-Putin organization: United Russia, which now included nearly every ambitious politician in the country.

Yabloko also suffered through a disastrous election cycle.[160] Yavlinskii first made an unlikely alliance with the hawkish former prime minister Stepashin as the number-two man on the party list, trying to woo nationalists and supporters of a strong state. But Yavlinskii then decided to stake out a campaign position – albeit one he did not always express unambiguously – as a partisan critic of Putin's conduct of the war in Chechnya, trying to woo liberals concerned about the growing militarization of Russian politics. This inconsistent strategy quickly alienated Stepashin, thoroughly demoralized what remained of the party's activist base in the regions, and ultimately led to a bitter personal split between Yavlinskii and Igrunov. Only 6 percent of Russian voters backed Yabloko in the proportional representation voting, and the party's Duma faction was down to twenty members.[161] Once again, Yabloko had paid dearly for its lack of ideological consistency in a time of high regime uncertainty.

Meanwhile, Gaidar, Chubais, and other pro-state liberals had managed to weld several smaller parties together to form the new Union of Rightist Forces (URF). The party leadership made the frankly instrumental decision to tie itself completely and openly to Putin, positioning the party as the one likely to provide future economic advice to Yeltsin's charismatic presidential successor. In a memorable television debate, Chubais even accused Yavlinskii of being a "traitor" for his criticism of Putin's strategy in Chechnya – making any electoral reconciliation between the two parties impossible.[162] Putin returned the favor, consenting to appear in a television ad for URF in which he was seen nodding approvingly when shown the party's new economic plan. The result was a resounding short-term electoral victory for the pro-Kremlin liberals: the URF easily surpassed the 5 percent barrier for proportional representation, attaining nearly 9 percent of the vote.[163] However, the URF's instrumental alliance with Putin now left the party entirely dependent on Kremlin support. When Putin later decided to turn against both nonideological liberal parties, they could neither unite with each other nor mount any effective campaign of resistance on their own.

In this respect, recent analyses from a rational choice perspective of the weakness of Russia's political party system in the 1990s by Hale and Smyth

---

[160] Henry Hale, "Yabloko and the Challenge of Building a Liberal Party in Russia," *Europe-Asia Studies* 56(7, November 2004): 993–1020.
[161] Colton and McFaul, *Popular Choice and Managed Democracy*, p. 8.
[162] White, *The Russian Democratic Party Yabloko*, p. 90.
[163] Colton and McFaul, *Popular Choice and Managed Democracy*, p. 8.

contain a great deal of insight. Hale demonstrates that by the latter part of the decade, political parties had failed to "close out" the political "market," in large part because of increasingly successful competition by "party substitutes" – that is, political machines sponsored by local governors, powerful oligarchs, and the Kremlin itself – which could help candidates win elections even more effectively than most Russian party organizations. Under such circumstances, rational Russian politicians had no reason to remain loyal to parties.[164] Smyth shows that in a context where most Russian party organizations failed to survive even a single election cycle and where party weakness rendered campaign positions inconsistent and contradictory, even repeated elections failed to produce any durable increase in political capital for party organizations – creating a vicious cycle in which the persistent political uncertainty facing ordinary voters further undermined democratic consolidation.[165] What these excellent analyses miss, however, is that the failure of rational political actors in Russia to overcome the collective action problems involved in building national party organizations reflects the broader historical failure of any partisan ideological project to achieve political hegemony in the post-Soviet context. After all, instrumental political coalitions backed by self-interested economic elites worked to undermine the cohesion of ideological parties in the early French Third Republic and in Weimar Germany, too; yet, in the end, parties did manage either to corner the market for electoral goods (as in France) or to destroy the organizational basis of political competition altogether (as in Germany).

Seen in comparative-historical perspective, the victory of the Kremlin-created Unity Party in the parliamentary elections of 1999 should not be interpreted as a final breakthrough toward relatively successful national party building – as Hale and Smyth both argue – but instead as the first step in the final destruction of Russia's independent political party system and its replacement by a weakly consolidated presidential autocracy. The mechanism by which the Kremlin overcame the collective action problem of national party organization in the 1999–2000 electoral transition depended solely on the mobilization of positive affect for Putin, along with top-down state incentives for participation and loyalty, and did not involve any independent value-rational motivation for fidelity to political principles among party members as in the case of the ideological parties we have analyzed. Given this frankly instrumental organizational foundation, Unity (and its successor, United Russia) could survive only so long as relative certainty about central-state patronage as a reward for party loyalty was maintained. Any move by the Kremlin to provide equal support to rival party organizations, or any sign that the Kremlin's power to reward loyalists might diminish, was bound to lead the instrumentally rational members of Unity to rethink their partisan affiliation and to explore the costs and benefits of association with rival groupings – threatening the pro-Kremlin

---

[164] Hale, *Why Not Parties?*
[165] Regina Smyth, *Candidate Strategies and Electoral Competition in the Russian Federation: Democracy without Foundation* (Cambridge: Cambridge University Press, 2006).

"party of power" with the same fate that befell Russia's Choice after 1993 and Our Home Is Russia after 1995.[166] To ensure that Unity would succeed where these previous top-down party organizations failed thus logically required the gradual elimination of the space for independent partisan competition in the Russian Federation.

Given the absence of effective ideological movements to compete with presidential power, the process whereby Putin gradually rebuilt the Russian state along authoritarian lines can thus quite easily be explained in rational choice terms. After Putin's easy electoral victory in March 2000 – beating Ziuganov by a huge margin according to official figures, 53 to 29 percent – the new president launched an explicit program of recentralizing and strengthening the Russian state, primarily by reestablishing what the Kremlin called the "vertical of power" (*vertikal' vlasti*) linking local officials to regional ones and regional officials to the central administration.[167] According to Putin's conception of *gosudarstvennost'* – loosely translatable as "loyalty to the state" – anyone who tried to oppose state centralization should be seen as unpatriotic at best, and perhaps treasonously in league with external enemies.[168] Coincidentally, too, Russia's economy began to rebound strongly just as Putin came to power, largely because of the combined effects of skyrocketing global energy prices and the beneficial effects for domestic producers of the ruble's devaluation in August 1998. The Kremlin suddenly had ample resources to pay off supporters and punish opponents – as Berezovskii and Gusinskii soon discovered when they tried to block Putin's early consolidation of state power; they were both stripped of their empires and forced to flee the country by the end of Putin's first year in office. Putin also quickly established seven new "federal districts," each led by a Kremlin loyalist (generally from the military or FSB) to bring previously powerful regional politicians in line. Finally, Putin tacitly encouraged the formation of a growing personality cult, promoting the idea of the Russian leader as tough, brilliant, competent, and even sexy – further cementing the association of the Russian state with the presidential persona.

Parallel tactics of state patronage or punishment were used to gain full control over the Russian parliament. Regional governors were denied their formerly automatic seats in the upper house, the Federation Council, and replaced by appointees who could be more easily controlled by the Kremlin. The merger

---

[166] Stephen E. Hanson, "Instrumental Democracy: The End of Ideology and the Decline of Russian Political Parties," in Vicki Hesli and William S. Reisinger, eds., *Elections, Parties, and the Future of Russia* (Cambridge: Cambridge University Press, 2003), pp. 163–185.

[167] For good general accounts, see Peter Baker and Susan Glasser, *Kremlin Rising: Vladimir Putin's Russia and the End of Revolution* (New York: Scribner, 2005); and Richard Sakwa, *Putin: Russia's Choice* (London: Routledge, 2004).

[168] Stephen E. Hanson, "Strategic Partner or Evil Empire?" in Ashley Tellis and Michael Wills, eds., *Strategic Asia, 2004–05: Confronting Terrorism in the Pursuit of Power* (Seattle: National Bureau of Asian Research, 2004), pp. 163–195; Valerie Sperling, "The Last Refuge of a Scoundrel: Patriotism, Militarism, and the Russian National Idea," *Nations and Nationalism* 9(2, 2003): 235–253.

of Unity and FAR to form United Russia created an overwhelming pro-Kremlin majority that ensured quick passage of legislation favored by the executive branch. The CPRF, initially still a formidable opposition force, was lulled into complacency through a deal in early 2000 to share parliamentary committee chairs with Unity, excluding Yabloko, the URF, and the LDPR; then, once the formation of United Russia was complete, the Kremlin reneged on the deal and left the CPRF in a powerless position. The window of structural opportunity for effective partisan resistance to top-down Kremlin control had now passed: no Russian party other than the CPRF could claim any serious degree of social support, much less passionate conviction, and even the CPRF itself was quickly fading into political irrelevance.

By the time of the 2003–2004 electoral cycle, the process of Kremlin domination over both the parliament and the party system was complete. After a farcical campaign in which state-controlled television and local bureaucracies trumpeted the virtues of United Russia night and day, the pro-Kremlin "party" attained a two-thirds majority of Duma seats – now allowing it to amend the Russian Constitution as needed without parliamentary resistance. The arrest of Mikhail Khodorkovskii at a Siberian airport in October 2003 eliminated the last major business empire willing to provide funding to opposition parties; this had a devastating effect not only on Russia's two liberal parties but also on the CPRF, which had resorted to cultivating ties with Khodorkovskii's Yukos empire in order to attain funding for the 2003 Duma campaign. In the end, neither Yabloko nor the URF was able to surpass the 5 percent barrier to proportional representation, and both parties were subsequently almost totally deprived of funds and media exposure as a result. The CPRF limped into the Duma with just 13 percent of the proportional representation vote and only twelve single-member district seats. The LDPR, meanwhile, recovered from the fiasco of 1999 to poll 11 percent of the proportional representation vote – but like Ziuganov, Zhirinovskii still commanded the loyalty of only a small minority of Russian voters.[169] As had been the case since the 1990s, only a minuscule percentage of Russian citizens professed any trust whatsoever in political parties as an institution, and – at least until an all-out campaign by the state to formally enlist members of the United Russia Party as the 2007–2008 elections approached – an even tinier fraction actually claimed to be party members.[170] Thus, Putin was only expressing the sentiments of the vast

---

[169] By May 2006, only 9 percent of Russians polled expressed support for the CPRF, while only 6 percent supported the LDPR. See Levada Analytical Center Survey, "Public Opinion and the Duma," howrussiavotes.org, accessed on June 25, 2006.

[170] See Richard Rose, *New Russia Barometer XIV: Evidence of Dissatisfaction*, Studies in Public Policy No. 402 (Glasgow: Centre for the Study of Public Policy, University of Strathclyde, 2005). For an interesting account of the different membership figures reported by Russian parties to the media and to the Russian Justice Ministry, see "How Many Party Members? Depends on Who's Asking," *Radio Free Europe/Radio Free Liberty Russian Political Weekly* 3(3, January 17, 2003), http://www.rferl.org/content/article/1344336.html, accessed on January 9, 2010. According to the figures Russia's party leaders gave to the media in 2002, all

majority of his countrymen when he declared his opposition to allowing any sort of party influence over the creation of the cabinet: "A party government? The lessons of history tell us that everything is possible, but I am against introducing such a measure into Russian politics today. I am deeply convinced that in the former Soviet Union, where the economy is developing, the state is being strengthened, and the principles of federalism are finally taking root, we need a firm presidential authority."[171]

But if Putin's authoritarian rule could be considered more or less consolidated by his second term in office, the absence of any underlying ideology to legitimate Russian state power remained a long-term organizational problem. Certainly Putin himself offered no clear and consistent political definition of the Russian polity – its mission, core principles of membership, and place in the world. On the contrary, Putin's efforts to build legitimacy for his regime involved an eclectic mixing and matching of contradictory symbols that, if anything, were even less coherent than Boris Yeltsin's ideological platform. Putin simultaneously called for renewed pride in Soviet-era accomplishments and approved the ostentatious reburial of White Russian general Anton Denikin. He trumpeted the need to "rebuild the Russian state" and warned darkly of conspiracies to destroy the nation – but he simultaneously upheld the importance of "civil society" and European values.[172] He termed the collapse of the USSR the "biggest geopolitical catastrophe of the century" but then publicly lauded Boris Yeltsin for bringing "freedom" to the Russian people.[173] Even the new official state symbols approved early in the Putin era reflected an underlying ideological ambivalence: the old Soviet national anthem was restored with new, ideologically neutral words; the communist red flag was approved for the military, along with the tricolor flag of Russian anticommunists for everyone else. Russia's presidential authoritarianism under Putin thus had an odd, hollow quality, not standing for or against any identifiable ideological

---

major parties in Russia together had a total of 1,669,900 members, or just over 1 percent of Russia's population. However, according to the figures Russian parties reported to the Justice Ministry that year, there were only 189,700 party members in all. In contrast, by early 2006 United Russia announced that it had reached the 1 million mark in party members; see "Russia's Main Pro-Kremlin Party Posts One Million Members," *Mosnews.com*, March 6, 2006, http://www.mosnews.com/news/2006/03/06/unitedmillion.shtml, accessed on June 25, 2006.

[171] Putin Press Conference, January 31, 2006. Full text available at www.kremlin.ru.

[172] Sergei Medvedev, "Juicy Morsels: Putin's Beslan Address and the Construction of the New Russian Identity," Program on New Approaches to Russian Security, Policy Memo No. 334 (Washington, DC: Center for Strategic and International Studies, November 2004); Vladimir Putin, "Speech at the First Plenary Session of the Public Council of the Russian Federation," January 22, 2006, www.kremlin.ru, accessed on August 18, 2008.

[173] Vladimir Putin, "Speech to the Federal Assembly," April 25, 2005, www.kremlin.ru, accessed on August 18, 2008; "Yeltsin, 75, Enjoys Bash at the Kremlin," *St. Petersburg Times* 1142(8, February 3, 2006), http://www.sptimes.ru/index.php?action_id=2&story_id=16636&highlight=yeltsin%2075%20enjoys%20bash%20at%20kremlin, accessed on January 9, 2010.

principles.[174] This did not pass unnoticed by Putin's closest advisers, who by 2006 had redoubled their efforts to construct a viable new ideology that might somehow bolster the regime's legitimacy in advance of the approaching 2008 elections.[175] Putin's ultimate decision to name his protégé Dmitrii Medvedev as his presidential successor, while retaining personal power as the new Russian prime minister, was in this context a sign of the continuing uncertainty about, and incoherence of, even basic Russian state institutions – now more than a decade and a half after the collapse of the USSR.

[174] Kathleen E. Smith, *Mythmaking in the New Russia: Politics and Memory during the Yeltsin Era* (Ithaca, NY: Cornell University Press, 2002); James H. Billington, *Russia in Search of Itself* (Washington, DC: Woodrow Wilson Center Press; Baltimore: Johns Hopkins University Press, 2004).

[175] See, in particular, the February 2006 speech of Deputy Director of the Russian Presidential Administration Vladislav Surkov, reprinted as "General'naia Liniia," *Moskovskie Novosti* 7 (March 3–9, 2006): 10–11; and "General'naia Liniia," *Moskovskie Novosti* 8 (March 10–16, 2006): 10–11.

7

Conclusion

Bringing Ideology Back In

The evidence presented in this book suggests that the role of ideology as a causal variable in the early stages of party formation has been seriously underestimated by political scientists to date. Out of sixteen political parties examined, fifteen fit the central hypothesis advanced here: namely, that under conditions of intense institutional and social uncertainty, parties must have ideologies – that is, clear and consistent definitions of the principles governing membership in their preferred polity – to succeed in overcoming the collective action problems involved in creating national organizations of party activists, while nonideological parties fail to do so as a result of instrumentally rational free riding among party members. This hypothesis explains the otherwise puzzling success of the initially marginalized republicans and legitimists in France after the defeat at Sedan, and the concomitant organizational failure of the comparatively well-established Orléanists and Bonapartists. It explains the relative strength and endurance of the Social Democratic Party and monarchist German National People's Party in the 1920s, in comparison with the splintering of the German People's Party, the German Democratic Party, and the Independent Social Democrats; similarly, it explains the emergence of the Nazis and Communists in Weimar Germany – originally on the very fringes of political life – as the two major contenders for power in the late Weimar Period. Finally, our central hypothesis is borne out in post-Soviet Russia, where the relatively ideological Communist Party of the Russian Federation and Liberal Democratic Party of Russia managed to sustain their party organizations throughout the first sixteen years of the Russian Federation, while less ideologically consistent liberal parties and "parties of power" fractured – at least until the authoritarian regime of Vladimir Putin decided to build a pliable pro-Kremlin party from the top down (see Table 7.1).

Other than Putin's United Russia, which exists solely as a creation of the state and therefore does not qualify as an independent electoral party, the only party in this study that managed to sustain its national activist organization without articulating a clear and consistent definition of the polity for

TABLE 7.1. *Party Formation in Post-Imperial Democracies*

Country Case	Party Name	Party Type	Outcome
Third Republic France	Republican Party	Ideological	Organizational success
	Legitimist Party	Ideological	Organizational success
	Orléanist Party	Nonideological	Organizational failure
	Bonapartist Party	Nonideological	Organizational failure
Weimar Germany	KPD	Ideological	Organizational success
	SPD	Ideological	Organizational success
	DNVP	Ideological	Organizational success
	NSDAP (Nazi Party)	Ideological	Organizational success
	USDP	Nonideological	Organizational failure
	DNP	Nonideological	Organizational failure
	DVP	Nonideological	Organizational failure
	Catholic Center Party	Nonideological	Organizational success
Post-Soviet Russia	CPRF	Ideological	Organizational success
	LDPR	Ideological	Organizational success
	Yabloko	Nonideological	Organizational failure
	"Parties of Power" (Russia's Choice, NDR, FAR)	Nonideological	Organizational failure

which it stood is the German Catholic Center Party. This disconfirming result, I have argued, can be explained in part when we consider that Center activists had no other plausible partisan options open to them, given the explicit anti-Catholicism of the competing Weimar parties. Yet even in this case, instrumental decisions by leading Center Party elites generated serious and damaging organizational splits over regional and sectoral issues. Ultimately, most Center activists defected relatively quickly once Hitler's rise to power shifted power away from parliamentary parties altogether – especially as compared to the SPD and KPD, which did manage to mount at least some organized resistance to the Nazis after 1933.[1]

A final piece of evidence for the importance of ideological commitments in the formation of post-imperial party systems emerges when we examine the policy orientations of victorious parties after they are in a position to direct the state. While ideology alone clearly does not explain precisely which parties will ultimately win state power – this depends upon structural conditions that predispose political, economic, and military elites to support one party ideology over another during moments of crisis – the remarkable fidelity of Gambetta's Republicans and Hitler's National Socialists to their initial political visions after attaining power surely lends additional weight to the argument advanced here. Were ideology simply a tool adopted by elites to position themselves

---

[1] Ivan Ermakoff, *Ruling Oneself Out: A Theory of Collective Abdications* (Durham, NC: Duke University Press, 2008).

advantageously in temporary political battles, one would not expect the launching of costly national programs in France during the late 1870s and 1880s to produce secular, patriotic French citizens through mass public education – precisely as had been promised by Gambetta in the Belleville Program of 1869. Were ideology irrelevant to the rise of the Nazis, one would not predict Hitler's consistent efforts after 1933 to build a "racial state" designed to enslave, and ultimately to murder, Jews and other targeted minorities, at incalculable cost not only to humanity as a whole but also to his own grip on power.[2]

In terms of regime outcomes, the case of Russia under Putin is the exception that proves the rule: ideology plays a crucial role in generating committed national partisan organizations, so nonideological authoritarian states should be relatively poor at maintaining their organizational integrity and ability to mobilize the masses. This appears to be precisely what we see in contemporary Russia. Given the comparatively weak party organizations established by Ziuganov and Zhirinovskii in the 1990s – reflecting in part the relatively low levels of ideological commitment among party members in post-Soviet Russia, as compared to those of ideological activists in Third Republic France or Weimar Germany – the financial collapse of August 1998 resulted in a political crisis in which a newly designated presidential "heir" with no ideology of his own was able to triumph over all partisan opponents. Having gained supreme state power after March 2000, President Putin proceeded to build a "pragmatic" authoritarian state buttressed by a reliably pro-Kremlin party, United Russia, which explicitly abjured ideological principles. The use of selective incentives imposed by the presidential state to weld together United Russia activists, however, did not produce a "political party" in the Sartorian sense – that is, an organization formed explicitly for the purpose of competing for the public vote. Rather, United Russia was sustained internally through state payoffs to loyalists, and its outwardly impressive results at the ballot box were generated only with the help of increasingly undemocratic forms of electoral manipulation. Such a party of purely instrumental rational actors would, like previous "parties of power" in post-Soviet Russia, hold together only so long as direct state patronage could be maintained.[3]

Alternative Explanations

In comparison with the Weberian theoretical approach to party formation set out in this study, rival theories do not appear to fit the evidence nearly as well. To begin with, as has already been emphasized, the three political

---

[2] Michael Burleigh and Wolfgang Wippermann, *The Racial State: Germany, 1933–1945* (Cambridge: Cambridge University Press, 1991).

[3] The results of our country studies thus confirm the widespread hypothesis among political scientists that democratic consolidation is impossible in the absence of an institutionalized party system – as well as Sartori's caveat that strongly polarized party systems, too, may become dangerously unstable. See Juan Linz and Alfred Stepan, *Problems of Democratic Transition and Consolidation* (Baltimore: Johns Hopkins University Press, 1995); Giovanni Sartori, *Parties and Party Systems: A Framework for Analysis* (Cambridge: Cambridge University Press, 1975).

But the condition of society in some of these countries were more favorable than

contexts we have chosen for analysis help to control for many of the most common alternative explanations for party success or failure. Explanations for the dynamics of the party systems of Third Republic France, Weimar Germany, and post-Soviet Russia based on cultural norms, imperial legacies, or presidential-parliamentarianism are thus shown to be flawed or incomplete in comparative perspective.

Culturalists ascribe Russia's relative failure in party formation simply to that nation's long history of autocracy and weak postcommunist civil society. But, as we have seen, most observers of nineteenth-century France and twentieth-century Germany also tended to describe their political cultures as authoritarian and their civil societies as relatively weak. Indeed, the majority of specialists on Soviet and Russian "political culture" in the 1980s and early 1990s argued – on the basis of Parsonian logic – that decades of Soviet modernization had provided a strong basis for Russian civil society, which augured well for the success of democratic institutions.[4] The clear tendency in this literature is to define a country's political culture by observing its political outcomes, rendering any explanation based on supposedly "essential" national characteristics tautological.

Historical institutionalists have ascribed defeats for democratic parties in both Weimar Germany and post-Soviet Russia as evidence for the constraining power of inherited institutional legacies. Yet France in the 1870s hardly appeared at the time to be an auspicious country for democratic institution building either; nevertheless, the prodemocratic republicans ultimately forged the most powerful party organization in the country. Moreover, deleterious past legacies alone do not explain why Weimar Germany was taken over by parties led by ideological extremists, while the state ultimately marginalized ideological partisan activists in the Russian Federation.[5]

Finally, our case selection calls into question the common assumption among comparativists that the choice of a presidential-parliamentary system is the key "design flaw" that undercuts the party system, leading to institutional breakdown and the rise of presidential autocracy. In France, as we have seen, an initial system of precisely this sort gave way instead to parliamentary sovereignty and multiparty competition once the compromise Constitution of 1875 was reinterpreted by the victorious Gambettists in the spirit of republican principles. In Germany, while the presidential emergency powers granted in Article 48 of the Weimar Constitution clearly played an important role in the downfall of the competitive Weimar party system, it hardly preordained the rise to power of a genocidal dictatorship. Lest institutionalist determinism be taken too far, it is worth remembering that, after Hitler's rise to power, the post of

4 Moshe Lewin, *The Gorbachev Phenomenon* (Berkeley: University of California Press, 1988); S. Frederick Starr, "The Soviet Union: A Civil Society," *Foreign Policy*, no. 70 (Spring 1988): 16–41; Francis Fukuyama, "The Modernizing Imperative: The USSR as an Ordinary Country," *National Interest* 20 (Spring 1993): 10–18.
5 Stephen E. Hanson and Jeffrey S. Kopstein, "The Weimar/Russia Comparison," *Post-Soviet Affairs* 13(3, July–September 1997): 252–283.

president was simply abolished as irrelevant. Seen in this comparative context, the victory of President Putin and the creation of a pliant parliament after 2000 appears less as the inevitable result of bad constitutional design and more as the consequence of the weakness of ideologically committed Russian political parties that might have otherwise helped to rein in presidential power – either to consolidate Russia's formal democratic institutions, as in France, or to replace them with an openly ideological form of dictatorship, as in Germany.

Naturally, not every alternative explanation for the success or failure of political parties is "controlled for" in this book. Yet other salient institutional and social differences among the three countries studied here do not seem to constitute plausible alternative causal variables explaining which political parties succeeded or failed in their efforts to build national activist organizations, nor do they correlate in any clear way with the ultimate regime outcomes these dynamics helped to generate. Among the additional factors that might be brought to bear on our case studies, five in particular seem most important: electoral rules, changes in media technology, macroeconomic performance, agricultural commercialization, and the effects of "world time." I deal with each of these variables in turn.

First, probably the most important rival theoretical framework that might call the results of this study into question is the large literature on the effects of electoral rules on party systems – and, in particular, the argument that other things being equal, proportional representation (PR) will tend to generate a stronger multiparty system than elections based on single member districts, because PR elections privilege nominations by party list, allow party leaders to reward party members with higher positions on these lists, and award seats in parliament even to minority parties.[6] No doubt the effects of electoral rules are important, as the results of our case studies show: party organizations in general were stronger in Weimar Germany, with its pure PR system, than in France, which utilized a modified list system in the 1871 elections and a district-based system for the 1875 and 1879 campaigns (albeit one that allowed prominent politicians to run in several districts simultaneously). In Russia, too, the role of parties was much stronger in elections for the PR portion of the mixed Russian ballot; the vast majority of Duma deputies elected in single-member districts (SMDs) through the Putin era were nonpartisan independents.[7]

Still, electoral rules alone cannot explain the variance between successful and unsuccessful party organizations in each of our three countries, because

[6] Maurice Duverger, *Political Parties: Their Organization and Activity in the Modern State* (London: Methuen; New York: Wiley, 1954); Giovanni Sartori, *Comparative Constitutional Engineering: An Inquiry into Structures, Incentives, and Outcomes* (New York: New York University Press, 1994); Gary Cox, *Making Votes Count: Strategic Coordination in the World's Electoral Systems* (Cambridge: Cambridge University Press, 1997); Arend Lijphart, *Patterns of Democracy: Government Forms and Performance in Thirty Six Countries* (New Haven: Yale University Press, 1999).

[7] Thomas F. Remington, *The Russian Parliament: Institutional Evolution in a Transitional Regime, 1989–1999* (New Haven: Yale University Press, 2001).

within each of these contexts the effects of electoral rules are the same for all. In the French Third Republic, taking the district-based voting rules into account seems to make the decline of the Bonapartists and Orléanists easier to explain, but this simultaneously makes the achievements of Gambetta's republicans in mobilizing committed activists in repeated parliamentary elections even more remarkable. In the Weimar Republic, the strict PR system, with no thresholds to limit the representation of splinter parties, helps to account for the success of some of the minuscule regional factions in the Reichstag – but PR voting alone hardly explains why initially powerful national parties such as the German Democratic Party and German National People's Parties so quickly lost their organizational cohesion, while the Nazis and Communists, with voting shares in the single digits for much of the 1920s, suddenly broke through to dominate the parliament after 1932.[8] The peculiarities of Russia's mixed PR-SMD ballot help to explain why dozens of ambitious politicians created "sofa parties" in the 1995 and 1999 elections, utilizing the free media time these parties received to bolster their own electoral chances in SMDs.[9] However, electoral rules alone cannot explain the relative success of the Communist Party of the Russian Federation throughout the 1990s in obtaining significant numbers of seats in both the PR and SMD balloting, nor the persistent failure of such parties as Yabloko or Our Home Is Russia to do the same.

Finally, it should be remembered that in all three countries examined here, prominent political actors themselves repeatedly miscalculated the probable effects of electoral rules. De Broglie in the 1870s thought that indirect elections for a powerful Senate in 1875 would strengthen the hand of moderate monarchists; instead, an alliance between hard-line legitimists and Gambettists gave a significant share of seats in the upper house to the republicans. The ruling republicans, in turn, chose to adopt proportional representation for the 1885 parliamentary elections, thinking that this would finally eliminate the power of local notables in conservative districts; instead, these elections saw a major comeback for the far right, leading to the quick restoration of district voting.[10] In Germany, Weber argued in 1919 that a powerful presidency would serve to legitimate an otherwise uninspiring parliamentary system; instead, the election of the war hero Hindenburg as president in 1925 played an important part in undermining public support for democracy. In Russia, Yeltsin's advisers in 1991 felt that early elections would cause political instability that would detract from market reform; instead, the members of the Russian Congress

---

[8] As Michael Bernhard points out too, even higher thresholds for parliamentary representation in the Reichstag would not have prevented the Nazi Party electoral breakthrough of 1930, because the Nazis ended up with such a large percentage of the vote. Bernhard, *Institutions and the Fate of Democracy: Germany and Poland in the Twentieth Century* (Pittsburgh: Pittsburgh University Press, 2005).

[9] Robert G. Moser, *Unexpected Outcomes: Electoral Systems, Political Parties, and Representation in Russia* (Pittsburgh: Pittsburgh University Press, 2001).

[10] R. D. Anderson, *France, 1870–1914: Politics and Society* (London: Routledge and Kegan Paul, 1977), p. 68.

of People's Deputies utilized the powers granted to them under the Brezhnev-era Russian Constitution to undermine Yeltsin and his government. Similarly, Russia's mixed PR-SMD electoral system was originally designed to curtail the power of the communists and to promote the parliamentary representation of Gaidar's Russia's Choice party; the unexpected result was to ensure stable CPRF representation in local districts while allowing for a massive victory in the PR balloting by Zhirinovskii's LDPR.[11] The question arises, then: if elites in these post-imperial democracies were consistently unable to calculate correctly the future political effects of electoral rules, why would they nevertheless have behaved in the ways predicted by formal neo-institutionalist theory? The evidence of our party case studies suggests, instead, that reactions to formal electoral rules in times of enormous institutional uncertainty were driven instead by the differing time horizons of competing political leaders: pragmatists found themselves unable to stick to any long-term strategy at all, while ideologically driven party leaders evaluated the effects of electoral rules in the context of their long-term political visions – in ways that ultimately helped to determine the long-term stability of electoral institutions themselves.

A second group of scholars would argue that analysis of party formation across a century and a half must somehow take into account changes in media and communications technology, which many political scientists see as a key reason for the decline in mass partisanship in the late twentieth and early twenty-first centuries.[12] Surely it makes a difference, this line of reasoning goes, whether would-be party builders must rely on door-to-door canvassing of voters and the distribution of printed pamphlets, or can instead mount sophisticated television campaigns in which entire electorates can be reached simultaneously? From this point of view, we might explain the general weakness of French political parties as a result of the low levels of electoral technology available in the 1870s, the notable organizational strength of Weimar parties as a consequence of the development of modern party bureaucracies and mass communication, and the disastrous performance of Russian parties as the effect of the "postmodern" world of TV news and sophisticated "image" management.[13]

There is no question that the effects of technology on campaign strategies and party organization must be taken seriously. Again, however, a macro-comparison of the three post-imperial democracies does not explain variations of party success or failure within each country. At the same technological levels, Gambettists and legitimists were able to distribute partisan propaganda

[11] Moser, *Unexpected Outcomes*; Michael McFaul, *Russia's Unfinished Revolution: Political Change from Gorbachev to Putin* (Ithaca, NY: Cornell University Press, 2001).

[12] There is by now a vast literature on this subject, beginning with Samuel J. Eldersveld, *Political Parties: A Behavioral Analysis* (Chicago: Rand McNally, 1964).

[13] Ellen P. Mickiewicz, *Changing Channels: Television and the Struggle for Power in Russia* (New York: Oxford University Press, 1997); Sarah Oates, *Television, Democracy, and Elections in Russia* (London: Routledge, 2006); Andrew Wilson, *Virtual Politics: Faking Democracy in the Post-Soviet World* (New Haven: Yale University Press, 2005).

and turn out the vote in local elections successfully, while for the most part Orléanists and Bonapartists could not do so with any consistency. Hitler and Thälmann both utilized modern mass technology to generate sophisticated electoral propaganda that grabbed the psyches of significant portions of German society – but so did the Social Democratic Party and the DNVP; indeed, the latter party fell apart precisely when it was taken over by the influential media magnate Hugenburg. Post-Soviet Russia is particularly anomalous for advocates of technological determinism: the most successful party of the 1990s, Ziuganov's CPRF, largely abjured television advertising in favor of old-fashioned campaigning at the "grass roots," while even the most expensive high-tech campaigns of uninspiring "parties of power" such as Our Home Is Russia generated precious little electoral return.

Third, social scientists of a materialist bent might question the results arrived at here by emphasizing the importance of macroeconomic variables that shape support for, or opposition to, antiliberal ideological projects. Surely the Nazi rise to power could not have happened except in the context of a massive global depression in which more than a quarter of Germans were unemployed? If so, isn't the success of democratic and antidemocratic ideology alike dependent on deeper material forces that make political ideologies plausible to large numbers of people?[14]

Upon closer examination, however, the cases presented in this book do not conform neatly to the expectations of materialist scholarship. To begin with, we must take into account the fact that a severe depression also hit France in the early years of republican political hegemony. The phylloxera plague of the 1870s wiped out a significant percentage of French wine production, and by the 1880s continental Europe as a whole experienced a prolonged period of industrial recession.[15] Indeed, economic crisis in the early Third Republic did catalyze anticapitalist parties, propelling the rapid expansion of the communist Guesdistes and, by the mid-1880s, the first manifestations of what would eventually become the French "New Right."[16] Despite these undemocratic trends, however, core republican institutions remained in place, and various offshoots of the republican party continued to dominate the Chamber of Deputies throughout these years. Turning to Russia, we see yet another macroeconomic counterexample to the Weimar case: multiparty democracy, however fragile, was launched and maintained despite the economic crisis of the 1990s – a period when the Russian economy shrank nearly by half and the Russian banking system failed not once but twice; democracy was then

[14] For one influential analysis that proceeds along these lines, see Peter A. Gourevitch, *Politics in Hard Times: Comparative Responses to International Economic Crises* (Ithaca, NY: Cornell University Press, 1986).

[15] R. D. Anderson, *France, 1870–1914: Politics and Society* (London: Routledge and Keegan Paul, 1977), p. 84.

[16] Zeev Sternhell, *Neither Right nor Left: Fascist Ideology in France* (Berkeley: University of California Press, 1986).

gradually eliminated during the Putin era, when GDP gro 7 percent per annum for nearly a decade.[17] In sum, ther causal relationship between macroeconomic trends and these three cases. It goes without saying, then, that mac at this level of analysis also fail to explain the variations we have tra organizational success or failure of individual parties competing within each post-imperial democracy.

A fourth line of argumentation would also advance a materialist critique of the argument here but from a structuralist point of view. Such scholars would argue that not only overarching macroeconomic performance but also the structure of class conflicts would seem to be crucial in understanding the diverging fates of democracy in France, Germany, and Russia. Specifically, as Barrington Moore argued in his classic work, we should examine the extent to which each country in question managed to commercialize its agricultural sector, making a class alliance between the rising bourgeoisie and the independent peasantry a political winning coalition.[18] From this point of view, France provides a classic case of "revolutionary breakthrough" to democracy; Weimar Germany saw an "incomplete revolution" in which the power of feudal elites blocked any consolidation of bourgeois democracy; and post-Soviet Russia remained tied to its uncompetitive structure of statist industry and collective farming, generating a clientelist political economy in which independent party building in general became extremely difficult.[19]

This explanation, I would argue, makes an important contribution to the analysis of the macropolitical outcomes we have observed in the Third Republic, Weimar, and the Russian Federation. There is no question that the precise outcomes of the pivotal regime crises in France in 1877, Germany in 1929, and Russia in 1998–1999 were greatly affected by the specific shape of economic interests and class alliances prevailing in these countries at those points. In the French case, Gambetta's ability to mobilize independent farmers as well as urban elites on behalf of the republican cause would have been extremely difficult had land tenure arrangements continued in the feudal patterns of the ancien regime. In the German case, Junker hatred of the Weimar Constitution, coupled with the bourgeoisie's fear of communism, certainly did pressure Hindenburg's inner circle to respond to the crisis of the Great Depression in reactionary ways. Finally, in the Russian case, the weakness of the post-Soviet capitalist class and its close ties to state officials predisposed it to side with the

17 Anders Aslund, *Russia's Capitalist Revolution: Why Market Reform Succeeded and Democracy Failed* (Cambridge: Cambridge University Press, 2007).

18 Barrington Moore, *Social Origins of Dictatorship and Democracy: Lord and Peasant in the Making of the Modern World* (Boston: Beacon, 1966); see also Bernard, *Institutions and the Fate of Democracy.*

19 Gregory Luebbert, *Liberalism, Fascism, or Social Democracy: Social Classes and the Political Origins of Regimes in Modern Europe* (New York: Oxford University Press, 1991); M. Steven Fish, *Democracy Derailed in Russia: The Failure of Open Politics* (Cambridge: Cambridge University Press, 2005).

ﬁlin once Putin elected to reimpose central authority over all autonomous
ﬁitical forces.

Structuralist analysis of this sort, however, does not fare so well in explaining why particular political elites in each country were able to mobilize these
preexisting socioeconomic coalitions effectively. Structural variables may provide opportunities for forging powerful new political coalitions, but to explain
why only some political actors manage to overcome collective action problems
in order to seize such opportunities requires attention to the individual level
of analysis. Here the theory of ideology advanced in this book fills important
gaps in structuralist historical accounts. The French Revolution's break with
feudal agriculture, after all, took place a full century before the consolidation of
republican democracy. Indeed, the structural change in French society in 1789
led not to democracy but instead to decades of empire, monarchy, revolution,
and dictatorship. It took a committed ideological organization of republican
activists in the 1870s and 1880s to build institutions that fully incorporated
the French farmer into the democratic body politic. Similarly, Junker nobles
and authoritarian capitalists may have aided and abetted the destruction of
Weimar democracy after 1929, but they played no direct role in the formation
of the Nazi Party itself. Ultimately, the Nazi regime, acting on its ideological beliefs about "racial struggle," destroyed every value that the Junkers and
German big business held dear. Finally, while the Russian oligarchs ultimately
deferred to Putin, before his full consolidation of power they had appeared
equally willing to back liberal, nationalist, or even Communist Party organizations. It was the comparative weaknesses of all these partisan groupings that
compelled Russia's nascent bourgeoisie to side so unequivocally with the state.
In sum, while socioeconomic structures and class power may indeed make
the formation of democratic, authoritarian, or revolutionary regimes more or
less likely, the presence or absence of mobilization of ideologically motivated
parties and associated social movements appears to be the proximate cause
of the precise timing and shape of regime formation in periods of high social
uncertainty.

This brings us to a final counterargument about the regime outcomes we
have traced in this book. Isn't the fate of party ideologies in each of these countries ultimately itself traceable to larger trends in world history? Can we really
treat parties in the early Third Republic, Weimar Germany, and post-Soviet
Russia as comparable "cases," ripped out of historical and cultural context?
After all, the ideological arguments made by party builders in all three post-
imperial democracies examined here were clearly shaped by the larger geopolitical environments in which they were situated. French republicans were able
to promote successfully the ideal of universal, secular citizenship as a form of
patriotism in part because France's main enemy, Prussia, was an authoritarian monarchy. In contrast, German liberals were undermined by the fact that
the hated occupier, France, was a republic – making it much more difficult to
forge a patriotic German republicanism, and encouraging the belief that the
destruction of democracy would allow Germany to rise to greatness again.

Finally, the world-historical context in which the Russian Federation emerged at the end of the twentieth century assured that would-be party builders in the post-Soviet context faced a society with a profound distaste for ideologies of every sort.[20] Marxism-Leninism in the wake of the collapse of the Soviet Union had become laughable. Fascist nationalism was still widely held responsible for the deaths of tens of millions of Russians and other Soviet citizens during World War II. Even liberalism, which first appealed to supporters of Yeltsin as a vehicle to promote Russian sovereignty from decaying communist institutions, soon became profoundly unpopular because of the often strongly anti-Russian "liberal" nationalism of most Central and East European postcommunist states, resentment of the United States as the "world's only superpower," and Russia's disastrous economic performance under what were perceived by most Russians as "neoliberal" policies designed by Western advisers. In this milieu of relative ideological exhaustion, even relatively successful ideologues like Ziuganov and Zhirinovskii felt compelled to assure their supporters that they were opposed to "extremism." The result, however, was a situation in which no organization of party activists could be mobilized to fight against the imposition of presidential authoritarianism.

Is "world time," then, the ultimate "cause" of the regime outcomes we have traced in this study?[21] The evidence suggests that while geopolitical and historical contexts do play a role in shaping the visions of ideologues, they do not determine them entirely. Supporters of legitimism in 1870s France, for example, found their rival interpretation of defeat in the Franco-Prussian War as a punishment for France's sins far more plausible than the call to return to the values of 1789 proposed by Gambetta and his followers. Had Gambetta never been born, Chambord's dedicated followers in the early 1870s might well have confronted only the relatively weak partisan oppositions of the Orléanists and Bonapartists – in which case, under the reign of "Henri V," the legitimist version of French history might have become authoritative for some period of time. Rival versions of German history after World War I, too, were certainly possible. In 1919, if we judge by the electoral results of that year, far more German citizens perceived the new Weimar Republic as the logical culmination of decades of patient civic effort by the Social Democratic Party than as a regime imposed through a conspiracy by traitorous Jews. Had Hitler never been born, the battle for power after the onset of the Great Depression might have come down to a choice between the SPD and KPD – with the SPD the likely winner. In that case, German history after 1933 might well have been written in official textbooks to paint Bebel and Kautsky as heroes who prophetically foresaw the future destiny of the nation as an evolutionary social democracy.

If this logic is correct, the fate of post-Soviet Russian democracy was hardly predetermined by world-historical conditions in 1991. While the task

---

[20] Svetlana Boym, *The Future of Nostalgia* (New York: Basic Books, 2001).
[21] Theda Skocpol, *States and Social Revolutions: A Comparative Analysis of France, Russia, and China* (Cambridge: Cambridge University Press, 1979).

of inventing a successful Russian party ideology in the wake of Marxism-Leninism's collapse was admittedly difficult, greater attention by leading Russian democrats to the importance of articulating and disseminating a clear and consistent vision of Russia's future as a civic nation might have helped to catalyze the formation of powerful organizations of democratic activism throughout the country – ultimately inspiring even the most instrumentally rational Russian politicians to join in. In short, the meaning of "world time" can be interpreted in different ways, through various sorts of ideological lenses. Thus, it is ideology, and not world-historical context itself, that is causally primary.

Is the case for ideology as a causal variable proved beyond all reasonable scientific doubt? Naturally, the comparative case study evidence provided here, mostly relying on qualitative historical evidence, will not convince every skeptic. To begin with, the failure of the Catholic Center Party to confirm the central hypothesis demonstrates that a strictly deterministic reading of the claim "no ideology, no parties" cannot be sustained. In the real world – as opposed to the "ideal-typical" world of complete uncertainty taken as a theoretical starting point here – important political actors may occasionally be able to weld together effective coalitions even through periods of intense social crisis simply by relying on the partisan loyalties of old friends and colleagues, by mobilizing the economic resources of particularly powerful business interests, or by both methods. Moreover, this is by necessity a "medium *n*" study. The nature of the evidence does not allow for a robust statistical test of the relative importance of ideological clarity and consistency in generating party organizations in times of high uncertainty – not only because of the small number of cases but also because constructing a composite quantitative measure of party organizational strength that would be valid across such diverse historical and political contexts would be problematic in the extreme. It would be salutary, too, to test the hypothesis here in an analysis of party formation in other cases of post-imperial democracy, such as Austria and Hungary in the interwar period or Portugal in 1974, which also experienced high initial institutional and social uncertainty along with repeated free and fair elections after imperial collapse.

These caveats aside, the fact that fifteen out of sixteen parties examined here do fit the initial hypothesis – in cases and observations chosen for theoretical reasons and not because of any "selection on the dependent variable" – would seem to constitute a major challenge to mainstream social science theories that deny the possibility that ideology might ever play an independent causal role. Given this overwhelming confirmation, the burden of proof would seem to shift to those who would wish to disprove the hypothesis that ideology can catalyze relatively successful collective action to form political parties in times of high uncertainty by artificially elongating the time horizons of party activists.

Comparative Implications

What does this analysis imply about the role of ideology in political life in more stable environments? One important implication of the analysis here is that we should *not* expect ideological activism based on value-rational action to be the key determinant of institutional outcomes under ordinary social conditions. As Weber argued a century ago, where institutions are stable and predictable, everyday decision making will typically be governed by habit and short-term instrumental rationality. Under such conditions, actors who articulate clear and consistent definitions of alternative future polities are likely to appear bizarre or deranged. For understanding individual conduct in strong institutional settings, then, rational choice models may be an excellent first step toward scientific understanding.[22]

However, it would be a grave error to assume that ideology plays no political role whatsoever except in periods of extraordinary regime transformation, for three reasons. First, the concept of "certainty" about the institutional future is a relative one. Much of the population of the developing world today lives in environments where institutional corruption is endemic, changes in regime frequent, and the long-term political and social future murky at best. Indeed, in the context of the global financial crisis that emerged in the fall of 2008, genuine social uncertainty has also begun to affect the functioning of key domestic and international institutions in the liberal capitalist West. Even in stable settings, different individuals may have markedly different discount rates in evaluating the payoffs from fidelity to existing institutional rules. Indeed, for some marginalized individuals in every social setting, the world may subjectively appear to be utterly chaotic and unpredictable. An unusual level of skepticism about the future of existing institutions may emerge for psychological reasons, as in the case of abused children who cannot develop lasting relations of ordinary interpersonal trust; for sociological reasons, as with oppressed or socially excluded populations such as slaves, ethnic outgroups, or members of the "subproletariat" living in ghettos or shanty towns; or for intellectual reasons, as among highly educated elites whose institutional environments reward rather than punish speculative thinking about long-term historical change. For members of such groups, leaders who articulate ideological visions of the political future may inspire enough "conversion" to form identifiable ideological movements with chiliastic or revolutionary goals, even in otherwise quite stable and wealthy societies. In some cases, such ideological movements may adopt pictures of the future that are so at odds with prevailing social norms that their members must cut themselves off from ordinary society entirely in order to sustain their fidelity to their chosen conception of political community. This process produces ideological sects such as anarchist and eco-terrorist groups that prophesy the "inevitable" disintegration of the modern capitalist state, quasi-religious "cults" such as Heaven's Gate or Jonestown, and radical intellectual associations that may also engage in revolutionary politics such as Sendero Luminoso in Peru. Most such sects must remain on the margins of

---

[22] Max Weber, *Economy and Society*, trans. and ed. by Guenther Roth and Claus Wittich (Berkeley: University of California Press, 1978).

ordinary political life. Yet, as the later international impact of minor ideological sects such as Lenin's Bolshevik Party before 1914 or Osama bin Laden's al-Qaeda before September 11, 2001, demonstrates, it is a mistake for social scientists to ignore them – even when their contemporary influence appears to be negligible.

Second, the dynamics of ideological conversion to new long-term visions of the political future can play an important role even within the context of established political institutions. To the extent that ideologically motivated activists in stable polities see political change as requiring cooperation with established organizations and interests, they may choose a strategy of "temporary" political engagement rather than isolation – while remaining committed to long-term regime transformation. Thus, a methodologically individualist approach to ideological collective action can help to augment our understanding of the common finding in established democracies that party activists tend to adopt more extreme positions on the left-right partisan spectrum than do ordinary voters. At least in some cases, such findings may reflect not simply the intensity of political preferences on the "far left" and "far right" but rather the distinctive long-term goals of partisan activists who have embraced ideological projects that are ultimately at odds with the maintenance of the regime status quo. In relatively stable democracies, to be sure, it may often be analytically useful to treat such activists as lying at the extreme points of a unidimensional political spectrum, as is required by the median voter theorem. Under conditions of rapid institutional change, however, what was once seen as the "far left" or "far right" may later emerge as the "centrist" or "orthodox" position in a newly established political order – as in the case of the gradual mutation of Gambetta's "radical republicans" into the "opportunists" of the mature Third Republic, or the transformation of Yeltsin's "leftism" in the Gorbachev era into the center-right policy of the Russian Federation. The promotion by party leaders of clear and consistent definitions of the political future, then, can under conditions of rising uncertainty rapidly introduce unexpected new dimensions into environments that previously appeared to feature a normal distribution of political preferences.

Third, the notion of a final "end of ideology" on a global scale is surely fanciful.[23] As Tetlock has dramatically illustrated, despite remarkable recent advances in statistical analysis, database construction, and formal methodology, even the ability of trained experts to predict the political future remains woefully limited.[24] We can hardly expect ordinary people paying very limited attention to politics to do a better job of distinguishing ideological prophecies

---

[23] The phrase originally comes from Daniel Bell, *The End of Ideology: On the Exhaustion of Political Ideas in the Fifties* (Glencoe, IL: Free Press, 1960) – although Bell did not predict such an outcome on a global scale, as did Francis Fukuyama, "The End of History?" *National Interest* 16 (Summer 1989): 3–16.

[24] Philip E. Tetlock, *Expert Political Judgment: How Good Is It? How Can We Know?* (Princeton, NJ: Princeton University Press, 2005).

from scientific prognostications. While ideologues in stable societies may at first appear laughably out of touch with their depictions of future utopias and dystopias, they may suddenly sound quite sensible to large numbers of people in the wake of unexpected institutional collapse. An "end to ideology," then, could occur only in a world where individuals presenting clear and consistent definitions of the political future were always ignored, and the vast majority of people rationally accepted the essential inscrutability of the course of human history. But because, as has been shown in this study, agnostic individuals will typically be less capable of organizing collective action in times of crisis than their ideologically self-confident competitors, the rational view of history, even if correct scientifically, is destined to lose out politically.

A Weberian Understanding of Structure and Agency

If this analysis is correct, the time has surely come for social scientists to take individuals' subjective beliefs far more seriously in causal analysis. To be sure, the assumption that all individual social action can be seen as instrumentally rational has taken us very far over the past several decades – calling into question unjustifiable Western stereotypes about everyday life in "traditional societies"; undercutting the functionalist assumption that societies necessarily "adapt" to the inexorable forces of "modernization"; and forcing analysts to think much harder about the microfoundations of explanations for macropolitical outcomes. Indeed, much of the analysis set out in this book is perfectly compatible with standard rational choice theory, which has long argued that collective action dilemmas can be solved when the rate at which individuals discount future payoffs for present action is sufficiently low. To understand fully the dynamic process through which ideology inspires collective action, however, we must integrate other sorts of human motivation into our theoretical framework. The evidence shows that ideologues succeed in attaining clarity and consistency in their statements about political membership, in large part because they actually believe what they say. Many of their earliest followers, it appears, join primarily because of their emotional attachment to the leader. In the end, the most successful ideologies gain widespread social acceptance simply because their principles become habitual. We can incorporate such value-rational, affectual, and habitual types of social action along with instrumental rationality with very little loss of parsimony by making theoretically explicit what seems obvious from personal introspection: namely, that both the degree to which human actors deliberate about their courses of action and the degree to which they care about the temporal implications of their conduct can vary – which logically generates four main types of social action, not just one. This more supple and robust understanding of individual motivation is also far more likely than standard rational choice theory to allow for exciting connections to new research in neuroscience on the functioning of the human brain, which has already demonstrated quite clearly the inadequacy of the assumption of universal "utility maximization."

The Weberian analysis of ideology developed and tested in this book also clearly demonstrates that individual human agency is profoundly important as a causal factor in political life – but not exactly in the way this point has usually been posed. Debates between advocates of structuralism and supporters of agent-based explanations in social science tend to be framed in zero-sum terms: either "deeper," underlying social conditions are seen as constraining the ability of isolated individuals to effect their will in changing political and social institutions, or, conversely, able leaders and "crafters" of new institutions are held to be the true "engineers" of political and social life, irrespective of historical and geopolitical context.[25] A third, equally unsatisfying position simply maintains that "structure" and "agency" are "mutually constitutive," without defining clearly or precisely just how such a process of mutual constitution comes about.[26]

The Weberian approach to comparative historical analysis points the way toward a more compelling resolution of the structure-agency relationship. On the one hand, like other comparative-historical theorizing, Weberianism emphasizes how little control individual agents usually have over the inherited institutional and social environments they inhabit. In almost all cases, it is organized collective action, not the decisions of isolated individuals, that truly changes human history. Thus, efforts at "institutional engineering" that fail to take into account the spatial and temporal contexts of the societies they analyze will usually run aground in the face of unanticipated social resistance to the imposition of new institutional rules.[27] Yet in periods of institutional turbulence and social uncertainty, existing patterns of collective action can sometimes break down sufficiently to allow a decisive reordering of political and economic institutions. Social "chaos" does not automatically promote effective individual agency, of course; even in highly uncertain environments, most individuals will find themselves powerless and overwhelmed in the face of rapidly changing events. For a small number of individuals who have positioned themselves in prior, more stable periods as credible proponents of a new ideological order, however, such "critical junctures" provide the opportunity

---

[25] For classic statements of each position, see Skocpol, *States and Social Revolutions*; Guiseppe DiPalma, *To Craft Democracies: An Essay on Democratic Transitions* (Berkeley: University of California Press, 1990); and Peter C. Ordeshook, "What Is the Study of Politics? Science or Engineering," in Jeffrey Friedman, ed., *The Rational Choice Controversy: Economic Models of Politics Reconsidered* (New Haven: Yale University Press, 1996), pp. 175–188.

[26] Anthony Giddens, *The Constitution of Society: Outlines of a Theory of Structuration* (Cambridge: Polity Press, 1984). The limitations of Giddens's "dialectical" approach to the structure-agency problem have been persuasively criticized by Jack Goldstone, *Revolution and Rebellion in the Early Modern World* (Berkeley: University of California Press, 1991).

[27] Grzegorz Ekiert and Stephen E. Hanson, "Time, Space, and Institutional Change in Central and Eastern Europe," in Ekiert and Hanson, eds., *Capitalism and Democracy in Central and Eastern Europe: Assessing the Legacy of Communist Rule* (Cambridge: Cambridge University Press, 2003), pp. 15–48; Stephen E. Hanson and Jeffrey S. Kopstein, "Regime Type and Diffusion in Comparative Politics Methodology," *Canadian Journal of Political Science* 38(1, March 2005): 69–99.

to "convert" and mobilize large numbers of people – sometimes with powerful future consequences for domestic and international politics.[28] The articulation by individuals of new political ideologies, then, should be seen as a subset of the kind of charismatic leadership that Weber saw as providing the "specifically creative revolutionary force of history."[29]

Even ideologues, however, do not control their ultimate political fate. As has been emphasized throughout this work, adopting a clear and consistent definition of one's preferred future polity may be a necessary condition for mobilizing collective action and forming national activist organizations in times of massive social uncertainty, but it is not a sufficient condition to ensure political success. In fact, most would-be ideological leaders fail to persuade many converts at all, while even among the small number of such leaders who do become politically significant, there are far more Chambords, Westarps, and Ziuganovs than there are Gambettas and Hitlers. In the final analysis, individual political agents can control only one thing, imperfectly – namely, their own political beliefs and actions.

The fact that ideologues tend to be "selected for" in turbulent social environments nevertheless has profound implications for our understanding of the role of agency in designing new social institutions. Mainstream political science has tended to assume that evolutionary competition in history invariably promotes strategically rational individuals and efficient institutions, while weeding out ideologues and their "crazy" projects.[30] If I am right, and individuals who act according to "timeless" value-rational principles have an evolutionary advantage in uncertain environments, many of the central simplifying assumptions of materialist and functionalist theorizing must be reexamined. Agency in the design of new institutions can no longer be assumed merely to reflect the strategic interests of actors who try to set up institutions that benefit them personally, because instrumentally rational individuals of this sort will typically fail to overcome the initial collective action problems involved in mobilizing others to enforce and defend new institutional rules.[31] Nor can the introduction of new "dimensions" in partisan competition in situations of high political uncertainty be assumed to reflect the self-interested calculations of "herestheticians" – that is, specialists in the art of strategic political manipulation.[32] Instead, we must take seriously the possibility that our effort to introduce parsimony in social science by assuming the strategic insincerity of political rhetoric has led us seriously astray in understanding institutional change. Indeed, the greatest theoretical parsimony and precision may, in the end, be achieved by embracing

---

[28] Giovanni Capoccia and Daniel Keleman, "The Study of Critical Junctures: Theory, Narrative and Counterfactuals in Historical Institutionalism," *World Politics* 59(3, April 2007): 341–369.

[29] Weber, *Economy and Society*, p. 1117.

[30] This argument goes back to the seminal article by Armen A. Alchian, "Uncertainty, Evolution, and Economic Theory," *Journal of Political Economy* 58(3, June 1950): 211–221.

[31] Jack Knight, *Institutions and Social Conflict* (Cambridge: Cambridge University Press, 1992).

[32] William H. Riker, *The Art of Political Manipulation* (New Haven: Yale University Press, 1986).

exactly the opposite assumption: most individual actors really do mean what they say. In any case, given the high likelihood that the twenty-first century will be as filled with dramatic institutional changes and unexpected revolutions as was the twentieth, we must surely begin to pay greater analytic attention to the ways in which political actors articulate and disseminate their own subjective views of the political future.

Finally, the Weberian theory of ideology developed here provides new insight into the old question of whether committed democrats are necessary to achieve democratic consolidation. The finding that political ideology is a necessary but not sufficient condition for establishing national networks of party activists in times of high uncertainty suggests that this question is often wrongly posed as a dichotomous one – that is, either one must show that all democracies can be traced back to heroically democratic founders, or one can safely assume (as do most political scientists today) that democratic value-rationality is irrelevant to democratic institution building. But as we have seen, the causal relationship between ideology and democracy is far more complex than this. In structural environments characterized by relatively high social certainty, leadership by clear and consistent democratic ideologues may be wholly unnecessary for or even damaging to democracy's progress. Moreover, most politicians who pay lip service to democratic ideals are hardly "democratic ideologues" in the sense described in this book; thus, their general failure to follow up on their empty, instrumental democratic rhetoric once in power should hardly surprise us. Taken together, the easily observed facts that democratic consolidation sometimes succeeds in countries that lack any clear and consistent democratic ideology, and that supposed "democrats" frequently behave autocratically once in power, have combined to generate a deep cynicism among social scientists about the causal impact of democratic values more generally.

In the three cases of post-imperial democracy examined in this book, however, environments of sustained social turbulence made the value-rational commitments of key party builders crucial to the success or failure of democratic institutions. Without a Gambetta to catalyze committed republican partisanship during the early years of the Third Republic, France would have likely suffered either another monarchical restoration or a new round of instrumental authoritarian rule under President MacMahon. Conversely, had someone like Gambetta been present in the early years of the Weimar Republic to form an ideologically committed German democratic party, the disintegration of Germany's moderate political organizations and the rise of the radical right might have been avoided. Thus, in countries like post-Soviet Russia, which still lack powerful political ideologies of any sort and in which state institutions are characterized by instability, corruption, and illegitimacy, clear and consistent visions of the political future promoted by creative individuals may still hold the power to reshape the destinies of millions of people – for good or for ill.

Index

Other Books in the Series (*continued from page iii*)

Michael Bratton and Nicolas van de Walle, *Democratic Experiments in Africa: Regime Transitions in Comparative Perspective*

Michael Bratton, Robert Mattes, and E. Gyimah-Boadi, *Public Opinion, Democracy, and Market Reform in Africa*

Valerie Bunce, *Leaving Socialism and Leaving the State: The End of Yugoslavia, the Soviet Union, and Czechoslovakia*

Daniele Caramani, *The Nationalization of Politics: The Formation of National Electorates and Party Systems in Europe*

John M. Carey, *Legislative Voting and Accountability*

Kanchan Chandra, *Why Ethnic Parties Succeed: Patronage and Ethnic Headcounts in India*

José Antonio Cheibub, *Presidentialism, Parliamentarism, and Democracy*

Ruth Berins Collier, *Paths toward Democracy: The Working Class and Elites in Western Europe and South America*

Christian Davenport, *State Repression and the Domestic Democratic Peace*

Donatella della Porta, *Social Movements, Political Violence, and the State*

Alberto Diaz-Cayeros, *Federalism, Fiscal Authority, and Centralization in Latin America*

Thad Dunning, *Crude Democracy: Natural Resource Wealth and Political Regimes*

Gerald Easter, *Reconstructing the State: Personal Networks and Elite Identity*

Margarita Estevez-Abe, *Welfare and Capitalism in Postwar Japan: Party, Bureaucracy, and Business*

Henry Farrell, *The Political Economy of Trust: Institutions, Interests, and Inter-Firm Cooperation in Italy and Germany*

M. Steven Fish, *Democracy Derailed in Russia: The Failure of Open Politics*

Robert F. Franzese, *Macroeconomic Policies of Developed Democracies*

Roberto Franzosi, *The Puzzle of Strikes: Class and State Strategies in Postwar Italy*

Geoffrey Garrett, *Partisan Politics in the Global Economy*

Scott Gehlbach, *Representation through Taxation: Revenue, Politics, and Development in Postcommunist States*

Miriam Golden, *Heroic Defeats: The Politics of Job Loss*

Jeff Goodwin, *No Other Way Out: States and Revolutionary Movements*

Merilee Serrill Grindle, *Changing the State*

Anna Grzymala-Busse, *Rebuilding Leviathan: Party Competition and State Exploitation in Post-Communist Democracies*

Anna Grzymala-Busse, *Redeeming the Communist Past: The Regeneration of Communist Parties in East Central Europe*

Mark Irving Lichbach and Alan S. Zuckerman, eds., *Comparative Politics: Rationality, Culture, and Structure,* second edition

Evan Lieberman, *Race and Regionalism in the Politics of Taxation in Brazil and South Africa*

Pauline Jones Luong, *Institutional Change and Political Continuity in Post-Soviet Central Asia*

Julia Lynch, *Age in the Welfare State: The Origins of Social Spending on Pensioners, Workers, and Children*

Doug McAdam, John McCarthy, and Mayer Zald, eds., *Comparative Perspectives on Social Movements*

Beatriz Magaloni, *Voting for Autocracy: Hegemonic Party Survival and Its Demise in Mexico*

James Mahoney and Dietrich Rueschemeyer, eds., *Comparative Historical Analysis and the Social Sciences*

Scott Mainwaring and Matthew Soberg Shugart, eds., *Presidentialism and Democracy in Latin America*

Isabela Mares, *The Politics of Social Risk: Business and Welfare State Development*

Isabela Mares, *Taxation, Wage Bargaining, and Unemployment*

Anthony W. Marx, *Making Race, Making Nations: A Comparison of South Africa, the United States, and Brazil*

Bonnie M. Meguid, *Party Competition between Unequals: Strategies and Electoral Fortunes in Western Europe*

Joel S. Migdal, *State in Society: Studying How States and Societies Constitute One Another*

Joel S. Migdal, Atul Kohli, and Vivienne Shue, eds., *State Power and Social Forces: Domination and Transformation in the Third World*

Scott Morgenstern and Benito Nacif, eds., *Legislative Politics in Latin America*

Layna Mosley, *Global Capital and National Governments*

Wolfgang C. Müller and Kaare Strøm, *Policy, Office, or Votes?*

Maria Victoria Murillo, *Labor Unions, Partisan Coalitions, and Market Reforms in Latin America*

Maria Victoria Murillo, *Political Competition, Partisanship, and Policy Making in Latin American Public Utilities*

Ton Notermans, *Money, Markets, and the State: Social Democratic Economic Policies since 1918*

Aníbal Pérez-Liñán, *Presidential Impeachment and the New Political Instability in Latin America*

Roger Petersen, *Understanding Ethnic Violence: Fear, Hatred, and Resentment in Twentieth-Century Eastern Europe*